Contributions to Management Science

More information about this series at http://www.springer.com/series/1505

Florinda Matos • Valter Vairinhos •
Isabel Salavisa • Leif Edvinsson •
Maurizio Massaro
Editors

Knowledge, People, and Digital Transformation

Approaches for a Sustainable Future

Springer

Editors
Florinda Matos
Lisbon, Portugal

Isabel Salavisa
Lisbon, Portugal

Maurizio Massaro
Venice, Italy

Valter Vairinhos
Lisbon, Portugal

Leif Edvinsson
Vienna, Austria

ISSN 1431-1941 ISSN 2197-716X (electronic)
Contributions to Management Science
ISBN 978-3-030-40389-8 ISBN 978-3-030-40390-4 (eBook)
https://doi.org/10.1007/978-3-030-40390-4

This Springer imprint is published by the registered company Springer Nature Switzerland AG.
The registered company address is: Gewerbestrasse 11, 6330 Cham, Switzerland

Foreword

Why Should You Read This Book?
In short, you will get ingredients for your own thinking on what digitalisation means for you and what are the societal impacts of digitalisation.

Digitalisation and globalisation have changed the business world in recent years. This change is not over, but it is speeding up. The world has moved to an era of true value networks, competition and advantage, where innovation and knowledge brokering will take place in increasingly open, shared settings. Companies and other organisations create value through networks in which they cooperate and compete simultaneously. The new key success factor is the regional innovation ecosystem. The future depends increasingly on innovation actors' abilities to connect and manage their talent, partnerships, clusters and practical innovation processes, for integrating the local knowledge base into the global innovation power grid. Active networking relationships with global top-runner innovation environments boost local abilities to attract a continuous flow of global players and global collaboration.

Lessons to Learn: Parliament's Committee for the Future

Let me take a view based on the Finnish Knowledge and Welfare Society development in the last 20 years. Change, especially positive change, does not happen easily. As clearly stated in this book, as well as research studies show, digitalisation is the driver of change, which is occurring much faster than 10 or 20 years ago.

How to invent the desired future is a question which has been broadly and thoroughly tackled in Finland. Evidence of this is the work of a parliamentary committee: The Committee for the Future of the Parliament of Finland. Along a renewed Constitution, the Finnish Parliament decided, in 1999, to establish this committee with a permanent status among the Parliament's committees, each typically with 17 Members of Parliament (MPs) elected for a 4-year term.

There are several key analytical lessons that can be learned from the Finnish experience—and of course, experiences of other countries. These lessons should be sources of reflection and inspiration for other countries and regions of the world. Knowledge is universal.

A good example coming from the *Committee for the future* is how they focused on five special issues in 2003–2007, chaired at that time by MP Jyrki Katainen, now the Vice-President of the European Union (EU) Commission:

1. The Future of the Finnish Information Society Model
2. The Future of Public Health Care
3. Human Security as an Extensive Long-term Phenomenon
4. Regional Innovation Systems
5. Social Capital in View of Future Risks for Children and Young People

The Finnish model has used incentives, strategic planning and participatory mechanisms. The combination of deregulation and an effective role of the state, as well as cities, in providing and facilitating the public infrastructure has stimulated growth. The state has acted as a promoter of technological innovation, as a public venture capitalist and as a producer of knowledge labour, thus creating the conditions under which Finnish businesses could restructure themselves and compete globally. Today, the role of cities is changing rapidly mainly due to digitalisation—they are more and more catalysers of public–private–people partnerships and enablers of societal innovations, rather than simply service providers to citizens.

The main statement of the Parliament's Committee for the Future under MP Katainen's leadership, i.e. their approach to information/knowledge society, was "The development of technology will help only when it is combined with changes in the underlying structures". My advice to you, the readers of this book, is to think about these chapters in a deeper sense—digitalisation and knowledge management are instrumental for intellectual capital.

Based on this, I have read several chapters of this book with enthusiasm, reviewing the messages especially from three angles: how knowledge management has changed during the last two decades; how digitalisation has challenged cities to rethink and renew their societal role and their processes; and, thirdly, what the European Union should do to speed up the development of positive opportunities provided by digitalisation, in general, and the digital single market, in particular.

Five years ago, the European Committee of the Regions made, based on my proposal as the rapporteur on "Closing the Innovation Divide", the following statement: "*Digitisation drives change, and convergence towards digital services is speeding up. New business ecosystems and value creation arenas are often driven by new consumer behaviours—as a result of user-centric designs and openness. They challenge top-down construction approaches inherited from the old, analogue world. While digitisation is making service development more global than ever, Europe's position is not optimal: we are not the ones leading the way in this global race.*"

The European Commission policy papers on the digital society phenomena highlight real-life action, and it is clear, from my experience, that significant transformation takes place from the bottom-up, that is, close to the citizens. Let me clarify this by writing a short version of the Espoo Innovation Garden story with the focus on digitalisation.

Lessons to Learn: The City of Espoo as a Forerunner

My city, Espoo, with our 300,000 inhabitants, is the fastest growing city in Finland. We are the western part of the capital region, Helsinki. It is not a traditional city with one city centre, but a network city of five city centres, all close to nature. We have a sea with 165 islands, as well as forests, rural areas and 100 lakes. According to an international comparative study conducted by Tilburg University, during the Dutch Presidency of the EU in 2016, Espoo is the most sustainable city in Europe. Sustainability was measured using economic, sociocultural and ecologically sustainable development metrics. A follow-up study, in 2017, ranked Espoo again as the most sustainable city in Europe. Espoo aims to continue being at the top of sustainability in Europe. This purpose is consistent with the city's history and strategy for the current 2017–2021 city council term.

Espoo Innovation Garden is the European forerunner in innovation. The heart of our Innovation Garden is in the Keilaniemi-Otaniemi-Tapiola area of 5 km^2 being the number 1 concentration of high-tech focused research, business and learning in Northern Europe. It is the home of Aalto University, VTT Technical Research Centre of Finland and the headquarters of companies like Kone, Fortum, Neste Oil, Rovio and Nixu, among many others. It has the hottest Startup Sauna on the planet, inspiring cultural and sports activities, as well as a renowned community of scientists and researchers. The area has a strong international character, thanks to more than 100 different nationalities that are working, studying or living there. Innovation Garden is an open collaboration and entrepreneurship network of residents, companies and communities. One does not even have to live or work in Espoo to join this initiative as an innovation gardener.

In September 2017, the City Council set that Espoo's main strategic goal is to reach carbon neutrality already by 2030. The necessary measures are planned, not only by the city, but also by all other public authorities—and the actions are implemented with the help of large-scale public–private collaboration and multi-stakeholder partnerships. Citizens play a crucial role.

Espoo was awarded as "The Most Intelligent Community in the World" in June 2018. In July 2018, the UN invited Espoo to join SDG 25 + 5 Cities Leadership Program as a forerunner city, to reach the United Nations Agenda for Sustainable Development goals already by the year of 2025.

Resilient work towards a smart and sustainable future based on advanced digitalisation has been a joint effort of the city, companies, research and educational institutions and citizens. This ongoing and continuously developing cooperation at different levels has developed into a unique way of collaboration, targeting strategically towards sustainable solutions. In Espoo, all four levels needed for successful sustainability work are present: Espoo city strategy is aiming strongly towards a more sustainable city; novel operational models enable new ways of working and cooperation; projects and solutions created in wide collaboration are truly making a difference. Then, there is the fourth level, which is the most important: people. Espoo city staff, as well as business representatives and collaborators, and the most important stakeholders, our citizens, are making sustainability happen in Espoo today.

A Few More Guidelines on Digitalisation

Europe needs pioneering innovation regions—in most cases, digitalisation is the driver of this transformation. The European Committee of the Regions has called for pioneering regions to form European consortiums integrating different capabilities to create groundbreaking societal innovations for Europe-wide use. It also calls for increased performance capabilities of regions and cities to use the Horizon 2020 Programme, EU Cohesion Funds and other similar initiatives. The focus should be, in particular, on making full use of digitalisation and new key enabling technologies to modernise regional innovation policies. Furthermore, the European Committee of the Regions (CoR) encourages the regions to move towards open innovation, with a human-centred vision of partnerships between public and private sector actors, with universities and other knowledge institutions playing a crucial role.

A Europe built on innovative regions is a Europe of many possibilities, resilient in the face of societal challenges, global competition and financial uncertainty. A Europe of diverse regions, moving at different speeds along distinct paths, can leverage diversity in the future. This is the reality faced by the Innovation Union. Within this diversity, different regions will play different roles on the road forward. One role of crucial importance is that of the pioneer, the region that explores new ground, sets examples, shows the way and prepares the ground for others.

Cloud technologies provide access to the best service available, independently of time and place. This way of developing and producing services will, in the next few years, replace a considerable number of traditional services, in which being physically face-to-face connected is still a defining factor. It will no longer be necessary to have hardware in every corner. This will also entail managing and developing the ICT services and global networked cooperation of businesses, public administration and other communities. The European Commission should encourage local and regional level e-leadership development through active European partnership programmes.

What Is Next?

To implement what is written in this book is not an easy task. We also need to ensure that the human capital investment potential of regions, cities and citizens is fully unlocked. It is up to all levels of government to facilitate actions that have positive effects on citizens' lives and support achieving all the 17 Sustainable Development Goals of the United Nations Agenda 2030. In this regard, digitalisation, increasingly driven by cities and regions, is of key importance in providing smart and sustainable solutions and scaling up their European and global dissemination. This requires extensive innovation, especially in the operation of cities, companies and the entire civil society, with a special focus on energy and transport systems.

Furthermore, this also requires European wide collaboration, including transparent action plans of every Member State, towards digital priorities, from the transfer of digital innovations across all sectors of the economy, to boosting the European innovation capacity, through the support of tomorrow's digital innovation hubs and industrial platforms. The EU's strategy to digitise industry, including public services, aims to ensure that any business in Europe, big or small, wherever located and in whatever sector can fully benefit from digital innovations to upgrade its products, improve its processes and adapt its business models to the digital change.

Brussels, Belgium Markku Markkula

About the Book

Why publish a book with the title *Knowledge, People and Digital Transformation: Approaches for a Sustainable Future*?

This book is a contribution to the discussion about digital transformation and how it is dominating all sectors of society. Knowledge and digital transformation have a causal relationship that connects them mutually. However, this connection is balanced by one fundamental factor: The People. Effectively, this book is also an alert for the urgent need to put People and the "Good" at the epicentre of digital transformation, towards a sustainable future, where the fundamental element is the People.

This book integrates some of the most relevant papers published in the Proceedings of the GFIC 2019—Global Forum of Intellectual Capital, whose goal was to explore the challenges of digital transformation and find how it can lead to a more sustainable future.

Moreover, some chapters are the result of contributions from invited authors, whose work and ideas are relevant to the topic of digital transformation.

Much remains to be written about this issue and this work is just an overview. Other publications focusing on different issues of digital transformation may follow this book.

Lastly, this is the first step towards a winding road that is intended to lead to the establishment in Portugal of an Intellectual Capital Observatory.

The Editors

Contents

About the Editors

Florinda Matos is the founder and the president of the Intellectual Capital Association (ICAA), whose mission is to help transform intellectual capital into added value by contributing to sustainable development. She holds a PhD in Social Sciences (Organisational Behaviour Studies) from the University of Lisbon (Portugal). She teaches in graduate and postgraduate courses at ISCTE—Instituto Universitário de Lisboa and in several other higher education institutions.

Currently, she is an associate research fellow of DINÂMIA'CET-IUL—Centre for Socioeconomic and Territorial Studies. She was also a Post-Doc researcher in the area of the Social Impacts of Additive Manufacturing and, presently, she is leading the project "KM3D—Knowledge Management in Additive Manufacturing: Designing New Business Models", in a national consortium. She is a member of the New Club of Paris, an international organisation whose main objective is to create awareness about the knowledge economy. As a knowledge management expert, she is the ambassador for Europe of the International Conference on Knowledge and Innovation (CIKI), organised by Universidade Federal de Santa Catarina (Brazil). Moreover, she is a member of the Observatory on Knowledge Management and Innovation in Public Administration of IPEA—Institute for Applied Economic Research of the Brazilian Government. Her main research interests are intellectual capital, knowledge management, measuring of intangibles, sustainability, innovation, entrepreneurship, additive manufacturing and sustainable development.

Valter Vairinhos is a retired Portuguese Navy officer, where he served as a naval engineer from 1964 to 2009. He got his Naval Engineer Degree from the Portuguese Naval School, an Applied Mathematics Degree and a Master´s Degree in Statistics and Operations Research from Faculdade de Ciências, University of Lisbon, and a Doctoral Degree in Multivariate Data Analysis, from the Statistics Department of the Salamanca University. Currently, he shares his investigation activity between ICAA, CINAV—Naval Research Centre, Portuguese Naval School and the Statistics Department of Salamanca University.

His main research interests are related to graph data mining and automatic synthesis of results from multivariate data analysis, being the author of a methodology, based on intersection graphs, to generate automatic synthetic descriptions of results from multivariate data analysis and its implementation through a software (BiplotsPMD), where those ideas are put into use.

Isabel Salavisa, PhD, is Associate Professor of Economics at ISCTE—Instituto Universitário de Lisboa, in Lisbon.

Her research is conducted at DINÂMIA'CET-IUL—Centre for Socioeconomic and Territorial Studies, of which she has been Director (2004–2013). Currently, she works on the SPLACH project—Spatial Planning for Change (2017–2019).

Her research areas are economics of innovation, sustainability transitions and welfare state policies.

Leif Edvinsson is a key pioneering contributor to the theory and practice of Intellectual Capital (IC). He is the world's first Director of IC in 1991. He was prototyping in 1996 the Skandia Future Center as Lab for Organisational design. In 1998, he was awarded by Brain Trust "Brain of the Year" award, UK; listed in Who's Who in the world; earlier associate member of the Club of Rome; and Co-founder and Founding Chairman of the New Club of Paris. In 2013, he was awarded the Thought Leader Award by the European Commission, Intel and Peter Drucker Association. In 2015, he was appointed Advisory Board to JIN—the Japan Innovation Network. He was appointed in 2016 to the Advisory Board of Norway Open Innovation Forum. Together with the UN he was awarded the KM Award 2017, in Geneva Palais des Nations, by km-a.net.

Maurizio Massaro, PhD, is Associate Professor at Ca' Foscari University of Venice. Before joining academia, he was the founder and CEO of multiple consultancy firms. He has also served as a research centre Vice-President in the field of metal analysis. He has been a Visiting Professor at Florida Gulf Coast University (USA) and Leicester University (UK). He enjoys several contacts and research partnerships with universities in the USA, continental Europe, UK, Asia and Australia. His research interests include knowledge management, intellectual capital, strategy and research methods. His research has been applied in multiple research contexts. He is the representative in Italy for the MIKE—Most Innovative Knowledge Enterprise Award.

Introduction

Florinda Matos, Valter Vairinhos, Isabel Salavisa, Leif Edvinsson, and Maurizio Massaro

We must consider the type of world that we want the next generation to live in. We must work together so that the digital space that they inherit is safe, fair and inclusive.
António Guterres, UN Secretary-General
June 10, 2019

The impacts of digital transformation on society, and particularly on people's lives, are increasing the debate between policy-makers, researchers, the industry and thinkers in general.

Digital transformation and its accompanying processes of automation, robotics, Internet of Things (IoT), augmented reality and artificial intelligence (AI) are becoming one of the central concerns in the contemporaneous social evolution.

F. Matos (✉)
Instituto Universitário de Lisboa (ISCTE-IUL), DINÂMIA'CET-ISCTE, Lisbon, Portugal

ICLab - ICAA - Intellectual Capital Association, Santarém, Portugal

The New Club of Paris, Vienna, Austria
e-mail: florinda.matos@iscte-iul.pt

V. Vairinhos
ICLab - ICAA - Intellectual Capital Association, Santarém, Portugal

CINAV – Naval Research Centre Escola Naval, Almada, Portugal
e-mail: valter.vairinhos@icaa.pt

I. Salavisa
Instituto Universitário de Lisboa (ISCTE-IUL), Lisbon, Portugal
e-mail: isabel.salavisa@iscte-iul.pt

L. Edvinsson
The New Club of Paris, Vienna, Austria

M. Massaro
Dipartimento di Management, Università Ca' Foscari, Venice, Italy
e-mail: maurizio.massaro@unive.it

F. Matos et al. (eds.), *Knowledge, People, and Digital Transformation*, Contributions to Management Science, https://doi.org/10.1007/978-3-030-40390-4_1

People and governments are confronted not only with the opportunities suddenly open to individuals and societies, but also with the potential problems that are emerging from them, for which there is not yet a clear formulation and ideas about their consequences and solutions.

All aspects of people's lives and society are being affected: employment, education, governance, social life, sustainability, values, economy, democracy, among others.

The objective of this book is *to explore the challenges* of this new revolution, pointing out solutions and showing how knowledge management (*knowledge navigation)* can enable the transition process, associated with the digital transformation, and guided by principles of sustainability.

The book is composed of 18 chapters that address some of the most relevant aspects of digital transformation, namely: artificial intelligence and robotics; the relationship between Man's evolution, knowledge and technology; smart cities; digital transformation in agriculture and health and the emergence of new business models; governance aspects and knowledge management models; cybersecurity and security issues; sustainable management; key competencies for digital transformation in the workplace; digital transformation and entrepreneurship in education; digital transformation in banking; knowledge management and blockchain platforms; and digital transformation in industry, namely through the use of additive manufacturing technology.

Many other issues concerning the relationship between digital transformation, people, and knowledge management could have been addressed in a more exhaustive work. Nevertheless, the purpose of this book is not to list the different impacts of digital transformation, but to nudge readers' interest for the topic by demonstrating how digital transformation is surgically entering every aspect of our daily lives.

This book also intends to appeal to the need of effectively managing intangible assets, namely intellectual capital (IC). This asset is "understood as an intangible, a renewable and a manageable asset, available at micro-level (individuals and organisations) and at a macro level (cities, regions and countries), that can be managed to create sustainable wealth" (Matos et al. 2019, p. 4).

Considering the relevance of this infinite, but misused asset in society, this book also aims to propose the thesis that the impact of digital transformation is closely related to intellectual capital management. Thus, depending on whether the management of this asset is positive (for good) or negative (for evil), this transformation will have positive or negative effects on society.

To demonstrate this thesis, one can consider the composition of intellectual capital, according to Edvinsson (1997, 2002) and Lin and Edvinsson (2011), which divides intellectual capital into two categories: human capital and structural capital.

Structural capital corresponds to databases, manuals, customer lists, hardware, software, organisations' structure, patents, among others, that support digital transformation. This capital also includes the relational capital that supports all the interaction (*network*) of systems and relationships of organisations. This interaction can be of type *system–system*, *system–individual–system*, *system–individual*, or *individual–system*, giving rise to multiple interactions. An example of this is the Smart Cities or Customer Relationship Management (CRM) systems.

Human capital is the capital of an organisation's members. In our perspective, it can include the use of digital transformation, as a multiplier of the IC impact on society, for the people's benefit, for example by improving people's skills, knowledge and welfare.

Another essential factor to consider is time. In fact, digital transformation acts as a time accelerator. Information and knowledge flow faster and can accelerate all intellectual capital management processes. The problem is that this acceleration can be positive or negative. That is, digital transformation can influence positively or negatively the management of intellectual capital.

As a moderator (*IC Navigator*) of this influence comes the ethics and social responsibility of people and organisations. These seem to be the main factors that balance the impacts of digital transformation on society. Therefore, people and society, in general, have to focus on these moderators (*Navigation Nodes*).

It seems clear that digital transformation will improve many aspects of society, such as facilitating the most difficult and dangerous tasks, speeding up processes, improving the quality of life, creating new jobs and new types of work, making cities safer, democratising access to scientific and technological knowledge, etc. However, a question arises: Will digital transformation be oriented towards a more people-centred society?

Several thinkers do not doubt that this is the only possible path to digital transformation: people-centred and sustainability-focused. An example of this is the Japanese Society 5.0 (UNESCO 2015, p. 642). Society 5.0 is a concept of society that combines the cyberspace and the physical space, balancing the economic aspects with social ones, in order to benefit social diversity in general, and contribute to sustainability.

Additionally, for many other thinkers, it is also clear that digital transformation will happen faster than people's ability to adapt, resulting in a massive disappearance of jobs, due to AI (Russel and Norvig 2010), and a significant gap between more developed countries and least developed countries.

Even though the most optimistic thinkers consider that this gap will not be relevant, the reality seems quite different. Therefore, some organisations are working in special programmes, such as the European Commission Program on Upskilling (Probst and Scharff 2019).

Indeed, many governments do not have enough funding to invest in the different aspects of digital transformation, particularly AI, providing citizens with the skills and security to reduce the impacts of this change. In fact, the adequate skills to meet the challenges of the labour market and the use of the new technologies, and new security-related issues, are perhaps the most complex aspects of this process (Acemoglu and Restrepo 2018; Chiacchio et al. 2018; Graetz and Michaels 2018). The problem is that the boundary between Work 3.0 (in which robots replace humans in productive processes, namely manual work) and Work 4.0 (digitalisation of processes, increase of interconnectedness among machines, and the emergence of machines able to replace cognitive work and take decisions) is very tenuous, and there is not enough time for people to learn and adapt.

The debate has flourished essentially around robotics and its impacts on the workplace. Despite some sectorial studies (Acemoglu and Restrepo 2018; Chiacchio et al. 2018; Graetz and Michaels 2018), this issue is still in an early stage, particularly regarding the impacts on developing countries. These countries usually have economies based on cheap workforce, so the impacts of robots on employment and society can be very significant, especially because the investments in education and training are very limited.

In addition, the concerns of developed countries to shorten supply chains, due to economic and ecological reasons, and the use of large-scale technologies (e.g. additive manufacturing) can affect the off-shoring production, with economic implications for countries with weaker economies (see, for example, United Nations 2017).

Furthermore, the digital transformation can quickly generate situations of digital illiteracy, job loss, and loss of jobs' control, which will have an impact on people's lives and on their mental and physical health. However, these issues are still little studied, and a question remains: Will society be prepared to deal with these new situations? Probably not.

There seems to be a time gap between clock time and decision/management time. In addition, the skills and leadership ability of managers are crucial for them to be able to narrow the gap between these two-time scales and to prepare the workers for the use of new and disruptive technologies. The decision-makers and policy-makers need to identify the skills for this new transition, training workers and creating systems that ensure a fair distribution of the benefits and a more effective talent attraction and retention. In this context, knowledge, its creation and sharing can be fundamental, in order to facilitate the transition to this new Digital Society, which should be more people-centred and sustainability-focused. An example of this can be found in the idea of Japanese Society 5.0 and in the Wiseplace, which are spaces for knowledge sharing and innovation, based on the idea of knowledge "Ba" (Nonaka and Konno 1998; Konno 2013), that is, shared spaces that facilitate the gathering, creation and transfer of knowledge between knowledge producers and users.

Moreover, there is no precise knowledge about the impact that digital transformation will have on a fair society, democracy and sustainability issues. Positive and negative impacts need to be identified. For example, it is challenging to know what kind of impacts algorithm-based systems, such as China's social scoring system, will have on society, democracy and citizens' right to privacy. Access to knowledge represents power, and dictatorships—based on the ability to access and manipulate knowledge and to use technology-based control, are more likely than ever to succeed, calling into question a fairer and more democratic society.

It seems evident that a well-used digital transformation can be an ally for sustainable development (e.g. in the climate area), but it presents new challenges for society's cohesion and democracy and, therefore, requires better governance and greater citizen social intervention.[1]

The 2030 Agenda of United Nations (2015) can benefit with further democratisation of access to knowledge but, at the same time, it can also be undermined by digitalisation (e.g. lack of digital skills, widening inequalities of gender and diversity aspects, etc.).

Another relevant aspect for which there is no consensus yet is the change in taxation policies on companies replacing their traditional systems with digital ones. Thus, it is necessary to promote regulated economic systems by increasing taxes on companies that opt for more digital business models or replace people with highly robotic solutions. However, the fair way in which these taxes can be applied has not yet reached unanimity among decision-makers.

Considering the issues linked to sustainability and the Sustainable Development Agenda (United Nations 2015), there is still a question to be answered: How digital transformation can contribute to environmental objectives (e.g. mobility, pollution or energy issues)?

Finally, the economic issue is a relevant aspect of the digital transformation. Does the digital transformation increase the levels of business productivity (Brynjolfsson et al. 2019) and efficiency? Can it contribute to more economically balanced economies, providing citizens with better welfare? As with other aspects of digital transformation, the economic aspect still raises many questions, and it is difficult to make an accurate prediction about the impacts of this new age on society and on people's lives.

In conclusion, the identification of significant topics related to the digital transformation impacts on people's lives and society is an important contribution of this book. Nevertheless, there are still a considerable number of unknown aspects. Thus, a set of questions related to the digital transformation impacts and perspectives remains unanswered.

The next chapters of this book are, therefore, also a challenge for editors and authors, who want to contribute to unlocking the secrets behind the *crystal ball* that is digital transformation itself.

References

Acemoglu D, Restrepo P (2018) The race between man and machine: implications of technology for growth, factor shares, and employment. Am Econ Rev 108(6):1488–1542. https://doi.org/10.1257/aer.20160696

Brynjolfsson E, Rock D, Syverson C (2019) The productivity J-curve: how intangibles complement general purpose technologies. SSRN Electron J. https://doi.org/10.2139/ssrn.3346739

[1]See, for example, the agenda of The New Club of Paris on "Societal Innovation" at http://new-club-of-paris.org/

Chiacchio F, Petropoulos G, Pichler D (2018) The impact of industrial robots on EU employment and wages: a local labour market approach. McKinsey Globa Inst 10(March):1–28. https://doi.org/10.3390/su10020490

Edvinsson L (1997) Developing intellectual capital at Skandia. Long Range Plan 30(3):366–373

Edvinsson L (2002) Corporate longitude: what you need to know to navigate the knowledge economy. Financial Times Prentice Hall, London

Graetz G, Michaels G (2018) Robots at work. Rev Econ Stat 100(5):753–768. https://doi.org/10.1162/rest_a_00754

Konno N (2013) Revisiting the 'knowledge creating firm' in the 'post-capitalist society' context BT. In: von Krogh G, Takeuchi H, Kase K, Cantón CG (eds) Towards organizational knowledge: the pioneering work of Ikujiro Nonaka. Palgrave Macmillan, London. https://doi.org/10.1057/9781137024961_12

Lin CY-Y, Edvinsson L (2011) National intellectual capital: a comparison of 40 countries. Springer, New York. https://doi.org/10.1007/978-1-4419-7377-1

Matos F, Vairinhos V, Selig P, Edvinsson L (eds) (2019) Intellectual capital management as a driver of sustainability perspectives for organizations and society. Springer, Cham. https://doi.org/10.1007/978-3-319-79051-0

Nonaka I, Konno N (1998) The concept of "Ba": building a foundation for knowledge creation. Calif Manag Rev 40(3):40–54. https://doi.org/10.2307/41165942

Probst L, Scharff C (2019) Upskill - 6 steps to unlock economic opportunity for all. Clink Street Publishing, New York

Russel S, Norvig P (2010) Artificial intelligence: a modern approach, 3rd edn. Prentice Hall, Upper Saddle River, NJ

UNESCO (2015) UNESCO science report: towards 2030. Retrieved from https://unesdoc.unesco.org/ark:/48223/pf0000235406

United Nations (2015) Transforming our world: the 2030 agenda for sustainable development - sustainable development knowledge platform. Retrieved from https://sustainabledevelopment.un.org/content/documents/21252030Agenda for Sustainable Development web.pdf

United Nations (2017) UNCTAD annual report 2016: a commitment to inclusive trade. Retrieved from https://unctad.org/en/PublicationsLibrary/dom2017_en.pdf

People, Intangibles and Digital Transformation

Valter Vairinhos, Florinda Matos, and Leif Edvinsson

Abstract This chapter seeks to characterise the main issues of Digital Transformation (DT) and to relate this concept with National Intangible Capital (NIC), having in mind people's attitudes and reactions to this transformation process, which is affecting the basic foundations of social life and civilisation. Previous technological revolutions replaced physical attributes of Man by the force of mechanical systems, and, later, machines were used to carry out repetitive, painful and dangerous tasks. With the present DT, intrinsic and noble characteristics of the human being, the mental characteristics, are being replaced or intended to be replaced by machines. This replacement is frequently made according to a logic that does not always put the Human Capital (HC) as the recipient and main beneficiary.

Moreover, one of the main objectives of this work is to show that, despite the extraordinary complexity of social life and the relations between nations, technologies and science, DT is based on a small number of simple concepts, very stable over time and with universal meaning. This explains, in a great measure, the DT economic success and its potential for transforming all aspects of social, economic, political and cultural life. Furthermore, this is an illustration of the Intangible Capital (IC) or Artificial Intelligence (AI) multiplier effect.

V. Vairinhos (✉)
ICLab - ICAA - Intellectual Capital Association, Santarém, Portugal

CINAV – Naval Research Centre Escola Naval, Almada, Portugal
e-mail: valter.vairinhos@icaa.pt

F. Matos
Instituto Universitário de Lisboa (ISCTE-IUL), DINÂMIA'CET-ISCTE, Lisbon, Portugal

ICLab - ICAA - Intellectual Capital Association, Santarém, Portugal

The New Club of Paris, Vienna, Austria
e-mail: florinda.matos@iscte-iul.pt

L. Edvinsson
The New Club of Paris, Vienna, Austria

F. Matos et al. (eds.), *Knowledge, People, and Digital Transformation*, Contributions to Management Science, https://doi.org/10.1007/978-3-030-40390-4_2

1 Introduction and Objectives

For the first time in history, it is possible to represent ideas, data, problems, methods to solve them, plans to construct material and immaterial systems, as well as all spoken and written literature and other intellectual manifestations, using a single paradigm and language: the Universal Turing Machine (TM). This paradigm covers problem identification and formulation, algorithms to solve them and a single computational model. Not surprisingly, this simple logic–mathematical device encompasses the fundamental ingredients of human reasoning: data, world representation and computations. This fact, coupled with almost free access in real time to the generated knowledge by individuals and organisations, produces an increasing acceleration of all the involved processes, shrinking the time scale, which accelerates the accumulation of Intangible Capital (IC) at all levels. This time scale, while being the source of new problems of adaptation for Man and society, creates impaired opportunities for finding new solutions. Furthermore, this also means a colossal reduction of entropy associated with the implicit standardisation of all creative human and social activities.

In this perspective, IC means a potential for transformation, knowledge and innovation creation, translated in capabilities to find future solutions for significant survival problems and, in synthesis, a vital dynamic value creation process for the relevant organisations.

Nowadays, the process of evaluation or measurement of an organisation's IC corresponds to the ability to predict, from observational and experimental data, the future behaviour of the unit, in terms of its capability to produce new knowledge, innovations, and solutions for future, critical and vital problems.

For an economy and society based on information and knowledge, this feature is by far more critical than the prediction of future financial flows. The reason is that, in this setting, the future earnings are a consequence of IC, not its cause. Therefore, what makes sense is to measure or predict IC future value, since it acts as a cause for future economic value, innovation, financial flows and strategic social value (Vairinhos et al. 2019), not the reverse.

Digital Transformation and the associated large-scale use of Artificial Intelligence (AI) can be shown as an outstanding example of IC development, specifically of National Intangible Capital development. DT is the generalised use, based in data, computation and analytics of digital technology in all fields of scientific, technologic and economic activities; Data means observed facts about the world; Computation is the realisation of logic and mathematical operations according to specific algorithms, using computers. The problems to be solved and decisions to be taken are formulated according to scientific knowledge and, consequently, involving world knowledge expressed by data. What is remarkable is that all of those algorithms that in last resort tell computers what they must do (compute) are expressible by a universal language, symbolised by a very limited set of words. These algorithms are translated by texts, called programs, that specify tasks executed by computers that are all instances of the TM. Effectively, the TM can be considered the theoretical founding concept of

Computer Science, and a necessary condition for DT (Turing 1937). One of the main DT technologies is AI, entirely dependent on computation and whose origins can also be traced back to Turing (1950).

The main objective of the present chapter is to identify essential issues of DT, as well as, sources of literature which can be used to understand the main consequences of DT, both on society and human lives. At the same time, aims to understand what people are thinking about this digital revolution and to identify and characterise the principal attitudes of the OECD and the EU countries towards DT, relating these attitudes with NIC scorings.

The structure of this chapter is as it follows: Sect. 2 identifies some important sources of knowledge, addressing key issues of DT and predicting its consequences; in Sect. 3 are presented the data and methods used in the comparative study of countries attitudes about DT relating these attitudes with NICs and other predictors; Sect. 4 describes the results of the data analysis and its interpretation; and in Sect. 5, the conclusions and future work are presented.

2 DT: Promises, Realities, Dangers and Risks

Digital Transformation (DT) refers to the process of introduction and use of digital technology in all domains of human activity, where that makes sense, from the scientific, economic and computational points of view. This embraces almost all human activities.

The DT process had its origins associated with the first developments of digital computers, both in the United Kingdom and the United States, consequence of World War II (WWII). These efforts manifested in high concentrations of Intangible Capital (IC) under the form of groups of first-rate civilian and military scientists, mathematicians and engineers, in places such as Bletchley Park in England or at the Institute of Advanced Studies (IAS) in Princeton, USA. This IC concentrations led to innovations such as the decipher of the German code machine called *Enigma*, in the United Kingdom, which contributed meaningfully to abbreviate the end of WWII, to the creation of the first digital computer and, to the advent of Artificial Intelligence (AI) (Dyson 2012; Turing 1937, 1950).

As already mentioned, one of the leading players for these developments was Alan Turing who, in his paper published in 1937, introduced the logical and mathematical foundations of what is known as Computer Science (Dyson 2012; Turing 1937).

The ideas and contributions of Turing are more present than ever in current DT, through his concept of TM, the prototype of every digital computer and, consequently, digital computation.

The universal diffusion of computational power and telecommunications, lead, eventually, to the creation, using the infrastructure of the Internet, in 1989 of the World Wide Web (WWW), the other big innovation associated to the DT (Berners-Lee 1990). Curiously, this was also a major global innovation laid down by a British computer scientist, Tim Berners-Lee, working in the massive concentration of Intellectual Capital that is CERN in Geneva.[1]

DT universal relevance and importance is now recognised and expressed in a series of investigations and official publications of prestigious world institutions (OECD 2017a, b, c, 2018, 2019b). These publications seek to identify, measure and characterise the issues, trends, policies and effects associated with the DT in main society domains. From this series of documents, we single out, by its relevance and coverage, OECD (2019a), published in the context of OECD's project Going Digital.[2]

Given its scope and deep effects, current DT is already a great revolution, since it is changing the paradigms in business, economy, science, technology, society, human behaviour, among others. Given the possibilities resulting from the fact that available data is doubling each year (Helbing et al. 2017), this means that society, firms, organisations and individuals have now access and can interact with an increasing stream of information and knowledge as it is being created. Consequently, this leads to ever-increasing access to innovations and new action possibilities, in an exponentially accelerating process of time scale shrinking.

Just to mention two components of this process, Big Data and AI are transforming at an increasing pace, governance and science, opening opportunities for new activities, theories formulation and its empirical verification.

This explains the justified expectations and promises issued by public investigations and political organisations, as the OECD and the EU (OECD 2019a, b).

Those possibilities are also open to its use by destructive forces that seek not the good of society, but its control, domination or destruction. These include potent risks hardly foreseen some years ago, and for which society and democracy are unprepared (Benkler et al. 2018; Brundage et al. 2018; Ding 2018; Kremer and Müller 2012; Shao et al. 2018; Yang et al. 2019).

Furthermore, Social Networks have already transformed meaningfully social relations, among billion of individuals, with deep impacts on ethical values, social behaviour and consequences, not yet handled, in education. As is evident from a mere daily media examination, its unethical use by influential organisations allows the unthinkable, such as social experimentation, involving entire societies, and the formulation of some decision processes that can end in war or domination from some nations over others. Prohibition of social experimentation has been one universal accepted principle for ethical behaviour of scientific corps. That principle, there is now plenty of evidence, is not being fully respected by some crucial players (Helbing et al. 2017; Shao et al. 2018). It is relatively simple to subject, during an "adequate" time, specific populations, previously characterised, to some specific stimuli and, after that, to observe the results expressed in individual decisions with meaning for the specific aim of the experience: advertising, political decisions, attitudes, etc.

---

[1]Tim Berners-Lee original document proposing this concept can be read at https://www.w3.org/History/1989/proposal.html

[2]See: https://www.oecd.org/going-digital/

Recently, these kinds of risk have been reported, by some analysts, about the UK Brexit and the American presidential elections (Benkler et al. 2018).

The AI has, inherently, significant shortcomings that must be addressed at any decision process involving its potential use (Waldrop 2019). In this context, the war concept is open to new and more sophisticated interpretations. Indeed, to win a war is, for one of the opponents, to be able, for example, to have some degree of influence on the decision processes of its opponents. It seems that some decision-makers believe that this is obtainable, in the foreseeable future, by conditioning NIC's opponents, using AI and Analytics.

Given the apparent unpreparedness of society in relation to this kind of problems, risks and dangers manifested in recent experience, it is natural the emergence of institutions like the "Future of Humanity Institute" from the University of Oxford, which is devoted to the study of the impacts of future technology (Dafoe 2018; Ding 2018; Zhang and Dafoe 2019).

One big issue connected with DT is the future of employment and how the major components of it, AI and Robotics, will affect human skills and employment. Frey and Osborne (2013), in a study about the susceptibility of future of employment, predicted that, in America, about 47% of jobs were at risk. In this same work, a methodology was defined that allowed the calculation of the probability of a job to be replaced by a machine (700 jobs were analysed). These probabilities varied, in that reference, from 0.002829 for a recreational therapist, to 0.99 for a telemarketer. The practice has shown that those predictions were most exaggerated, but the evolution of DT has not dissipated the fears about the net effect of DT in future employment. Several studies documented the institutional concerns about this issue, such as Nedelkoska and Quintini (2018), in a study for OECD about Adult Skills, and EU (2017) the "Special Eurobarometer 460: Attitudes towards the impact of digitisation and automation on daily life". In addition to these European studies, it is noteworthy the American study, by Zhang and Dafoe (2019), the "Artificial Intelligence: American Attitudes and Trends". Both studies documented the same concerns in America and Europe.

3 Data and Methodology

In this section, a study about European Countries' attitudes concerning Digital Transformation (DT), using data from EU (2017) and other sources, is presented.

The primary data source is the "Special Eurobarometer 460 Report: Attitudes towards the impact of digitisation and automation on daily life", published in March 2017 EU (2017).

The other two sources are OECD (2016), the "Skills Matter: Further Results from the Survey of Adult Skills" and, data of National Intangibles Capital (NIC) from Lin and Edvinsson (2011), and Ståhle et al. (2015).

Table 1 Labels of countries according with EU (2017, p. 8)

	Label	Country		Label	Country
1	BE	Belgium	15	LT	Lithuania
2	BG	Bulgaria	16	LU	Luxembourg
3	CZ	Czech Republic	17	HU	Hungary
4	DK	Denmark	18	MT	Malta
5	DE	Germany	19	NL	Netherlands
6	EE	Estonia	20	AT	Austria
7	IE	Ireland	21	PL	Poland
8	EL	Greece	22	PT	Portugal
9	ES	Spain	23	RO	Romania
10	FR	France	24	SI	Slovenia
11	HR	Croatia	25	SK	Slovakia
12	IY	Italy	26	FI	Finland
13	CY	Rep. of Cyprus	27	SE	Sweden
14	LV	Latvia	28	UK	United Kingdom

EU (2017) already includes descriptive statistics of the data, resulting from answers to the full set of questions described in the methodology section of that reference.

The analysis presented, in this chapter, uses some selected tables of EU (2017, pp. 133–170), listed in Annex.

From each selected table, two columns were used, those corresponding to the aggregation of the extreme modalities' answers. For example, Table QD1.1 originated two columns in our data set: QD1-1_TP—Total Positive, and QD1-1_TN—Total Negative. Another example, from Table QD4.4, two columns were considered for our data set: QD44_TA—Total Agree, and QD44_TD—Total Disagree. For the other selected tables, the result is listed in Annex, which corresponds to 38 columns.

In addition to those 38 variables/columns, two more columns, with external information, were considered: NIC_S14, representing the intangible potential of a country, and MNP (Mean Numeracy Proficiency).

NIC_S14 was obtained from Lin and Edvinsson (2011), and Ståhle et al. (2015).

MNP was obtained from OECD (2016—Annex A, Table A2.11, Colum PIAAC).

MNP, being an indicator related to numeric skills, is also potentially related to the skills involved in DT and Artificial Intelligence (AI). Being easily obtainable from international surveys, it was decided to study its eventual usefulness, in conjunction with NIC_S14, as a predictor of answers to questions about those matters.

A data set with 28 rows, representing the EU 28 countries, by 40 columns was obtained. The meaning of those columns appears in Annex. The 28 rows of the final data set were labelled according to Table 1 (EU 2017, p. 8).

As the principal descriptive methodology, biplots, namely HJ-biplots (Gabriel 1971; Galindo 1986; Greenacre 2010), were used to synthesise the attitudes of EU's countries in relation to the aspects covered by the list of variables. Cluster analysis of countries and variables, performed on the coordinates of those biplots, were obtained, allowing a useful synthesis of meaning, both for sets of variables and countries. For the construction of all the biplots, presented in the next section, only variables observed by the Special Eurobarometer 460 Report (EU 2017) were used. The two additional variables (NIC_S14 and MNP) were used as supplemental variables, not contributing to the topology of the obtained plots. The software used to obtain the graphical results was BiplotsPMD (Vairinhos 2003).

4 Results of Data Analysis

Figure 1 shows the biplot of the countries, which are identified by points with blue labels, according to Table 1. The variables are represented as by red arrows and labelled according to Annex. Small angles between the variables mean that the variables have high correlations; while large angles (>90°) mean variables with small and negative correlations. The orthogonal arrows mean the variables that are not correlated (Gabriel 1971; Galindo 1986; Greenacre 2010).

If two countries, for example, Sweden (SE) and Netherlands (NL), are represented by near points, that means that answers coming from those countries

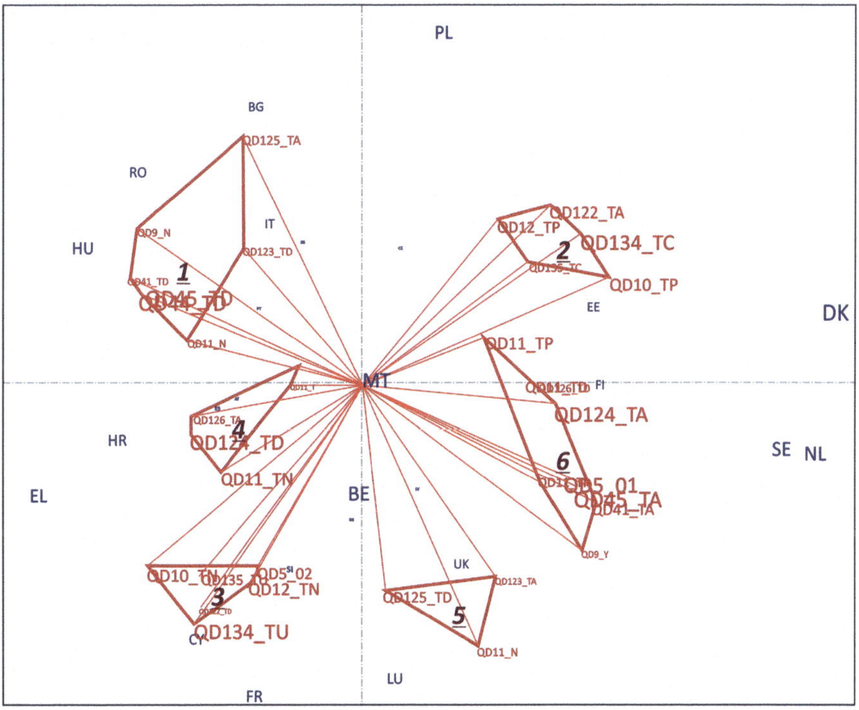

Fig. 1 Biplot relating questions' answers (red) with countries (blue). Polygons: clusters formed by highly correlated answers

are similar. If the distance between the two countries is considerable, for example, Denmark (DK) and Hungary (HU), it means that answers coming from those countries are very distinct.

Using the coordinates of the variables on the biplot, these were automatically clustered using Ward Method. The result of this procedure is shown, also, in Fig. 1. The clusters obtained, formed by sets of similar answers to the questions identified, are numbered from 1 to 6.

Each variable cluster can be interpreted as a “kind” of answer, “attitude” or “feeling” to the content of the questionnaire about Digital Transformation (DT), Artificial Intelligence (AI) and the use and effects of Robots, within the 28 EU countries.

The contents of each one of the clusters with the variables (questions answers), labelled from 1 to 6, in Fig. 1, and its suggested interpretation, based on the meanings of the questions listed in Annex (remember that the meanings of the suffixes are: TA—Total Agree, TD—Total Disagree, TP—Total Positive, TN—Total Negative, TC—Total Comfortable, TU—Total Uncomfortable, Y—Yes, and N—No), is shown in Table 2.

Figure 2 contains four clusters of countries, represented as blue polygons numbered from 7 to 10. These clusters were obtained automatically using the Ward method, operating with countries coordinates on the biplot.

Table 3 presents the contents of blue clusters in Fig. 2, labelled 7, 8, 9, 10, formed by countries, and its suggested interpretation, given its relative positions to the red clusters of variables, labelled from 1 to 6 in Fig. 2.

In addition, for each cluster, the result of an automatic description, using the observed variables, is presented. In those descriptions, the numbers mean percentages of answers.

The descriptions of the clusters, both variables and countries, have been constructed exclusively using the answers given to questions in the Special Eurobarometer 460 Report (EU 2017).

Figure 3 tries to answer the question: is there any evidence that the EU countries' attitudes in relation to DT (expressed by the variables in Annex) can be predicted by the NIC (measured by the variable NIC_S14)? In Fig. 3, the group of countries with label 31 is formed by countries where the NIC_S14 is valued below the first quartile. The group of countries with label 32 is formed by countries where the NIC_S14 is valued above the third quartile.

Examining the numeric labels for points representing countries, in Fig. 3, it can be observed that cluster 31 contains countries such as {EL, HR, HU, RO, BG, IT}, where there is a negative attitude of distrust and preoccupation with DT when employment is considered.

On the other hand, cluster 32 contains countries like {LU, UK, SE, DK, EE, FI}, where the general attitude about DT is positive. This means that there is evidence supporting the idea that NIC_S14 can be used to predict the general attitude of countries about DT, expressed by people's answers to this specific questionnaire. In other words, countries with greater NIC_S14 tend to accept better DT matters.

Table 2 Variables clusters' meaning interpretation

Cluster label	Variable label	Variable meaning
1	QD125_TA	Totally agrees that the EU is ahead of other world regions in relation to DT and AI at the year of 2015
	QD123_TD	Totally disagrees with the idea that Robots and IA must have a careful management
	QD 14_N	Disagrees with the idea of having access to Medical Health Records
	QD9_N	In the last 12 months, did not hear or see about IA
	QD41_TD	Disagrees with the idea of being sufficiently skilled in the daily use of digital technologies
	QD45_TD	Disagrees with the idea of being sufficiently skilled to benefit from digital technologies
	Cluster synthesis	Formed by people that consider themselves rather away from digital technologies or who do not have the skills to allow a useful use of digital technologies
2	QD135_TC	Is comfortable with being driven in the traffic by a driverless car
	QD12_TP	Is positive about the current impact of digital technologies on the society
	Q10_TP	Has a positive view about Robots and AI
	QD134_TC	Is comfortable about receiving goods by Drone or Robot
	QD122_TA	Robots and AI are good things for society and help people in daily life
	Cluster synthesis	Formed by people with positive feelings about the impact of DT, AI and Robotics
3	QD5_02	Do not trust stories published in social networks
	QD12_TN	See as totally negative the impact in society of DT
	Q10_TN	Has negative feelings about Robots and AI
	QD135_TU	Is uncomfortable with the idea of being driven in the traffic by a driverless car
	QD122_TD	Disagrees with the idea that IA and Robotics are good things
	QD134_TU	Is totally uncomfortable with the idea of receiving goods delivered by Drone or Robot
	Cluster synthesis	Formed by people with negative feelings about Robots and AI and who do not trust in its use
4	QD11_Y	Think that his current job can be done by a Robot in future
	QD1-1_TN	Think that digital technology has a negative effect on the Economy
	Q124_TD	Does not agree with the idea that Robots and AI are necessary to realise jobs too hard and dangerous for humans
	QD126_TA	Agrees with the idea that AI and Robots steel people's jobs
	QD121_TA	Agrees with the idea that more jobs will disappear, than new jobs will be created by DT
	Cluster synthesis	Formed by people that fear and are uncomfortable with the idea that Robots and AI will eliminate more jobs, than will create new ones
5	QD11_N	Think that his current job cannot be done by a Robot
	QD125_TA	Agrees that the EU is ahead of other world regions in DT
	QD123_TA	Robots and AI require careful management
	Cluster synthesis	Formed by people who are not very enthusiastic about DT

(continued)

Table 2 (continued)

Cluster label	Variable label	Variable meaning
6	QD11_TP	Has a positive view about the impact of DT on Economy
	QD124_TA	Agrees with the need of Robots, because they can do hard and dangerous tasks for people
	QD126_TD	Disagrees with the idea that Robots and AI steel people's jobs
	QD121_TD	Disagrees with the idea that more jobs will disappear, than will be created
	QD14_Y	Would like to have access to Medical Health Records
	QD5_01	Believes that a story is trustworthy if it comes from a reliable source
	QD9_Y	In the last 12 months, has hear or see something about AI
	QD41_TA	Considers himself sufficiently skilled to use digital technology
	QDA45_TA	Considers himself sufficiently skilled to benefit from digital technology
	QD44_TA	Considers himself sufficiently skilled to use online public services
	Cluster synthesis	Formed by people with a positive and confident attitude and skills about DT and its personal use of digital technologies

Using the variable MNP, a similar question was formulated: is there any evidence that countries attitudes in relation to DT can be predicted from MNP?

Proceeding in the same way, but using as external information, the MNP variable, Fig. 4 shows countries labelled with MNP values. The center of Fig. 4 corresponds to an MNP average value of 267.2.

Also, in Fig. 4, cluster 33 corresponds to countries with MNP below the first quartile and cluster 34 corresponds to countries with MNP above the third quartile. Once more, it is shown that there is an increasing gradient in the positive attitude about DT when crossing the plot from cluster 33 to cluster 34. However, why would MNP variable even be used? One reason is because it can be used as a rough predictor for people's attitudes concerning DT, for countries in the EU.

Furthermore, Fig. 4 shows that, in the case of MNP, a considerable intersection or confounding zone exists. This means that the prediction with NIC_S14 has better quality, since the "confounding" zone is empty in this case, existing a clear separation of countries with lower values, from the countries with higher values, as seen in Fig. 3.

5 Conclusions

This study, using data from the EU (2017), identifies and characterises, in a holistic way, the European countries' attitudes to Digital Transformation (DT) and, specifically, in relation to Robotics and Artificial Intelligence (AI). From this study

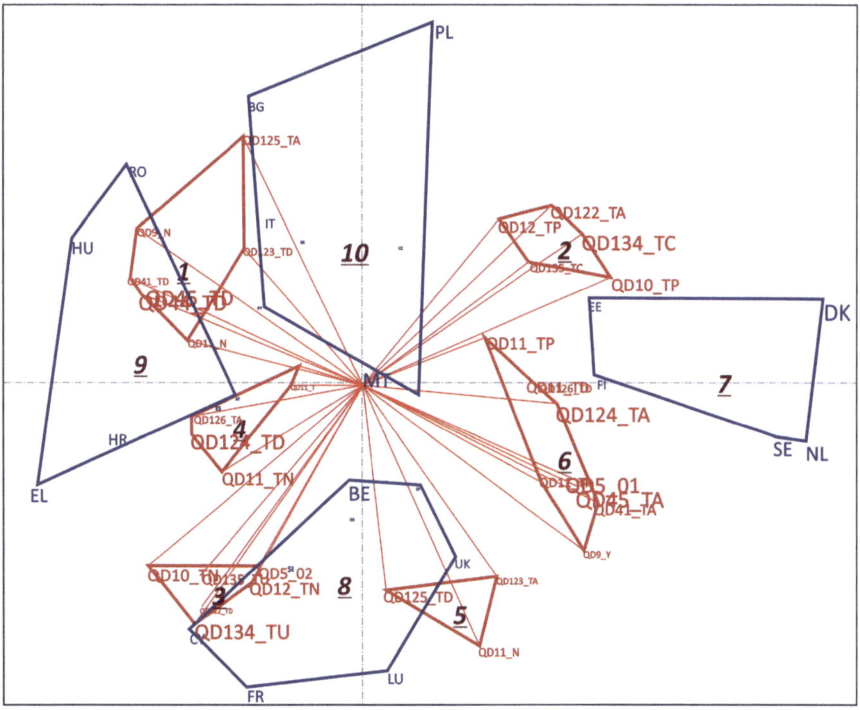

Fig. 2 The plot shows simultaneously cluster for variables (1–6, in red) and clusters to countries (7–10, in blue)

emerges a general picture of some concern about the future consequences for people's employment. However, in general, it does not point out strong opposition to DT.

There is evidence that National Intangible Capital (NIC_S14) and Mean Numeracy Proficiency (MNP) can be used, also, as rough predictors of the EU countries' attitudes about DT. Smaller values of NIC_S14 and MNP point to countries with negative attitudes concerning DT; whereas, large values of NIC and MNP point to countries with positive attitudes in relation to DT, with NIC_S14 being a better predictor than MNP.

Another interesting finding is that informed people in some advanced countries manifest negative feelings and distrust to AI and Robotics. This is the inherent understanding of the Intangible Capital multiplier effects of AI and DT. This was, also, already illustrated by the late economist from the Lund University, Professor Knut Wicksell, who stated in his research that Innovation and Technology are the best friends of the Man (Humphrey 2004).

As a final remark, an idea remains: digital transformation is underway, the process cannot be stopped. Society must derive maximum benefit from this process by knowing how to place "boundaries" that respect the harmonious development that places the Planet and the People at the centre of decisions.

Table 3 Countries' clusters interpretation

Cluster label	Country	Cluster meaning
7	FI—Finland DK—Denmark E—Sweden NL—Netherland EE—Estonia	Given the position of this group of countries between the cluster 2 (attitude: Positive feelings about impact of DT) and 6 (attitude: Positive and confident attitude about DT and its personal use of digital technologies) we see that these countries correspond to advanced societies that accept, understand and have positive attitudes in relation to DT; its effects in society are seen as positive and desirable. Authomatic synthesis: (48 <= QD5_01 <= 61) AND (46 <= QD126_TA <= 60) AND (73 <= QD9_Y <= 81)
8	CY—Cyprus FR—France SI—Slovenia DE—Germany BE—Belgium LU—Luxembourg UK—United Kingdom LV—Latvia	Attitudes between those of clusters 3 and 5: 3: Formed by people with negative feelings about Robots and AI and not trusting in its use. 5: Not very enthusiastic about DT. Distrust seems an adequate description for the general attitude of this cluster. Authomatic synthesis: (28 <= QD5_01 <= 41) AND (31 <= QD9_N <= 58) AND (25 <= QD125_TA <= 43)
9	RO—Romania HU—Hungary HR—Croatia EL—Greece AT—Austria SP—Spain	Attitudes between those of clusters 1 and 4: 1: This group is formed by people that considers himself rather away from digital technologies or not having the skills allowing a useful use of digital technologies. 4: With Fears and uncomfortable with the idea that Robots and AI eliminates more jobs than create new ones. Authomatic synthesis: (33 < 0 QD11_N < 45) AND (13 < QD1-1_TN <= 22) AND (58 <= QD9_N >= 75)
10	LT—Lithuania CZ—Czech Republic MT—Malta IE—Ireland PL—Poland BG—Bulgaria PT—Portugal SK—Slovakia IT—Italy	Attitudes between those of clusters 1 and 2: 1: Formed by people that considers himself rather away from digital technologies or not having the skills and information allowing a useful use of digital technologies. 2: Formed by people with positive feelings about impact of DT. Authomatic synthesis: (19 <= QD10_TN < 31) AND (68 <= QD122_TA <= 86)

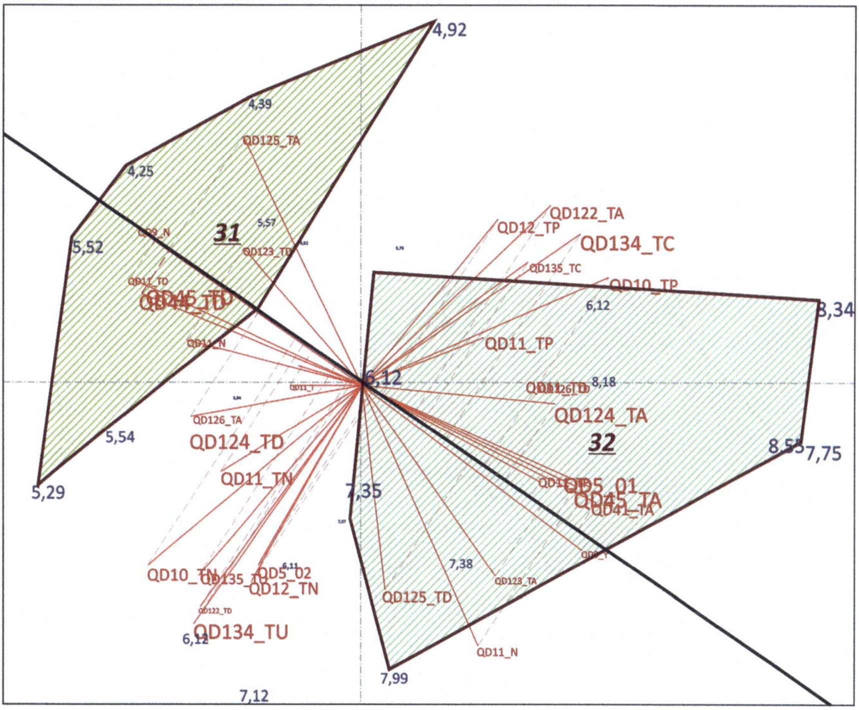

Fig. 3 Countries' labels replaced with values of variable NIC_S14. Countries with NIC_S14 below the first quartile (label 31) and above the third quartile (label 32) are clustered

Annex: Correspondence of the Variables Used in the Data Set and Some of the Variables Included in the Questionnaire of EU (2017, pp. 121–171)

QD1.1 In your view, what impact do the most recent digital technologies currently have on: The economy (%).
Resulting columns in data set: QD1-1_TP—Total "Positive" QD1-1_TN—Total "Negative".

QD1.2 In your view, what impact do the most recent digital technologies currently have on: The society (%).
Resulting columns in data set: *QD12_TP—Total "Positive" QD12_TN—Total "Negative".*

QD4.1 To what extent do you agree or disagree with the following statements regarding your skills in the use of digital technologies: You consider yourself to be sufficiently skilled in the use of digital technologies . . . in your daily life (%).
Resulting columns in data set: *QD41_TA—Total "Agree" D41_TD—Total "Disagree".*

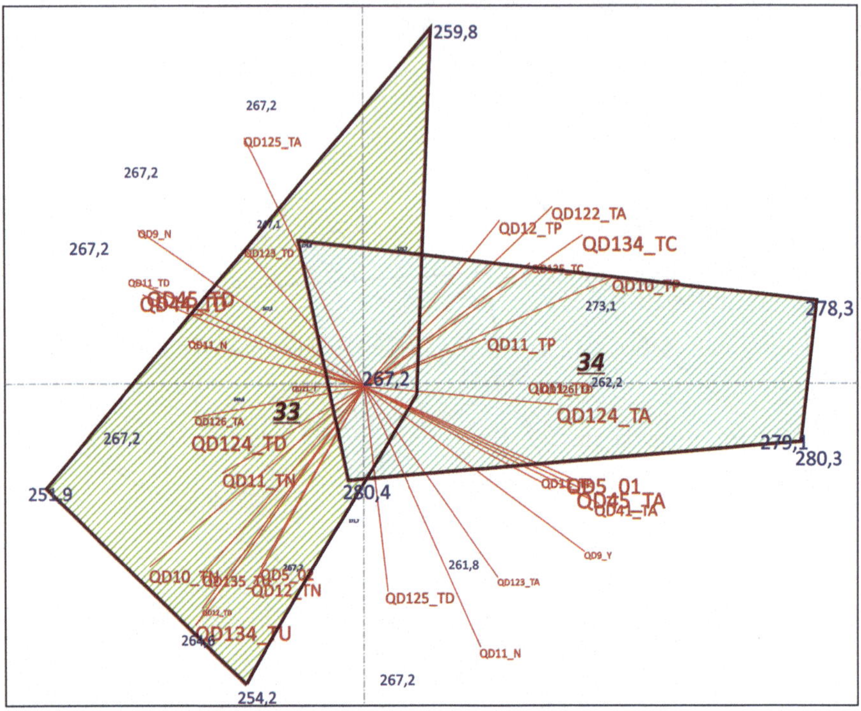

Fig. 4 Countries labels replaced with values of variable MNP. Countries with MNP below the first quartile (label 33) and above the third quartile (label 34) are clustered

QD4.4 To what extent do you agree or disagree with the following statements regarding your skills in the use of digital technologies: You consider yourself to be sufficiently skilled in the use of digital technologies … to use online public services, such as filing a tax declaration or applying for a visa online (%).
Resulting columns in data set: *QD44_TA—Total "Agree" QD44_TD—Total "Disagree"*.

QD4.5 To what extent do you agree or disagree with the following statements regarding your skills in the use of digital technologies: You consider yourself to be sufficiently skilled in the use of digital technologies … to benefit from digital and online learning opportunities (%).
Resulting columns in data set: *QD45_TA—Total "Agree" QD45_TD—Total "Disagree"*.

QD5 When you see or read a story published on online social networks, what makes you consider the story trustworthy? (MAX. 2 ANSWERS) (%) *(IF 'ONLINE SOCIAL NETWORKS USERS', CODE 1 TO 5 IN D62.5)*. Resulting columns in data set:
Resulting columns in data set: *QD5_01—The story comes from a reliable source (e.g. media, brand or organisation) Q D5_02—You generally do not trust stories published on online social networks.*

QD6 Have you ever used a fact checking website, for example to check if a story you read on online social networks was trustworthy? (%).
(IF 'ONLINE SOCIAL NETWORKS USERS', CODE 1 TO 5 IN D62.5).
Resulting columns in data set: *QD6_N—No, never Q D6_Y – Total "Yes"*

QD9 In the last 12 months, have you heard, read or seen anything about artificial intelligence? (%).
Resulting columns in data set: *QD9_Y—Yes Q D9_N—No.*

QD10 Generally speaking, do you have a very positive, fairly positive, fairly negative or very negative view of robots and artificial intelligence? (%).
QD10_TP—Total "Positive" QD10_TN—Total "Negative".

QD11 Do you think your current job could be done by a robot or by artificial intelligence in the future? (%).
(IF "CURRENTLY WORKING", CODE 5 TO 18 IN D15a).
Resulting columns in data set: QD11_Y—Yes, entirely QD 11_N—No, not at all.

QD12.1 Please tell me to what extent you agree or disagree with each of the following statements. Due to the use of robots and artificial intelligence, more jobs will disappear than new jobs will be created (%).
Resulting columns in data set: *D121_TA—Total "Agree" QD121_TD—Total "Disagree".*

QD12.2 Please tell me to what extent you agree or disagree with each of the following statements. Robots and artificial intelligence are a good thing for society, because they help people do their jobs or carry out daily tasks at home (%).
Resulting columns in data set: *QD122_TA—Total "Agree" QD122_TD—Total "Disagree".*

QD12.3 Please tell me to what extent you agree or disagree with each of the following statements. Robots and artificial intelligence are technologies that require careful management (%).
Resulting columns in data set: *QD123_TA—Total "Agree" QD123_TD—Total "Disagree".*

QD12.4 Please tell me to what extent you agree or disagree with each of the following statements. Robots are necessary as they can do jobs that are too hard or too dangerous for people (%).
Resulting columns in data set: *QD124_TA—Total "Agree" QD124_TD–Total "Disagree".*

QD12.5 Please tell me to what extent you agree or disagree with each of the following statements. The EU is ahead of other world regions when it comes to the digital transformation of industry (%).
Resulting columns in data set: *QD125_TA—Total "Agree" QD125_TD—Total "Disagree".*

QD12.6 Please tell me to what extent you agree or disagree with each of the following statements. Robots and artificial intelligence steal peoples' jobs (%).
Resulting columns in data set: *QD126_TA—Total "Agree" QD126_TD—Total "Disagree".*

QD13.4 Here is a list of things that could be done by or with robots. For each of them, please tell me, using a scale from 1 to 10, how you would personally feel about it. On this scale, "1" means that you would feel "totally uncomfortable" and "10" means that you would feel "totally comfortable" with this situation. Receiving goods delivered by a drone or a robot (%).
Resulting columns in data set: *QD134_TC—1 Totally Comfortable QD134_TU—10 Totally Uncomfortable.*

QD13.5 Here is a list of things that could be done by or with robots. For each of them, please tell me, using a scale from 1 to 10, how you would personally feel about it. On this scale, "1" means that you would feel "totally uncomfortable" and "10" means that you would feel "totally comfortable" with this situation. Being driven in a driverless car in traffic (%).
Resulting columns in data set: *QD135_TC—1 Totally Comfortable QD135_TU—10 Totally Uncomfortable.*

QD14 Would you like to have online access to your medical or health records (health data, prescriptions and medical records about you) allowing you to consult them at any time wherever you are? (%).
Resulting columns in data set: *QD14_Y—Yes QD14_N—No.*

References

Benkler Y, Roberts H, Faris R (2018) Network propaganda: manipulation, disinformation, and radicalization in american politics. Oxford University Press, Oxford. https://doi.org/10.1093/oso/9780190923624.001.0001

Berners-Lee T (1990) Information management: a proposal. CERN

Brundage M, Avin S, Clark J, Toner H, Eckersley P, Garfinkel B, Dafoe A, et al (2018) The malicious use of artificial intelligence: forecasting, prevention, and mitigation. https://doi.org/10.17863/CAM.22520

Dafoe A (2018) AI governance: a research agenda. Center for the Governance of AI, Future of Humanity Institute, University of Oxford, Oxford. https://www.fhi.ox.ac.uk/wp-content/uploads/GovAIAgenda.pdf

Ding J (2018) Deciphering China's AI dream: the context, components, capabilities, and consequences of China's strategy to lead the world in AI. Center for the Governance of AI, Future of Humanity Institute, University of Oxford, Oxford

Dyson G (2012) Turing's cathedral: the origins of the digital universe. Vintage Books, New York

EU (2017) Special eurobarometer 460: attitudes towards the impact of digitisation and automation on daily life, directorate-general for communication. http://data.europa.eu/euodp/en/data/dataset/S2160_87_1_460_ENG

Frey CB, Osborne M (2013) The future of employment: how susceptible are jobs to computerisation? University of Oxford, Oxford

Gabriel KR (1971) The biplot graphic display of matrices with application to principal component analysis. Biometrika 58(3):453–467

Galindo MP (1986) Una alternativa de representación simultánea: HJ-Biplot. Quaderns d'Estadística, Sistemes, Informatica i Investigació Operativa, Questiió

Greenacre M (2010) Biplots in practice (edited by editorial: Rubes). Fundación BBVA, Madrid. https://www.fbbva.es/publicaciones/biplots-in-practice-2/

Helbing D, Frey BS, Gigerenzer G, Hafen E, Hagner M, Hofstetter Y, Hoven J van den, et al (2017) Will democracy survive big data and artificial intelligence? Sci Am. https://www.scientificamerican.com/article/will-democracy-survive-big-data-and-artificial-intelligence/

Humphrey TM (2004, Fall) Ricardo versus Wicksell on job losses and technological change. Econ Q, Federal Reserve Bank of Richmond 90(4):5–24

Kremer J-F, Müller B (2012) Cyber security: developing a framework to understand the emerging challenges to states in an interconnected world. British International Studies Association and International Studies Association Joint International Conference, Edinburgh

Lin CY-Y, Edvinsson L (2011) National intellectual capital: a comparison of 40 countries, national intellectual capital: a comparison of 40 countries. Springer, New York. https://doi.org/10.1007/978-1-4419-7377-1

Nedelkoska L, Quintini G (2018) Automation, skills use and training. OECD, Paris. https://doi.org/10.1787/2e2f4eea-en

OECD (2016) Skills matter: further results from the survey of adult skills. OECD, Paris. https://doi.org/10.1787/9789264258051-en

OECD (2017a) Key issues for digital transformation in the G20. OECD, Paris. https://www.oecd.org/g20/key-issues-for-digital-transformation-in-the-g20.pdf

OECD (2017b) OECD digital economy outlook 2017. OECD, Paris. https://doi.org/10.1787/9789264276284-en

OECD (2017c) OECD science, technology and industry scoreboard 2017: the digital transformation. OECD, Paris. https://doi.org/10.1787/9789264268821-en

OECD (2018) OECD science, technology and innovation outlook 2018: adapting to technological and societal disruption. OECD, Paris. https://doi.org/10.1787/sti_in_outlook-2018-en

OECD (2019a) Going digital: shaping policies, improving lives – summary. OECD, Paris. http://www.oecd.org/going-digital/going-digital-synthesis-summary.pdf

OECD (2019b) Measuring the digital transformation: a roadmap for the future. OECD, Paris. https://doi.org/10.1787/9789264311992-en

Shao C, Hui P-M, Wang L, Jiang X, Flammini A, Menczer F, Ciampaglia GL (2018) Anatomy of an online misinformation network. PLoS ONE 13(4):e0196087

Ståhle P, Ståhle S, Lin CYY (2015) Intangibles and national economic wealth – a new perspective on how they are linked. J Intellect Cap 16(1):20–57. Emerald Group Publishing Limited

Turing AM (1937) On computable numbers, with an application to the Entscheidungsproblem. Proc Lond Math Soc s2-42(1):230–265

Turing AM (1950, October) Computing machinery and intelligence. In: Mind, vol 59. Oxford University Press, Oxford, pp 433–460

Vairinhos VM (2003) Desarrollo de Un Sistema de Minería de Datos Basado En Los Métodos de Biplot. Universidad de Salamanca, España

Vairinhos V, Matos F, Matos AJ (2019) National intellectual capital influence on innovation and sustainability. In: Matos F, Vairinhos V, Selig P, Edvinsson L (eds) Intellectual capital management as a driver of sustainability: perspectives for organizations and society. Springer, Cham, pp 221–237

Waldrop MM (2019) News feature: what are the limits of deep learning? Proc Natl Acad Sci 116 (4):1074–1077

Yang K-C, Varol O, Davis CA, Ferrara E, Flammini A, Menczer F (2019) Arming the public with artificial intelligence to counter social bots. Hum Behav Emerg Technol 1(1):48–61

Zhang B, Dafoe A (2019) Artificial intelligence: american attitudes and trends. Center for the Governance of AI, Future of Humanity Institute, University of Oxford, Oxford

Knowledge and Technology: Man as a Technological Animal

Inês Salgueiro

Abstract Technology is a prominent projection of human reason upon the world. It is an attempt to make the world fit in with what we imagine to be the ideal for us. Human beings, unlike other animals, are capable of understanding their limitations and can not only reflect on these limitations but also envisage what the human condition should be. This chapter argues that, given it is not possible for us to reject these ideals of reason, we can infer that to be technical beings is a characteristic of human nature. We shall analyse some issues belonging to our relationship with technology throughout history and show that technology should be viewed as a specific desire prompted by the very nature of human rationality. More than that, technology is an attempt to fill the gap between the limitations of our nature and a continuous increase in our knowledge. This chapter is not about the connections between technology and science, morality, politics, economy, society and culture, but about technology as a metaphysical urge of the human condition. We conclude that man is not simply a rational or political animal but a technological animal as well. In our era of global technology, it is possible to see clearly what the reality of our condition has always been.

1 Introduction

Technology is present in almost all aspects of human lives. It is closely related to the creation of artefacts. Almost all human activities require artefacts. Starting from an extended definition of artefact, understanding artefacts as a human construction, this chapter aims to show that creating artefacts corresponds to the true essence of thought. There are not only physical artefacts, but there are also mental artefacts. Thus, it is intended not only to show the relation of thought to the artefacts it has created, but also to discuss the true nature of technology. This analysis will allow us to infer that the human being is a technological animal.

I. Salgueiro (✉)
IFILNOVA, Faculdade de Ciências Sociais e Humanas, Universidade Nova de Lisboa, Lisbon, Portugal

F. Matos et al. (eds.), *Knowledge, People, and Digital Transformation*, Contributions to Management Science, https://doi.org/10.1007/978-3-030-40390-4_3

The chapter is structured as follows: after this introduction, the second section describes the relationship between technology and the human mind. Subsequently, the third section presents some issues belonging to our relationship with technology throughout history. The fourth section aims to prove that technology is not just applied to science. The fifth section analyses the phenomenon of technology itself, or, in other words, focuses on the metaphysics of technology. The conclusion summarises the main ideas.

2 The Relation Between Technology and the Human Mind

Technology is a projection of human reason in the world. Human reason needs to establish synthesis, which means that it is not purely analytical but synthetic; in other words, it is part of the nature of the human mind to create syntheses and to make a rational comprehension of the world possible. When Man reflects upon nature, he does not limit himself to analysing this nature but observes its faults and its limits and imagines ideal circumstances. He studies nature as the condition of the possibility of something new. This is the great anthropological difference. While other animals analyse the world around them and act only according to what is given to them, man synthesises the data and transforms it into something new—he creates artefacts. Artefacts are the visible effect of the synthetic nature of human thought. Human thought cannot be reduced to a mere connection of predefined rules. It is not a simple formal system in which the concepts are logically related. Human thought is creative; it is work. Human thought is, in its essence, the work of the intellect that uses the raw material given by nature in potency and transforms it into an act. Thus, creating artefacts corresponds to the true essence of thought. Without this creative activity, human thought does not fulfil its nature. Without the creative activity of artefacts, thought is reduced to mere consciousness. Without work, human reason is limited to the field of use. There is only true thinking when there is work. Thought and work are one. Thought is only revealed in work. Artefacts are a manifestation of the work of thought. Unlike other beings, who have an existence independent of man, artefacts, in order to live, must first be thought in the human mind. The creation of artefacts is the manifestation of the spontaneity of reason. It is the capacity to initiate a new series of causal phenomena, anthropological distinction par excellence. It is almost true freedom in the sense that it creates entities while moulding what it is. This ability allows the updating of ideas through the creation of new entities. These new beings cooperate in the knowledge of the world and in the knowledge of the mind. Such aptitude for creation is referred to as technique. Technique has several characteristics that should be emphasised. First and foremost, it allows thought and work, but it also allows knowledge. Without technique, knowledge is not possible. It is technique that enables the understanding and acquisition of the world by setting limits to the unlimited real. Technique increases the efficiency of thought and, above all, allows men to understand part of nature because it enables a progressive path for the mind and human life. Technique is creation.

Aristotle says in *Physics* that "generally art in some cases completes what nature cannot bring to a finish, and in others imitates nature" (Aristotle 1984, *Phys.* 199 a 15). It is indeed easy to observe in history that it is so. Let us look at two examples: the first the creation of basic tools, the second the creation of the airplane. As far as the first example is concerned, what was at stake was clearly completing nature. In the Palaeolithic, the creation of chipped stone tools and in the Neolithic the creation of polished stone tools show, precisely, a recognition of one's limits and a capacity to overcome these limits. There is in this technique a visible synthetic unit of prediction of an artefact, according to the specific objective of a task, the need the same task presents and the apprehension of a human limitation one wishes to abolish. The creation of the airplane is a good example to illustrate this point. Although there is no dating possible for man's desire to fly, it is believed that since prehistory man has desired to fly because he wishes to fly. Despite the benefits of flying, the first interest is the desire to imitate a competence. Whether technology completes or imitates nature, it is certain that it is due to the work of the person who thinks. Technology is the foundation of thought. There is a reciprocal relationship between thought and technology. Without technology, thought would be impossible. Thought needs technology to present itself, to strengthen itself and to manifest itself. Thought and technique are one. Technique and technological development allow *episteme*. Episteme appears to the human mind as the object of desire par excellence. It corresponds to an ideally conceived synthesis which is still recognised at a childish and confusing stage and, therefore, intends to develop new learning procedures. Under the domain of this desire for knowledge, technique allows a kind of epistemology. We say "kind of" because we are in a stage of little enlightenment, which only allows us to show that we make certain judgements without knowing what exactly these judgements correspond to because we do not have total evidence. Only technology admits revisions and successive approximations to the truth. Only technology will allow, through an adequate methodology, the escape from partial epistemology. Only technology can overcome dogmatism, whether sceptical or naive. In fact, knowledge of things and the awareness of our situation transcends us, and so we are not able to either certify or repudiate data with apodictic evidence. Technology makes it possible, in the first place, to persist in the possibility of future enlightenment and secondly, it allows an adaptation of our finite point of view to the immensity of the world through successive technical developments. This capacity is the sign of the anthropological difference to the supposed inferences of other animals. All epistemology begins with technique. Without technique, no work is possible. Without technique, it is not possible to think. Technique allows knowledge of the world. The human cognitive condition is a technological condition. It is only through technology that man is allowed some comprehension of the self and some comprehension of others. Technology is a metaphysical activity. Without metaphysics and without projection of synthetic ideals, the progress of knowledge is not possible. Metaphysics and technology are one. Technology is present in almost all aspects of human lives, not only in our contemporary world but always.

3 Some Issues Belonging to Our Relationship with Technology Throughout History

The analysis of the creation of the artefacts "time measurements", "language", "writing", "numbers", "papyrus", "press", "computer" and "internet" will help us to understand technology as a specific desire prompted by the very nature of human rationality.

Time measurements are an extremely useful artefact. By looking at the sky, men divided the world into two parts—the day and the night. Once again, a synthesis is observed. There had never been days and nights before human existence. This creation was the first step in counting time. It is believed that in the year 2000 B. C., through the projection of the shadow of a given object, the Sun's time was quantified. The solar clock was the first time-reckoning. The moon allows us to count how many days each phase lasts and its intervals of 7 days. When the lunar periods come to an end, this represents a month. Leap years result from the inadequacy of the technical model adopted for counting time in relation to reality. Our planet takes about 365.2422 days to circle the Sun, but we do not count the decimal part because, as noted earlier, we work with days and nights. Thus, the decimal part is added to the following year. After the Earth has circled the Sun four times, 1460.9688 days have passed. Four years correspond to 1460 days, and therefore the remainder corresponds to approximately 1 day. It was for this reason that it was decided to add an extra day every 4 years. The month of February was chosen to contain only 28 days and every 4 years to contain 29 days, with the latter year being designated as a leap year because in mathematical terms it is the year divisible by four. Measuring time brought immense advantages and conferred benefits on man's organisation in terms of achieving greater clarity in planning. It made understanding and communication between men possible and, above all, it developed human intelligence which began to operate on the technical basis of temporality.

Language is a human-made artefact. It is the way in which man thinks and knows almost everything real. It is not known for certain when language first emerged; there are only easily questionable theories. The theory of continuity (Chomsky 1996) argues that the origin of language has not been taken from its final form; in other words, language must have evolved from prelinguistic systems present in primates. The theory of discontinuity (Pinker 1994) argues that language is a unique feature and, to that extent, cannot be compared to anything. It must have appeared suddenly in humans. Regardless of how the language technique was developed, the benefits and advantages of the human condition's progress are undeniable. Language corresponds to a technique for abbreviating things and, therefore, it makes us move. Imagine a world without language, a mental world without concepts. This is impossible, which proves our technological nature.

The invention of writing is another great technological development. The development of the *cuneiform* system of writing by the Sumerians corresponds to an evolution not only political and intellectual, but above all technical.

Numbers are another example of the brilliant synthetic faculty of human reason. It is believed that they arose from the need to count animals about 30,000 years ago. The first numbering system dates to 1500 BC in Egypt and Greece. Without numbers, mathematical calculation would be impossible, and calculation is present in almost every situation of our day-to-day lives. Mathematics is a science supported by the causal connections we make, and proof of this is the concept of a decade conceived with base ten because we have ten fingers on our hands. Mathematics allows an epistemic path to the development of knowledge. Mathematics is a form of knowledge whose process leads to the establishment of relations between terms through an integrative calculation that is manifestly synthetic. It is applied in almost every area of knowledge. Mathematics is a technical knowledge in constant technological development. Mathematics is a technical modelling and, in this sense, allows computation, but this modelling does not correspond to accuracy; it is a human-made system. Hilbert's aim at the International Congress of Mathematics in 1928 (Hilbert 1929) was to point out the shortcomings of Russell and Whitehead's *Principia Mathematica* (Whitehead and Russell 1925, 1927). Hilbert wondered if it was possible to demonstrate what *Principia Mathematica* claimed. His main question was whether or not mathematics is complete and, if so, whether this is possible to demonstrate. Gödel was able to prove that arithmetic is incomplete (Gödel 1986). Starting from the set of *integers* defined by *Peano's* axioms,[1] Gödel enlarged them through a complex theory of types so that "the obtained system could represent sets of integers" (Pereira 2007, p. 64). Thus, Gödel proved that the property of being demonstrable is as arithmetical as classifying numbers as natural, whole, rational, irrational or integer, for example. All arguments offered as proofs in mathematics are not demonstrations. Therefore, there are mathematics statements that are taken as true,[2] but cannot be proved to be true. What Gödel attests is that this is not demonstrable. In fact, mathematics is not demonstrable because it is a technical model created by man. It is a limitation that gives synthesis to the analytical base from which we begin—logic. Logic is the core of human thought. Mathematics is a construction of the human mind, and because it is a construction, it only allows epistemic approximations, but these approximations cannot be demonstrated from themselves. We would have to jump out of our building models so that we can say whether our models are appropriate. In other words, we cannot understand outside the model of understanding we construct to understand. Mathematics starts from definitions; definitions describe the meaning of a term. From our definitions follow all axioms, which are the starting point for reasoning and, in this sense, must be assumed as true. A theorem is a statement that we prove to be true based on previous statements. The proof will be obtained by previously defined valid rules. All these are mere technical models of cognitive approximation to the real and to an ideal

[1]Jeff Paris and Leo Harrington (1977) provided an example of the incompleteness of Peano's arithmetic that does not require the numerical code of notions of logic, or in other words, a strictly mathematical example of incompleteness.

[2]For further discussion see Salgueiro (2012).

whose exact nature we do not know. To want to demonstrate that mathematics itself is true or false requires another observer. It would have to be possible for us to recognise arithmetic in its entirety, which would imply not only the apprehension of all parts of arithmetic, but also the meaning and position of each arithmetical element. A similar position is presented by Quine (1961) in *Two Dogmas of Empiricism* regarding the distinction between analytic and synthetic made by Kant (1998) and maintained by Carnap (1967). Quine considers that to be able to establish a difference between analytic and synthetic, one would have to be in possession of an absolute epistemic point of view, otherwise this distinction is empty of any epistemological determination. In other words, the concept of analytic is itself a meaning because it is understood based on a position of enlightenment we do not possess. What is at stake in Quine's analysis is that the relation existing in a given linguistic universe must presuppose knowledge of the rules of a given linguistic universe for which an assertion can be considered analytic or synthetic. When we try to clarify an analytic relationship, we assume the existence of previously defined semantic rules, but the very expression "semantic rule" is not released from the need for clarification. This makes the difference between analytical and synthetic propositions unnecessary. That is to say, for Quine, any assumption cannot hold a valid meaning and therefore cannot correspond to knowledge free of dogma.

Papyrus is another excellent example of technology. It was invented by the Egyptians over 5000 years ago and is made from the fibres of an aquatic plant found on the banks of the River Nile in Egypt. It was the first support for writing, essential for the extension of memory and the transmission and acquisition of knowledge.

Gutenberg's press was one of the greatest contributions to our development. We are beings with little time, and the dissemination of knowledge using manuscripts took a long time. Enabling texts to be printed contributed not only to the diffusion but also to the progress of knowledge. It is one of the best examples of technological involvement with human thought. The press allowed the creation of more libraries. Libraries are a technological extension of memory and mind.

The Turing machine is one of the most intelligent synthetic projections of human reason. It is, in our view, the best example of technological creation existing in the history of humankind. It allowed, among other things, data processing and storage as well as large-scale calculations. It is a computational function by mathematical algorithms, and it made it possible to determine solutions to complex problems through a finite number of steps (Turing 1950).

The Internet connects the world, extends possibilities never before achieved and provides access to information and knowledge. Through the Internet, we can search for data and satisfy our curiosity in a very short time. The Internet gives us the ability to gain knowledge very quickly. It makes it possible to discuss ideas with people who work in our research area or in other fields through a network of links. Through the Internet, we can know, without having to go to a bookstore or a library, that new approaches exist for solving a given problem in our scientific area. We can download articles and books that interest us. The Internet has democratised knowledge. If there is free access to the Internet, everyone is able to seek and acquire knowledge, regardless of race, sex, social status or country of birth.

The analysis of these questions, which belong to our relation with technology throughout history, allows us to infer that technology is a specific desire caused by the very nature of human rationality. More than this, technology is the attempt to fill the gap of the limitations of our nature through a continuous increase not only in knowledge but in skills. We think with technology, and technology and man are so intertwined that it is not possible to separate man from the artefacts he has created. Man, without artefacts, is an irrational animal. In fact, his rationality begins with the creation of the artefact of language. We are not just political and rational animals as Aristotle claims in *Politics* (Aristotle 1984, *Pol.* 1253 a 3), but technological animals as well. What Aristotle claims cannot be denied, but man is only a political animal thanks to technology. Technology unites, and has always united, society. It is an anthropological force. It is the most elementary phenomenon of humankind. Man is a technological animal.

The evolution of technology allows human evolution. Darwin shows the evolution of the different species of nature over time (Darwin 1859). The evolution that Darwin focuses on can be classified as interspecific because it corresponds to an evolution to a different species; the human evolution made possible by technology is of a different order and can be classified as intraspecific. Technology enables human intraspecific evolution. No other species evolve intraspecifically because no other species has a technological nature, and only a technological nature has the capacity to do so.

4 Technology Is Not Applied Science

Technology is not applied to science. To claim that technology is merely applied science corresponds to a hasty judgement. In fact, science depends on technology and not the other way around. Technology precedes and is fundamental to science. It is not a chronological priority, as it is the very essence of thought to be technical. We think with technology whereas science only exists because man has created artefacts that have allowed him to think better, to be smarter and to have faster reasoning with improved effectiveness. The scientific-technological development model is as follows:

Human mind ⇒ Creation of artefacts ⇒ Incorporation of the new artefact into the mind ⇒ Science ⇒ Human mind ⇒ Creation of new artefacts.

Simon (1969) in *The Sciences of the Artificial* argued that technology is different from science because science cares about what it is while technology is concerned with what it should be. This level of distinction seems appropriate to us because technology can be defined as a continuous attempt to approximate the world to what we desire. Ideas about what this should be are usually found to originate outside technology, that is, engineers are responsible for conceiving these ideas, that is, they have the quality, the talent, the genius and the creative ability. They are people who strive and can bring new things into existence owing to the identification of a gap and their effort, will, creativity, ingenuity and genius. Thus, technology is traditionally understood to have two dimensions, namely, productivity and instrumentality. While productivity is related to the production of new artefacts, instrumentality assists in production while at the same time mastering the surrounding environment. This view is incomplete. In fact, ideas about what it should be are inseparable from technology, and it is not possible for humans to think without artefacts, so without technology, there is no thought. This is so not only because some artefacts are so rooted in the human mind that they are inseparable from thought, but also because it is technology that provides certain technical skills indispensable to the acquisition of scientific knowledge. We are forced to admit the technological character of mind and human nature. When it is argued that technology is science applied to society, it should rather be thought that science only affects society through technology. Science is closely dependent on technology; in fact, if there were no technology, there would be no science. It is technology that allows scientific development and not the other way around. We will give a very concrete example—lenses. It was only thanks to the technological development of increasing vision through the lens that certain scientific developments became possible. If there were no technology, the atomic model would still be Democritus' model, and the developments of physics would still be in the field of philosophical reflection which, as Wittgenstein says, "mean something which stands above or below, but not beside the natural sciences" (Wittgenstein 1922, 4.111).

Technology has made it possible to clarify fundamental questions of classical epistemology, such as the reality of atoms, the question of causality and probability, space-time and the nature of the quantum world. Technology has made it possible to apply the experimental method to fields beyond human vision. Human-made particle accelerators, for example, have made it possible to achieve knowledge that could not be reached with naturally occurring particle sources. They provide high doses of energy so that the particles can break the force field that surrounds the atomic nucleus and hit it. Particles, when accelerated in the opposite direction, produce thousands of collisions per second. Detectors record the particle traces that result from each collision, and a computer selects the collisions to be analysed. Such technology has enabled the amazing observation of subatomic data and the consequent expansion of science. Technology is an open system because it manifests itself continuously. It depends on engineering and, because of this, can never be considered a closed system. For this reason, it must also be thought of as producing effects in the world. That is why many thinkers consider it important to reflect not on the phenomenon itself but on the relation of the phenomenon to morality, politics, culture, civilisation and the human condition. Any of these relations with technology are interesting and allow us to observe in detail some aspects of technological manifestation. But all these approaches correspond to peripheral visions, phenomena of visions of mere detail that do not allow us to grasp and understand what technology truly represents.

5 The Phenomenon of Technology Itself

Heidegger's essay "The Question concerning Technology" (Heidegger 1977) is the one that best approaches the technology phenomenon and, as such, presents some interesting aspects about its substance that need to be emphasised. First, Heidegger complains that for questioning to exist about technology, this questioning must be free and will only be free if it allows our existence to be open to the essence of technology. What Heidegger claims is that when one asks about the being of technology, one is not asking about machines and engineering processes, but about the phenomenon that is present in all technological aspects. The question about technology, the philosophical reflection on technology, cannot be a reflection on specific methodological processes. It is not a question about machines, but about being. It is about asking what it is that makes technique be technique. In other words, what is present in all technical artefacts that allows them to be identified as technological? What is the substance, the essence of technology? What form does technology have? Thus, the essence of technology cannot be identified with technology in the same way as when we look for the essence of a tree, we search for what is present in all trees and allows us to identify any tree as a tree, because in all trees is that precise thing that allows them to be trees. Thus, Heidegger complains that "the essence of technology is by no means anything technological" (Heidegger 1977, p. 4). Therefore, to understand this specific phenomenon, we cannot observe it with a neutral look of inquiry because it makes us blind to what we want to observe. Heidegger regards the view of the Ancient Greeks as correct. Thus, for the Ancient Greeks to understand something, it was necessary to identify its essence. Based on this assumption, he resorts to two statements that any man can identify—the first declares that technology is a means to an end and the second states that technology is a human activity. These two definitions complement one another. Indeed, postulating ends and using means to achieve them is a human activity. Heidegger says:

> [t]he manufacture and utilisation of equipment, tools, and machines, the manufactured and used things themselves, and the needs and ends that they serve, all belong to what technology is. The whole complex of these contrivances is technology. Technology itself is a contrivance, or, in Latin, an *instrumentum*. (Heidegger 1977, p. 4).

Instrumentum means here to build and to organise. Heidegger compares it with the noun *Einrichtung*; it is an invention. Thus, technology is an instrument, an *Einrichtung*. Heidegger considers, however, that such an understanding does not exhaust what technology is because it is an instrumental and anthropological view that does not capture its true essence. In fact, according to Heidegger, "the instrumental conception of technology conditions every attempt to bring man into the right relation to technology" (Heidegger 1977, p. 5). It is understood that Heidegger does not consider the instrumental definition of technology to be incorrect; it simply does not capture its essence. To grasp the substance, we must ask "What is the instrumental itself? Within what do such things as means and end belong?" (Heidegger 1977, p. 6). Heidegger's response is as follows:

> A means is that whereby something is effected and thus attained. Whatever has an effect as its consequence is called a cause. But not only that by means of which something else is effected is a cause. The end in keeping with which the kind of means to be used is determined is also considered a cause. Wherever ends are pursued, and means are employed, wherever instrumentality reigns, there reigns causality. (Heidegger 1977, p. 6).

Thus, to clarify the status of causality, it is necessary to understand what technology is. Causality enables synthesis between concepts and these syntheses allow knowledge to be understood as the revelation of something true. Heidegger says: "We are questioning concerning technology, and we have arrived now at *aletheia*, at revealing. What has the essence of technology to do with revealing? The answer: everything" (Heidegger 1977, p. 12). Once instrumentality is considered the fundamental characteristic of technology, it represents a means to revelation, to knowledge. Thus, all technological production relies on revealing something. Heidegger argues: "Technology is, therefore, no mere means. Technology is a way of revealing" (Heidegger 1977, p. 12). Heidegger resorts to the etymological origin of the word technology to support the idea of technology as a means of revealing the truth. The word comes from the Greek *technikon* and means what belongs to *techne*. Heidegger points out that *techne* is the name given not only to the craftsman's activities and skills but also to the arts of the mind and plastic arts. *Techne* belongs to appearance, to *poiesis*; it is poietic, it is work. Thus, there is a classic relationship between technology and work. By work, we understand thought in act. One cannot dissociate the act of thinking from technology, one cannot decompose thought and creative activity, and it is not possible to separate technique and emergence as one cannot separate poetry and work. These concepts are one and are closely linked to metaphysics and epistemology. Aristotle in the sixth book of *Nicomachean Ethics* distinguishes between *episteme* and *techne* (Aristotle 1984, *N.E.* 1139 b 18–1140 a 24). *Techne* is a way of *aletheuein*; it reveals what is not clear and is not before us. Technology allows revelation, and although what is revealed is not identical to what is revealed through *poiesis*, it is, in any case, a means of disclosure. Thus, technology is the sister of poetry, and both are not merely human acts:

> Modern technology as an ordering revealing is, then, no merely human doing. Therefore, we must take that challenging that sets upon man to order the real as standing-reserve in accordance with the way in which it shows itself. That challenging gathers man into ordering. This gathering concentrates man upon ordering the real as standing-reserve. (Heidegger 1977, p. 19).

The merely instrumental definition of technology is weak. Heidegger believes that if we represent technology as an instrument, we force the essence of technology, and we do not grasp it. If we understand its instrumental character *comes to presence* as a kind of causality, we understand this *coming to presence* as a revelation. If we understand that *coming to presence* occurs in something that man needs and uses, it is clear the essence of technology is ambiguous. As Heidegger says:

> There was a time when it was not technology alone that bore the name *techne*. Once that revealing that brings forth truth into the splendour of radiant appearing also was called *techne*. Once there was a time when the bringing-forth of the true into the beautiful was called *techne*. And the *poiesis* of the fine arts also was called *techne*. (Heidegger 1977, p. 34)

The metaphysical meaning of the essence of technology is creation. Only creation enables the manifestation of being. Thus "the essence of technology is by no means anything technological" (Heidegger 1977, p. 4). Technology is related to the creative process. The reflection on technology belongs to the metaphysical domain of philosophical speculation. Metaphysics is the home of philosophy. All philosophy must be metaphysical because the essence of philosophy is to go beyond limits. Metaphysics is at the basis of all technological developments. There is no technological advance without stretching the limits of what has already been thought. It is metaphysics that, as a creative activity, allows scientific developments. No creative thinking is free from metaphysics—it is a kind of probe that carries out the first mission of recognition for the establishment of knowledge. Philosophy is and always has been a metaphysical activity. There is no philosophy without metaphysics. The work of philosophy is first to be *recognition*. When this recognition becomes effective knowledge, there is emancipation from metaphysics. It is metaphysics that allows us to advance, it is what designs paths for scientific knowledge. All scientific knowledge is second knowledge. Metaphysics is the foundation of all possible knowledge.

6 Conclusion

To be technical beings is a characteristic of human nature. The technical creation of artefacts allows man to think better and to develop. Technology, as a projection of human reason in the world, allows intraspecific human evolution. The questions analysed in this chapter point to the complexity of our thought process, including creativity. The metaphysical meaning of technology is creation. Metaphysics is at the basis of all creation and for that reason is at the basis of all human knowledge. Metaphysics is the pillar on which human knowledge is built because it provides the first insights. We do not think only with logic; to include metaphysical language in all knowledge fields would be very important for the development of science, technology, ethics and sustainability. The first issue raised by this study is that human thought is so complex that we cannot dissociate it from the models we have created. This analysis allows us, however, not only to persist in searching for theoretical and practical knowledge but also to place man in relation to his abilities.

References

Aristotle (1984) The complete works of Aristotle (vols 1–2). Princeton University Press, Princeton, NJ

Carnap R (1967) The logical syntax of language. Routledge, London

Chomsky N (1996) Powers and prospects. Reflections on human nature and the social order. Pluto, London

Darwin C (1859) On the origin of species. John Murray, London

Gödel K (1986) On formally undecidable propositions of Principia mathematica and related systems I. In: Feferman S, Kleene S, Moore G, Solovay R, van Heijenoort J (eds) Kurt Gödel collected works. I: Publications 1929–1936. Oxford University Press, New York, pp 144–195

Heidegger M (1977) The question concerning technology. In: Lovitt W (Trans.) The question concerning technology and other essays. Harper and Row, New York, pp 3–35

Hilbert D (1929) Probleme der Grundlegung der Mathematik. Mathematische Annalen 102:1–9. Lecture given at the international congress of mathematicians, 3 Sept 1928. In: Mancosu P (ed) From Brouwer to Hilbert. the debate on the foundations of mathematics in the 1920s. Oxford University Press, New York, pp 227–233

Kant I (1998) Critique of pure reason. Cambridge University Press, Cambridge, UK

Paris J, Harrington L (1977) A mathematical incompleteness in Peano arithmetic. In: Barwise J (ed) Handbook for mathematical logic. North-Holland, Amsterdam, pp 1133–1142

Pereira L (2007) Gödel and computability. In: Neves J, Santos MF, Machado JM (eds) Progress in artificial intelligence: 13th Portuguese conference on artificial intelligence, EPIA 2007. Springer, Berlin, pp 63–72

Pinker S (1994) The language instinct. How the mind creates language. William Morrow, New York

Quine WVO (1961) Two dogmas of empiricism. In: From a logical point of view. Harper and Row, New York, pp 20–46

Salgueiro I (2012) Certainty and forms of life. In: Galvez JP, Gaffal M (eds) Doubtful certainties—language-games, forms of life, relativism. Ontos, Heusenstamm, pp 41–52

Simon H (1969) The sciences of the artificial, 3rd edn. MIT Press, Cambridge, MA

Turing A (1950) Computing machinery and intelligence. Mind 50(236):433–460

Whitehead A, Russell B (1925) Principia mathematica, vol 1, 2nd edn. Cambridge University Press, Cambridge, UK

Whitehead A, Russell B (1927) Principia mathematica, vol 2–3, 2nd edn. Cambridge University Press, Cambridge, UK

Wittgenstein L (1922) Tractatus logico-philosophicus (Ogden CK, Trans.). Routledge & Kegan Paul, London

Beyond Digitalization: "My Boss Is Artificial"

Elke Brucker-Kley and Thomas Keller

Abstract Imagine that one day we have reached technological singularity—the point when technological development has outpaced human development. The question of whether machine intelligence is on a par with human intelligence has long been answered. Does this constellation place human fate at the mercy of machines, or is there still room to maneuver?

This chapter aims to propose a research design to facilitate an interdisciplinary discourse on our digital futures. The research proposal aims to trigger and explore an interdisciplinary discourse on the designability of our digital future based on immersive scenarios. The main contribution of the immersive scenarios shall be that all experts are able to live through and comment on the same experiences. The domain of leadership in an organizational setting serves as an example that shall enable us to frame and discuss "possible futures" in a particular sphere of life.

1 Theoretical Background

A fundamental question in dealing with digital change is whether the relationship between human and machine can be deliberately shaped or whether, sooner or later, human destiny will inevitably be determined by superior machine intelligence. ***If we choose the constructive path and decide to accept our digital future as a design challenge, how can we formulate our vision and our requirements for a desirable state?*** And what is "desirable," or at least "acceptable" or "bearable"? What is "risky" or even "dangerous"—and from what perspective? What can be done to enable human and social sciences to articulate such perspectives and requirements? Through the mixed reality scenarios at the heart of this research proposal, which will portray the relationship between a machine superior and its human subordinates, experts will experience what our life could be like once technological singularity has been reached and once virtualization is far advanced in every aspect of our life

E. Brucker-Kley · T. Keller (✉)
ZHAW Institute of Information Systems, Winterthur, Switzerland
e-mail: brck@zhaw.ch; kell@zhaw.ch

F. Matos et al. (eds.), *Knowledge, People, and Digital Transformation*, Contributions to Management Science, https://doi.org/10.1007/978-3-030-40390-4_4

(Kurzweil 2005; Ohta and Tamura 2014; Siderius 2012; Vinge 1993). At this point in time, digital transformation is no longer an issue, everything ***is*** digitized, we are ***beyond digitization***.

Technological singularity is a hypothesis that conjures up an era in which exponentially advancing technological development will outpace human development and lead to superior machine intelligence, which will then optimize itself continuously and ultimately make human destiny unpredictable (Kurzweil 2005). The nature and arrival of technical singularity have been discussed (and continuously postdated) since the 1950s (Ulam 1958). The first predictions of information theorists and science fiction authors were vague (Ulam 1958), but with the achievements of the Internet age and artificial intelligence (AI), in particular, they became increasingly concrete and imaginable, including computers that are "awake" and superhumanly intelligent, distributed computer networks joining forces to form an intelligent entity, intimate human–computer interfaces that emulate or even replace social interactions (Vinge 1993). The terms trans- or posthumanism extend this vision to include technologies that enhance human biology and intelligence considerably, all the way to a complete fusion of human and machine existence (Kurzweil 2005; Sorgner 2016). And there are equally extreme counter-propositions that foresee a collective storm of "neo-Luddites" in the face of technological totalitarianism, as the only salvation for human self-determination (Jones 2006; Larnier 2011). Whether these potential realities of our digital future are utopias or dystopias, they have always triggered reflections as to whether technological singularity is avoidable, desirable, and, ultimately, shapeable from a human perspective (Helbing 2015; Vinge 1993).

Such reflections gain in substance whenever allusions to technological singularity are made, allowing us to sense what machine superiority might mean, even if its field of application is still limited to date. In February 2011, a machine competed against two people in the quiz show "Jeopardy." The machine, called Watson (Ferrucci 2012), combined various technologies from the fields of speech recognition (Yu and Deng 2015) and AI (Russell and Norvig 2016) to be able to participate in the quiz show under the same conditions as human participants. Watson won the game and demonstrated its superiority over its human opponents in this very narrow field of application. Facial coding algorithms such as Afdex, that analyze facial expressions, have become a common tool in market research able to recognize people's emotions, such as a sincere versus a fake smile, faster and more accurately than humans (McDuff and Kaliouby 2017; Sénéchal et al. 2013). Cancer researchers using AI to extract prognostic information from tissue morphology came to the conclusion that state-of-the-art deep learning technologies outperform the results of experienced human observers (Bychkov et al. 2018). It is innovation news such as this that sheds new light on formerly fictional statements. Such as the famous quote from the science fiction movie "Matrix": "Never send a human to do a machine's job" (The Matrix 1999).

As a given for the scenarios, we further assume that the digitization and virtualization of the workplace (Colbert et al. 2016) will continue to advance and that a workplace will typically not have a physical location. Human and machine participants in any process will be seamlessly integrated and orchestrated in distributed networks. Mixed reality technologies will raise virtual cooperation continuously to a new level (Lanier 2017). Virtual spaces will not only enable the verbal and visual exchange of information, but also the interaction with virtual objects that represent the content of a discussion. A prototype example was developed based on the Master's thesis "Benefits and Practical Implications of using Mixed-Reality in the AEC Industry" (Sleegers 2018). Microsoft uses a three-dimensional video chat to market this approach as "holoportation" (Orts-Escolano 2016).

2 Research Design

We propose a multistage explorative and participatory research approach to develop, enrich, and evaluate scenarios for a setting in which human employees are guided, to varying degrees, by machines. The disciplines of economics (i.e., human resource management, law, business information technology), applied linguistics, and design (i.e., interaction design, immersive design) shall be employed in an interdisciplinary approach to create scenarios that allow to experience the human–machine relationship in such a setting. Experts from various fields of human and social science (e.g., psychology, philosophy, ethics) shall then immerse themselves in these scenarios to comment on and evaluate them against the background of their theories and models of human identity and behavior. Immersive technologies (i.e., mixed reality blending virtual and augmented reality) mediating the scenarios will be used to force the investigators to leave the role of the distanced observer and to dive into a subjective experience.

3 Research Questions

The proposed research plan is illustrated in Fig. 1. At the heart are the domains of leadership and law since our use case is an artificial boss. These two domains are complemented by IT and applied linguistics. IT sets the capabilities and behavior of an artificial boss whereas applied linguistics covers the human–machine communication styles. The four domains cover the scenario content. In a subsequent phase the scenario content is designed for immersion in a possibly virtual reality space. In this virtual reality space experts from different fields as indicated in the figure are able to live through and comment on the same experiences. These different perspectives then set the basis for the last phase: the scope for design of our digital future.

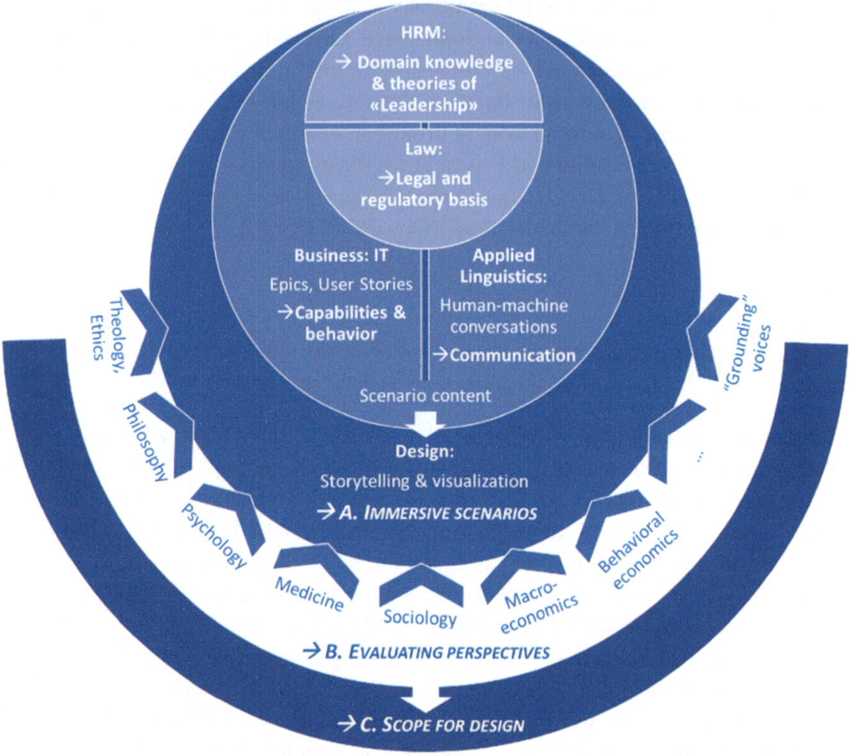

Fig. 1 Elements of the research plan

3.1 *How Does Digitization Change Social Ties?*

Imagine the following situation: Digitization has taken its course and all private sector and public services have been implemented intelligently using suitable technologies (Brucker-Kley et al. 2018). All your administrative procedures and transactions are fully automated. The vehicle that delivers your shopping moves autonomously. Your office has been completely virtualized. There is no longer any need for you to commute to work. Human and machine resources are perfectly orchestrated in fully digitized and networked processes. You communicate digitally with your co-workers. For this purpose, you and your co-workers have an infrastructure at your disposal that allows you to move around in virtual, three-dimensional spaces (Townsend et al. 1998). The majority of your co-workers have never actually seen you, and for them it goes without saying that your appearance in virtual space does not necessarily correspond to your physical shape (Muhammad et al. 2014).

Now you are told that your line manager, who you still know personally from earlier times, is about to retire. You are notified of her successor and are told, along with a name and contact details, that it is in fact a machine. You are perplexed; you do not want to report to a machine. On the other hand, a machine will be more rational than a human being. It will never be in a bad mood and it will evaluate your performance objectively. Nevertheless, you are somewhat uncomfortable with the idea of having a digital boss.

For many people, the role of employee and the relationship with one's direct superior is a fact of life. Even if the meaning and nature of work will most likely change, the leader–follower aspect will remain. According to the leader–member exchange (LMX) theory (Martin et al. 2016) leadership occurs when leaders and followers are able to develop effective relationships which result in mutual and incremental influence (Uhl-Bien 2006). The central principle of the LMX theory is that leaders develop different exchange relationships with their followers, in which the quality of the relationship affects various outcomes (i.e., performance or commitment) (Gerstner and Day 1997). The question arises how the employee role and thus the relationship between leaders and employees will evolve if leadership is fully or partially performed by machine intelligence (Chamorro-Premuzic 2016; Wildhaber 2016). The scenarios to be implemented aim to show variants of how the leader–follower relationship may be structured in the outlined setting and to what extent the leadership role may be filled or may be not filled by a machine.

3.2 *How Does Digitization Change the Economy?*

The concept of leadership is an integral part of today's economy. Reflections on future manifestations of this domain in the form of scenarios automatically include perspectives of how digitization may change the economy. In determining the key factors and driving forces of future relationships between the two actors defining such relationships, the human worker and his or her machine superior, emerging and potential alternative forms of organizational or economic structures will have to be taken into account. Today's companies typically have a hierarchical structure, and many management positions are partly justified by administrative responsibilities. However, the concept of a digital superior calls this organizational principle into question because restrictions due to human cognitive abilities and egotisms are eliminated and may give room for alternative bottom-up or loosely coupled organizational settings that are already emerging today such as holacracy, gig economy, or digital nomadism (Nash et al. 2018; Robertson 2015). The envisaged scenarios illustrate the settings for such alternative constellations.

3.3 *How Does Digitization Change Politics?*

The need for reform in legal frameworks, social security systems, education, and administration arising from digitization is already widely discussed today (Cachelin

2016; Frick and Höchli 2014). In this context, new challenges occur with regard to the legal provisions needed to correspond to the realities of digital change. Shaping the digital future requires guidelines that ensure clarity and legal certainty for all economic players. The domain of leadership as an object of the scenarios is well suited to demonstrate the significant impact of AI and virtualization on the world of work and on labor law (see Sect. 4). Legislators are called on to take account of the consequences of such developments and to anticipate the associated risks and opportunities with regard to regulatory issues (adaptation of existing or creation of new legal provisions; international cooperation; self-regulation of companies).

4 Research Object and Research Needs

As indicated in the previous section, the proposed research approach is intended to trigger and explore an interdisciplinary discourse on the designability of our digital future based on immersive scenarios. The domain of leadership in an organizational setting serves as an example to frame and discuss "possible futures" in a particular sphere of life.

The research questions stated at the beginning of Sect. 3 correspond to the following research needs:

(A) Need for immersive scenarios
(B) Need for a multi-perspective approach
(C) Need to identify the design scope (= room to maneuver to shape our digital future)

4.1 Need for Immersive Scenarios

If we accept our digital future as a design challenge, what is wanted and what is not wanted needs to be examined and defined from various perspectives. There is, however, no common ground of experience or perception to guide the formulation of such requirements or boundaries. Researchers have been studying the impact and people's acceptance of machine intelligence, but their findings are usually either limited to the current manifestations of machine intelligence, e.g., the impact of social robots on humans (Fong et al. 2002), or they rely on conventional survey techniques to explore human tolerance thresholds for hypothetical concepts such as working for an unbiased machine (Dare2 2016). The tangible scenarios at the heart of this research proposal are intended to close this gap and act as a reference point to enable an interdisciplinary discourse based on the same discoverable artifacts. In order for these scenarios to meet this requirement, answers to currently open questions must be anticipated in explorative and creative ways and implemented in the scenarios in a coherent manner. The aim is not to predict our digital future as accurately as possible, but to create a comprehensible and tangible image that can trigger specific reactions from the evaluating experts. To that end, the proposed research plan combines the domain knowledge of human resource management (HRM) and law with the competence of business information technology, applied linguistics, and design (immersive design) to create, iteratively, immersive scenarios for digitized leadership relationships (see Fig. 1).

Human resource management (HRM) reflects the research challenge to identify key factors and driving forces that may impact the future relationships between human workers and machine superiors based on socioeconomic developments and megatrends in the world of work (Colbert et al. 2016; Nash et al. 2018; Robertson 2015). The involvement of HRM will also ensure that the specific use cases in the scenarios will cover all relevant aspects of current and predicted leadership roles (Mintzberg 2015) and leadership skills based on state-of-the-art leadership theories (Judge et al. 2002; Martin et al. 2016; Yukl 1989).

Legal researchers will investigate the gaps that exist under the current regulatory framework, identify the need for adaptation, and outline what a new regulatory framework might look like in the scenarios. The use of AI in general and, in particular, the use of algorithms in employment relationships is a controversial legal issue and has led to a number of challenges and potential risks, which will be revealed in the scenarios: First of all, the use of algorithms raises numerous questions regarding the transparency, quality, and fairness of algorithm-based decisions and the protection of employees (Bundesrat 2017; European Parliament 2017; Reynard 2015; Schmidt 2017; Wildhaber 2017; Wildhaber and Lohmann 2017). For example, is an algorithm-based decision less biased than a human decision? Are algorithms black box systems? Algorithms are already used in the recruitment process to select suitable employees as well as in existing employment relationships to coordinate, monitor, and evaluate work (Wildhaber 2017). With regard to the present legal framework, the following research gaps arise, in particular: (a) Which provisions of law may apply to the use of AI in the recruitment process and in existing employment relationships? (b) Do existing national and international rules provide an appropriate means of achieving transparent and fair decision-making through the use of algorithms? (c) Is there a need for a right to obtain a human review of an automated decision or even an prohibition on automated decision-making (see Art. 22 of the GDPR of the European Union (Regulation (EU) *2016/679 of the European Parliament and of the Council of 27 April 2016 on the protection of natural persons with regard to the processing of personal data and on the free movement of such data, and repealing Directive 95/46/EC (General Data Protection Regulation)*, 2016))? (d) What are the requirements for programming these algorithms in order to comply with legal standards regarding data protection, equality, nondiscrimination, or personality protection? An essential contribution will be to identify protected goods and concerns, in other words, to identify who deserves protection under what circumstances and why. To this end, suitable criteria or a grid will be developed against which the regulatory measures can be measured and evaluated.

Business technology engineering will address the need to "ground" the scenarios through specific use cases (e.g., the screening of candidates in the context of staff recruitment) which make the division of labor and the interaction between humans and machines both tangible and coherent. For this purpose, a design-oriented approach to information systems research (Österle et al. 2011) and methods from user-centered design (Cooper et al. 2014) will be combined to define the technical capabilities and limitations presumed for the scenarios (Keller and Savarimuthu 2017) and to model the behavioral aspects and the interaction between humans and machines in the form of epics and user stories (Patton 2014).

Applied Linguistics: On the one hand, when people talk to each other, they use familiar patterns and practices from their traditional everyday and professional lives; on the other hand, they develop new ones and adapt them to the corresponding challenges. Such strategies appear, for example, in professional situations in which instructions play a role. Normally one has, e.g., a wide range of opportunities to give instructions and/or understand and respond adequately. Linguistic-orientated research papers in the context of organizational communication are available in a large number (Gardner and Jones 2007; Mayfield et al. 1998; Morand 2000). If a person talks to a machine, they will use both known and new strategies (Thar 2015). The aim of this research area is to investigate interdisciplinary and transdisciplinary, which pragmatic approaches are used, how they are adapted, and which patterns and practices are best suited for transfer.

Immersive Design as a design discipline will be key to realizing scenarios that will be comprehensible and tangible both for the evaluating experts and potentially a broader audience (see Sect. 4 on subsequent research perspectives). Increasing their emotional involvement is considered both a critical enabler and a major research challenge. To this end, the impact of immersive technologies to incite and intensify a discourse is to be explored and validated. Immersive technologies, blending virtual and augmented reality, have become an important addition to the media toolset of visualization. They have proven their superiority over other media to increase emotional involvement in different disciplines and for different purposes: They are increasingly used in psychological studies (increased control, validity (Blascovich et al. 2002)), medical learning (decreased ethical concerns (Roy et al. 2006)), professional training (increased safety, efficacy (Bailenson et al. 2008)), and historical recreations (learning effects (Dede 2009)). The lessons learned from the various levels of abstraction (Bailenson et al. 2008; Blascovich et al. 2002; Dede 2009; Roy et al. 2006) and their acceptance by viewers shall be applied and validated with regard to their effectiveness in stimulating a rich discourse. In this context, design criteria for avatars are a highly relevant research subject. In order to convey human emotions convincingly, avatars in virtual worlds are the logical environment in which to test interaction with AI (Martindale 2017). Due to recent advances in consumer technology, it is now feasible to record facial expressions and body movements and translate them into virtual worlds where a human operator can simulate interaction with an entity that cannot easily be identified as human or AI by the user (Amidi 2018).

4.2 *Need for a Multi-perspective Approach*

The expressions of concern about our digital future and calls for action from experts of all disciplines are numerous, diverse, and substantial (Helbing 2015; Schirmacher 2015; Sorgner 2016; Zicari no date). However, every expert has his or her own conception of the digital future and considers it against the background of the values and theories of his or her discipline. There is no doubt about the relevance of those perspectives and their capability to trigger a discourse, but they do not enforce it in a systematic manner. Valuable synergies in the search for design scope remain unexplored. This research proposal is based on a participatory and interdisciplinary approach both for creating the scenarios (human resource management, law, business information technology, linguistics, design) and for evaluating their impact with the help of experts from various disciplines (see Sect. 3).

4.3 *Need to Identify the Design Scope (= Room to Maneuver to Shape Our Digital Future)*

Valuable research initiatives to shape our digital future exist worldwide. Examples include the Privacy by Design movement that originated in Canada (Cavoukian 2011), the EU Horizon 2020 initiative for "Responsible Research and Innovation" (Horizon 2020—European Commission, no date), the "Wisdom Computing" Initiative of the Japan Science and Technology Agency (Japan Science and Technology Agency, no date), or the IEEE initiative for Ethically Aligned Design (*Ethically Aligned Design, Version 2 (EADv2)|IEEE Standards Association*, no date). The latter has already led to the development (work in progress) of specific standards, such as for a model process to address ethical concerns in system design (*IEEE SA—7000—Model Process for Addressing Ethical Concerns During System Design*, no date). Other approaches focus less on such implementation-oriented design guidelines rather than on the transformation of our socioeconomic system as a whole in order to retain control (Helbing 2015). In this context, a digital manifesto issued in 2015 by renowned experts from the field of computer science, AI, and social computer science promoted the need for a new social contract and self-determined bottom-up mechanisms (e.g., collective intelligence, open data, sharing economies, blockchain, participatory platforms such as "fablabs") (Helbing et al. 2015). In the context of the proposed research approach, it will be subject to explorative research whether to consider and implement such mechanisms and criteria already in certain scenarios in the sense of desirable visions or characteristics, or to capture such perspectives by involving social computer scientists, among other perspectives, in the evaluation of the scenarios.

4.4 Research Plan

In order to reach the goal to incite an interdisciplinary discourse on the designability of our digital future, we propose a transdisciplinary and participatory approach to construct and evaluate explorative scenarios. The research design encompasses three phases that correspond to the three major outcomes of the research plan as outlined in Fig. 1:

(A) Design and creation of immersive scenarios (→ mixed reality scenarios increasing emotional involvement)
(B) Investigation of scenarios (→ base on which to formulate risks and requirements)
(C) Formulating the scope for design (→ design guidelines, requirements, limitations, possibilities of influence)

Character and Format of the Scenarios to Be Developed

- *Possible futures, not forecasts*: The proposed approach to scenario thinking is all about thinking in alternatives and drafting holistic thought-provoking hypotheses for possible futures with a high degree of uncertainty (Müller and Müller-Stewens 2009; Schwartz 2005), not about precise forecasting.
- *Narrative and explorative, not normative scenarios*: The scenarios are designed to explore and portray possible future situations with human protagonists and comprehensible plots (Gaßner and Steinmüller 2004). The aim is not to portray preferable states, but to enable the experts to reflect on the desirability of the scenarios.
- *Static scenarios, not development scenarios*: The scenarios capture snapshots of the future, without referring to the developments that have led to this state (Steinmüller 2012).
- *Enabling immersive experiences, not just reading*: The scenarios are implemented using mixed reality technologies that are superior to textual stories when it comes to increasing emotional involvement (Bailenson et al. 2008; Blascovich et al. 2002; Dede 2009; Roy et al. 2006).

Method

To generate and investigate scenarios that comply with the characteristics and aspirations described above, a different set of methods will be applied than in normative scenario design or strategic forecasting, which focus on gathering and analyzing data and opinions to identify the most probable scenarios (Glenn and Gordon 2004). A participatory approach will be key in making these alternative images of the future more diverse and robust and to provide a creative frame of thought (Kerber et al. 2014; Steyaert et al. 2006). If HRM, law, linguistics, design and business information technology develop scenarios jointly and iteratively, theory triangulation will ensure a holistic view; investigator triangulation will ensure a rich discourse that will occur when experts from various disciplines experience and evaluate the scenarios (Gerhold 2012). Combining the constructive artifact-based set of methods from design science research, which is well established in the world of information systems research and immersive design, with the qualitative methods of empirical social research to guide and analyze the discourse, is considered a key asset of this transdisciplinary research proposal (Dresch et al. 2015; Hevner and Chatterjee 2010; Krausse and Lichtenstein 2001).

Since the 1990s, futures research has developed a rich set of qualitative and explorative methods that focus on alternative designable futures as an object of research (e.g., Delphi, multiple perspective assessment, agent modelling) (Bishop et al. 2007; Gerhold 2012). Developing explorative and narrative scenarios undoubtedly requires creativity in order to come up with sufficiently visionary and thought-provoking images. However, the design process will be governed by rigorous criteria (plausibility, concreteness, consistency) in order to produce coherent, high-quality scenarios (Steinmüller 2012). The definite mix of methods to be applied will be determined in the initial bounding phase of this project. Figure 2 illustrates the application of the four-quadrant scenario matrix technique (Heijden 2002), which is considered as the best option to develop a set of "extreme versions" of the digital future. To define conclusive axes for such matrices, key factors and drivers for our digital future in the selected domains of work and leadership will need to be identified (Gaßner and Steinmüller 2004; Steyaert et al. 2006) and put in relation to the main players (Bertrand et al. 2000), in our case machine and human. At least two matrices (resulting in eight scenarios) will be designed and roughly sketched to allow for reflection on the most relevant influencing factors and drivers. For implementation and evaluation, however, a restriction to four scenarios is recommended in order to control the level of complexity for the evaluation. Experiences from scenario projects indicate that dealing with more than four scenarios may be challenging for the investigators and may thus have a negative impact on the communication quality of the discourse (Müller and Müller-Stewens 2009).

The process to develop and evaluate the scenarios (Bradfield et al. 2005; Gaßner and Steinmüller 2004; Kerber et al. 2014; Steyaert et al. 2006) is structured according the following topics:

(A) Design and creation of immersive scenarios

1. Definition and bounding (team constellation), approach, and techniques to create and evaluate the scenarios, design criteria, assumptions about the setting of the scenarios (e.g., technical capabilities)
   Outcome: common ground for the collaborative creation of conclusive scenarios
2. Developing the scenario logic and deciding on the set of scenarios to be developed (key factors, drivers)
   Outcome: logic of the scenarios, set of scenarios, parameters, and assumptions for the scenarios
3. Exposé and story board for the scenarios (plot/epics, use cases: user stories, dialogs, legal conditions)
   Outcome: content and structure of the scenarios
4. Implementing the scenarios (mixed reality)
   Outcome: design and implementation of the scenarios

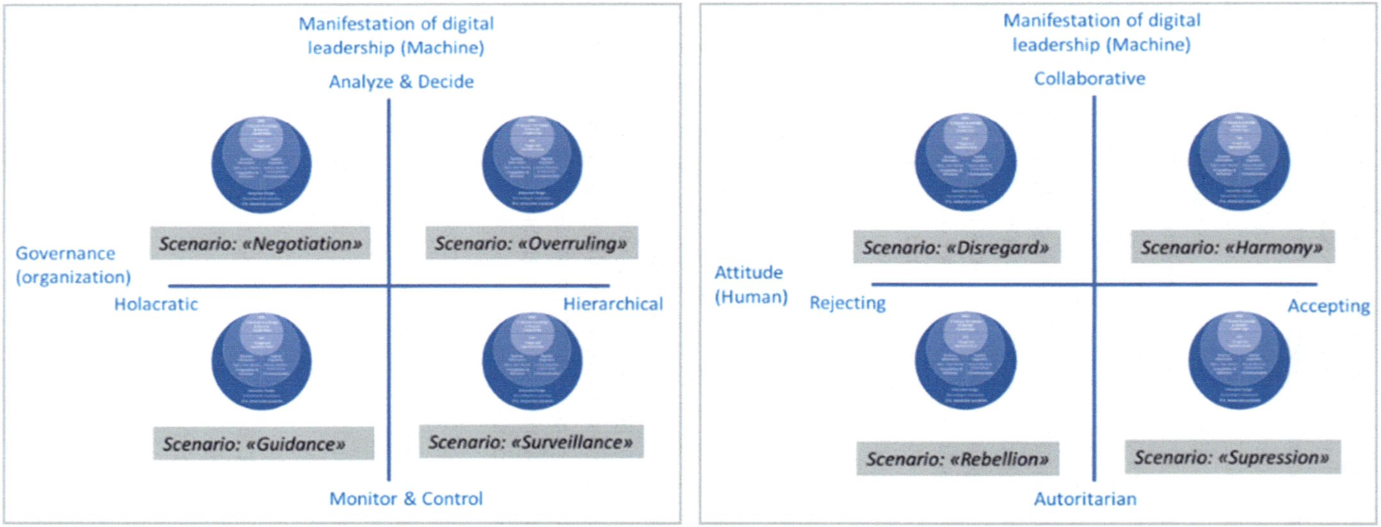

Fig. 2 Sample application of the four-quadrant scenario technique (illustrative)

(B) Investigation of scenarios

5. Immersion of the experts in the scenarios
   Outcome: Experiences (common ground for the discourse)
6. Enrich scenarios with experts' annotations
   Outcome: formulated perspectives of experts from different disciplines
7. Collecting voices (from MSc students in Business Information Technology, Linguistics, Law, and Design and from personalities with a less rational, less theoretical approach (e.g., artists, novelists))
   Outcome: "Grounding" feedback on the scenarios from a broader audience and a different age group (quantitative feedback in a limited setting based on a short online survey following the scenario experience; further empirical evidence is subject to subsequent research, see Sect. 4)
8. Facilitating and analyzing the interdisciplinary discourse of experts
   Outcome: interdisciplinary collage of requirements, risks, and opportunities

(C) Formulating the scope for design

9. Analysis and deduction of the scope for design
   Outcome: configuration options, design guidelines

(D) Dissemination

10. Documentation of research results
11. Vernissage (public access to the mixed reality scenarios and artifacts of the discourse)

5 Conclusions

Uncertainty and fear are not a fertile breeding ground for innovation. On the other hand, exaggerated belief in technology and a focus on technological feasibility can lead to relevant risks being ignored. Even though this research proposal is neither willing nor able to ultimately resolve such extreme positions, the scenarios and the expert opinions based on them are intended to address uncertainties and risks and to formulate concrete requirements and limits. This is a step toward an informed and constructive dialog that can drive responsible innovations in the world of work. More specifically, we see the following innovation potentials:

- *Ethics by design*: The outcomes and findings could be contributed to and further developed in running projects that are aimed at influencing the engineering community both in research and in the industry (e.g., the IEEE standardization projects currently ongoing in the context of the Ethically Aligned Design Initiative (*Ethically Aligned Design, Version 2 (EADv2) | IEEE Standards Association*, no date)). This would enable the results of the proposed research to be taken into account for concrete technology innovations or even product developments.

- *Input for required legal reforms and the related political processes*: Based on the identified protected goods and concerns and the developed criteria to evaluate regulatory measures, debates about necessary adjustments can be initialized.
- *Input for solution design*: Findings about the design of avatars with a focus on user acceptance and immersive impact can be used to innovate solutions that are based on virtual, augmented, or mixed reality (e.g., teleconferencing).
- *Inspiration for the contributing and evaluating disciplines*: Narrative scenarios are tools to foster creativity (Gaßner and Steinmüller 2004). We expect the immersive experiences to trigger creative thinking both on the part of the designers and on the part of the evaluators. This can have an impact on the quality and novelty of the discourse and the recommendations to be drawn up. In the medium and long term, the experience gained could broaden the view of the participating experts of digital change and thus contribute to new ideas and innovative solutions.
- *Inspiration for the application of immersive technologies in human and social sciences*: The proposed research approach would provide a unique experimental ground to explore the potential, limitations, and impact of immersive technologies for social and human sciences research and, specifically, for facilitating discourse.

Subsequently, the research design—validated and improved based on the quality of the discourse triggered—could be widened in scope and extended to a wider audience to enable further research:

- *Scope*: The research design can be applied to other subject areas and spheres of life beyond "leadership."
- *Empirical evidence*: Empirical research with a broad set of investigators (lay audience) could be initiated to study the influence of factors such as cultural background, age, gender, or education.
- *Formalization*: Specific frameworks or instruments, such as for holistic risk management in the context of digital change could be developed based on the identified areas of concern.

References

Amidi A (2018) See the results of this animator's homemade motion capture system using iPhone X. Cartoon Brew, 12 January. https://www.cartoonbrew.com/tools/see-results-animators-homemade-motion-capture-system-using-iphone-x-155924.html. Accessed 14 Apr 2018

Bailenson J, Patel K, Nielsen A, Bajscy R, Jung S-H, Kurillo G (2008) The effect of interactivity on learning physical actions in virtual reality. Media Psychol 11(3):354–376. https://doi.org/10.1080/15213260802285214

Bertrand G, Michalski A, Pench LR (2000) European futures: five possible scenarios for 2010. Edward Elgar, Cheltenham

Bishop P, Hines A, Collins T (2007) The current state of scenario development: an overview of techniques. Foresight 9(1):5–25. https://doi.org/10.1108/14636680710727516

Blascovich J, Loomis J, Beall AC, Swinth KR, Hoyt CL, Bailenson JN (2002) Immersive virtual environment technology as a methodological tool for social psychology. Psychol Inq 13 (2):103–124

Bradfield R, Wright G, Burt G, Cairns G, Van der Heijden K (2005) The origins and evolution of scenario techniques in long range business planning. Futures 37(8):795–812

Brucker-Kley E, Kykalova D, Keller T (eds) (2018) Prozessintelligenz. Gabler, Berlin. https://www.springer.com/de/book/9783662557044. Accessed 8 Feb 2018

Bundesrat (2017) Bundesrat verabschiedet bericht und massnahmen zu auswirkungen der digitalisierung auf den arbeitsmarkt, 8 November. https://www.admin.ch/gov/de/start/dokumentation/medienmitteilungen.msg-id-68708.html. Accessed 14 Apr 2018

Bychkov D, Linder N, Turkki R, Nordling S, Kovanen PE, Verrill C et al (2018) Deep learning based tissue analysis predicts outcome in colorectal cancer. Sci Rep 8(1):3395. https://doi.org/10.1038/s41598-018-21758-3

Cachelin JL (2016) Update!: warum die digitale Gesellschaft ein neues Betriebssystem braucht. Stämpfli, Bern

Cavoukian A (2011) Privacy by design. Information & Privacy Commissioner Ontario, Ontario. https://www.ipc.on.ca/wp-content/uploads/Resources/7foundationalprinciples.pdf

Chamorro-Premuzic T (2016) Why a robot could be the best boss you've ever had. The Guardian. http://www.theguardian.com/media-network/2016/sep/09/robot-boss-best-manager-artificial-intelligence. Accessed 27 Mar 2018

Colbert A, Yee N, George G (2016) The digital workforce and the workplace of the future. Acad Manag J 59(3):731–739. https://doi.org/10.5465/amj.2016.4003

Cooper A, Reimann R, Cornin D, Noessel C (2014) About face: the essentials of interaction design, 4th edn. Wiley, Indianapolis, IN

Dare2 (2016) Does your co-worker want your boss to be a robot? DARE2, 8 November. https://dare2.dk/future-of-work/. Accessed 27 Mar 2018

Datenschutz-Grundverordnung der Europäischen Union (no date) https://www.edoeb.admin.ch/edoeb/de/home/dokumentation/rechtliche-grundlagen/Datenschutz%20-%20International/DSGVO.html. Accessed 14 Apr 2018

Dede C (2009) Immersive interfaces for engagement and learning. Science (New York, NY) 323 (5910):66–69. https://doi.org/10.1126/science.1167311

Dresch A, Lacerda DP, Antunes Jr JAV (2015). Design science research. Springer, Cham. https://doi.org/10.1007/978-3-319-07374-3

Ethically Aligned Design, Version 2 (EADv2) | IEEE Standards Association (no date) EADv2—Ethics in action. https://ethicsinaction.ieee.org/. Accessed 8 Apr 2018

European Parliament (2017) Report on a European Agenda for the collaborative economy—A8-0195/2017. http://www.europarl.europa.eu/sides/getDoc.do?pubRef=-%2F%2FEP%2F%2FTEXT%2BREPORT%2BA8-2017-0195%2B0%2BDOC%2BXML%2BV0%2F%2FEN&language=EN. Accessed 14 Apr 2018

Ferrucci DA (2012) Introduction to "this is Watson". IBM J Res Dev 56(3.4):1:1–1:15. https://doi.org/10.1147/JRD.2012.2184356.

Fong T, Nourbakhsh I, Dautenhahn K (2002) A survey of socially interactive robots: concepts, design and applications. http://uhra.herts.ac.uk/handle/2299/3821. Accessed 4 Apr 2018

Frick K, Höchli B (2014) Die zukunft der vernetzten gesellschaft Neue spielregeln, neue spielmacher. Gottlieb Duttweiler Institute, Rüschlkon. http://www.gdi.ch/de/Think-Tank/Studien/Die-Zukunft-der-vernetzten-Gesellschaft/611. Accessed 8 Apr 2018

Gardner M, Jones E (2007) Problematic communication in the workplace: beliefs of superiors and subordinates. Int J Appl Linguist 9(2):185–203. https://doi.org/10.1111/j.1473-4192.1999.tb00172.x

Gaßner R, Steinmüller K (2004) Scenarios that tell a story; Normative narrative scenarios—an efficient tool for participative innovation-oriented foresight. EU-US seminar: new technology foresight, forecast & assessment methods, Seville, 13–14 May 2004, p 7

Gerhold L (2012) Methodenkombination in der sozialwissenschaftlichen Zukunftsforschung. Zukunft und wissenschaft. Springer, Berlin, pp 159–183. https://doi.org/10.1007/978-3-642-28954-5_8
Gerstner CR, Day DV (1997) Meta-analytic review of leader–member exchange theory: correlates and construct issues. J Appl Psychol 82(6):827–844
Glenn J, Gordon T (2004) Integration, comparisons, and frontier of futures research methods. ResearchGate. EU-US seminar: new technology foresight, forecast & assessment methods, Seville, 13–14 May 2004. https://www.researchgate.net/publication/253392093_Paper_7_Integration_Comparisons_and_Frontier_of_Futures_Research_Methods. Accessed 15 Apr 2018
Heijden K van der (2002) The sixth sense: accelerating organizational learning with scenarios. Repr. October. Wiley, Chichester
Helbing D (2015) The automation of society is next: how to survive the digital revolution. SSRN scholarly paper ID 2694312. Social Science Research Network, Rochester, NY. https://papers.ssrn.com/abstract=2694312. Accessed 6 Apr 2018
Helbing D, Frey BS, Gigerenzer G, Hafen E, Hagner M, Hofstetter Y et al (2015) IT-Revolution: Eine strategie für das digitale zeitalter—Spektrum der wissenschaft. https://www.spektrum.de/kolumne/eine-strategie-fuer-das-digitale-zeitalter/1376083. Accessed 8 Apr 2018
Hevner A, Chatterjee S (2010) Design research in information systems, Integrated series in information systems. Springer, Boston, MA. https://doi.org/10.1007/978-1-4419-5653-8
Horizon 2020—European Commission (no date) Responsible research and innovation, Horizon 2020. https://ec.europa.eu/programmes/horizon2020/en/h2020-section/responsible-research-innovation. Accessed 8 Apr 2018
IEEE SA—7000—Model process for addressing ethical concerns during system design (no date) http://standards.ieee.org/develop/project/7000.html. Accessed 8 Apr 2018
Japan Science and Technology Agency (no date) Wisdom computing: creative collaboration between humans and machines—ESOF 2016 Manchester. https://manchester2016.esof.eu/en/the-programme/event-information/wisdom-computing.html. Accessed 8 Apr 2018
Jones SE (2006) Against technology: from the luddites to neo-luddism. Taylor & Francis, New York
Judge TA, Bono JE, Ilies RG, Megan W (2002) Personality and leadership: a qualitative and quantitative review. J Appl Psychol 87(4):765–780
Keller T, Savarimuthu BTR (2017) Facilitating enhanced decision support using a social norms approach. J Electron Commerce Org 15:1–15. https://doi.org/10.4018/JECO.2017040101
Kerber H, Schramm E, Winker M (2014) Partizipative szenarioverfahren—zur methodischen ableitung von zukunftsbildern: das projekt SAUBER+ als Beispiel. https://publikationen.ub.uni-frankfurt.de/frontdoor/index/index/year/2014/docId/36072. Accessed 15 Apr 2018
Kurzweil R (2005) The singularity is near. Penguin, New York
Lanier J (2017) Dawn of the new everything: encounters with reality and virtual reality. Henry Holt, New York. https://us.macmillan.com/dawnofthenew everything/jaronlanier/9781627794091/. Accessed 8 Apr 2018
Larnier J (2011) You are not a gadget: a manifesto. Penguin, London
Martin R, Guillaume Y, Thomas G, Lee A, Epitropaki O (2016) Leader–member exchange (LMX) and performance: a meta-analytic review. Pers Psychol 69(1):67–121. https://doi.org/10.1111/peps.12100
Martindale J (2017) Nvidia shows off virtual reality-taught robots at SIGGRAPH 2017. Digital Trends, 1 August. https://www.digitaltrends.com/computing/nvidia-isaac-vr-training-dominoes-siggraph/. Accessed 14 Apr 2018
Mayfield JR, Mayfield MR, Kopf J (1998) The effects of leader motivating language on subordinate performance and satisfaction. Hum Resour Manag 37(3–4):235–248. https://doi.org/10.1002/(SICI)1099-050X(199823/24)37:3/4<235::AID-HRM6>3.0.CO;2-X
McDuff D, Kaliouby R (2017) Applications of automated facial coding in media measurement. IEEE Trans Affect Comput 8(2):148–160. https://doi.org/10.1109/TAFFC.2016.2571284

Mintzberg H (2015) The nature of managerial work (1973) & Simply managing: what manager do—and can do better (2013). M@n@gement 18(2):186–188. https://doi.org/10.3917/mana.182.0186
Morand DA (2000) Language and power: an empirical analysis of linguistic strategies used in superior-subordinate communication. J Org Behav 21(3):235–248
Muhammad AA, Shen C, Srivastava J, Contractor N (2014) Predicting real world behaviors from virtual world data. Springer, New York
Krausse J, Lichtenstein C (eds) (2001) Your private sky: R. Buckminster Fuller. Lars Müller, Baden, pp 7–43
Müller AW, Müller-Stewens G (2009) Strategic foresight: Trend- und zukunftforschung in unternehmen. Schäffer-Poeschel, Stuttgart
Nash C, Jaharri MH, Sutherland W, Phillips G (2018) Digital nomads beyond the buzzword: defining digital nomadic work and use of digital technologies. In: Transforming digital worlds. International conference on information, Lecture notes in computer science. Springer, Cham, pp 207–217. https://doi.org/10.1007/978-3-319-78105-1_25
Ohta Y, Tamura H (2014) Mixed reality: merging real and virtual worlds, 1st edn. Springer, Berlin
Orts-Escolano S (2016) Holoportation: virtual 3D teleportation in real-time. In: Proceedings of the 29th annual symposium on user interface software and technology. ACM (UIST '16), New York, pp 741–754. https://doi.org/10.1145/2984511.2984517
Österle H, Becker J, Frank U, Hess T, Karagiannis D, Krcmar H et al (2011) Memorandum on design-oriented information systems research. Eur J Inf Syst 20(1):7–10. https://doi.org/10.1057/ejis.2010.55
Patton J (2014) User story mapping. http://shop.oreilly.com/product/0636920033851.do. Accessed 8 Apr 2018
Regulation (EU) 2016/679 of the European Parliament and of the Council of 27 April 2016 on the protection of natural persons with regard to the processing of personal data and on the free movement of such data, and repealing Directive 95/46/EC (General Data Protection Regulation) (2016) OJ L. http://data.europa.eu/eli/reg/2016/679/oj/eng.
Reynard M (2015) Postulat 15.3854 | Automatisierung. Risiken und chancen | Geschäft | Das Schweizer Parlament. https://www.parlament.ch/de/ratsbetrieb/suche-curia-vista/geschaeft?AffairId=20153854. Accessed 14 Apr 2018
Robertson BJ (2015) Holacracy: the new management system for a rapidly changing world. Macmillan. https://us.macmillan.com/holacracy/brianjrobertson/9781627794282/. Accessed 6 Apr 2018
Roy MJ, Sticha DL, Kraus PL, Olsen DE (2006) Simulation and virtual reality in medical education and therapy: a protocol. Cyberpsychol Behav 9(2):245–247. https://doi.org/10.1089/cpb.2006.9.245
Russell SJ, Norvig P (2016) Artificial intelligence: a modern approach. Pearson, Malaysia. http://thuvienso.thanglong.edu.vn/handle/DHTL_123456789/4010. Accessed 3 Apr 2018
Schirmacher F (2015) Technologischer totalitarismus: Eine debatte. Edition suhrkamp. http://www.suhrkamp.de/buecher/technologischer_totalitarismus-_7434.html. Accessed 7 Apr 2018
Schmidt FA (2017) Digital labour markets in the platform economy: mapping the political challenges of crowd work and gig work. Friedrich-Ebert-Stiftung. http://www.voced.edu.au/content/ngv:76462. Accessed 14 Apr 2018
Schwartz P (2005) The art of the long view: planning for the future in an uncertain world [Repr.]. Wiley, Chichester
Sénéchal T, Turcot J, Kaliouby R (2013) Smile or smirk? Automatic detection of spontaneous asymmetric smiles to understand viewer experience. In: 2013 10th IEEE international conference and workshops on automatic face and gesture recognition (FG), pp 1–8. https://doi.org/10.1109/FG.2013.6553776
Siderius E (2012) A tautological singularity: Kurzweil, science fiction and the question of intelligence. The Starry Messenger, 21 September. https://edmundsiderius.wordpress.com/2012/09/

21/a-tautological-singularity-kurzweil-science-fiction-and-the-question-of-intelligence/. Accessed 7 Feb 2018

Sleegers M (2018) Benefits and practical implications of using mixed-reality in the AEC industry. ZHAW School of Management and Law. https://drive.switch.ch/index.php/f/839025345

Sorgner SL (2016) Transhumanismus: 'Die gefährlichste Idee der Welt'!? Herder, Freiburg im Breisgau. https://www.herder.de/philosophie-ethik-shop/transhumanismus-die-gefaehrlichste-idee-der-welt!-taschenbuch/c-27/p-5283/. Accessed 7 Apr 2018

Steinmüller K (2012) Szenarien—Ein Methodenkomplex zwischen wissenschaftlichem Anspruch und zeitgeistiger Bricolage. Zukunft und Wissenschaft. Springer, Berlin, pp 101–137. https://doi.org/10.1007/978-3-642-28954-5_6

Steyaert S, Lisoir H, Nentwich M (2006) Leitfaden partizipativer Verfahren—Ein Handbuch für die Praxis. Institut für Technikfolgenabschätzung. https://www.oeaw.ac.at/ita/publikationen/buecher/leitfaden-partizipativer-verfahren/. Accessed 27 Mar 2018

Thar E (2015) Ich habe Sie leider nicht verstanden: Linguistische Optimierungsprinzipien für die mündliche Mensch–Maschine-Interaktion (1st ed). Sprache in Kommunikation und Medien, Bern, Book 8

The Matrix (1999) Warner Bros.

Townsend AM, DeMarie SM, Hendrickson AR (1998) Virtual teams: technology and the workplace of the future. Acad Manag Perspect 12(3):17–29. https://doi.org/10.5465/ame.1998.1109047

Uhl-Bien M (2006) Relational leadership theory: exploring the social processes of leadership and organizing. Leadersh Q 17(6):654–676. https://doi.org/10.1016/j.leaqua.2006.10.007

Ulam S (1958) John von Neumann 1903-1957. Bull Am Math Soc 64(3, part 2):1–49

Vinge V (1993) The coming technological singularity: how to survive in the post-human era. https://edoras.sdsu.edu/~vinge/misc/singularity.html. Accessed 5 Apr 2018

Wildhaber I (2016) Der Roboter als Chef | NZZ. Neue Zürcher Zeitung, 1 June. https://www.nzz.ch/meinung/kommentare/robotik-am-arbeitsplatz-der-roboter-als-chef-ld.86082. Accessed 27 Mar 2018

Wildhaber I (2017) Robotik am arbeitsplatz: Robo-kollegen und robo-bosse. AJP-Aktuelle juristische Praxis (02)

Wildhaber I, Lohmann M (2017) Roboterrecht. AJP/PJA2|2017, pp 135–140

Yu D, Deng L (2015) Automatic speech recognition: a deep learning approach. CERN Document Server. https://doi.org/10.1007/978-1-4471-5779-3

Yukl G (1989) Managerial leadership: a review of theory and research. J Manag 15(2):251–289. https://doi.org/10.1177/014920638901500207

Zicari RV (no date) Machines of loving grace. Interview with John Markoff. ODBMS Industry Watch. http://www.odbms.org/blog/2016/08/machines-of-loving-grace-interview-with-john-markoff/. Accessed 7 Apr 2018

Smart Cities, Well-Being and Good Business: The 2030 Agenda and the Role of Knowledge in the Era of Industry 4.0

Diana Soeiro

Abstract Industry 4.0 represents the so-called fourth industrial revolution (4IR). In broad terms, the concept refers to our current stage where the biological, physical and digital boundaries blur. How does the 4IR impact cities? The notion of 'smart city' corresponds to the city perceived through the lens of the 4IR. The previous industrial revolution was mainly characterised by the advent of the digital (1960s–1990s) where the computer and the Internet played a pivotal role. The 4IR is about connectivity and networks (Internet of Things/IoT). In the realm of the specific challenges are: buildings, connectivity, data, energy, governance and transport.

Our claim is that in order for the 4IR to be integrated in cities, three criteria should be met. First, the concept of sustainability should go beyond ecology and economics, it should consider the Agenda 2030 as its framework, in particular the sector of health and well-being. A sustainable city must be a healthy city. Second, urban planning practice is vital to translate information into knowledge. How can we make spatial sense of an increasing amount of information? The practice used to encompass designing physical structures now; however, it needs to incorporate virtual networks, embedded in physical structures. Third, 'smart cities' depend on innovative businesses which respond to the challenges of the 4IR and are an indispensable part of the process.

We conclude that 'smart cities' need above all knowledgeable and innovative governance design strategies, as well as public policies that support and promote well-being, urban planning practice and good business.

D. Soeiro (✉)
DINÂMIA'CET-IUL - ISCTE-IUL, Instituto Universitário de Lisboa, Lisbon, Portugal

CIAUD - Research Centre for Architecture, Urbanism and Design, Faculty of Architecture, University of Lisbon, Lisbon, Portugal

F. Matos et al. (eds.), *Knowledge, People, and Digital Transformation*, Contributions to Management Science, https://doi.org/10.1007/978-3-030-40390-4_5

1 Introduction

The nature of this chapter is interdisciplinary. Based on my expertise of more than 10 years, I have found that informally, it is acknowledged that interdisciplinarity is vital in order to provide adequate solutions to today's complex problems and as a broad statement this seems to be consensual. However, in academia and at policy level it quickly becomes clear that an interdisciplinary approach often proves to be too challenging—a perspective often corroborated by fellow international research colleagues. In academia this approach seems to defy the logic of most funding systems available where a project needs to be presented within a specific area. This sometimes makes it almost impossible to choose an area where the project can fit adequately excluding many valuable ideas (and a lot of times the most innovative). The reality is that more and more, in order to provide an answer that can actually contribute to solve a societal problem, the approach must be interdisciplinary. At policy level the biggest challenge is governance. The articulation of policies and the collaboration between different ministries and actors can prove to be too demanding due to heavy administrative burdens in sharing a budget, or due to communication difficulties between human resources.

Bringing together smart cities, sustainability and business is acknowledged informally as a much-needed perspective in order to assure the future of each of these areas but, strangely enough, simultaneously, it is officially recognised as a pioneering (therefore unconventional) perspective (Blanck et al. 2019). This chapter aims to contribute, first and foremost, to formally recognise and validate the advantages of an interdisciplinary perspective.

The nucleus of this conceptual trio is 'smart cities'. Because since 2015, more than half the world population lives in urban areas and by 2025 the number is expected to reach to 58.2%. 'More developed regions' will have the highest percentage (80.4%); however, the fastest rate of change is among 'less developed regions' and 'least developed countries' (UN-Habitat 2016). This means that to rethink cities, the concept of what a city is and how it should be conceived is a question primarily posed by a demographic challenge.

Additionally, we are both undergoing a rapid technological advancement process and a change of technological paradigm. According to Professor Klaus Schwab (Founder and Executive Chairman of the World Economic Forum, the International Organization for Public–Private Cooperation) since the turn of the century we are living under the Fourth Industrial Revolution (4IR) (Schwab 2017). Briefly, the first industrial revolution spanned roughly between 1760 and 1840, encompassing the construction of railroads and the invention of the steam engine, which favoured mechanical production. The second (late nineteenth century–early twentieth century) was defined by the invention of electricity, which enabled mass production. The third industrial revolution started around the 1960s and main developments were semiconductors, mainframe computing (1960s), personal computing (1970s and 1980s) and the Internet (1990s). The 4IR is still deeply connected with digital technology but a mobile internet, a smaller scale, and a lower cost provides the opportunity both for worldwide massification/accessibility and for the integration of systems. This is what enables it to propel artificial intelligence and machine learning.[1,2]

Floridi (2014) claims that "(. . .) we are probably the last generation to experience a clear difference between online and offline environments. Some people already spend most of their time onlife" (Floridi 2014, p. 94).

How does this translate into the way we envision the future of cities and how does it affect urban design?

City planning increasingly involves planning at a physical level and at the virtual level. The physical architecture of the city is quickly merging with the architecture of the virtual, where the Internet of Things (IoT) becomes a key element. These virtual "Things" are embedded in physical structures, changing cities' morphology from the inside out. Thus, what lies behind the metamorphosis of the architecture of the city is partially visible and partially invisible. City-specific challenges are: buildings, connectivity, data, energy, governance and transport. The ways in which technology will propose to address these will demand an accommodation to the architecture of physical 'things'. Up to what point should traditional architecture of the physical 'things' surrender to technological advancements, defined by the architecture of IoT? The question is relevant in the sense that people inhabit the city and the human factor should prevail over technology when it comes to guiding the future of cities (Pelton 2019).

'Smart cities' encompass the challenge of integrating the use of artificial intelligence (AI), decentralised consensus, nanotechnology, robotics and autonomous vehicles—some of the main challenges of the 4IR. Which are the fundamental requirements so that the 4IR is integrated successfully in cities? Sustainability grounded in the promotion of health and well-being (i.e. Sedlak 2014); a successful articulation between the physical and virtual architecture and innovative businesses. We will now address each of them.

---

[1]Floridi (2014) also claims that we are living under the paradigm of a fourth revolution but the elements defining the advent of each one is of cultural nature: the first starts with Copernicus' claim, in the sixteenth century, that all planets revolve around the sun and not around the Earth; the second with Charles Darwin's publication of *On the Origin of Species by Means of Natural Selection* (1859) proving that all species of life have evolved over the years from common ancestors through natural selection; the third is represented by the work of Sigmund Freud (1856–1939) who claimed that the mind is also unconscious and subject to defence mechanisms such as repression; and the fourth, initiated by Alan Turing's (1912–1954) work that has revolutioned computer science, a task that once belonged to men and since then has belonged to the machine.

[2]Professor Klaus Schwab has also founded, in 1998, the non-profit association Schwab Foundation for Social Entrepreneurship in order to provide platforms at the country, regional and global levels to promote social entrepreneurship.

2 Methodology and Objectives

Relying on state-of-the-art literature addressing the 4IR, new challenges in urban planning where health and well-being are a growing concern and the future of work and innovative business, we aim at presenting an original perspective that clearly demonstrates that each of these elements is key to positively influence the other two.

Main goals are to confirm that besides a technological challenge, embodied by the 4IR, the social dimension is vital to materialise the 4IR, both through the ability to design innovative businesses and also to implement (and articulate) governance strategies. The city, and consequently urban planning, is unequivocally among the objects that is impacted by the complexity of these elements and therefore, we claim that it can have an active role in order to contribute to harmonise them.

3 Background and Discussion

3.1 Sustainable Cities

The word 'sustainability' was used for the first time in 1972. Kidd (1992), analysing the word's usage up until the late 1990s, identifies six different roots in its use: the ecological/carrying capacity root; the resource/environmental use; the biosphere root; the critique of technology root; the 'no growth-slow growth' root and; the most recent one, the ecodevelopment root, which includes values such as equity, broad participation in governance, and decentralised government. The word aimed at providing a frame to articulate rates of population growth, resource use, and their respective pressure on the environment, which became increasingly important since the 1950s.[3]

Having started as a term that was used to describe a physical reality in the realm of ecology and the environment, it quickly translated to economics and lastly to 'ecodevelopment', consequently including normative values.

Amartya Sen, having been awarded the Nobel Memorial Prize in Economic Sciences in 1998, published *Development as Freedom* the following year. In this seminal work, Sen adds the social dimension to the concept of sustainability aiming at investigating "the development process in inclusive terms that integrate economic, social and political considerations" (Sen 1999, p. 8). This means that a sustainable articulation of population growth, resources and environment that promotes development should actively encompass the social realm. The reason is briefly stated in this short statement: "Economic unfreedom can breed social unfreedom, just as social or political unfreedom can also foster economic unfreedom" (Sen 1999, p. 8).

Freedom becomes a key concept to nurture this interdependency and it is deeply embedded in Sen's understanding of social sustainability. The rationale is that the

[3]See also Du Pisani (2006).

more freedom institutions give to its citizens the more agency citizens will have this will in turn will reflect positively on economy (Fukuda-Parr 2001; Glasmeier and Christopherson 2015; Kaletsky 2011). The idea is that this process becomes a constant dialogue, creating a flow between both institutions and citizens. Institutions should therefore design and use instruments that empower the citizens' agency, and when that is put in place successfully, sustainable development ensues.[4]

Sen details which freedoms should citizens be given in order to actively exert free 'sustainable agency',[5] claiming that

> [e]ach of these distinct types of rights and opportunities helps to advance the general capability of a person. They may also serve to complement each other. Public policy to foster human capabilities and substantive freedoms in general can work through the promotion of these distinct but interrelated instrumental freedoms. (Sen 1999, p. 10)

He specifically addresses:

1. *Political freedoms* (opportunities that people are given to determine who should govern and on what principles)
2. *Economic facilities* (opportunities enjoyed by individuals to utilise economic resources for the purpose of consumption, production, or exchange)
3. *Social opportunities* (i.e. education, health, effective participation)
4. *Transparency guarantees* (the freedom to deal with one another under assurance of mutual trust through material disclosure)
5. *Protective security* (it includes fixed institutional arrangements such as unemployment benefits and statutory income supplements)

In that regard, how can we define what a sustainable city is? A sustainable city is a city that it does not hinder these freedoms, actively contributing for their implementation by design and governance (Kazmi et al. 2019).

To this we add our claim that a sustainable city must be a healthy city. Furthermore, that the health criterion is not but one amongst the many criteria, instead that it sits at the root itself of what a city should be. The analogy between the dynamics of a living organism and a city has often been asserted. Briefly, to quote a few examples, Rudolf Steiner (1861–1925) and Herbert Spencer (1820–1903) paved the way by declaring similarities between the social body and a living organism. Later on, architects Frank Lloyd Wright (1867–1959) and Christopher Alexander (*b.* 1936) took as foundational principles, in both their architectural practices, the dynamics of

---

[4]"What people can positively achieve is influenced by economic opportunities, political liberties, social powers, and the enabling conditions of good health, basic education, and the encouragement and cultivation of initiatives. The institutional arrangements for these opportunities are also influenced by the exercise of people's freedoms, through the liberty to participate in social choice and in the making of public decisions that impel the progress of these opportunities." (Sen 1999, p. 5)

[5]"With adequate social opportunities, individuals can effectively shape their own destiny and help each other. They need not be seen primarily as passive recipients of the benefits of cunning development programs. There is indeed a strong rationale for recognizing the positive role of free and sustainable agency-and even of constructive impatience." (Sen 1999, p. 11)

a living organism (Soeiro 2019). Therefore, the notions of health and well-being of a city go beyond the impact that it has in the human body. Being in itself a living body, the city can be conceived as an extension of the human body (Soeiro 2017). In that sense, architecture and spatial planning should consider the human body and its surrounding environment as a contiguous—i.e. something which Wright conceptualised as 'organic architecture'.

The United Nations' 2030 Agenda defines 17 Sustainable Development Goals. Among them are Goal 11, 'Sustainable cities and communities' and Goal 3, 'Health and well-being'. Each goal establishes several targets to be achieved. Nevertheless, when it comes to goals 11 and 3, both goals will mutually benefit if more public policies and businesses address them simultaneously since they are deeply interconnected. Let us proceed in order to strengthen our argument.

3.2 Smart and Sustainable Cities

The city of the future has been recently envisioned under the concept of 'smart cities', which translates the impact of the 4IR in the way we conceive our surrounding built environment. Because nowadays both sustainability and smart cities are concepts frequently addressed, it becomes an implicit expectation that a smart city is a sustainable city. However, it is important to keep in mind that both concepts are normative, meaning, they express goals to be attained. Against this background it becomes vital to clarify what is the dynamics, which is the process that keeps the link between both sustainability and smartness, contributing to edify the common nucleus, the city.

According to a recent literature review (Yigitcanlar et al. 2019) there is a consensus that first cities must become sustainable and only then can they be considered truly smart. This is so because smart cities face major challenges in delivering sustainable outcomes: (a) smart city policies are characterised by heavy technocentrism; (b) smart city practices involve complexities, and; (c) smart city notions are conceptualised in an ad hoc manner.

This means that there is a risk that technology is being implemented in cities (generating—apparently—smart cities) before we have assured that we have sustainable cities able to handle technology, or have defined what is our understanding of what a 'sustainable smart city' should be.

A smart city is unequivocally about technology and this should be embraced and encouraged. However, technology should not be the guiding force of its own implementation (Sassen 2018).

Favouring this perspective, Streitz (2019) from the Smart Future Initiative (Frankfurt am Main, Germany) argued that the 'smart-everything' paradigm should be replaced by a human-centred design approach resulting in the provision of 'people-oriented, empowering smartness'. In the same year an article dwelling on the impact of the Internet-of-Things (IoT) in several scientific and engineering application domains, presented a comprehensive literature review of key features and applications of IoT paradigm to support sustainable development of smart cities. Among its conclusions it claims:

> The other area that IoT will profoundly change in the near future is human habits and physical wellbeing. Therefore, it is vitally important to consider the social impacts of IoT-based technologies on individuals and communities as part of planning, design, and deployment (Alavi et al. 2018, p. 12).

This statement becomes increasingly relevant when we consider its context. In a literature review encompassing the most recent updates on the technological use of IoT authored by three engineers (Civil and Environmental Engineering, Mechanical Engineering and Applied Mechanics), one of the conclusions denotes something that is seemingly unrelated, belonging to a different area of knowledge. Nevertheless, the interdisciplinary nature of the statement and the acknowledgement that in future cities, urban design, and health and well-being are key areas that need to be addressed as a priority, agrees with the position we take in this chapter.

Recent topics addressed in the context of smart cities are big data and artificial intelligence (Acuto et al. 2019; Allam and Dhunny 2019; Artificial Intelligence and Life in 2030 2016; Tegmark 2017), automated mobility (Ang et al. 2019; Freudendal-Pedersen et al. 2019), blockchain and the need for reliable data and reliable sources (Brandão et al. 2019) and, the impact of smart cities in low density regions (Lopes and Guarda 2019).

All of these topics are based on how the technology of IoT can be used in the context of smart cities. IoT is the third wave of information technology, being preceded by the Internet and by mobile communication networks (Park 2019). The main focus of IoT is integration of different systems in order to create a unit. How can different technologies being implemented in cities integrate the interconnection via the Internet of computing devices embedded in everyday objects, enabling them to send and receive data? How can we make spatial sense of an increasing amount of information?

Nowadays, urban planning practice has a crucial role in translating information into knowledge. In order to do this it needs to balance technology with those who inhabit the city, keeping in mind that a human-centred design is the guiding force. The practice used to encompass designing physical structures and now it needs to incorporate virtual networks, embedded in physical structures. Again, we acknowledge that technological developments do influence urban design but citizens and citizens' needs should not be ignored.

Furthermore, spatial planners should create both a physical and virtual architecture that empowers citizens to take control over technology. Due to a growing hybridisation of space, the architecture of the physical surrounding space now comprises concurrently an 'architecture of governance'. Is architecture defined by technology (the virtual architecture) or by physical architecture? Urban planning has a crucial role in assuring the architecture of governance is human-centred instead of technology-centred having on its side the power to balance the virtual environment with physical structures. Urban planning should make use of technology, incorporating it in its physical structures but not surrender to the virtual.

The interaction between citizens and its surrounding environment, over technology, is vital in order to keep both healthy cities and healthy democracies. (Brundtland Commission Report 2008; Ross 2017; Sen 2013; Wang et al. 2017) Embodying the strong link between both we propose the concept of 'urban homeostasis', a dynamic open system that regulates a state of equilibrium in living organisms where citizens use responsible agency. Going back to Sen (1999) and his claim for citizens' empowerment, not only urban planners and decision-makers are important, citizens also have a crucial role in smart cities. Not in the sense that the technology of smart cities is user-oriented (which presupposes a passive/receptive role) but because they are an active element participating in the choice of which technologies exist, which needs and purpose should they serve and how cities should be organised (governance).

3.3 *Businesses and Human-Centred Solutions*

The use of information with no knowledge can have a strong destructive effect, particularly in the realm of spatial planning having a direct impact in our health and well-being. What is the intelligence behind the process of transforming information into knowledge? One thing is to assign to a machine the function to collect information and large bodies of information (big data). Something else is to decide what to do with it and how it should be used. To resolve that decisions can and should be made by machines themselves is what we should be very careful of. It becomes increasingly harder to establish the boundaries between where human decision-making ends and where machine decision-making starts. Concurrently, it becomes increasingly hard to establish the boundaries between where the architecture of the physical ends and where the architecture of the virtual starts.

Innovative businesses have a crucial role in establishing healthy boundaries, by creating and implementing human-centred design that encompasses citizens, because humans who are in charge of the decision-making orient businesses.

Businesses have always been a crucial part of human development at any stage. The era of the 4IR is no exception (Carvalho et al. 2018; Corea 2019).

Architecture as a profession has been strongly impacted by technology use since the 1990s, which consequently changed architectural practice itself. Yet, it was able to adapt and architectural structures would have surely be different had there been no technological development.

> As tasks have become digitized and easier to share out, building projects increasingly draw on a more disparate network of people—architects, structural engineers, mechanical and electrical consultants, designers, contractors and suppliers, ordinary people, and computerized systems—each of whom have their own models, collect their own data, and focus on different aspects of the building. This is a move away from the architect at the helm of the project, responsible for every task. (. . .) CAD or CAE software allows architects to design, and engineers to erect buildings that would have been unimaginable or unfeasible with a setsquare and a slide-rule (Susskind and Susskind 2015, pp. 97, 113).

The business of architecture is different because of technological advancements and traditional architects who learned and developed their practice before the 1990s had a hard time adapting to fast-paced changes in their profession. Not only because of technology use but also because what was expected from them, as architects, and their role within a project, also changed.

The impact of the 4IR in the workforce is one of the most complex factors influencing the way cities are planned. Not only architecture but every single profession as we know it is being challenged by speedy technological transformation. The mass of information we are required to deal with is progressively increasing, the way each profession relates with every other profession is different, the need for certain professions is disappearing, the need for others is increasing but in general, it is known that the need for such a high number people in the workforce is becoming unnecessary. The concept that is addressing all of these challenges in Germany, and to some extent in the European Union, is Arbeit 4.0 (Work 4.0). Associated, is the government programme 'Arbeiten 4.0—Arbeit weiter denken' (*Work 4.0—To further think work/Bundesministerium für Arbeit und Soziales*), running since April 2015, where several studies are being conducted in order find out how the world of work may change until 2030 and beyond, in response to the developments associated with Industry 4.0, including widespread digitalization.

Big corporations are known to sometimes have a tendency to defend their own interests even if they hinder the population's best interests. However, in a scenario where the dynamics and structure of the workforce is changing worldwide, the role of social entrepreneurship becomes increasingly relevant, acting more effectively at a smaller scale and promoting citizens' ownership (Ford 2018; Lester 2009).

This favours a workforce acting under the dynamics of a community-based structure, where nodes within a complex structure become densely connected internally. Community structure is therefore a concept that goes one step beyond complex networks because of nodes. In this future scenario, where the phenomenon of community-based structures becomes more common, sustainability can be good business.

Governments alone cannot do it. Private actors should engage and citizens should engage. We bring back to the table the idea that against what we might expect, smart cities and not necessarily sustainable, and that smart cities must be first sustainable cities. Behind this divide, between sustainability and smartness, there is a prejudice associated with it: the state takes care of sustainability and private actors take care of smartness. Why? Because sustainability is a non-profit activity and smartness is a profit-based activity. As much as smartness is about the future, suitable to visionaries who have broad horizons and sustainability is about some kind of nostalgia about how things used to be, always were and should continue to be.

Sustainability is not exclusively a matter of the state just as smartness is not exclusively about private actors. Leadership becomes key in public and private sectors, and in community-based structures able to acknowledge this (Kelly 2019). 'Smart cities' depend on innovative businesses that respond to the challenges of the 4IR and are an indispensable part of the process. All actors have a role to play working together, with access to relevant information in order to make informed choices.

Governments, companies and citizens should create structures, at governance level, that allow them to constantly be able to maintain a creative, positive and flexible dialogue where all are given a chance to have their input. Particularly when it comes to governance strategies in the context of smart cities, technology use should be carefully designed and monitored to serve urban homeostasis, i.e. the city and democracy. Only then we can assure that the future of cities is connected with the democratic process.

4 Concluding Remarks

We now highlight the main claims we have presented that aim to justify and foster an interdisciplinary approach, particularly between the realms of health and well-being, smart cities and good business.

Main goals are to confirm that besides a technological challenge, embodied by the 4IR, the social dimension is vital to materialise the 4IR, both through the ability to design innovative businesses and also to implement (and articulate) governance strategies. The city, and consequently urban planning, is unequivocally among the objects that is impacted by the complexity of these elements and therefore, we claim that it can have an active role in order to contribute to harmonise them:

1. Sen's concept of social sustainability does not deny previous understandings of sustainability rooted in economy, ecology and ecodevelopment (equity, broad participation in governance, and decentralised government). On the contrary, it encompasses all previous categories and identifies the social as the main propelling factor of all others, being the key to an all-encompassing sustainability.
2. Based on the understanding of a city as an extension of the human body, it is vital that the concept of sustainable cities take as its background the promotion of health and well-being. This connection should not be considered one among many. Health and well-being are mandatory, high-priority criteria to assess sustainability, to promote public policies and to develop good business.
3. Due to a growing hybridisation of the built environment, planners have a crucial role in assuring that the architecture of governance is human-centred instead of technology-centred having on its side the power to balance the virtual environment with physical structures. They should make use of technology, incorporating it in physical structures but not surrender to the virtual.
4. Consequently, innovative governance design strategies for smart cities should be human-centred instead of technology-centred. However, in order to promote sound 'sustainable smart cities' we need to go beyond a human-centred approach and claim for a citizens-first approach, where the population takes an active role and is empowered through governance design. To this corresponds the concept of 'urban homeostasis': healthy cities, healthy democracies. *A sustainable city is a*

city that promotes freedom, actively contributing for its implementation by design and governance.

5. An effective and efficient governance structure should design its framework in order to accommodate a collaborative interprofessional and interdisciplinary process where different areas of knowledge equally contribute to envision the future of cities.
6. Innovative businesses have a crucial role in creating and implementing human-centred design, and citizen-centred design, because businesses are in its essence based on human decision-making and run by humans.
7. In a scenario where community-based structures tend to replace complex networks, sustainability can be good business and citizens and small-scale businesses can be successful catering to nodes' specific needs. The prejudice that sustainability is a non-profit activity and smartness is a profit-based activity should be left behind.

This chapter aims at pointing the direction on how balance can be found between the 4IR, urban planning strategies and innovative businesses. As much as a more detailed approach would be desirable, the approach is necessarily general, mainly due to two reasons: a joint consideration of the three elements is still recent; each of the elements is going under a fast-paced transformation. Therefore, there is an opportunity for further research to be developed addressing governance design strategies on a case-by-case basis, investigating the best possible way to articulate these three elements that simultaneously impact and stimulate each other. The biggest development is expected to be the changes that are currently affecting the work force as we know it influencing daily migrations, urban flows, urban design and the way we design innovative businesses.

References

Acuto M, Steenmans K, Iwaszuk E, Ortega-Garza L (2019) Informing urban governance? Boundary-spanning organisations and the ecosystem of urban data. Area 51(1):94–103. https://doi.org/10.1111/area.12430

Alavi AH, Pengcheng J, Buttlar WG, Lajnef N (2018) Internet of things-enabled smart cities: state-of-the-art and future trends. Measurement 129:589–606. https://doi.org/10.1016/j.measurement.2018.07.067

Allam Z, Dhunny ZA (2019) On big data, artificial intelligence and smart cities. Cities 89:80–91. https://doi.org/10.1016/j.cities.2019.01.032

Ang L, Seng KP, Ijemaru GK, Zungeru AM (2019) Deployment of IoV for smart cities: applications, architecture, and challenges. IEEE Access 7(1):6473–6492. https://doi.org/10.1109/ACCESS.2018.2887076

Artificial Intelligence and Life in 2030 (2016) One hundred year study on artificial intelligence: report of the 2015-2016 study panel. Stanford University, Stanford, CA. Retrieved from https://ai100.stanford.edu/2016-report. Accessed 14 June 2019

Blanck M, Ribeiro JLD, Anzanello MJ (2019) A relational exploratory study of business incubation and smart cities—findings from Europe. Cities 88:48–58. https://doi.org/10.1016/j.cities.2018.12.032

Brandão A, Mamede HS, Gonçalves R (2019) A smart city's model secured by Blockchain. In Mejia J, Muñoz M, Rocha Á, Peña A, Pérez-Cisneros M (eds) Trends and applications in software engineering. CIMPS 2018. Advances in intelligent systems and computing, vol 865. Springer, Cham, pp 249–260. https://doi.org/10.1007/978-3-030-01171-0_23

Brundtland Commission Report (2008) The growth report strategies for sustained growth and inclusive development. Commission on growth and development. The International Bank for Reconstruction and Development/ The World Bank, Washington, DC

Carvalho LC, Rego C, Lucas MR, Sánchez-Hernández MI, Noronha AB (eds) (2018) Entrepreneurship and structural change in dynamic territories: contributions from developed and developing countries. Springer, Cham

Corea F (2019) Applied artificial intelligence: where AI can be used in business, 1st edn. Springer, Cham

Du Pisani JA (2006) Sustainable development—historical roots of the concept. Environ Sci 3 (2):83–96. https://doi.org/10.1080/15693430600688831

Floridi L (2014) The 4th revolution: how the infosphere is reshaping human reality, 1st edn. Oxford University Press, Oxford

Ford M (ed) (2018) Architects of intelligence: the truth about AI from the people building it, 1st edn. Packt, Birmingham

Freudendal-Pedersen M, Kesselring S, Servou E (2019) What is smart for the future city? Mobilities and automation. Sustainability (Switzerland) 11(1). https://doi.org/10.3390/su11010221

Fukuda-Parr S (2001) Making new technologies work for human development. United Nations Development Programme, Human Development Report. http://hdr.undp.org/en/content/human-development-report-2001. Accessed 14 June 2019

Glasmeier A, Christopherson S (2015) Thinking about smart cities. Camb J Reg Econ Soc 8 (1):3–12. https://doi.org/10.1093/cjres/rsu034

Kaletsky A (2011) Capitalism 4.0: the birth of a new economy in the aftermath of crisis, 1st edn. Public Affairs, New York

Kazmi A, Serrano M, Lenis A (2019) Smart governance of heterogeneous internet of things for smart cities. Proc Int Conf Sens Technol ICST. https://doi.org/10.1109/ICSensT.2018.8603657

Kelly R (2019) Construction leadership: swarm leadership and the fourth industrial revolution, 1st edn. Palgrave Macmillan, Cham

Kidd CV (1992) The evolution of sustainability. J Agric Environ Ethics 5(1):1–26. https://doi.org/10.1007/BF01965413

Lester R (2009) Plan B 4.0: mobilizing to save civilization, 1st edn. W.W. Norton, New York

Lopes IM, Guarda T (2019) The relationship between smart cities and the internet of things in low density regions. In Antipova T, Rocha A (eds) Digital science. DSIC18 2018. Advances in intelligent systems and computing, vol 850, pp 369–378. https://doi.org/10.1007/978-3-030-02351-5_42

Park JH (2019) Advances in future internet and the industrial internet of things. Symmetry 11 (2):244. https://doi.org/10.3390/sym11020244.

Pelton JN (2019) Preparing for the next cyber revolution: how our world will be radically transformed—again! 1st edn. Springer, Cham

Ross A (2017) The industries of the future, 1st edn. Simon & Schuster, New York

Sassen S (2018) Cities in a world economy, 1st edn. SAGE, Thousand Oaks

Schwab K (2017) The fourth industrial revolution, 1st edn. Penguin, New York

Sedlak D (2014) Water 4.0: the past, present, and future of the world's most vital resource, 1st edn. Yale University Press, New Haven

Sen AK (1999) Development as freedom. Random House, New York

Sen A (2013) The ends and means of sustainability. J Hum Dev Capabilit 14(1):6–20. https://doi.org/10.1080/19452829.2012.747492

Soeiro D (2017) The built environment as an extension of human biology: Alexander, Damásio, Bratton. In: Oliveira MJ, Osório FC (eds) Kine[SIS]tem, from nature to architectural matter, pp 314–323. http://hdl.handle.net/10071/13603. Accessed 14 June 2019

Soeiro D (2019) Urban Homeostasis: citizenship, democracy and urban design in the age of circular economy. In: Peleman D, Notteboom B, Dehaene M (eds) Journal for Architecture Oase #104: the urban household of metabolism/Het Stedelijk, Huishduden van het Metabolisme. Netherlands Architecture Institute. October. https://www.oasejournal.nl/en/Issues

Streitz N (2019) Beyond 'smart-only' cities: redefining the 'smart-everything' paradigm. J Ambient Intell Humanized Comput 10(2):791–812. https://doi.org/10.1007/s12652-018-0824-1

Susskind RE, Susskind D (2015) The future of the professions: how technology will transform the work of human experts, 1st edn. Oxford University Press, New York

Tegmark M (2017) Life 3.0: being human in the age of artificial intelligence, 1st edn. Alfred A. Knopf, New York

UN-Habitat (2016) World cities report 2016. Urbanization and development: emerging future. UN-Habitat, Kenya

Wang PK, Lee H, Kiat LW, Elara MR, Chae YM, Balasubramanian G et al (2017) Living digital 2040: future of work, education and healthcare, 1st edn. World Scientific, Singapore

Yigitcanlar T, Kamruzzaman M, Foth M, Sabatini-Marques J, da Costa E, Ioppolo G (2019) Can cities become smart without being sustainable? A systematic review of the literature. Sustain Cities Soc 45:348–365. https://doi.org/10.1016/j.scs.2018.11.033

Business Model Innovation and Transition to a Sustainable Food System: A Case Study in the Lisbon Metropolitan Area

Isabel Salavisa and Maria de Fátima Ferreiro

Abstract The food systems' transition toward sustainability involves structural changes, namely the emphasis on local production, short supply chains, and the preference for organic products.

The shift in the agri-food system is taking place through the creation of entirely new businesses and individual farms moving toward organic production. In both cases, the enterprises use a combination of well-established agricultural knowledge and techniques, new scientific knowledge on productive methods and new technological platforms for commercialization. These mixed sources permit the creation of innovative business models (BMs). They exemplify how traditional industries can absorb/generate innovation at technological and organizational levels, and become part of the new knowledge-based era.

The study has three objectives: to analyze the emerging agri-food businesses in the Lisbon Metropolitan Area (LMA); to characterize innovative sustainable BMs within the transition dynamics; to reflect on the challenges that the characteristics of the food system pose for the emergence of these BMs.

The study is part of an interdisciplinary project on Spatial Planning for Change (SPLACH). The analysis addresses the food system transition in a specific territory, namely the LMA. The chapter presents the results of the research conducted, focusing on the case of an organic food initiative, Quinta do Oeste.

1 Introduction

Transition to sustainability is at the top of the political and policy agenda in most countries. It requires structural transformations in several domains, involves distinct actors and organizations, and calls for new policies.

The various domains can be conceptualized as large socio-technical systems addressing major societal functions, such as the provision of energy, nutrition,

I. Salavisa (✉) · M. de F. Ferreiro
ISCTE – Instituto Universitário de Lisboa, Lisbon, Portugal
e-mail: isabel.salavisa@iscte-iul.pt; fatima.ferreiro@iscte-iul.pt

F. Matos et al. (eds.), *Knowledge, People, and Digital Transformation*, Contributions to Management Science, https://doi.org/10.1007/978-3-030-40390-4_6

housing, and transportation. Transitions arise from the alignment of niche innovations, socio-technical regimes, and the landscape. This is the perspective of the transitions literature, which combines innovation systems economics, contributions from the sociological literature on transitions, and from science and technology studies. In this field, most studies have focused on energy or transportation systems, with only a meagre percentage (3%) addressing the food system (Markard et al. 2012).

Low-carbon transitions in agriculture and the food system pose significant challenges. They involve a wide range of actors, from farmers to consumers. Niche innovations are still relatively incipient due to high costs, entrenched diet preferences, a powerful and reluctant incumbent industry, and weak policies (Geels et al. 2017). However, this is a domain where a variety of bottom-up experiments are taking place that involve consumers, producers, municipalities, associations, and public entities, thus making it a very interesting case.

The reasons and motivations underlying the emergence of these experiments include the search for better quality food, ethics, and environmental concerns; indeed, they quite often come together to induce the change in social practices related to nutrition, both on the consumer and producer sides.

This study has three main objectives: to identify and analyze the emerging agri-food businesses in the Lisbon Metropolitan Area (LMA); to characterize innovative business models (BM) within the transition dynamics toward sustainability; to reflect on the challenges posed by the characteristics of the food system for the emergence of innovative sustainable BMs.

Our focus is on the production side, that is, the organic farming business. To this end, the chapter is organized as follows: Sect. 2 presents the theoretical background; Sect. 3 describes the methodological options; Sect. 4 presents the case study; Sect. 5 concludes.

2 Theoretical Background

2.1 The Food System as a Multidimensional Reality

The food system is a complex and multifaceted reality, defined as a broad system made up of "the activities, infrastructure, and people involved in feeding the global population (e.g., the growing, processing, distribution, consumption, and disposal of foods). It includes the web of processes by which institutions, organizations, and individuals transform inputs into foods and individual ingredients into the food we consume" (Popkin 2017, p. 73). As Popkin (2017) points out, this system interacts with the environment, the society, the economy, and the political domain.

A food supply chain or value chain is a good example of a large system unfolding in time and space "from farm to fork" (Popkin 2017, p. 73). Some authors, however, prefer to distinguish two separate but closely interlinked systems, namely food production and food consumption (Green et al. 2003).

Fig. 1 Food value chain

In this chapter, we will retain the notion of a value chain, with different stages and important feedback loops between the various stages. Complementary activities, such as agrochemicals, packaging and transportation, to mention just the most relevant, are not depicted in the diagram (Fig. 1).

In most developed countries, processing and wholesale are dominated by a small number of large companies. Although large chains also dominate in retail, they coexist with small businesses (corner and convenience shops, traditional food outlets, and small groceries). However, farming and consumption involve thousands or even millions of actors.

Therefore, the transformation of this set of activities implies a multitude of actors with asymmetrical power. This is why the creation of networks, formal collaborations, and associations is so important for innovative producers. Policies also play a crucial role in setting the regulatory environment, boosting the emergence and deployment of new experiments and promoting healthier diets. As Popkin (2017) stresses, a strong intake of highly processed food affects the consumers' health, and this calls for a global shift in nutrition.

To sum up, change is motivated by the growing awareness of the environmental impact together with health concerns. Mention must also be made of ethical issues related to the extractive use of natural resources and the dominant systems of animal husbandry.

2.2 *Food System Transition*

In agriculture, transition means a shift from the "productivist regime" aimed at production growth and high yields to a regime built around the principles of sustainability (Brunori et al. 2013, p. 28).

The "productivist" paradigm is capital and agrichemicals-intensive, usually highly specialized or even single product, with strong mechanization and focused on increasing efficiency and productivity but with a disregard for soil conservation and landscape protection. Conversely, the post-productivist paradigm is multifunctional, locally embedded, more labor-intensive and aimed at balancing economic viability, high-quality food, environmental concerns, and a new lifestyle (Wilson 2008).

Due to the specificity of the food system, technological innovations may be "dismissed as a potentially productive analytical entry point for work on sustainability transitions in food and agriculture" (Hinrichs 2014, p. 147). This is due to both the intimate links of agriculture and food production with living land and bodies, and the capital-intensive trajectory of the system's modernization over the twentieth century (Hinrichs 2014). As a result, the nutrition transition has to rely on a broader framework than that of the energy system, which has been based mostly on the emergence and scaling up of new renewable energy technologies.

The transition will arise from the combination of numerous experiments (Sengers et al. 2019). Technological innovations play a less prominent role than in other sectors (Geels et al. 2017), and new and old elements coexist, particularly in farming and retail. Major transformations must be made to the dominant approach, due to the relevance of organizational and marketing innovations.

Organizational and marketing innovations, such as alternative food networks and the extensive use of internet for commercialization, are widespread in organic farms, along with new production technologies, such as inputs arising from biotechnological advances to improve cultivation methods and obtain quality products. These farms use tests for certification and achieve high-level quality parameters of their products. Meanwhile, they also use traditional knowledge about soil conservation and farming practices. In short, they create innovative business models that depend on supportive networks of customers, retailers, local authorities, and public entities. These networks are critical for the new businesses. They permit the sharing of knowledge and information and the creation of commercialization channels. In addition, they reinforce the sense of belonging to a group that has a strong identity and offers an alternative to the mainstream behavior and value patterns (Ingram et al. 2015).

In retail, new and old forms also combine through the creation of large and varied commercial networks involving farmers' markets, box schemes, traditional food shops, new organic product chains, and incumbents' departments devoted to organic products. The expansion of short supply circuits is a further example that minimizes the harm caused by long-distance transportation of commodities, sometimes overseas.

Public entities play a relevant role, in this case through the procurement of quality food by school and hospital canteens as well as public campaigns aimed at promoting healthy diets and ultimately boosting the market for quality food—fresh, seasonal, organic—with less impact on the environment (Bui et al. 2016; Cohen and Ilieva 2015).

In sum, the combination of distinctive sources of knowledge in production activities, the creation of organizational and marketing innovations, and the use of supportive networks are all essential to the transformation of the food sector toward sustainability. This shift is indissociable from the creation of innovative and sustainable business models.

2.3 Innovative Business Models for Sustainable Farming

Business models (BMs) correspond to the approach taken by firms, their partners and customers to create, deliver, and capture value (Kurucz et al. 2017, p. 193).

Methods used to achieve a "generic business model concept" (e.g., Boons and Lüdeke-Freund 2013, p. 11) include the identification of the following elements:

- Value proposition (a type of value embedded in product/service);
- Supply chain (characterization of relationships with suppliers);
- Customer interface (characterization of relationships with customers);
- Financial model (costs, benefits, and their distribution across business model stakeholders).

The BM concept has been reassessed in light of the transition pathways to sustainability. Recent research in this field highlights the different approaches to and models of BM and the innovation required to address social and environmental values, more sustainable supply chains, and customer interface. Indeed, the critical role played by BMs in the change toward sustainable societies constitutes the research topic of a number of studies (e.g., Bocken et al. 2014; França et al. 2017; Osterwalder and Pigneur 2010; Upward and Jones 2016). The main issues addressed by these studies are as follows: (1) types of BM and their link with sustainability; (2) innovation in BMs toward a transition pathway.

The literature on BMs and their relationship with sustainability goals identifies a number of limitations of conventional BMs. In fact, the primacy or exclusivity of monetary returns to shareholders via profits and other quantitative and financial metrics has tremendous negative externalities in social and environmental terms (Upward and Jones 2016). As pointed out by Kurucz et al. (2017), organizations are required to change their goals to account for these externalities. This shift, in turn, entails enhanced methods and tools that overcome this fundamental limitation of conventional approaches to business modelling. Specific adaptations and extensions must be made that align business models with sustainability objectives (Kurucz et al. 2017, p. 193).

The reasons for conventional BMs' failure to integrate the sustainability dimension (Boons and Lüdeke-Freund 2013; Upward and Jones 2016) are related to a poor understanding of the sustainability issue, the limited time and system scope, and insufficient collective action in sustainable business (Baumgartner and Korhonen 2010; Rohrbeck et al. 2013; Stubbs and Cocklin 2008). As a result, we witness a "lost opportunity for advancing and embedding sustainability throughout business-value creation processes via business models" (França et al. 2017, p. 156).

Therefore, BM innovation for sustainability purposes constitutes a critical aspect within paradigmatic transformations envisaging more sustainable societies. In this sense, and to overcome the limitations of conventional BM in this regard, we need to adopt a specific approach that is strategically and explicitly aligned with sustainability goals (Kurucz et al. 2017). According to Bocken et al. (2014), the BM shift involves "innovations that create significant positive and/or significantly reduced negative impacts for the environment and/or society, through changes in the way the organization and its value-network create, deliver value and capture value (i.e. create economic value) or change their value propositions" (Bocken et al. 2014, p. 44).

The Framework for Strategic Sustainable Development (FSSD) is the most prominent reference in the literature focused on BM and sustainability. According to França et al. (2017), we are dealing with "a unifying framework for sustainability analyses, planning, cross-disciplinary and cross-sector cooperation, and cohesive use of the myriad sustainability tools, methods and concepts" (França et al. 2017, p. 155). In their comprehensive description of the FSSD, Broman and Robèrt (2017) consider the need to combine and adopt multiple tools, methods, and concepts through the following principles:

- Necessary, but avoiding excesses (e.g., restrictions and controversial aspects);
- Sufficient (covering all the important principles);
- General (context and scale of application);
- Concrete (real-life problems);
- Non-overlapping (facilitating understanding and assessment).

Bearing these principles in mind, the definition of sustainability proposed was elaborated in collaboration with natural and social scientists. According to this proposal, the essential aspects that need to be accounted for in natural and social terms include "assimilation capacity, purification capacity, (. . .) production capacity, climate regulation capacity, and diversity. (. . .). trust between people and between people and societal institutions, diversity of personalities, ages, gender, skills, etc., common meaning, capacity for learning, and capacity for self-organization" (Broman and Robèrt 2017, p. 23).

FSSD is operationalized through a four-step procedure (known as ABCD) (França et al. 2017) that can be summarized as follows: (A) design of a global sustainability challenge (core purpose, core values, and overall long-term goals); (B) assessment of the entity/organization under analysis and assets to deal with sustainability goals; (C) creative thinking and co-creation in order to close the gap between A and B; (D) "a stepwise approach" guaranteeing effective advancements in the transition path. According to the authors, "this logic creates the opportunity for pragmatic leadership, not only looking at the promise of an improved bottom-line in the future, but also considering short-term profits designed in a way that opens up the potential for the longer-term profits. This way, the FSSD allows for the above-outlined self-benefit of sustainability proactivity to be captured by businesses" (França et al. 2017, p. 160).

Innovation in the design of a BM with sustainability goals corresponds to the second domain in the BM research identified above. As already mentioned, FSSD is the central framework in the research on transforming BM into a sustainability tool (França et al. 2017; Karlsson et al. 2018; Kurucz et al. 2017; Rosca et al. 2017; Upward and Jones 2016). Product–service systems (PSS), Business Model Canvas (BMC), Strongly Sustainable Business Model Canvas (SSBMC), and Future-Fit Business Benchmark (F2B2) are the most common approaches mentioned in the literature.

The Product–Service Systems approach reassesses the functional value to end users of a mix of products and services, where "value creation is less about sales and ownership of individual products and more of a focus on the ongoing delivery of the service-value embedded in that product" (França et al. 2017, p. 156). Modern information and communication technologies and supply webs are important tools.

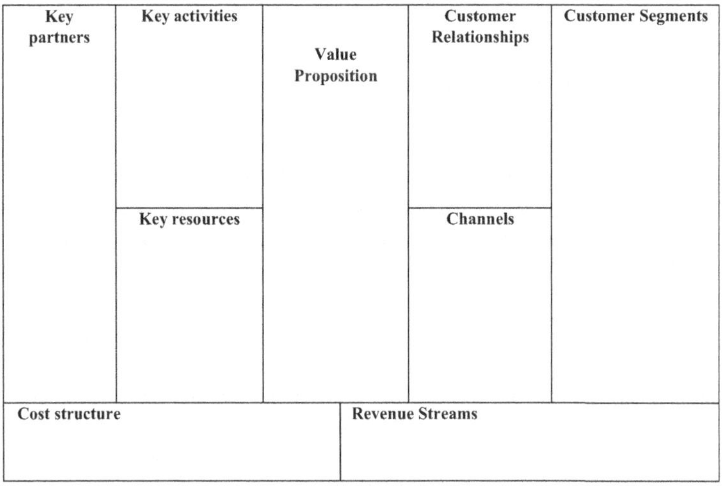

Fig. 2 The business model canvas (adapted) (França et al. 2017)

In the case of food systems, the recovery of local and seasonal products, and short supply chains (e.g., local markets), and the direct contact between farmers and consumers, for instance, are integrated with advanced technology such as web services and other information and communication technologies, fuelling the demand for products and access to relevant information on the products consumed.

The Business Model Canvas is a tool that allows the visualization of the business model on a canvas. The components and their interactions are designed in a single page through nine blocks. They make it possible to visualize how an organization creates, delivers, and captures value, covering the four main areas of the business: customers, value offer, infrastructure, and financial viability (França et al. 2017, p. 157) (Fig. 2).

The Strongly Sustainable Business Model Canvas (SSBMC) seeks to "help organizations of all kinds to identify opportunities for developing new and transforming existing business models in ways that increase the possibility for contributions to strategic sustainability" (Kurucz et al. 2017, p. 193). Finally, the Future-Fit Business Benchmark (F2B2) proposes an assessment framework to overcome the perceived limitations of the methods currently used in sustainability reporting, ratings, and standards (Kurucz et al. 2017, p. 193). In sum, all these management tools endorse the FSSD concepts and principles in order to overcome the BM's limitations regarding sustainability values.

Research by Kurucz et al. (2017) highlights the role of "relational leadership" and knowledge in the implementation of strategic sustainability (FSSD), through both the SSBMC and the F2B2. In the SSBMC, collective meaning-making is "enabled by a shared language based on an integrative view of the complex knowledge of environmental, social and economic value co-production for stakeholders into a limited number of questions situated in their necessary contexts". In the F2B2, collective meaning-making is "supported by translating complex knowledge from the natural and social sciences into a limited number of business principles" (Kurucz et al. 2017, p. 190).

Conversely, other authors stress the strategic importance of using different forms of knowledge and science. For example, Upward and Jones (2016) defend an "enterprise framework compatible with natural and social sciences." This framework resorts to ecological economics "derived from natural, social, and system sciences" and uses suitable concepts for strongly sustainable business models, namely the "selection of stakeholders with moral justice" and "governance design" (Upward and Jones 2016, pp. 97 and 105).

In the case of the agri-food sector, conceptualizing BM innovation toward sustainability poses a number of challenges. In fact, it is necessary to take the sector's specificities into account, namely the strong interdependence of human-animal-nature elements, the connection with different territories and geographic aspects, and special characteristics of the food supply chain (e.g., the very different size and sustainability focus of companies) (Cagliano et al. 2016; Ulvenblad et al. 2018). Therefore, an interdisciplinary approach is needed.

In addition, the combination of old and new knowledge is particularly important in the food sector transition. In the case of organic farms, for instance, the use of ICT is often combined with traditional knowledge (e.g., soil conservation). Research on the resilience of agriculture, food systems, and rural areas also draws attention to this combination of "old" and "new." Some authors who call for a deeper understanding of knowledge and innovation in this sector, identified four related challenges for the future: "first, to make agricultural knowledge systems more responsive to contemporary challenges; second, to perceive knowledge and innovation as drivers of development; third, to move beyond old paradigms based on linear approaches and conventional assumptions; and fourth, to integrate ecological and social concerns with economic aspects" (Rivera et al. 2018, p. 204).

Despite these findings, and quite surprisingly, the case of the food sector is practically absent from the literature on BM innovation for sustainability. In fact, the sector has a strong environmental and ecological impact related to natural resources usage (e.g., water, soil, biodiversity) and the consequent negative externalities. That is why it is so important and urgent to understand and systematize the sector's BMs, namely the innovation needed to overcome its "unsustainability" expressed by increasing globalization, changes in consumption patterns (out of season products processed in global chains), and the retailers' accrued concentration of power (Fritz and Matopoulos 2008).

According to Tell et al. (2016), the exceptions to the research gap are Beuchelt and Zeller (2012), Bocken et al. (2014), Markowska et al. (2011), and Teece (2010). The authors conclude that it is a new but expanding subject (Tell et al. 2016, p. 9). Indeed, recent systematic literature reviews, participative methods, and case studies (Barth et al. 2017; Ulvenblad et al. 2018, 2019; Tell et al. 2016) permit the identification of some key aspects in the debate on BM innovation for sustainability in the case of the food sector. However, and according to Ulvenblad et al. (2018, p. 3), for instance, it is important to conduct more research on the subject.

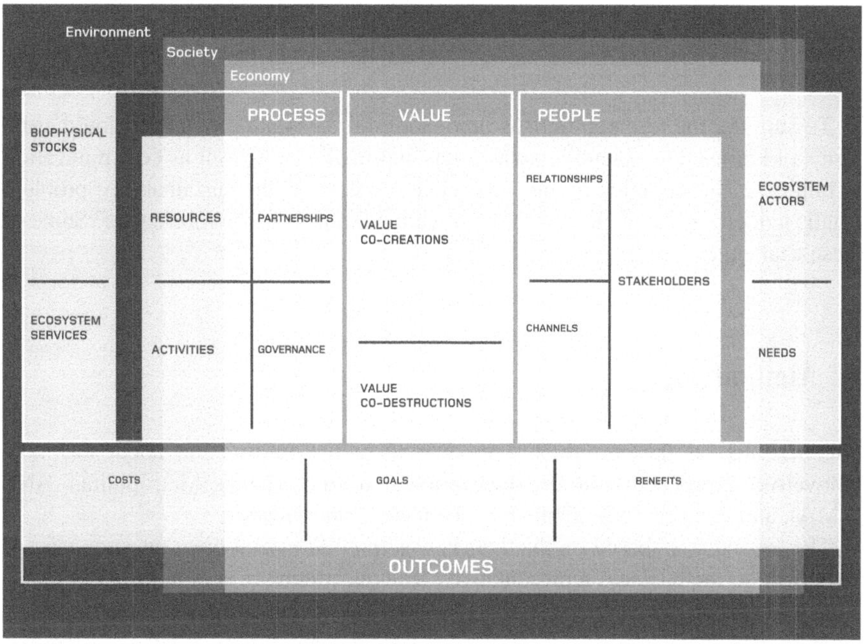

Fig. 3 The business model canvas (adapted) (Karlsson et al. 2018)

An interesting exception is Karlsson et al.'s (2018) study of a Swedish biogas-producing farm cooperative (Fig. 3) which proposes to include the environment, society, and economy. These dimensions have a hierarchical relationship: the environment encompasses society, and the society encompasses the economy. The systemic view is one of the interesting aspects of their model as economic life is considered in social terms and society is approached in its environmental framework. This systematization corresponds to a change in the BM concept, which aims not only to benefit shareholders through profit maximization but also to foster social and environmental values (Karlsson et al. 2018).

As a preliminary conclusion, the research on BM innovation allowed key elements in the transition pathways to be identified, namely in the food sector. These include:

- The need to adopt a sustainability definition (FSSD) in order to systematize the main aspects of the process of business change.
- The role of environmental (and social) outputs as central in business design, as opposed to the exclusivity of monetary and financial metrics.
- The utility of participatory and clear methods in order to identify the main components of BM. Product–Service Systems, BMC, and SSBMC are interesting tools of business design.

- The need to consider various forms of knowledge and different sciences (e.g., natural, social), in order to clearly understand what is at stake in sustainability pathways.

To sum up, the research on BM innovation for sustainability goals should cross forms of knowledge, scientific areas, tools and methods, as well as communication techniques. The complexity and problematic nature of the sustainability problem entails numerous challenges for BM innovation, notably in the food sector. Some of these challenges will be presented in Sect. 4.

3 Methodology

The first step of the empirical study was to gather information about the most innovative experiments in organic farming in the Lisbon Metropolitan Area (LMA), and to select individuals for face-to-face interviews.

The second step, based on the theory, was to build a semi-open questionnaire to be applied to the business representatives. The questionnaire is organized in blocks, namely on the origins and evolution of the experiment; the profile and motivations of the interviewee; the existence of public support for the initiative; the characterization of the activities and the distinct business model dimensions, notably the productive and commercialization strategies, including the relationships and networking with suppliers, customers, and similar producers; and the technological options in farming and commercialization.

The third step consisted of a scheduled visit to the venue and facilities of the selected farm (cultivated plots, greenhouses, warehouses, transformation facilities, farm shop, and restaurant), and applying the questionnaire in a face-to-face interview with the farm's main representative. After obtaining permission, pictures were taken, and the interview audiotaped. The products were tasted at a meal in the farm restaurant. Finally, the tape was transcribed and interpreted in the light of similar experiments reported in the literature.

4 The Case Study

Quinta do Oeste, a family organic farm business located in the Lisbon Metropolitan Area (LMA) was selected for our case study. A visit was made to the farm in October 2018, when we conducted a semi-structured interview with the farm's main representative (owner and manager) and had an organic food meal at the restaurant in the farm complex.

When Quinta do Oeste was acquired by the present owners' family in the late 1960s, it was dedicated to fruit production. Between 2007 and 2009, the heirs began the process of converting part of the farm to an organic production system with a view to incorporating differentiated products and creating a registered trademark. It is interesting to note that this shift was motivated by the interviewee's desire to adopt a lifestyle driven by sustainability values in farming. This is very much in line with the shift toward post-materialist values of a significant proportion of the population observed in many affluent societies (Tibbs 2011).

The farm currently has 14 ha dedicated to organic farming. A further 13 ha, essentially the old orchard which they have not been able to reconvert, is farmed using conventional methods.

They produce, transform, and distribute agri-food products and provide environmental and awareness training through workshops and field trips, including schools. They hold a biological certification of cultivation methods.

In addition to their own production, they also buy from intermediaries to complete their offer (e.g., fruit, potato, onion, and carrot). They sell 600 hampers a week in LMA through home delivery. They also sell directly to the public in their own store and local markets (e.g., Príncipe Real, and Campo Pequeno, in Lisbon; and Cascais). The farm's main activities are complemented by a restaurant on-site where they serve high-quality meals made of organic products.

In 2010, they obtained financing from the PRODER program to convert facilities (greenhouses and plant processing/packaging). More recently, they received support from LEADER-Local Action Group to remodel the restaurant. Both programs rely on European Union funds (Common Agricultural Policy). This means that public funding has been important to the success of this initiative.

The interviewee also noted the importance of informal collaborative networks with other organic producers not only for the exchange of knowledge and information but also for the supply of products to complete their offer. This seems to be a common trait of this emerging sector in Portugal and elsewhere (Seyfang 2006). These networks enhance the strong sense of belonging to a new community that assumes full responsibility for environmental matters. Reference was also made during the interview to customers' growing awareness of sustainability values, which has allowed Quinta do Oeste start the process of using alternatives to plastic in hampers more quickly.

The bet on brand development and communication was essential to the business strategy. Social networks (Facebook, Instagram, etc.) were just emerging when the project began, but it is now essential both to feed these channels and to get their input in the company's website. Together, they also function as virtual stores. The marketing strategy also targets big companies by sending newsletters to firms that act as delivery points, such as Roche, Microsoft, EDP, etc., and offering their employees discounts. This illustrates how Quinta do Oeste has built a sustainable business model.

The new value proposition consists of quality organic products. It relies on both traditional knowledge—in some cases ancient practices such as crop rotation to ensure soil fertility—and new technologies, namely the technological platforms in the commercialization stage (Boons and Lüdeke-Freund 2013). In the newly configured value chain, the producer has close control of the process along a much-shortened path to the market. The value capture is improved because the products are relatively expensive and, unlike traditional farming, they do not compete via prices, and margins are not smashed by big retailers. The customer interface is fully

Table 1 The case study value chain

Value chain	What	Where	How
Production	Seasonal organic vegetables and fruit	Local farm (14 ha; owner) Other producers located in other places of the same region or other Portuguese regions (depending on the products)	Traditional techniques New techniques Informal networks (trust-based)
Transformation	Seasonal organic vegetables and fruit	Local farm and restaurant	Traditional techniques New techniques
Commercialization	Seasonal organic vegetables and fruit	Local and regional (LMA) Local shop (owner)	Internet consumer registration and orders Domestic and enterprise delivery (own vehicles)
Consumption	Seasonal organic vegetables and fruit	Local restaurant, local and regional consumers (LMA)	

modified. The producer maintains a direct relationship with buyers, who have become active supporters and are also committed to health, food security, and sustainability values and practices. The aim is not to maximize profit but to obtain a reasonable return to secure the economic health of the business and provide fair revenues for the owners and workers. Land ownership is a very important asset as the business might not otherwise be viable. In addition, supportive networks of suppliers, customers, producers and local entities, based on trust and shared values and goals, are a new element of this solution.

Table 1 depicts the particular business model of Quinta do Oeste and shows the main elements and relationships along the value chain.

The case is characterized by options and values involved in the different steps of the value chain. In fact, the BM has been designed through the combination of the entrepreneur's personal values and options (e.g., ecological and environmental values) and sound management principles and rules. The entrepreneur's education in management is an important aspect of her approach to business and explains the development of complementary activities, like the workshops and field trips, the local restaurant and the shop. In fact, the business revenues are stabilized by these multiple activities.

Therefore, the key elements of the new sustainable BM of this case are as follows:

- Land ownership.
- Local production combined with production from other Portuguese regions within informal and trust-based networks. These networks allow the delivery of products that are temporarily unavailable or not produced at Quinta do Oeste. In addition, they permit to share information, knowledge and encouragement.

- Seasonal products, allowing natural cycles and the environment (land, ecosystems, water) to be respected.
- The integration of different parts of the value chain under the same enterprise: production, transformation, commercialization, and consumption.
- The centrality of the web platforms, which allows them to offer consumers and the community a range of important services: registration as a customer, weekly orders of hampers, information on seasonal products (e.g., their life cycle, nutrients and importance to health), information about other activities at the farm (restaurant, cooking workshops).
- The multidimensionality of this case regarding the option for a sustainable business in the food system: economic (production, transformation, commercialization and consumption), environmental (organic production), and social (field trips and knowledge dissemination within a large community).

To sum up, integration and diversity are keywords in this case, namely in terms of knowledge (old and new), communication tools (informal, web), sustainability goals (economic, social and environmental), and value chain components (production, transformation, commercialization, consumption). Based on these principles, the sustainability, economic and social dimensions of this experience have proved to be successful.

5 Conclusions

The analysis has shed light on the specificity of the food system. It is a territory-based system where new experiments to transform agricultural practices have to draw on both new and old knowledge. This is clearly illustrated by the Quinta do Oeste case study. The new business model draws on the new technological platforms to advertise and commercialize the farm's products and rejects the prevalent chemical-intensive farming practices. This shift is driven by the quest for quality food and sustainable practices, but has also proved to be very successful in economic and social terms.

Quinta do Oeste has tackled the uneven competition—their products are more expensive than those of "industrialized" agriculture—by developing a multifaceted strategy with distinct elements:

1. Participation in informal networks of organic farmers, consumers, associations, etc., to share knowledge, information and encouragement and to complete their offer.
2. Targeting a specific market segment that is very sensitive to food quality and sustainable farming practices rather than to food price.
3. Capture of a higher share of the value created through a sales scheme based on short supply chains (direct delivery, own shop, and participation in farmers' markets).
4. Complementary activities, such as a restaurant and a shop in the farm complex and the organization of field trips and cooking workshops.

An important conclusion is that support from public agencies is relatively modest in this sector, unlike others. This issue will be developed in future research. In our view, it is only possible to speed up the food system transition with much stronger public commitment and a reorientation of current policies, incentives and regulations not only in relation to sustainable agri-production and commercialization, but also all kinds of unsustainable agri-food related activities.

In addition to identifying the need for a territorial-based approach and greater public intervention, the case studied allowed us to identify other key aspects of the transition to more sustainable business models in the food sector. Firstly, critical reflection must take place on the theoretical frameworks available, in order to understand the dynamics of the transition pathway. In fact, and unlike sectors such as energy, the food system involves a huge number of very diverse actors in terms of type, size, and power. The specificity of the food system also entails the need to include the consumer side and societal values such as concern for the planet, health, and quality of life. This means that research on transition pathways in this sector should develop new theoretical and methodological frameworks that suit the specificity of these critical dimensions of social life.

A final conclusion is that agri-food transition requires an integrated solution encompassing innovative business models, the creation of sustainability-oriented technological innovation in conjunction with the recovery of ancient knowledge, a new generation of policies, and stronger public commitment.

The main limitation of this analysis is that it relies on a single case study. Future research will compare several case studies, corresponding to different business models at different stages of the value chain, in order to draw sounder conclusions that can be generalized. In addition, we will try to provide a theoretical contribution to the relationship between the sustainable business models approaches and the transition literature, taking into account the singularity of the food sector. Finally, we will analyze the adequacy of existing policies and formulate recommendations.

References

Barth H, Ulvenblad PO, Ulvenblad P (2017) Towards a conceptual framework of sustainable business model innovation in the agri-food sector: a systematic literature review. Sustainability 9(9):1620

Baumgartner RJ, Korhonen J (2010) Strategic thinking for sustainable development. Sustain Dev 18(2):71–75

Beuchelt T, Zeller M (2012) The role of cooperative business models for the success of smallholder coffee certification in Nicaragua: a comparison of conventional, organic and organic-fairtrade certified cooperative. Renew Agric Food Syst 28(3):195–211

Bocken NM, Short SW, Rana P, Evans S (2014) A literature and practice review to develop sustainable business model archetypes. J Clean Prod 65:42–56

Boons F, Lüdeke-Freund F (2013) Business models for sustainable innovation: state-of-the-art and steps towards a research agenda. J Clean Prod 45:9–19

Broman GI, Robèrt KH (2017) A framework for strategic sustainable development. J Clean Prod 140:17–31

Brunori G, Barjolle D, Dockes AC, Helmle S, Ingram J, Klerkx L, Tisenkopfs T (2013) CAP reform and innovation: the role of learning and innovation networks. Eurochoices 12(2):27–33
Bui S, Cardona A, Lamine C, Cerf M (2016) Sustainability transitions: insights on processes of niche-regime interaction and regime reconfiguration in agri-food systems. J Rural Stud 48:92–103
Cagliano R, Worley CG, Caniato FF (2016) The challenge of sustainable innovation in agri-food supply chains. In: Cagliano R, Caniato FF, Worley VG (eds) Organizing supply chain processes for sustainable innovation in the agri-food industry. Emerald Group, Bingley
Cohen N, Ilieva RT (2015) Transitioning the food system: a strategic practice management approach for cities. Environ Innov Soc Trans 17:199–217
França CL, Broman G, Robèrt KH, Basile G, Trygg L (2017) An approach to business model innovation and design for strategic sustainable development. J Clean Prod 140:155–166
Fritz M, Matopoulos A (2008) Sustainability in the agri-food industry: a literature review and overview of current trends. In: Proceedings of the 8th international conference on management in agri-food chains and networks
Geels FW, Sovacool BK, Schwanen T, Sorrell S (2017) The socio-technical dynamics of low-carbon transitions. Joule 1(3):463–479
Green K, Harvey M, Mcmeekin A (2003) Transformations in food consumption and production systems. J Environ Policy Plann 5(2):145–163
Hinrichs CC (2014) Transitions to sustainability: a change in thinking about food systems change? Agric Hum Values 31(1):143–155
Ingram J, Maye D, Kirwan J, Curry N, Kubinakova K (2015) Interactions between niche and regime: an analysis of learning and innovation networks for sustainable agriculture across Europe. J Agric Educ Ext 21(1):55–71
Karlsson NP, Hoveskog M, Halila F, Mattsson M (2018) Early phases of the business model innovation process for sustainability: addressing the status quo of a Swedish biogas-producing farm cooperative. J Clean Prod 172:2759–2772
Kurucz EC, Colbert BA, Luedeke-Freund F, Upward A, Willard B (2017) Relational leadership for strategic sustainability: practices and capabilities to advance the design and assessment of sustainable business models. J Clean Prod 140:189–204
Markard J, Raven R, Truffer B (2012) Sustainability transitions: an emerging field of research and its prospects. Res Policy 41(6):955–967
Markowska M, Saemundsson RJ, Wiklund J (2011) Contextualizing business model developments in Nordic rural gourmet restaurants. In: Alsos G, Carter S, Ljunggren E (eds) Handbook of research on entrepreneurship in agriculture and rural development. Edward Elgar, Cheltenham, pp 162–179
Osterwalder A, Pigneur Y (2010) Business model generation: a handbook for visionaries, game changers, and challengers. Wiley, Hoboken, NJ
Popkin BM (2017) Relationship between shifts in food system dynamics and acceleration of the global nutrition transition. Nutr Rev 75(2):73–82
Rivera M, Knickel K, de los Rios I, Ashkenazy A, Pears DQ, Chebach T, Šūmane S (2018) Rethinking the connections between agricultural change and rural prosperity: a discussion of insights derived from case studies in seven countries. J Rural Stud 59:242–251
Rohrbeck R, Konnertz L, Knab S (2013) Collaborative business modelling for systemic and sustainability innovations. Int J Technol Manag 63(1/2):4–23
Rosca E, Arnold M, Bendul JC (2017) Business models for sustainable innovation—an empirical analysis of frugal products and services. J Clean Prod 162:S133–S145
Sengers F, Wieczorek AJ, Raven R (2019) Experimenting for sustainability transitions: a systematic literature review. Technol Forecast Soc Chang 145:153–164
Seyfang G (2006) Ecological citizenship and sustainable consumption: examining local organic food networks. J Rural Stud 22(4):383–395
Stubbs W, Cocklin C (2008) Conceptualizing a "sustainability business model". Organ Environ 21 (2):103–127

Teece DJ (2010) Business models, business strategy and innovation. Long Range Plan 43 (2–3):172–194

Tell J, Hoveskog M, Ulvenblad P, Ulvenblad PO, Barth H, Ståhl J (2016) Business model innovation in the agri-food sector: a literature review. Br Food J 118(6):1462–1476

Tibbs H (2011) Changing cultural values and the transition to sustainability. J Futures Stud 15 (3):13–32

Ulvenblad P, Barth H, Björklund JC, Hoveskog M, Ulvenblad PO, Ståhl J (2018) Barriers to business model innovation in the agri-food industry: a systematic literature review. Outlook Agric 47(4):308–314

Ulvenblad PO, Ulvenblad P, Tell J (2019) An overview of sustainable business models for innovation in Swedish agri-food production. J Integr Environ Sci 16(1):1–22

Upward A, Jones P (2016) An ontology for strongly sustainable business models: defining an enterprise framework compatible with natural and social science. Organ Environ 29(1):97–123

Wilson GA (2008) From 'weak' to 'strong' multifunctionality: conceptualising farm-level multifunctional transitional pathways. J Rural Stud 24:367–383

Digital Transformation and Brazilian Agribusiness: An Analysis of Knowledge Management in the Sector

Cinthya Mônica da Silva Zanuzzi, Paulo Maurício Selig, Roberto Carlos dos Santos Pacheco, and Graciele Tonial

Abstract Smart farming is the application of digital transformation technologies in agribusiness. Big Data, IoT, robotics, nanotechnology, and artificial intelligence have brought new scenarios to productivity in this sector. The introduction of such innovations, however, requires new human, structural, and operational capacities. In this study, these factors are analyzed by knowledge management (KM). We adapted the questionnaire proposed by APO (Knowledge management: facilitators guide. Tokyo; 2009), to evaluate the KM in the Brazilian agribusiness sector, delimiting four main dimensions: Leadership, People, Processes, and Technology. The questionnaire was validated with 11 experts, and we performed a pretest with 5 from poultry farms. The data were collected from 240 managers from poultry farms. The results reveal that KM practices are known to livestock sector managers of the Brazilian poultry industry, but are implemented in isolation, either without leadership, strategic management or with neither of the two. The People dimension presented the lowest KM average and shows a dependency on external technical assistance. The dimension Process has the highest KM average, confirming previous work about the agility, quality, and innovative capacity of the Brazilian poultry sector. The results indicate that, in order to introduce smart factoring, Brazilian agribusiness need more investment in farmer's schooling, partnerships to share knowledge with stakeholders, and the introduction of new technologies based on KM practices.

Keywords Knowledge management · Smart farming · Poultry farming

C. Mônica da Silva Zanuzzi (✉) · P. M. Selig · R. C. dos Santos Pacheco · G. Tonial
Department of Engineering and Knowledge Management, Federal University of Santa Catarina (UFSC), Florianopolis, Santa Catarina, Brazil
e-mail: rpacheco@egc.ufsc.br; graciele.tonial@unoesc.edu.br

F. Matos et al. (eds.), *Knowledge, People, and Digital Transformation*, Contributions to Management Science, https://doi.org/10.1007/978-3-030-40390-4_7

1 Introduction

In the last 50 years, agribusiness has been the most productive economic sector, changing Brazil from an importer to one of the world's largest exporters of food (Vieira Filho and Fishlow 2017). Research, innovation, and knowledge management (KM) have been among the successful strategies to reach such results.

More recently, however, the agribusiness sector is facing new challenges: the increase in the world's population that is expected to reach 10 billion by 2050, increasing food demand by 60% compared to 2013, and by the worsening global environmental crisis (Food and Agriculture Organization of the United Nations [FAO] 2017).

These, among other factors, have required new knowledge as well as alternative and varied forms of sustainable production.

For authors such as Massruhá and Leite (2017), Massruhá et al. (2014), Pivoto et al. (2018), Wolfert et al. (2017) and for the World Economic Forum [WEF] (2018) technological innovations in agribusiness have been identified as an alternative to face such challenges. These innovations should promote the digital transformation of agribusiness through the use of Big Data, IoT (Internet of Things), artificial intelligence, robotics, and nanotechnology, all of which are part of the Smart Farming (SF) concept.

Pivoto et al. (2018) point to the concept of SF, as a set of technologies that aim to make processes and decision-making digital, faster, and more efficient in agriculture, heading toward automating agricultural processes and generating innovations and improvements in the sector.

To adopt innovations, the productive agribusiness sector will need new management models, and manage the fact that the same technology differs among rural producers, due to their capacity to absorb knowledge (Vieira Filho and Silveira 2016).

In this scenario, the productive return differs due to the KM that assists in the decision-making process. This was already seen by Angeloni (2009), who verified that modern Brazilian organizations were changing the traditional management models in order to meet the society of information and knowledge demands. KM is perceived as strategic to integrate the new management models o of the organizations that work in the agribusiness (Rossetti 2009). According to the Asian Productivity Organization [APO] (2010), KM is an integrated approach that allows the use, creation, sharing and application of knowledge to increase productivity, profitability, and organizational growth.

Within context, the goal of this study was to evaluate the KM in the Brazilian agribusiness, in the face of the challenges regarding digital transformation.

As a basis, we used the KM evaluation method proposed by the Asian Productivity Association [APO] framework (2009), which is formed by three levels: accelerators, KM process, and results. For this study, the first framework level was delimited: the accelerators level. The other levels will be dealt with in a posterior stage of this research.

The data collector instrument from APO (2009) was adapted for the context of this research, which analyzes the production units from the livestock sector of the Brazilian poultry industry, and its relationship with new digital technologies, supported by the Smart Farming concept.

The practical contribution of this study is the validation of an initial proposal for the evaluation of KM in vertically integrated production units of Brazilian poultry. This will, therefore, allow the use of different strategies, driving digital transformation from the concept of Smart Farming.

2 Knowledge Management in Agribusiness

According to APO (2010), KM is an integrated approach that allows the use, creation, sharing and application of knowledge to increase productivity, profitability, and organizational growth. Additionally, it provides a global set of processes that are put in place to identify relevant data sources and information for organizations (Lakshman 2009). This enables, through the management of their intellectual assets and knowledge, the generation of value and competitive advantage (Uriarte 2008).

The positive effects of the application of knowledge management processes in the various agribusiness sectors are already highlighted in the research of (Bruisma 2003; Eastwood et al. 2012; Feliciano 2013; Kokate et al. 2013; Lwoga et al. 2010).

For Vieira Filho and Silveira (2016), the managerial capacity of the farmer is fundamental in the process of exploring the competitive advantages and productive gains of technological knowledge, as well as for decision-making. However, the challenge is to manage these processes, innovations, people and knowledge for the development of sustainable agribusiness.

In this regard, Kokate et al. (2013) recommend that actions of innovation in knowledge management in agriculture be focused on organizational practices through Information and Communication Technology (ICT), Communities of Practice (CoP) and other networked tools.

In this context, the concept of Smart Farming (SF), treated by the literature as a set of technologies aimed at making processes and decision-making in agriculture faster, more efficient and digital, goes toward the automation of agricultural processes (Pivoto et al. 2018).

The concept deals with precision agriculture technologies and information technology already used, as well as emerging technologies and innovations in robotics, artificial intelligence, Big Data and IoT. For Vieira Filho and Fishlow (2017) the incorporation of technology in agricultural activities is crucial to increase the production of different agricultural products.

The agricultural and economic benefits that Smart Farming can generate have been studied by Gelb and Voet (2009), and are understood as: (1) better production and farm management; (2) dissemination of important information; (3) improvement in the planning, monitoring, and pacing of production; (4) access to the latest research results in the area; and, (5) automation of activities.

However, in accordance with Pivoto et al. (2018), the adoption of innovations and technologies in agribusiness presents some challenges, such as those related to socioeconomic factors. These refer to the individual characteristics of the decision-maker (age, schooling, amount of experience in the activity). The challenges related to information dissemination can occur through consultants, mass media (TV, radio, Internet), technical assistance services and through ICTs such as social networks. Finally, there are the institutional factors: agricultural policies, public technical assistance, and legislation to encourage adoption. The authors also point out that the available network infrastructure (internet) is a challenge in adopting Smart Farming.

3 KM Evaluation Method

The APO (2009) developed a reference method known as the APO KM Framework, which deals with a worldwide reference method to evaluate KM. The method allows measurement of the efforts and efficiency of knowledge processes supported by the factors which are considered critical for success in KM initiatives. The objective of the APO's approach to implementing knowledge management is to develop competencies for the application of its approach to the framework and, as a result, the formulation of action plans for its implementation (APO 2010).

The implementation of knowledge management by the APO (2009) consists of the following steps: discover, design, develop, and implement. The method presents a referential framework consisting of three levels: accelerators; process of knowledge management; and results. It also presents a data collection tool (questionnaire) that is part of the framework to manage the complete implementation process of KM in an organization and not just the diagnosis. The questionnaire is flexible to customizations and has been tested in various public and private organizations in the United States, Europe, and Asia (APO 2010).

The KM "accelerators level" from the APO framework is formed by Processes, People, Technology, and Leadership, being recognized as dimensions that boost the KM initiative. Dalkir (2005) supports that the driving elements and facilitators of KM projects are based on the Leadership, Processes, People, and Technology dimensions. Therefore, in this research, it is understood that these dimensions theoretically support the KM analysis for the analyzed context.

In the Processes dimension, the effective and systemized processes that can contribute to improving the productivity, rentability, quality, and organizational growth are analyzed. In the People dimension, the users and generators of knowledge are recognized as the ones responsible for the creation and the ones who own the intellectual capital. In the Technology dimension, the way that technology accelerates the knowledge processes through effective usage of tools and techniques capable of retaining and promoting knowledge is analyzed. Moreover, the Leadership dimension comprehends the conduction of KM initiatives, providing alignment with the organization's strategy (APO 2009).

Table 1 KM analysis dimensions and variables

Dimension	Variables
People	Training and capacitation programs that increase knowledge.
	Policies regarding the protection of knowledge.
	Practices to spread KM information to new employees.
	The production system includes teamwork.
	Formal processes, assistance, consulting and technical assistance.
Processes	Sharing of best practices and lessons learned.
	Modeling of its working systems and processes to aggregate value.
	Continuous evaluation of the processes, with a result-based view.
	Internal and external benchmarking to improve performance and innovate.
Leadership	Promote, recognize, and reward the improvement of performance and learning.
	Incentivize the sharing of knowledge and collaborative work.
	Promote the creation of knowledge and innovation.
Technology	Usage of technology as a means to share knowledge.
	Usage of technology as a means of knowledge or technological efficiency.
	Characterization of the Internet as a source of knowledge processes to solve problems at work.

Source: Adapted from APO (2009)

Table 1 presents the four dimensions of analysis adapted for this research, with the description of the variables.

Therefore, these dimensions and variables were adapted and compose the collection instrument to evaluate the KM within the Brazilian agribusiness sector's poultry industry.

4 Brazilian Poultry Industry

The sector chosen as the object of this study was the livestock sector of the Brazilian poultry industry. It was chosen for its representativeness in the international market, and for its use of a system of partnership between the agribusiness industry and the farmer for production. Brazil is the second-largest producer, and the largest exporter of chicken meat in the world (Ministério da Agricultura, Pecuária e Abastecimento [MAPA] 2018).

All poultry production in Brazil is regulated mainly by the legislation that defines norms in food safety, health and animal welfare, the environment, and by specific requirements of clients, i.e., the market (Martins 2018). The compliance with these rules enables the Brazilian agribusinesses of chicken meat to produce for the domestic market and to export to more than 150 countries. According to the Brazilian Association of Agribusiness [ABAG] (2017), the expressive numbers of the Brazilian agribusiness are also demonstrated by its share of the Brazilian Gross Domestic Product (GDP), for which it was responsible for 23.5% in 2017.

This sector adopts the agroindustrial vertical coordination system for the production of animals, which occurs through a partnership between the rural producers (poultry farmers) and the poultry slaughterhouses. Therefore, the poultry production units are delimited as the analysis level for this study.

5 Methodology

This study adopts a quantitative research approach, since it uses the quantification of data, information gathering, and processing of data by means of descriptive statistical techniques (Richardson 2017).

After defining the adoption of the APO reference model (2009), the KM assessment tool (questionnaire) was adapted in order to adjust it to the real situation of the poultry production units, by the following steps.

Step 1: Adaptation of the questionnaire based on the APO (2009) model: In this stage, the analysis was delimited just to the four dimensions stated by the APO (2009), supported and comprehended by Dalkir (2005) as driving elements for the implementation of a KM project, which are: Leadership, Processes, People, and Technology, as described in Table 1.

Step 2: Validation of the questionnaire: In this stage, the questionnaire proposed to analyze the KM of the poultry production units was validated. Primarily, the experts were chosen accordingly by the following criteria: have knowledge about the theme discussed; have a full higher academic background; know the Brazilian agribusiness sector. The goal was that the experts could verify the relevance, pertinence, and clarity of the questionnaire, pointing out possible inconsistencies and making suggestions. The group was formed of 11 experts, 2 of them being doctors representing universities; 2 researchers of the research institution called *Embrapa*; 6 technicians from agroindustries; and a representative from the Santa Catarina Poultry Farming Association.

Step 3: After the validation stage, the pretest was applied (with five poultry farmers).

Therefore, the questionnaire was formed of 27 questions, with 15 of them being made to evaluate the KM of production units as presented in Table 1, 10 questions to characterize the sample, and 2 questions to identify the KM practices used by the sample. All of them use a Likert scale, from 1 to 5 points, corresponding to inexistent (1), insufficient (2), adjusted (3), good (4), and excellent (5).

After this stage, the analysis and reliability test of the questionnaire was carried out, in order to measure the reliability of the data collection instrument. The reliability analysis dimensions were evaluated using Cronbach's alpha. The result was judged to be adequate, since the figure was above 0.6 in all dimensions. According to DeVellis (2016), in social sciences, adequate values are those above 0.6. In this research, all dimensions were above this value as shown in Table 2.

The data collection stage was carried out on-site by 49 technicians who were agroindustries employees, and that accepted to participate in the study. Firstly,

Table 2 Dimensions reliability analysis ($n = 240$)

Dimensions	Cronbach's alpha
Leadership	0.696
Processes	0.619
People	0.712
Technology	0.633

Source: Research data (2019)

online training with all the technicians was carried out. The selection of the producing units took place at random, following the daily working routine of the technicians, and 240 questionnaires were completed by the managers of the production units. The data collection period occurred between November and December of 2018.

The collected data were individually reviewed, with the purpose of identifying possible inconsistencies or gaps that could compromise the analysis. The data were treated in a quantitative way and were analyzed using the software "Microsoft Excel" (Microsoft Office) and SPSS (Statistical Package for the Social Sciences) version 20.

The descriptive statistical analysis of the variables had the purpose of identifying measures of the distribution and location of the sample. In this way, it was possible to characterize it and make inferences of the variables, analyzing information regarding maximum, minimum, mean, frequency, and standard deviation values.

5.1 Population and Sample

Brazil is divided into 26 federal states, and this research was conducted in Santa Catarina state, which is recognized as the second-largest producer and primary exporter of chicken in Brazil, according to Brazilian Association of Animal Protein [ABPA] (2018). It has nearly 6684 poultry units and poultry slaughter businesses, according to Agricultural Research and Rural Extension Company of Santa Catarina [EPAGRI] (2017).

After getting in touch with businesses located in Santa Catarina, three of them agreed to participate in the research, with these three representing nearly 90% of the poultry production units in the state.

For greater precision in the estimation and size of the sample, the probabilistic sampling calculation according to Richardson (1999) was used, considering that the three main businesses in the state represent 90% of the industry, which resulted in the population of 6015 production units when the total was multiplied by 90%. The reliability level adopted was 95%, the sampling error was 6%, and the minimum sample for the study was 219 production units.

However, it must be stated that the researched production units were selected in a non-probabilistic way, which characterize the sample by convenience, because they were chosen from criteria such as accessibility and typicity. The subjects of this research are the managers (poultry farmers), responsible for each production unit.

After the field research conducted on-site by the 49 technicians, the results were represented in 240 questionnaires, the number that makes up the sample of this study's analysis.

5.1.1 Characterization of the Surveyed Subjects and Production Units

The descriptive statistics of the total sample analyzed ($n = 240$) showed the age of the poultry farmers with a variation of 21 and 71 years, a mean of 47 years and a standard deviation of 10.91. The variation can be compared with the results of the Brazilian Institute of Geography and Statistics [IBGE] (2017), in which the age of rural producers in Brazil ranges from 30 to 60 years (Brazilian Institute of Geography and Statistics [IBGE] 2018). The poultry farmer's mean amount of experience in the activity is 20 years, ranging from 1 to 59 years of experience.

The education of the respondents is represented by different percentages: 56.25% have primary education, 36.67% have secondary education, only 2.92% have higher education, 1.92% have postgraduate studies, while 2.08% said they are illiterate. These numbers demonstrate the low level of schooling of poultry farmers who were part of this sample. However, when compared to rural producers in Brazil, ascertained by the Agro Census 2017, the level of schooling is even lower −15.5% of producers said they had never attended school and 79.1% of them did not go beyond the Elementary level (IBGE 2018).

The characterization of the producing units in this study is represented by the most common type of aviaries (house poultry) used by the studied agroindustries, the conventional and automated, which are related to the adopted technologies. In the conventional, there is less control of the internal environment (as an example, the temperature and humidity), because it is manual. However, in the air-conditioned aviary, there is a greater internal control as it is automated. The results of the research show that 56.6% of the sample has only conventional aviaries (manual); 34.58% have automated aviaries, and 8.33% of the sample have both types. It is noticed that the conventional low-tech aviary still predominates, since the automated aviary assumes a greater investment, according to Sartin (2016).

6 Analysis and Presentation of Results

6.1 Knowledge Management Diagnosis

The data of this research were analyzed using the descriptive statistic technique, based on a Likert scale from 1 to 5 points. Firstly, the average of the questions related to each dimension was calculated, which resulted in the average, mode and standard

Table 3 Result relative to the four KM dimensions ($n = 240$)

Dimension	Mean	Trend	Mean standard deviation
Leadership	3.41	4	1.09
Processes	4.01	5	1.06
People	3.08	4	1.20
Technology	3.33	3	0.96
Maturity degree			

Source: Research data (2019)

deviation of the four dimensions (Leadership, Process, People, and Technology), and the results are presented in Table 3.

It is highlighted that the highest mean (4.01) was the Processes dimension. For APO (2009), this dimension accelerates the processes of knowledge through an effective use of techniques and tools of ICT. This dimension may have presented the best mean, as in the vertical integration system, the processes are established by integrating agroindustries and passed on to poultry farmers. In addition, the processes are accompanied by technical assistance. The lowest mean (3.08) was the People dimension. The results of the dimensions will be presented next.

6.2 *Process Dimension Analysis*

Regarding the aspects, the Process dimension involves how they are systematized and articulated to assist in the acquisition and sharing of knowledge in poultry production units. This dimension presents a mean of 4.1, being the highest mean of all dimensions. The result corroborates with Dos Santos et al. (2017), which demonstrates that the greater agility and quality of poultry processes are related to innovations in the means of production.

Making decisions based on the information collected in the activity processes is indicated by 66.53% of the respondent managers. The collection of this data can be manual or automated but is a routine practice. However, 27.54% claim only to collect the information and not to use it to make decisions, while 5.93% do not perform data collection. For Helou (2015), the knowledge that underlies decision-making is based on the need to empower people within the organization, so that the decision can be taken more accurately, in a decentralized manner and with agility. Therefore, it is understood as paramount that managers rely on relevant information about the production process for future decisions.

Another issue addressed in the study concerns how the manager tracks information regarding technological changes to improve avian productivity. Of the respondents, 23.56% said that they have already heard about the technological changes and that they try to understand how they work through conversation with the integrators, participation in the fairs, and through the demonstrations made by the suppliers of the technologies. Those who say that they keep track, understand, and are evaluating the adoption of technologies represent 18.67% of poultry farmers. The results of the survey indicate that 50.66% of respondents already use technologies to improve the performance of their aviaries, such as sensor installation. The others, 0.89%, have never heard of the technology, and 6.22% have heard of it, but do not understand how it works.

6.2.1 Analysis of the Leadership Dimension in Knowledge Management

With regard to the aspects of leadership, whether it is aligned and committed to the purpose of KM of the poultry producing units or not has been assessed. Considering the Leadership dimension, we can see that it presents the second-best mean, 3.41, in relation to the other dimensions surveyed.

In this dimension, the aspects of how the sharing of goals by the leadership with the other members of their team was evaluated. Of the total respondent poultry farmers, 83.41% said that the goals are discussed with all of their staff. However, 13.10% of respondents affirmed that they only have the goals, and do not discuss them with the team. There are still 3.49% of respondents who said that they do not have production targets. Leadership plays a crucial role in the implementation and sustainability of knowledge management in organizations as they influence people, giving them direction and purpose, while at the same time gaining consistency and precision in knowledge management initiatives (Herrera 2008).

The research also addresses the incentive given by the leader to the team to learn and share knowledge about the activity among team members. From the poultry farmer respondents, 90.05% consider that the leader gives incentive. Meanwhile, to 7.69%, the incentive is rare. To 2.26%, no incentive is given. For Helou (2015), the leadership functions as a conductor of the new actions to be implemented and to ensure the use of KM in processes. The leadership of the poultry production units must both anticipate initiatives of practices that motivate the cooperation in the day-to-day work and the exchange of knowledge to reach the goals established by the integrating agroindustry.

6.2.2 Analysis of the Technology Dimension in Knowledge Management

The Technology dimension verifies if it is being used as a means to accelerate the processes of knowledge, and as a consequence to improve the performance of the poultry units. This dimension presents the second-best mean of the dimensions analyzed, of 3.33. The use of technology was approached in the research, regarding the adoption of technological equipment (for example sensors of humidity control and temperature, among others) for the aid of day-to-day activities in the aviaries.

For more than half of the poultry farmer respondents or 69.44%, technological resources have helped in the activities, and have improved performance. The poultry farmers who say they do not use technological resources are 7.53% of the respondents, and those who have the technological resources but are still learning to use them are 5.44%. For Sartin (2016), technological innovation is a differentiating factor in poultry production and improves the production performance of poultry farmers.

For Artuzo (2015) and Pivoto et al. (2018), even if producers have expectations of adoption of technologies, these expectations have some limitations to their adoption, such as the cost of technology, the lack of qualified personnel, and the lack of information about technology.

The survey also questions about the use of the Internet for communication. The results of respondents are: do not use the Internet 6.96%; use the Internet in some cases as a source of communication (for example, WhatsApp and e-mail), 19.13%; use the Internet daily to communicate (for example, with the technician of the integrator, with other poultry farmers), 39.57%; use the Internet to search for new information about the activity, 28.70%; and 5.75% use it to train themselves (they take courses through the Internet). The significant increase in Internet access of Brazil's agricultural establishments is corroborated with the data of the Agro Census 2017, with a growth of 1790.1% in relation to the 2006 Census. However, for Pivoto et al. (2018), the speed of input and signal quality are still factors that limit the adoption of Smart Farming technologies in Brazil.

6.2.3 Analysis of the People's Dimension in Knowledge Management

Regarding aspects related to the People dimension, it is important to highlight that the majority of staff members are members of the family and they are the ones who create, share, and transfer their knowledge in the poultry production units. The People dimension was highlighted by the lowest results in relation to all other dimensions, presenting a mean of 3.08. The issues dealt with in the People dimension address the acquisition of knowledge, through some practices inherent to the vertically integrated production system or the poultry farmer's own initiatives.

The technical assistance provided by the agroindustry was analyzed as a practice of knowledge sharing. All respondents claim to receive technical assistance and to take their doubts and acquire new knowledge through this practice. In the study conducted by Carrer et al. (2017), technical assistance is a form of information transfer that increases the knowledge of farmers and their employees about the availability of new production and management technologies.

Technical assistance provided by the agroindustry occurs through visits by a technician to the agricultural properties, aiming to broaden the reach of this technical assistance, as well as the frequency of visits by the technician. This can be innovated through the adoption of communication technologies such as video conferencing, social networks, and videotapes. Different practices of KM can also be adopted according to the level of maturity of poultry farmers.

The existence of training for new employees (or family members) before taking part in the activity was addressed in the survey. Among the respondents, 28.57% said that there is no training or the question does not apply; 16.01% only talk to the new employee and pass on the routine information of the activity; but for 55.42% of respondent poultry farmers, training is given, and they are accompanied by another employee with experience. For Sartin (2016), the knowledge accumulated by poultry farmers, combined with the technological advances, instigates the increase of labor productivity. For Fialho et al. (2007), the new business models require different approaches from the organizations, which require new cognitive skills of the worker and more competence in the effective management of the knowledge that the worker possesses.

The People dimension deserves attention both from integrating agroindustries and from managers, since people are the owners and users of the knowledge needed to meet production requirements. They are the decision-makers. Thus, agroindustries and managers can adopt KM practices aimed at increasing the acquisition and sharing of knowledge. Some practices are pointed out in the literature, such as encouraging experienced poultry farmers to transfer their knowledge to the less experienced—training in model properties (benchmarking).

6.3 *Knowledge Management Versus Smart Farming*

Although the digital transformation of agribusiness studied by the concept of Smart Farming is innovative, for these technological innovations to occur it is necessary to analyze some factors related to the implementation of the concept, such as those highlighted by Pivoto et al. (2018), which deal with:

Socioeconomic Factors are related to the individual characteristics of the main decision-maker of the farm (producing unit). Based on research by De Souza Filho et al. (2011), Pierpaoli et al. (2013), and Tey and Brindal (2012), the main variables and socioeconomic determinants generally analyzed in the technology adoption process are age, schooling, experience, and time spent on agricultural activity.

The results of this study demonstrate the low level of education of the respondents. This may be correlated with the low adoption of technology in the activities. However, in contrast, 69.44% of the respondents say that technological resources helped in the activities and improved the performance. Still, 66.53% of respondents mention that the decision-making process is based on the information collected in the activity processes.

The explanation for this, according to the authors, is that more educated farmers expressed greater demand for information and more ability to assess the benefits of using computers as a tool to support management in decision-making, which tends to increase marginal efficiency of technology (Carrer et al. 2017). Some studies demonstrate the positive effect of education on the process of technology adoption in agriculture (Abdulai and Huffman 2005; Abdulai et al. 2008; Ashraf et al. 2009; Carrer et al. 2017).

Experience with agricultural activity is another variable that can affect the process of technology adoption. This study presents a mean of 20 years of experience and mean age of 47 years for the respondents. On the one hand, more experience with agricultural activity measured by age or years of work with agriculture, is a positive factor in the adoption of technologies, since it is related to better management skills

(De Souza Filho et al. 2011). However, older producers may have a short-term planning horizon, especially if they do not have a successor in the production unit. Younger producers are more easily attracted to novelties and are likely to adopt technologies first, especially in the context of Smart Farming. Age can also negatively influence the process of technology adoption.

The results of this study relate two of the factors influencing the diffusion of information that influence the adoption of the technological innovations pointed out by Pivoto et al. (2018). The first one in the existence of technical assistance, where 100% of the poultry production units are provided with the service, and the second that deals with the use of the Internet for communication, since only 6.96% of the respondents say they do not use the Internet. A study carried out by Carrer et al. (2017) indicates that the presence of technical assistance has a positive impact on the adoption of technology. Technical assistance is a form of information transfer that increases the knowledge of poultry farmers and their employees about the availability of new production and management technologies. A recent study by the Brazilian Agricultural Research Corporation [EMBRAPA] (2018, p. 135) shows that the agricultural sector has experienced significant changes due to the migration of the information society, as well as knowledge to the society of the digital age. Around 90% of the rural producers already use cell phones in their daily activities (personal and professional). There is also a growing use of digital media and social networks (Facebook, Instagram, Twitter) in rural businesses.

The institutional factors pointed out by Pivoto et al. (2018) are agricultural policies, public technical assistance, and legislation to encourage the adoption of technologies. In this study, it was identified that the participation of poultry farmers in representative institutions such as a union, a producers' association, or a cooperative leadership was only 18.57%, which shows the low participation in entities that represent farmers (poultry farmers) against their demands, such as agricultural policies. This result can strengthen the indication of dependence of the poultry farmer both in the knowledge sharing of the activity and in the adoption of technologies of the partner agroindustry.

It should be noted that Smart Farming is a relatively new concept, and knowledge about its applications and implications for research as well as its development is still scarcely diffused in the literature, according to Wolfert et al. (2017). However, the analysis of the challenges pointed out by Pivoto et al. (2018), together with the results of this study, indicate that knowledge management by having a systematic approach to increasing productivity and organizational sustainability through practices and methods (tools) can help with challenges of the digital transformation of agribusiness.

7 Final Considerations

This study evaluated how KM supports and gives the potential to the digital transformation factors of the Brazilian agribusiness through the combination of the APO framework accelerated dimensions, adopted to the sector's context.

The findings of this research reveal significant variation between the average of the People, Leadership, Technology, and Processes dimensions, showing that the production units are still organized within the traditional management and production model.

In relation to the KM practices, they are known and implemented separately, without leadership or management direction. This is noticeable, especially when the analyses indicate the People dimension as the lowest average and show a dependency on external technical assistance. This factor is highlighted by Pivoto et al. (2018) as a negative influence in the process of adopting new technologies and in the conduction of effective KM practices.

The Processes dimension presented the highest average between the analyzed KM dimensions, confirming previous studies that highlight the agility, quality, and innovative capacity of the sector in Brazil over recent years.

Other relevant findings concern the effectiveness of the partnership model between the farmer and the agroindustry in the studied production chain, which proves to be a model that has helped in the sharing of knowledge and in the adoption of technological innovations. The results indicate that to introduce Smart Farming, the Brazilian agribusiness needs investment in the education of farmers, partnerships to share knowledge with stakeholders and the introduction of new technologies such as Big Data, IoT (Internet of Things), artificial intelligence, robotics, and nanotechnology.

This study contributes to the advances of research in the area of KM, corroborating with studies already performed. It is understood that KM can help agribusiness in the identification, creation, use, and storage of the knowledge necessary for the sustainable development of the sector, promoting its digital transformation, with KM evaluation being a possible strategy to be used.

A limitation of the study is the fact that the production unit's characteristics are specific, which do not have a formal organizational structure. Therefore, the KM evaluation methods and models proposed by the literature must be adapted to analyze the sector's context.

Therefore, it is suggested that future works may propose models for the assessment of KM, defining scales, dimensions and specific variables for agribusiness. Other works can also identify barriers and facilitators for the implementation of KM in agribusiness.

Additionally, can expand the application of the method to all segments of the agricultural sector of the other animal protein production chains, such as pig and cattle breeding.

References

Abdulai A, Huffman WE (2005) The diffusion of new agricultural technologies: the case of crossbred-cow technology in Tanzania. Am J Agric Econ 87(3):645–659

Abdulai A, Monnin P, Gerber J (2008) Joint estimation of information acquisition and adoption of new technologies under uncertainty. J Int Dev 20(4):437–451

Agricultural Research and Rural Extension Company of Santa Catarina (2017) https://www.epagri.sc.gov.br/index.php/a-epagri/documentos-institucionais/

Angeloni MTA (2009) Gestão do conhecimento no Brasil: casos, experiências e práticas de empresas privadas. Qualitymark

Artuzo FD (2015) Análise da eficiência técnica e econômica da agricultura de precisão a taxa variável de fertilizantes na cultura da soja no RS. (Dissertação de Mestrado). Programa de Pós-Graduação em Agronegócios, Centro de Estudos e Pesquisas em Agronegócios. Universidade Federal do Rio Grande do Sul, Porto Alegre

Ashraf N, Giné X, Karlan D (2009) Finding missing markets (and a disturbing epilogue): evidence from an export crop adoption and marketing intervention in Kenya. Am J Agric Econ 91 (4):973–990

Asian Productivity Organization (2009) Knoweledge management: case studies for small and medium enterprises. Tokyo

Asian Productivity Organization (2010) Knowledge management: facilitators guide. Tokyo

Brazilian Agricultural Research Corporation (2018) Visão 2030: o futuro da agricultura brasileira. Embrapa, Brasília, DF. https://www.embrapa.br/busca-de-publicacoes/-/publicacao/1090820/visao-2030-o-futuro-da-agricultura-brasileira

Brazilian Animal Protein Asociation (2018) http://abpa-br.com.br/setores/avicultura/publicacoes/relatorios-anuais

Brazilian Association of Agribussines (2017) http://www.abag.com.br/sala_imprensa/interna/abag-agronegocio-contribui-com-23-do-pib-1

Brazilian Institute of Geography and Statistics (2017) https://www.ibge.gov.br/estatisticas-novoportal/economicas/agricultura-e-pecuaria/21814-2017-censo-agropecuario.html?=&t=resultados

Brazilian Institute of Geography and Statistics (2018) https://www.ibge.gov.br/estatisticas-novoportal/economicas/agriculturae-pecuaria/21814-2018-censo agropecuario.html?=&t=resultados

Bruisma J (2003) World agriculture: towards 2015/2030: an FAO study. Routledge, London

Carrer MJ, de Souza Filho HM, Batalha MO (2017) Factors influencing the adoption of farm management information systems (FMIS) by Brazilian citrus farmers. Comput Electron Agric 138:11–19

Dalkir J (2005) Knowledge management in theory and pratice. Elsevier, Butterworth-Heinemann

De Souza Filho HM, Buainain AM, da Silveira JMFJ, Vinholis MDMB (2011) Condicionantes da adoção de inovações tecnológicas na agricultura. Cadernos de Ciência & Tecnologia 28 (1):223–255

DeVellis RF (2016) Scale development: theory and applications, vol 26. Sage, Newbury Park, CA

Dos Santos TO, Castanha ET, Monteiro JJ, Benfatto AC, Cittadin A (2017) Reflexos da tecnologia de automação nos resultados econômicos de aviários integrados a uma empresa do ramo avícola. In: Anais do Congresso Brasileiro de Custos-ABC. November

Eastwood CR, Chapman DF, Paine MS (2012) Networks of practice for co-construction of agricultural decision support systems: case studies of precision dairy farms in Australia. Agric Syst 108:10–18

Feliciano AM (2013) Extensão rural: criação, estratégias de uso e retenção do conhecimento. Tese de Doutorado. Programa de Engenharia e Gestão do Conhecimento. Universidade Federal de Santa Catarina, Florianópolis, SC

Fialho FAP, Montibeller Filho G, Macedo M, Mitidieri TDC (2007) Empreendedorismo na era do conhecimento. Visual Books, Florianópolis

Food and Agriculture Organization of the United Nations (2017) The future of food and agriculture—trends and challenges. Rome. http://www.fao.org/3/a-i6583e.pdf. Accessed 15 Jan 2018

Gelb E, Voet H (2009) ICT adoption trends in agriculture: a summary of the EFITA ICT adoption questionnaires (1999–2009). Abrufbar unter, 20. http://departments.agri.huji.ac.il/economics/voet-gelb.pdf.Letzter Zugriff

Helou ARHA (2015) Avaliação da maturidade da gestão do conhecimento na administração pública. (Tese de Doutorado). Curso de Programa de Pós-Graduação em Engenharia e Gestão do Conhecimento. Universidade Federal de Santa Catarina, Florianópolis, SC

Herrera CGN (2008) El liderazgo en la gestión del conocimento. Manizales: Universidad de Manizales, 25

Kokate K, Vijayaragavan K, Adhiguru P, Kumbhare N, Sangeetha V (2013) Proceedings of international conference on innovative approaches for agricultural knowledge management: global extension. International Society of Extension Education & Indian Council of AGricultural Reaerch, Nova Deli

Lakshman C (2009) Organizational knowledge leadership: an empirical examination of knowledge management by top executive leaders. Leadersh Org Dev J 30(4):338–364

Lwoga ET, Ngulube P, Stilwell C (2010) Managing indigenous knowledge for sustainable agricultural development in developing countries: knowledge management approaches in the social context. Int Inf Libr Rev 42(3):174–185

Martins AF (2018) Estruturas de Governança na Produção de Suínos: Os Diferentes Mecanismos que Coordenam a Qualidade. Revista Suinocultura Industrial 282(3):12–19

Massruhá SMFS, Leite MDA (2017) Agro 4.0-rumo à agricultura digital. In Embrapa Informática Agropecuária-Artigo em anais de congresso (ALICE). In: Magnoni Júnior L, Stevens D, Silva WTL, Vale JMF, Purini SRM, Magnoni MGM et al. (Org) JC na Escola Ciência, Tecnologia e Sociedade: mobilizar o conhecimento para alimentar o Brasil, 2nd ed. Centro Paula Souza, São Paulo

Massruhá SMFS, Leite MDA, Luchiari Junior A, Romani LAS (2014) Tecnologias da informação e comunicação e suas relações com a agricultura. Embrapa Informática Agropecuária-Livro científico (ALICE), Brasília, DF

Ministério da Agricultura, Pecuária e Abastecimento (2018) Economia e Emprego. http://www.brasil.gov.br/economia-e-emprego/2017/03/carnesbrasileiras-sao-reconhecidas-internacionalmente

Pierpaoli E, Carli G, Pignatti E, Canavari M (2013) Drivers of precision agriculture technologies adoption: a literature review. Procedia Technol 8:61–69

Pivoto D, Waquil PD, Talamini E, Finocchio CPS, Dalla Corte VF, de Vargas Mores G (2018) Scientific development of smart farming technologies and their application in Brazil. Inf Proc Agric 5(1):21–32

Richardson RJ (2017) Pesquisa Social: Métodos e Técnicas, 4th edn. Atlas, São Paulo

Richardson RJ et al (1999) Pesquisa Social: métodos e técnicas, 3rd edn. Atlas, São Paulo

Rossetti A (2009) Um modelo conceitual de gestão do conhecimento para Unidades organizacionais de pesquisa agropecuária sob a ótica da interdisciplinaridade. Tese de Doutorado. Programa de Pós-Graduação em Engenharia e Gestão do Conhecimento. Universidade Federal de Santa Catarina, Florianópolis, SC

Sartin KR (2016) Escala de produção, tecnologia e desempenho da avicultura de corte em goiás. Dissertação de Mestrado. Universidade Federal de Goiás, Goiânia, GO

Tey YS, Brindal M (2012) Factors influencing the adoption of precision agricultural technologies: a review for policy implications. Precis Agric 13(6):713–730

Uriarte FA (2008) Introduction to knowledge management: a brief introduction to the basic elements of knowledge management for non-practitioners interested in understanding the subject. ASEAN Foundation, Jakarta

Vieira Filho JER, Silveira JMFJ (2016) Competências organizacionais, trajetória tecnológica e aprendizado local na agricultura: o paradoxo de Prebisch. Econ Soc 25(3):599–629

Vieira Filho JER, Fishlow A (2017) Agricultura e indústria no Brasil: inovação e competitividade. IPEA, Brasília, DF

Wolfert S, Ge L, Verdouw C, Bogaardt MJ (2017) Big data in smart farming—a review. Agric Syst 153:69–80

World Economic Forum (2018) Innovation with a purpose: the role of technology innovation in accelerating food systems. http://www3.weforum.org/docs/WEF_Innovation_with_a_Purpose_VF-reduced.pdf. Accessed 1 Oct 2018

Sustainable Business Models and Artificial Intelligence: Opportunities and Challenges

Korinzia Toniolo, Eleonora Masiero, Maurizio Massaro, and Carlo Bagnoli

Abstract This chapter aims to shed light on the pivotal role played by artificial intelligence (AI) in supporting sustainable business models' development.

To achieve this objective, the chapter starts by illustrating relevant previous studies about sustainable business models with a specific focus on the economic, social, and environmental (ESG) dimensions of sustainability and by briefly exploring the literature about AI and its potential impacts on business models.

Subsequently, the chapter deepens the investigation by developing specific subsections about the implications of adopting AI for each ESG dimension. Each subsection provides an explicative example illustrating how a multinational company (each located in a different country—the United States, Spain, Italy) has implemented AI techniques toward sustainability performance.

These examples provide an empirical view and yield insights about sustainable business models' development, driving general implications for practitioners. The study also illustrates future research opportunities for academics about the link between sustainability and artificial intelligence.

1 Introduction

The increasing relevance of sustainability topics at global level resulted, in 2015, in the launch of the Sustainable Development Goals through which the business world is called upon contributing to the global sustainability Agenda 2030 (European Commission [EC] 2017; United Nations [UN] 2015a). Working toward sustainable development implies challenging simultaneously National Governments, the International Community, and companies toward collaborating to ensure progress without neglecting environmental, social, and governance (ESG) matters. At the same time, adopting a sustainable development approach implies, for companies, a profound shift in their way of doing business considering their impact on the

K. Toniolo (✉) · E. Masiero · M. Massaro · C. Bagnoli
Dipartimento di Management, Università Ca' Foscari, Venice, Italy
e-mail: korinzia.toniolo@unive.it; eleonora.masiero@unive.it; maurizio.massaro@unive.it; bagnoli@unive.it

F. Matos et al. (eds.), *Knowledge, People, and Digital Transformation*, Contributions to Management Science, https://doi.org/10.1007/978-3-030-40390-4_8

environment, on the society, and their approach toward governance. To achieve a greater long-term social and environmental sustainability, organizations have to consider innovating their business models to make them sustainable (Bocken et al. 2014).

Business models are a means for explaining how organizations create, deliver, and capture value (Nielsen et al. 2018; Osterwalder and Pigneur 2010; Zott et al. 2011) and for consenting managers' envision and implementation of their business' strategy (Bagnoli et al. 2018; Biloslavo et al. 2018). As observed by Osterwalder and Pigneur (2010, p. 246), the innovation of a business model "rarely happens by coincidence. It is something that can be managed, structured into processes, and used to leverage the creative potential of an entire organization." Often, developing a new business model represents, for companies, a challenge and may fail (Geissdoerfer et al. 2018). To effectively implement strategies and practices toward sustainable development, businesses should be thoughtful about their values and willing to embrace possibilities related to sustainability (Fleming et al. 2017). In this regard, Artificial intelligence (AI) is among the most important enablers for developing a sustainable business model (Manyika 2017).

The role of technology in supporting and driving a sustainable development was already being empathized in 1987 when the United Nations presented the Brundtland Report. Thirty years later, in 2015, the World Economic Forum underlined the importance of a technological shift, recognizing AI as a fundamental technology playing a key role in the next years (Espinel et al. 2015). Accordingly, in a recent paper, Brynjolfsson and Mcafee (2017, pp. 19, 3) underlined how AI "is the most important general-purpose technology of our era," explaining that "[i]n the sphere of business, AI is poised to have a transformational impact, on the scale of earlier general-purpose technologies." Given the rapid progress of this highly disruptive technology, business leaders must adopt a mindset and new practices that accept and embrace this change, translating technological possibilities into business value for customers, partners, and society (Biloslavo et al. 2018; Teece 2010).

With a potential contribution of $15 trillion to the world economy by 2030 (Rao et al. 2017), AI is listed as the number one strategic technology (Panetta 2018). The Gartner survey 2018 showed that 59% of organizations are still gathering information to build their AI strategies, while the remainder has already made progress in piloting or adopting AI solutions (Panetta 2018). AI will come to act as a preponderant element in the transformation and reconfiguration of organizational and management elements, such as strategy, processes, structure, and culture (Mendonça and Andrade 2018). "Executives in companies around the world are increasingly looking to AI to create new sources of business value" (Ransbotham et al. 2018, p. 1). This chapter aims to shed light on the increasingly relevant role played by technology, and specifically by AI in supporting sustainable business models' development.

2 Sustainability and Sustainable Business Models

The concept of sustainable development, from which the one of sustainability originates, was initially defined by the United Nations World Commission for Environment and Development in the Brundtland Report (Holden et al. 2014; Manes-Rossi et al. 2018; Marx and Ahmed 2014). Published in 1987, the report of the United Nations (1987, p. 24) explained that: "Humanity can make development sustainable to ensure that it meets the needs of the present without compromising the ability of future generations to meet their own needs."

More than 30 years later, the European Union still adopts this definition when recalling that sustainability is "at the heart of the European project" (European Commission [EC] 2018, p. 9). Since the Brundtland Report, the trend toward sustainable development has been increasingly supported by global leaders through the signing of Kyoto Protocol in 1997, the Copenhagen Conference in 2009, and the Paris Agreement in 2015 (Alrazi et al. 2016; Falkner 2016; Massaro et al. 2018a). With the launch of the Sustainable Development Goals (SDG), in 2015, the European Union explicitly called upon the business world to contribute to the Global Sustainability Agenda 2030 (EC 2017; UN 2015a).

Following the United Nations' (UN) Agenda 2030 for Sustainable Development (United Nations [UN] 2015b) and the UN's principles for responsible investments, the European Parliament and Council introduced the Environmental, Social and Governance (ESG) factors into guidelines for sustainable investments decision-making and for the nonfinancial disclosure (Directive 2014/95/EU) guiding organizations through the harmonization of their business' models (EC 2018; European Parliament and Council 2014). Widely accepted concepts, the ESG factors are defined by the EC (2018, p. 10) as follows: "Environmental (E) issues related to the quality and functioning of the natural environment and natural systems; Social (S) issues related to the rights, well-being, and interests of people and communities; Governance (G) issues related to the governance of companies and other investee entities." These actions toward a sustainable economy are in line with the increasing international concerns for a genuinely sustainable economic growth (Beltramello et al. 2013) and with the fears for the social and environmental consequences of climate change and global warming (Alrazi et al. 2016; Capstick et al. 2015).

Transitioning toward a sustainable economy implies for companies embracing, or rethinking, their way of doing business by innovating themselves through acting upon environmental, social, and governance matters. Thus, firms' integration of a sustainability approach can be enacted through innovating their business model allowing "re-conceptualizing the purpose of the firm and the value-creating logic and rethinking perceptions of value" (Bocken et al. 2014, p. 43). More precisely, companies should develop a business model "that creates competitive advantage through superior customer value and contributes to the sustainable development of the company and society" (Lüdeke-Freund 2010, p. 23). Thus, a sustainable business model seeks to align interests and to create value for a broad range of stakeholders, including the society and the environment (Bocken et al. 2013, 2014).

3 Artificial Intelligence

According to the Brundtland Report, technology can be "managed and improved to make way for a new era of economic growth" (UN 1987, p. 24). Thirty years later, the role of technology in supporting and driving a sustainable development not only is still being emphasized, but it is getting momentum. For instance, in 2015, the World Economic Forum remarked the need for a technological shift illustrating how specific elements, such as AI will profoundly change the society during the future 10 years (Espinel et al. 2015). Considered as one of the most important technologies for developing sustainability (Panetta 2018), AI enables new ways of creating, delivering, and capturing value among stakeholders, affecting all the business models' dimensions (Ransbotham et al. 2018). Accordingly, the Global Reporting Initiative (GRI 2011, p. 2) evidenced that the progress in knowledge and technology not only contribute to the economic development in a broad sense, but also support the resolution of "risks and threats to the sustainability of our social relations, environment, and economies." The adoption of advanced technologies implies business disruption and reshape (Manyika 2017).

The term AI was coined in 1956 by John McCarthy during the first academic conference on the subject at Dartmouth College to develop the concept around thinking machines (Marr 2018). Today, AI has become an umbrella term that can refer to various computer science technologies and applications, ranging from neural networks to speech and pattern recognition, genetic algorithms and deep learning (Bughin et al. 2017; Jarrahi 2018; Ransbotham et al. 2018). An accurate picture of the AI field is hampered by the lack of a precise and universally accepted definition (Stanford University 2016). However, adopting the Oxford English Dictionary's definition, AI can be described as "the theory and development of computer systems able to perform tasks normally requiring human intelligence, such as visual perception, speech recognition, decision-making, and translation between languages."[1] A widely accepted distinction is between strong and weak AI (KPMG 2018a). Strong AI refers to systems with complete human or superhuman intelligence, which still do not exist at present (Hengstler et al. 2016). Weak AI, or narrow AI, refers to specific tasks that require single human capabilities, e.g., visual perception, understanding context, probabilistic reasoning, and dealing with complexity (Russel and Norvig 2010). Currently, only weak AI is implemented in commercial applications, such as expert systems, or knowledge-based systems, which include tools for medical diagnosis, loan approval, insurance underwriting, decision-making support (Duan et al. 2019; KPMG 2018b).

Interestingly, AI allows finding new ways of generating and sharing value affecting business models (Ransbotham et al. 2018), constituting a major source of innovation (Russel and Norvig 2010). For example, AI provides several significant research opportunities to change the role of resources within a company's business model (Biloslavo et al. 2018). Consistent with the digital transformation of

[1] See www.oed.com

businesses, we are witnessing extensive automation of physical tasks and production processes, putting practical technologies to work (Baccala et al. 2018). On the bright side, AI will expand companies' intuition and peoples' creativity (Ferràs-Hernández 2018). On the dark side, the workplace environment will experience a paradigm shift through the replacement of jobs with robots and intelligent machines (Huang and Rust 2018). Similarly, looking at products and services, AI is making them more intelligent, providing new applications and functionalities (Rosenberg 2008). For example, smartphones now incorporate AI characteristics such as speech recognition and understanding, completing words when writing, and providing customized advice (Makridakis 2017).

AI also offers new ways of analyzing, interpreting, and using customer data with significant implications for developing customer loyalty and a more competitive value proposition (Huang and Rust 2018). For example, in the retail industry, the entire online and physical shopping experience is being revolutionized (Grewal et al. 2017), as AI forecasting algorithms enable companies to project demand accurately and to reach the right target customers through new forms of distribution and communication channels, like personalized marketing and advertising (Bughin et al. 2017). Considering the extended network of relationships outside the company (Biloslavo et al. 2018), AI can enable the development of new approaches for capturing value in the ecosystem beyond company boundaries providing a new research context for sustainability and stakeholder engagement. For example, swarm intelligence algorithms can detect information and patterns behaviors in online community platforms facilitating the systematization of knowledge and the understanding of a company's activity impact on society (Martinez-Torres and Olmedilla 2016).

The disruptive potential embedded in AI technologies is a key driver for innovating business models toward sustainability, allowing companies to fulfil ESG criteria. In the following section, the potential applications of AI for the environment, society, and governance in companies are described.

4 Artificial Intelligence for Sustainable Business Models

4.1 Environmental Sustainability

Six of the seventeen UN Sustainable Development Goals apply directly to the environment and humans' influence over it: fighting climate change, using the ocean and marine resources wisely, managing forests, fighting diversification, reversing land degradation, developing sustainable cities and providing clean, affordable energy (Waughray et al. 2018). Companies can apply AI tools to fulfil environmental criteria to turn their business models toward environmental sustainability. To increase energy efficiency in operations, organizations are starting to adopt smart grids which take full advantage of AI techniques supporting real-time demand response and delivering power that is stable and affordable (Bassiliades and

Chalkiadakis 2018). Indeed, with more complex grids gathering energy from different sources, both nonrenewable and renewable, AI can analyze massive datasets, improving the management of these sources toward higher grid stability and autonomy (CBInsights 2018).

Energy efficiency is a primary concern in manufacturing: the growing interest in environmentally friendly manufacturing is pushing the industry to adopt cleaner production processes (Kristianto et al. 2017). This translates into the development of supply chain optimization models, raising concern for energy consumption to the entire global manufacturing (Elia et al. 2011; You et al. 2012). Artificial Intelligence can support the development of decision support systems, which help to minimize energy costs while maximizing the technological innovation that could reduce energy consumption and the environmental impact (Kristianto et al. 2017).

Similarly, AI techniques may help support pollution and waste management (Khakurel et al. 2018). In the agriculture and food industry, post-harvest loss and food waste are the two major problems in the supply chain management and logistics (Gustavsson et al. 2011; James and James 2010). Artificial Intelligence in sensors and communication technologies provide the foundations for the development of smart supply chain systems and intelligent food logistics (Haass et al. 2015). For example, data gathered from GIS and smart devices based on sensor technologies allow supply chain managers to automate the shipping and the delivery of goods by monitoring and forecasting the perishability of the cargo travelling in intelligent containers (Bogataj et al. 2017; Haass et al. 2015). Additionally, signals from the smart measurement devices can be transmitted to a decision support system, which helps supply chain professionals regarding the final use and the changed price of the cargo or by anticipating the cargo rerouting decisions, enabling the cut of logistics cost and time (Bogataj et al. 2017). In Example 1 we illustrate the application of AI inside a multinational company that, following the EC (2018, p. 10) definition of sustainability, allowed to improve environmental issues related to the quality and functioning of the natural environment and system.

Example 1 Xcel Energy

Xcel Energy Inc. is a utility company based in Minnesota, which creates electricity from burning coal plants in Texas.[2] One major by-product of this activity is nitrous oxide emissions, a greenhouse gas that contributes heavily to climate change. Xcel has started to look at different artificial intelligence techniques to become more sustainable. To reduce emissions of nitrous oxide, the company uses artificial neural networks, that simulating the human brain, allow to quickly analyze the data that results from the processes of coal combustion. This system provides accurate recommendations about

(continued)

[2]Company website: https://www.xcelenergy.com/

Example 1 (continued)
how to adjust the plant's operations to reduce the negative emissions and operate at peak efficiency.

Additionally, Xcel is the first utility company in the United States to systematically use drones with machine learning algorithms to automatically inspect its infrastructures for potential failures. To address the issue of intermittency and forecasting error, the company has also partnered with the National Centre for Atmospheric Research to use machine learning to provide more accurate wind forecasts, providing data from sensors on hundreds of wind turbines. Thanks to artificial intelligence techniques, Xcel Energy has been able to reduce costs to end customers by $60 million and to reduce annual CO_2 emissions from fossil-reserve power generation by more than a quarter of a million tons per year (Schiermeier 2016).

4.2 *Social Sustainability*

Social responsibility plays an important role in the differentiation of companies: fulfilling social criteria improves their reputation and promotes their market share, gaining an opportunity for superior competitive advantage (Massaro et al. 2018a; Zhao 2018). There are many social issues AI can contribute to, such as workforce development, gender diversity, employees' safety, and working conditions (Makridakis 2017). It is acknowledged that the advent of artificial intelligence will reshape the workplace environment by replacing many jobs: 30% of jobs are at potential risk of automation by mid-2030s (Rao et al. 2017). However, the more jobs being automated, the greater the skills that would be required to perform the remaining tasks adequately (Makridakis 2017). This means that companies can employ AI to free people from repetitive, monotonous, and hard jobs to use their competencies and capabilities to more meaningful and creative occupations (Davenport and Ronanki 2018; Dignum 2016).

Interestingly, these new opportunities bring new challenges for the whole higher educational system (Lombardi et al. 2019; Secundo et al. 2018). For example, at Amazon's warehouses, employees who previously lifted and stacked objects are becoming robot operators, monitoring the automated arms and resolving issues such as an interruption in the flow of objects (Wingfield 2017). The reduced workload can enhance working conditions, contributing to employees' well-being inside and outside the organization (Rosenberg 2008). Looking at safety conditions, AI has been present in the manufacturing industry for years through assembly-line robots that replace humans where hazards may be present, and risks may be high (Manyika and Sneader 2018).

Concerning safety issues, Cisco, for example, has partnered with Cortexica, an AI start-up, to develop an automated intelligent system which combines real-time video analysis with advanced algorithms and machine learning to ensure that employees are correctly wearing the personal protective equipment required by safety regulation (Chrissos 2018). At the same time, AI tools can be used to train and reskill the workforce, promoting efficient collaboration between humans and machines, especially when tackling complex decision-making (Jarrahi 2018). Miller (2018) calls for a new human–machine symbiosis, where humans and machines need to work symbiotically to augment and enhance each other's capabilities. Additionally, AI can help to close the gender gap in the workplace, bringing a data-driven view of the issue. For example, AI techniques can identify inequity in pay and promotion recommendations before they reach the employee, allowing managers to make more equitable decisions (Wielgosz 2018).

Similarly, tools and technologies driven by AI can help reduce biases in the recruitment process by following a standardized and objective candidate assessment methodology (Strohmeier and Piazza 2015). This fosters a culture of transparency and collaboration, which is critical to engage a productive workforce and to promote the company's reputation (Grbac and Lončarić 2009). In Example 2, we illustrate how the application of AI inside a multinational company allowed to improve social issues relating to the rights, well-being, and interests of people and communities (EC 2018, p. 10).

Example 2 Telefónica

Telefónica[3] is a Spanish multinational telecommunications company and one of the largest telephone operators and mobile network providers in the world. In 2018, its pioneer company in integral security technology, Telefónica Ingeniería de Seguridad, has partnered with AnyVision,[4] the world's leading designer and developer of artificial intelligence and recognition platforms. Both companies share a deep commitment to creating safer and smarter environments all over the world (Telefónica 2018). The partnership enabled Telefónica to integrate its technologies with AnyVision's advanced AI solutions of face, body, and object recognition across a variety of verticals, such as homeland security, transportation, critical infrastructures, and smart cities. The two companies are working together on major projects in airports, smart cities, stadiums, and banks providing onboarding and authentication solutions, as well as seamless access control solutions, among other services. Together with AI techniques, Telefónica is also making use of IoT and Big Data to develop smart city initiatives. For example, gaining data from traffic movement sensors, it is possible to report on the intensity of vehicles' movement through a city and enable flexible parking tariffs and intelligent signage which reacts in real time to help citizens plan their day's journeys.

Similarly, data from monitoring stations and weather data are used to inform decisions on when motorway speed limits should be put in place to

(continued)

[3]Company website: https://www.telefonica.com/

[4]Company website: http://www.anyvision.co/

Example 2 (continued)
stop pollution levels becoming high in an area. In Valencia, Telefónica is monitoring car parking using sensors to gain information on the density of parking across the city in real time (Marr 2017). This helps set parking fees to achieve a fairer distribution of parking, reduce CO_2 emissions, and fuel consumption. Telefónica's Valencia Smart City project aims to improve citizens and tourists' quality of life through AI, IoT, and Big Data.

4.3 Governance Sustainability

The general definition of corporate governance includes the mechanisms, processes, and relations by which corporations are controlled and directed (Shailer 2004). Many corporate governance issues have been identified in the literature which refers to bankruptcy, money laundering, corruption, bribery, gender diversity of the board, auditing, and decision-making (Bonime-Blanc 2018; Liang et al. 2016). AI techniques like statistical and machine learning algorithms can be used, for example, to develop bankruptcy prediction models assisting financial institutions in making better lending decisions (Liang et al. 2016). Chang and Wang (2013) employed the learning ability of artificial neural networks and the optimization ability of the evolution strategies for the development of an evaluation model linking accounting and non-accounting information, to identify true corporate value, providing a relevant reference both for enterprises and investors.

AI may also serve to address the gender imbalance in the board and drive an organizational culture change, as men still dominate the boardrooms (Stephens 2013). For example, the introduction of AI in daily operations can make the issues of biased data and inaccurate results more visible, therefore, resulting in more transparent decision-making processes, especially in recruitment pools (Sutherland 2019). Indeed, AI can enhance complex decision-making processes in the board and create sophisticated tools to monitor and analyze behaviors and activities in real time, improving organizations' capabilities in areas such as corporate governance, regulatory compliance, and risk management (Ferràs-Hernández 2018; Libert et al. 2017). The ability of AI to handle Big Data, identify patterns and detect anomalies or bias makes it a potential anti-corruption, anti-fraud, and anti-money laundering tool (Chang and Wang 2013; Salehi et al. 2017).

Detecting management fraud is a difficult task when using normal audit procedures; there are too many transactions in most companies for auditors to go through manually (Forbes 2019). By introducing machine learning techniques at different stages of the transaction monitoring process, AI offers immediate opportunities to reduce operational costs with no loss of effectiveness (Singh et al. 2018). Additionally, AI engines like data mining may be able to stop violations before they happen rather than catching them after the fact (Forbes 2019). In Example 3, we illustrate the application of AI for developing sustainable business models that affected the governance of the company and other investees.

Example 3 Generali
Generali is a multinational group, a major player in the global insurance industry.[5] In line with its innovation and digitalization strategies, in January 2018, Generali signed an agreement with Expert System,[6] a company specialized in text mining solution, for implementing, during the first trimester 2018 in Spain, an AI technology named Cogito. Cogito is a text analytics and cognitive computing software designed to autonomously operate 24 h per day and enabling to rapidly classify a large amount of information, thus accelerating decision processes, reducing costs, and improving business processes. Despite starting with the aim of optimizing the registration and processing of clients' refund applications, Generali's objective is to extend this AI technology to other business units (La Cava 2018). Discussing AI and digital transformation, Alessandra Chiuderi, Head of Generali's Analytics Solutions Centre, underlined the changes brought by AI to the insurance sector, from processes' automatization to frauds prevention. In this regard, she explained: "The projects we are working on together with our Business Units range from providing new insights for product definition to strengthening existing fraud detection systems, from back-office automation to claims management streamlining, from identifying the best Customers for specific products to helping the NGOs that are part of The Human Safety Net. Given Generali's activity toward digital transformation, on March 2018, Generali Italia (the Italian branch) was awarded for its adoption of AI and robotics as a means for reshaping the business insurance sector (Agalliu et al. 2018)."

5 Conclusion

This chapter illustrates how digital technologies, and specifically AI, play a pivotal role in the development of sustainable business models. The aim is to emphasize the reason behind the necessity for companies to align with the technological change effectively contributing to the sustainability goals.

The chapter opens with the definition of sustainable business model briefly illustrating the present state of the literature and recalling the ESG criteria. Subsequently, the investigation expands, exploring previous studies investigating the AI topic and its potential implications for innovating business models. In this stage, the authors deepen the analysis investigating the application of the AI techniques in the environmental, in the social, and in the governance dimensions, respectively. Additionally, to provide a concrete demonstration of how AI can be adopted to enhance sustainability, the authors present three examples selecting, for each, a multinational

[5]Company website: https://www.generali.com/

[6]Company website: https://www.expertsystem.com/

company based in different countries (the United States, Spain, Italy). Each example reports the sources used to transparently inform the reader (Massaro et al. 2018b).

Each example describes the impact that the adoption of AI has on a specific ESG aspect. More specifically, the authors explain how the partnerships between the AI companies and the multinational ones allowed the latter to implement AI techniques inside their organizations, thus improving and reshaping their business models toward sustainability. By demonstrating how AI techniques can be implemented in the different ESG dimensions, these examples provide an empirical view and yield insights about sustainable business models' development.

The study drives general implications for practitioners by illustrating the potentiality of the AI techniques for sustainable business models' development from the environmental, social, and governance perspectives. More specifically, the chapter presents explicative examples for managers who want to approach AI. As the examples demonstrate, by creating partnerships with AI companies or start-ups, managers can best achieve their needs and are provided with the technical know-how to innovate their business models toward sustainability. From the academic perspective, given the scarcity of the literature about AI, future challenges for academics may be to undertake broader literature reviews, extending the knowledge about the topic. Additionally, a better understanding of how to improve sustainability through AI can derive from undertaking further empirical analyses. For instance, a multiple-case study approach may allow to collect and compare best practices regarding the application of AI techniques for reshaping business models toward sustainability.

References

Agalliu R, Di Leva C, Bollea E (2018) A Generali Italia il Premio Innovazione Smau. https://www.generali.it/272748/03-27_NS-Premio-Innovazione-SMAU.pdf. Accessed 29 May 2019

Alrazi B, De Villiers C, Van Staden CJ (2016) The environmental disclosures of the electricity generation industry: a global perspective. Account Bus Res 46(6):665–701

Baccala M, Curran C, Garrett D, Likens S, Rao A, Ruggles A, Shehab M (2018) 2018 AI predictions—8 insights to shape business strategy. https://doi.org/10.1007/s12193-015-0195-2

Bagnoli C, Massaro M, Dal Mas F, Demartini M (2018) Defining the concept of a business model: searching for a business model framework. Int J Knowl Syst Sci 9(3):48–64

Bassiliades N, Chalkiadakis G (2018) Artificial intelligence techniques for the smart grid. Adv Build Energy Res 12(1):1–2

Beltramello A, Haie-Fayle L, Pilat D (2013) Why new business models matter for green growth. OECD Publishing, Paris

Biloslavo R, Bagnoli C, Edgar D (2018) An eco-critical perspective on business models: the value triangle as an approach to closing the sustainability gap. J Clean Prod 174:746–762

Bocken NMP, Short S, Rana P, Evans S (2013) A value mapping tool for sustainable business modelling. Corp Gov 13(5):482–497

Bocken NMP, Short SW, Rana P, Evans S (2014) A literature and practice review to develop a sustainable business model archetypes. J Clean Prod 65:42–56

Bogataj D, Bogataj M, Hudoklin D (2017) Mitigating risks of perishable products in the cyber-physical systems based on the extended MRP model. Int J Prod Econ 193:51–62

Bonime-Blanc A (2018) AI and reputational risk: an ESG perspective. Ethical Boardroom Winter:116–118

Brynjolfsson E, Mcafee A (2017) The business of artificial intelligence: how AI fits into your data science team. Harv Bus Rev 2017:1–20

Bughin J, Hazan E, Ramaswamy S, Chui M, Allas T, Dahlström P et al (2017) Artificial intelligence: the next digital frontier? McKinsey Global Institute. https://doi.org/10.1016/S1353-4858(17)30039-9

Capstick S, Whitmarsh L, Poortinga W, Pidgeon N, Upham P (2015) International trends in public perceptions of climate change over the past quarter-century. WIREs Clim Chang 6:35–61

CBInsights (2018) 5 Ways the energy industry is using artificial intelligence. https://www.cbinsights.com/research/artificial-intelligence-energy-industry/. Accessed 6 May 2019

Chang YH, Wang SC (2013) Integration of evolutionary computing and equity valuation models to forecast stock values based on data mining. Asia Pac Manag Rev 18(1):63–78

Chrissos N (2018) Introducing AI-SAFE: a collaborative solution for worker safety. Cisco UK & Ireland Blog. January 23. https://gblogs.cisco.com/uki/introducing-ai-safe-a-collaborative-solution-for-worker-safety/. Accessed 17 May 2019

Davenport TH, Ronanki R (2018) Artificial intelligence for the real world: don't start with moon shots. Harv Bus Rev 96(1):108–116

Dignum V (2016) Social and ethical impact of artificial intelligence. Delft University of Technology, Delft

Duan Y, Edwards JS, Dwivedi YK (2019) Artificial intelligence for decision making in the era of Big Data—evolution, challenges and research agenda. Int J Inf Manage 48:63–71. Elsevier

Elia JA, Baliban RC, Xiao X, Floudas CA (2011) Optimal energy supply network determination and life cycle analysis for hybrid coal, biomass, and natural gas to liquid (CBGTL) plants using carbon-based hydrogen production. Comput Chem Eng 35(8):1399–1430

Espinel V, Brynjolfsson E, Annunziata M, Brechbuhl H, Cao R, Crawford S et al (2015) Deep shift: technology tipping points and societal impact. World Economic Forum, Geneva

European Commission (2017) The 2030 Agenda for sustainable development and SDGs. http://ec.europa.eu. Accessed 26 Mar 2019

European Commission (2018) Commission staff working document impact assessment. https://eur-lex.europa.eu/legal-content/EN/TXT/?uri=SWD%3A2018%3A141%3AFIN. Accessed 26 Mar 2019

European Parliament and Council (2014) Directive 2014/95/EU of the European Parliament and of the Council of 22 october 2014 amending Directive 2013/34/EU as regards disclosure of non-financial and diversity information by certain large undertakings and groups. Off J Eur Union 2014:1–9

Falkner R (2016) The Paris agreement and the new logic of international climate politics. Int Aff 5:1107–1125

Ferràs-Hernández X (2018) The future of management in a world of electronic brains. J Manag Inq 27(2):260–263

Fleming A, Wise RM, Hansen H, Sams L (2017) The sustainable development goals: a case study. Mar Policy 86:94–103

Forbes (2019) Can AI help companies do the right thing? Forbes Insights. https://www.forbes.com/sites/insights-intelai/2019/03/27/why-ethical-ai-is-a-critical-differentiator/#19f4a16963ab. Accessed 17 May 2019

Geissdoerfer M, Vladimirova D, Evans S (2018) Sustainable business model innovation: a review. J Cleaner Prod 198:401–416. Elsevier

Global Reporting Initiative (2011) RG. Sustainability reporting guidelines

Grbac B, Lončarić D (2009) Ethics, social responsibility and business performance in a transition economy. EuroMed J Bus 4(2):143–158

Grewal D, Roggeveen AL, Nordfält J (2017) The future of retailing. J Retail 93(1):1–6

Gustavsson J, Cederberg C, Sonesson U (2011) Global food losses and food waste. Food and Agriculture Organization of the United Nations, Rome

Haass R, Dittmer P, Veigt M, Lütjen M (2015) Reducing food losses and carbon emission by using autonomous control—a simulation study of the intelligent container. Int J Prod Econ 164:400–408. Elsevier

Hengstler M, Enkel E, Duelli S (2016) Applied artificial intelligence and trust—the case of autonomous vehicles and medical assistance devices. Technol Forecast Soc Chang 105:105–120

Holden E, Linnerud K, Banister D (2014) Sustainable development: our common future revisited. Glob Environ Chang 26(1):130–139

Huang MH, Rust RT (2018) Artificial intelligence in service. J Serv Res 21(2):155–172

James SJ, James C (2010) The food cold-chain and climate change. Food Res Int 43(7):1944–1956

Jarrahi MH (2018) Artificial intelligence and the future of work: human-AI symbiosis in organizational decision making. Bus Horiz 61(4):577–586

Khakurel J, Penzenstadler B, Porras J, Knutas A, Zhang W (2018) The rise of artificial intelligence under the lens of sustainability. Technologies 6(4):100

KPMG (2018a) Trust in artificial intelligence. https://doi.org/10.1177/1064804618818592

KPMG (2018b) Rethinking the value chain. A study on AI, humanoids and robots. https://assets.kpmg.com/content/dam/kpmg/xx/pdf/2018/09/rethinking-the-value-chain.pdf

Kristianto Y, Gunasekaran A, Helo P (2017) Building the 'triple R' in global manufacturing. Int J Prod Econ 183:607–619

La Cava D (2018) Generali punta su intelligenza artificiale di Expert System per gestione processi aziendali. https://www.finanza.com/Finanza/Notizie_Italia/Italia/notizia/Generali_punta_su_intelligenza_artificiale_di_Expert_System_-485674. Accessed 29 May 2019

Liang D, Lu CC, Tsai CF, Shih GA (2016) Financial ratios and corporate governance indicators in bankruptcy prediction: a comprehensive study. Eur J Oper Res 252(2):561–572. Elsevier BV

Libert B, Beck M, Bonchek M (2017) AI in the boardroom: the next realm of corporate governance. MITSloan Management Review. October 19. https://sloanreview.mit.edu/article/ai-in-the-boardroom-the-next-realm-of-corporate-governance/. Accessed 17 May 2019

Lombardi R, Massaro M, Dumay J, Nappo F (2019) Entrepreneurial universities and strategy: the case of the University of Bari. Manage Dec. https://doi.org/10.1108/MD-06-2018-0690

Lüdeke-Freund F (2010) Towards a conceptual framework of business models for sustainability. In: Proceedings of the knowledge collaboration & learning for sustainable innovation, Conference, Delft, vol 49, pp 1–28

Makridakis S (2017) The forthcoming artificial intelligence (AI) revolution: its impact on society and firms. Futures 90:46–60

Manes-Rossi F, Tiron-Tudor A, Nicolò G, Zanellato G (2018) Ensuring more sustainable reporting in Europe using non-financial disclosure—De Facto and De Jure Evidence. Sustainability 10:1162. https://doi.org/10.3390/su10041162

Manyika J (2017) What's now and next in analytics, AI and automation. San Francisco: McKinsey Global Institute. May

Manyika J, Sneader K (2018) AI, automation, and the future of work: ten things to solve for. McKinsey Global Institute. June. https://www.mckinsey.com/featured-insights/future-of-work/ai-automation-and-the-future-of-work-ten-things-to-solve-for. Accessed 17 May 2019

Marr B (2017) How telefonica is using IoT and big data to build smart cities. Forbes. May 19. https://www.forbes.com/sites/bernardmarr/2017/05/19/how-telefonica-is-using-iot-and-big-data-to-build-smart-cities/#5205bc347e60. Accessed 28 May 2019

Marr B (2018) The key definitions of artificial intelligence (AI) that explain its importance. Forbes. https://www.forbes.com/sites/bernardmarr/2018/02/14/the-key-definitions-of-artificial-intelligence-ai-that-explain-its-importance/#4f4220b4f5d8. Accessed 9 April 2019

Martinez-Torres R, Olmedilla M (2016) Identification of innovation solvers in open innovation communities using swarm intelligence. Technol Forecast Soc Chang 109:15–24

Marx B, Ahmed M-H (2014) Emerging trends in reporting: an analysis of integrated reporting practices by South African top 40 listed companies. J Econ Financ Sci 7(1):231–250

Massaro M, Dumay J, Bagnoli C (2018a) Transparency and the rhetorical use of citations to Robert Yin in case study research. Meditari Account Res 27(1):44–71. https://doi.org/10.1108/MEDAR-08-2017-0202

Massaro M, Dumay J, Garlatti A, Dal Mas F (2018b) Practitioners' views on intellectual capital and sustainability: from a performance-based to a worth-based perspective. J Intellect Cap 19 (2):367–386

Mendonça CMC, Andrade AMV (2018) Dynamic capabilities and their relations with elements of digital transformation in Portugal. J Inf Syst Eng Manage 3(3). https://doi.org/10.20897/jisem/2660

Miller S (2018) AI: augmentation, more so than automation. Asian Manag Insights 5(1):1–20

Nielsen C, Lund M, Montemari M, Paolone F, Massaro M, Dumay J (2018) Business models: a research overview. Routledge, New York

Osterwalder A, Pigneur Y (2010) Business model generation, 30. Wiley. https://doi.org/10.1523/JNEUROSCI.0307-10.2010

Panetta K (2018) Gartner top 10 strategic technology trends for 2019. https://www.gartner.com. Accessed 11 Mar 2019

Ransbotham S, Gerbert P, Reeves M, Kiron D, Spira M (2018) Artificial intelligence in business gets real. MIT Sloan Manag Rev. https://doi.org/10.1145/2063176.2063177

Rao AS, Verweij G, Cameron E (2017) Sizing the prize: what's the real value of AI for your business and how can you capitalise? PwC. https://www.pwc.com/gx/en/issues/analytics/assets/pwc-ai-analysis-sizing-the-prize-report.pdf

Rosenberg RS (2008) The social impact of intelligent artefacts. AI Soc 22(3):367–383

Russel S, Norvig P (2010) Artificial intelligence a modern approach, 3rd edn. Pearson. https://doi.org/10.1017/S0269888900007724

Salehi A, Ghazanfari M, Fathian M (2017) Data mining techniques for anti money laundering. Int J Appl Eng Res 12(20):10084–10094

Schiermeier Q (2016) And now for the energy forecast. Germany works to predict wind and solar power generation. Nature 535(14):212–213

Secundo G, Massaro M, Dumay J, Bagnoli C (2018) Intellectual capital management in the fourth stage of IC research: a critical case study in university settings. J Intellect Cap 19(1):157–177

Shailer G (2004) An introduction to corporate governance in Australia. Pearson Education, French Forest

Singh R, Fernandes M, Lim N, Ang E (2018) The case for artificial intelligence in combating money laundering and terrorist financing, Deloitte

Stanford University (2016) Artificial intelligence and life in 2030: one hundred year study on artificial intelligence. Stanford University. https://ai100.stanford.edu

Stephens N (2013) Addressing the boardroom gender gap. It is time to give more women the opportunities they deserve. Hum Resour Manag Int Dig 21(2):41–44

Strohmeier S, Piazza F (2015) Artificial intelligence techniques in human resource management—a conceptual exploration. In: Intelligent techniques in engineering management. Springer, Cham, pp 149–172

Sutherland S (2019) Why AI could correct the gender imbalance right up to the boardroom. EY Global Center for Board Matters. March 8. https://www.ey.com/en_gl/women-fast-forward/why-ai-could-correct-the-gender-imbalance-right-up-to-the-boardroom. Accessed 17 May 2019

Teece DJ (2010) Business models, business strategy and innovation. Long Range Plan 43 (2–3):172–194

Telefónica (2018) AnyVision and Telefónica announce integration partnership. http://ingenieriadeseguridad.telefonica.com/news/2018/12/05/AnyVision-and-Telefónica-Announce-Integration-Partnership.html. Accessed 28 May 2019

United Nations (1987) Report of the world commission on environment and development

United Nations (2015a) SDG compass—the guide for business action on the SDGs. www.sdgcompass.org

United Nations (2015b) United Nations Summit on Sustainable Development 2015. https://sustainabledevelopment.un.org

Waughray D, Herweijer C, Leape JW (2018) Fourth industrial revolution for the earth. Harnessing artificial intelligence for the earth. PwC. https://www.pwc.com/gx/en/services/sustainability/publications/ai-for-the-earth.html

Wielgosz A (2018) How artificial intelligence can solve the issues surrounding gender equity. Medium. May 24. https://medium.com/@agnes.wielgosz/how-artificial-intelligence-can-solve-the-issues-surrounding-gender-equity-c97197839cde. Accessed 17 May 2019

Wingfield N (2017) As Amazon pushes forward with robots, workers find new roles. The New York Times. September 10. https://www.nytimes.com/2017/09/10/technology/amazon-robots-workers.html. Accessed 17 May 2019

You F, Tao L, Graziano DJ, Snyder SW (2012) Optimal design of sustainable cellulosic biofuel supply chains: multiobjective optimization coupled with life cycle assessment and input–output analysis. AICHE J 58(4):1157–1180

Zhao WW (2018) How to improve corporate social responsibility in the era of artificial intelligence? IOP Conf Ser Earth Environ Sci 186(6). https://doi.org/10.1088/1755-1315/186/6/012036

Zott C, Amit R, Massa L (2011) The business model: recent developments and future research. J Manag 37(4):1019–1042

Strategy Innovation, Intellectual Capital Management, and the Future of Healthcare: The Case of Kiron by Nucleode

Francesca Dal Mas, Daniele Piccolo, Leif Edvinsson, Miran Skrap, and Stanislao D'Auria

Abstract The growing development of new technologies has a substantial impact on Intellectual Capital (IC) and strategy innovation. Healthcare is one of the most affected sectors by digital technologies. We analyse the case of Nucleode, an innovative company based in the northeastern part of Italy, which can be defined as a knowledge organisation. The company aims to provide new technologies regarding hospital management, taking healthcare to the future. Analysing Nucleode's Kiron project, the chapter aims to discuss the future of healthcare, considering the digital transformation and intangible assets management, especially considering the value created for the various stakeholders.

1 Introduction and Objective of the Study

In the 1990s, the concepts of "innovation" and "Strategy" have attracted scholars and practitioners fostering a growing production of scientific papers in the fields, representing those concepts as two different aspects of the same coin (Schlegelmilch et al. 2003). On the one side, strategy has been focused on the way to compete within a specific market sector and to define the field of action of the organisation to achieve its goals. On the other side, the literature on innovation has focused its attention on

F. Dal Mas (✉)
Lincoln International Business School, University of Lincoln, Lincoln, UK
e-mail: fdalmas@lincoln.ac.uk

D. Piccolo
Dipartimento di Neuroscienze, Università degli Studi di Padova, Padua, Italy

Nucleode Srl, Gorizia, Italy
e-mail: daniele@nucleode.com

L. Edvinsson
The New Club of Paris, Vienna, Austria

M. Skrap · S. D'Auria
Azienda Sanitaria Universitaria Integrata di Udine, Udine, Italy
e-mail: skrap@asuiud.sanita.fvg.it; stanislao.dauria@asuiud.sanita.fvg.it

F. Matos et al. (eds.), *Knowledge, People, and Digital Transformation*, Contributions to Management Science, https://doi.org/10.1007/978-3-030-40390-4_9

the product and process innovation (Schlegelmilch et al. 2003). We can state how the literature on strategy studies the overall aims of the organisation, whilst, on the contrary, innovation has been seen as a tool to achieve organisational goals.

From the 1990s, the concepts of innovation and strategy have started to become more linked, thanks to the introduction of the idea of strategic innovation (Schlegelmilch et al. 2003). Strategic innovation is the process of developing or reinventing the organisational strategy, i.e. Structural Intellectual Capital. Organisations can achieve strategic innovation through the development of new products or services, presented or combined in an original way, to create a radically new experience for clients/end users, involving them also at an emotional level. Additionally, strategic innovation can also arise from the reconfiguration of the sector's value chain to change the rules of the game—exploiting, for example the possibilities offered by new technologies to enhance the distinctive competencies of the company (Buaron 1981).

According to the Resource-Based View theory, companies need to have access to distinctive resources to support Strategic Innovation, and Intellectual capital (IC) has been considered as one of the most important resources. Since its first development, IC is defined as the set of intangible assets that the firm owns or has access to (Edvinsson and Malone 1997). Traditionally, IC has been divided into three pillars: *human capital (HC)*, which represents the employees' knowledge, skills and experience (Abeysekera and Guthrie 2004; Dal Mas 2019; Edvinsson 2000; Massaro et al. 2018); *structural capital (SC)* which is about the organisation's codified knowledge, databases, and culture (Bontis 1998; Massaro et al. 2017); and *relational capital (RC)* which represents the knowledge embodied in the networks of internal and external relationships that the company manages (Dal Mas et al. 2019b; Massaro et al. 2014b; Peng and Bewley 2010; Secundo et al. 2018). IC has several distinctions. One of them is the Intangibles. Another is more dynamic as Future Earnings Capabilities. And a more simplistic view is as Roots for the Fruits (Grafstrom and Edvinsson 1996). Recently this view is also expanding into the IC of Nations (Lin and Edvinsson 2011).

According to Prof. Edvinsson, one of the fathers of IC, since the 1990s, the dominant investment flow, both in the United States and Sweden, have gone into intangibles, such as R&D, Intellectual Property Rights, education and competencies, IT software and the Internet (Edvinsson 2000, 2002), and this is also reflected by companies' stock value, A Galaxy of Intangible Value emerges, that might be structured by the Value Scheme of IC, in above-mentioned booklet. Edvinsson defined the phases of the pattern of market capitalisation growth and IC global growth. The example comes from his early experience and prototyping at Skandia AFS. At Skandia, the IC value grew from a very minimal value in the early 1990s to some US$15 billion at the beginning of the year 2000.

Each phase, as defined by Edvinsson, resulted, for Skandia, in a stock market appreciation shift, based on increased transparency, as well as new expectations from the future value creation of the intangibles investment. The following figure shows the market capitalisation value over time according to Edvinsson's framework (Fig. 1).

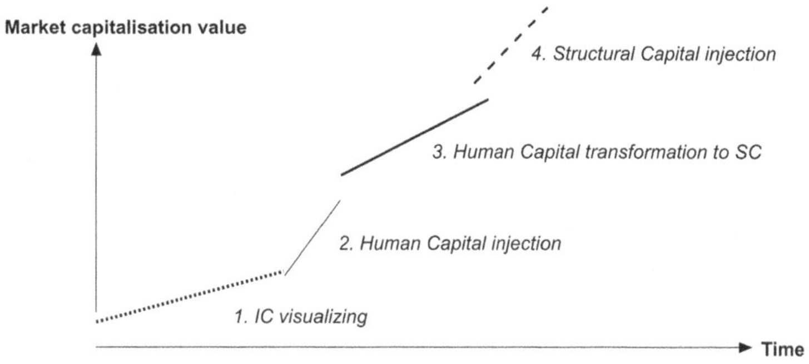

Fig. 1 Market capitalization value pattern over time. Source: Edvinsson (2000, p. 15)

The first phase is about the visualisation of intangibles from a reporting perspective. The second phase is about the human capital injection, adding skills, and competencies, also in a knowledge management perspective (knowledge sharing, IT-based knowledge systems, . . .). The third phase concerns the systematic transformation of human capital into structural capital as a multiplier, which leads to more sustainable earnings potential for the organisation. The fourth phase requires an external structural capital injection. The effect of the fourth phase can be defined as a "turbo effect" on the IC multiplier by combining different types of structural capital constellations for co-creation of new opportunities. These phases of IC growth have the power of gradually increasing the value creation potential of organisations.

The growing development of new technologies has a substantial impact on IC and therefore on strategy innovation (Bagnoli et al. 2018; Bagnoli et al. 2019; Nielsen et al. 2018). Healthcare in general and surgery, in particular, are among the sectors which are most affected by new technologies (Christensen et al. 2000; Iacopino et al. 2018; Lucas 2015; Mascia and Di Vincenzo 2011; Snowdon et al. 2015). Starting from this premise, our chapter aims to discuss the future of surgeons' work, considering the digital transformation and intangible management in healthcare.

2 Research Method

To investigate our research goal, we employ a case study approach (Yin 2009). Case studies are particularly relevant when "the impetus of our research project lies in some broad, familiarising, questions about a social process" (Swanborn 2010, p. 24). According to Bolton and Stolcis (2003, p. 628) practitioners have "preference for case studies and research derived from practice experience" and therefore the use of more qualitative approaches could help to speed the application of research studies among practitioners (Dal Mas et al. 2019a; Massaro et al. 2014a). A similar approach is proposed by Dumay and Garanina (2013), who actively invite scholars to "get their hands dirty within organisations". As suggested by Mouritsen (2006) some managerial dilemmas require more detailed approaches that are not possible within the traditional statistical analysis. To ensure transparency, we tried to be as rigorous as possible in our analysis (Massaro et al. 2019).

The case study is about the Kiron project, carried on by Nucleode Srl, an innovative start-up company in the field of technology and healthcare based in Gorizia, Italy. We chose to analyse the case of Nucleode since it is an innovative company working in one of the sectors which are most affected by a digital transformation swift, that of healthcare. Moreover, Nucleode can be defined as an intense knowledge company, since it relies on its Intellectual Capital to reach its success. Its Human Capital is one of the key resources of the organisation, with high skilled professionals of different fields (Medicine, Engineering, IT, Graphic Design, and Communications). Its CEO has a double degree in Engineering and Medicine, and he is a neurosurgery resident. The company relies on its Structural Capital, which is the core of its product development. At the same time, the organisation uses the top technologies coming from multinational companies like Microsoft. Relational Capital is also a relevant resource. Nucleode works closely with hospitals, private clinics, universities, and doctors, to ensure the best connections and trials to the end-users of its products. The context in which Nucleode works makes it ideal for studying the impact of new digital technologies in healthcare. Data acquisition was made involving several people for the company, and all materials coming out from the interviews were double-checked with the company's CEO.

3 The Company, Project Idea, and Vision

Nucleode Srl[1] is an innovative start-up based in Gorizia, in the north-east of Italy, active in the field of new technologies related to healthcare. The company was founded in March 2017 by six young professionals characterised by different skills: Medicine and Surgery, Engineering, IT, Graphic Design, and Communications. The vision of Nucleode can be summarised as "better healthcare for everyone". The mission of the company is to drive the healthcare environment into the future, helping physicians, researchers, and patients to take advantage of the last technology innovations, in particular using Industry 4.0 technologies such as Cloud Computing and Mixed Reality. More in detail, cloud computing is a type of computing that relies on shared computing resources rather than having local servers or personal devices to handle applications. In its most simple description, cloud computing is taking services ("cloud services") and moving them outside an organisation's firewall. Mixed reality, sometimes referred to as hybrid reality, is the merging of real and virtual worlds to produce new environments and visualisations where physical and digital objects coexist and interact in real time.

[1]Company website: https://nucleode.com/

The project "Kiron"[2] is a perfect example about the importance of the heterogeneous skills of the team, conceived and developed together with professor Miran Skrap M.D. and Stanislao D'Auria M.D., Neurosurgery Department, University Hospital of Udine, Italy. The project aims at improving the current navigation systems, offering surgeons more sophisticated and thus more useful information bringing Augmented Reality and Cloud Computing technologies to the operating room. The goal is to be able to visualise for the first time in a 3D space both in the planning phase of the intervention and during surgery a brain with some pathology such as a tumour, a vascular, or anatomical malformation.

Image-guided neurosurgeries systems (IGNS), so-called neuronavigation systems, were introduced into neurosurgery in the late 1980s and early 1990s, earlier than they were later introduced into other surgical areas. In IGNS, surgical tools are tracked in real time and displayed on a navigation system in the correct location and orientation with respect to a virtual patient model. Commercial IGNS systems such as Medtronic's StealthStation and BrainLab's Curve are routinely used in the operating room for various neurosurgical interventions and have proven to be important neurosurgical tools (Inoue et al. 2013). However, these systems have several shortcomings in terms of registration, visualisation, and surgeon–computer interactions: ergonomics of such devices are still not optimal, technical, and user-experience choices are not always adequate in an increasingly specialised context of use (Drouin et al. 2017). The most popular type of neuronavigation system is the optical system (a reflection of infrared light) (Enchev 2009). The most popular type of neuronavigation system is the optical system (a reflection of infrared light). One of the shortcomings of this optical system is that neurosurgeons must look away from the surgical field to see the navigation display since the navigation monitors are located far from the lens tubes of the microscope and monitors of the neuroendoscope. Then, the operator is required to transfer the information from the "virtual" environment of the navigation system to the real surgical field. This mental 3D exercise is repeated several times during a surgical procedure.

Kiron aims to give a new dimension to neuronavigation, projecting directly on the patient in holographic form all the anatomical details that may be needed during the operation, without the need to look away from the operating field. The technology exploits the possibilities of Mixed Reality and allows the neurosurgeon an immersive experience, allowing him/her to observe the objects of interest directly within the patient and decreasing the surgical times, as it is no longer necessary to look away to check the exact position of the neuronavigation on the monitor. A further advantage is the easier and more precise preoperative planning, carried out directly on the patient. Furthermore, it is also necessary to consider how some types of surgical operations, such as the placement of ventricular drainage, temporary, or definitive, do not currently enjoy the advantages of neuronavigation and rely exclusively on anatomical findings and the experience of the surgeon. The possibility of directly visualising the ventricular system within the patient using holographic

[2]Project website: https://kiron.nucleode.com

technology makes the intervention easier, minimising the risks of failure and overcoming anatomical limits of the individual patient, all taking advantage of cheap and routine radiological examinations, such as the brain scan, at no additional cost.

Surgical planning for a brain tumour done with Mixed Reality starts from data acquired from high-field magnetic resonances to create a 1:1 scale 3D model that faithfully reproduces the patient's brain, both with regard to the cortical surface and the deep structures, including vascularisation. DTI and tractography data, as well as data acquired with functional brain MRI, are added to the anatomical data, providing all the information useful for the neurosurgeon to conduct the operation within a single three-dimensional model. Those steps are done in a secure cloud platform with an integrated 3D viewer with advanced features, then securely transferred to the holographic device for usage before and during surgery.

Before surgery, Kiron allows improving the planning and preoperative preparation, as it accelerates the acquisition of specific 3D anatomic knowledge, which is usually based upon the surgeon's long-time experience. The quality of information available during preoperative briefings is of increasing importance for surgery outcomes. In this respect, Oishi et al. (2013) showed that performing surgical planning on computer graphic devices and in 3D is more useful than using 2D devices in 44% of cases. Augmented reality planning generally contributes to reducing the surgeon's guesswork and enables surgical procedures to be tailored for specific anatomical considerations, concerning craniotomy and bone resection, surgical trajectory, and spatial relationships of the surgical target among surrounding structures. Usually, an unpredictable variety of vessels, structural shapes, and cranial nerves obstruct the surgical route, which makes detailed planning mandatory for determining the best surgical approach for each patient.

Using the device during surgery provides the surgeon with additional information on the patient and the lesion directly on the field of vision, thus ensuring total visibility of the surgical field all the time, without any interference or the need to move the focus away from the patient to look at the monitor. It is also possible to add other three-dimensional models positioned to the side of the patient's head with further data, such as a magnification of the tumour mass and its spatial relationships with the adjacent vascular structures. In the same way, it is possible to insert further information, for example the diagnostic data of the magnetic resonance, the data coming from neurophysiological monitoring or clinical data such as arterial pressure and heart rate.

Mixed Reality blends real world and virtual content into hybrid environments where physical and digital objects coexist and interact. It is the next evolution in human, computer, and environment interactions, and it is made possible by advancements in computer vision, graphical processing power, display technology, and input systems. Mixed Reality places a digital object, such as a hologram, in the physical world with environmental understanding capabilities, as if it is really there. Holograms add light to the user world, which means that he or she can see both the view from the digital object and the light from his/her surroundings. The device used by Nucleode for Mixed Reality development is Microsoft's HoloLens.[3]

Cloud Computing, intended as a flexible and cost-effective model for the supply of ICT services, represents a tool for saving and optimising IT resources through economies of scale. The infrastructure developed by Nucleode is suited for healthcare usage, and it is constructed ground up with privacy by design and privacy by default methodologies, packed in Docker's[4] containerised applications that are orchestrated by Kubernetes.[5]

The development of a project based on cutting-edge technology is surely stimulating but not always easy to carry out, given the lack of references. Furthermore, the adoption of new technology such as Mixed Reality involves the development of 3D Graphical User Interface unlinked from the existing development paradigms for products used on two-dimensional supports. To overcome these new problems, the network on which Nucleode can rely is fundamental, which allows the company to give beta versions directly to the neurosurgeons, end users of the project, gathering fundamental feedbacks from the earliest stages of development.

The development to date has made it possible to collect several feedbacks that have guided the project up to a first test in the operating room. At the end of 2018, it was possible to test the Mixed Reality tool directly in a neurosurgery operating room for a scheduled operation on a 72-year-old lady with a right parasagittal meningioma.

The test, although still at an early stage, was received extremely positively by the neurosurgeons involved, who were able to use the Mixed Reality in parallel with the neuronavigation for better pre-surgical planning (Figs. 2 and 3).

4 The Impact of Digital Transformation and Intellectual Capital Management in Healthcare

The case of Kiron can be seen as an innovation in healthcare through the application of two digital technologies belonging to Industry 4.0: Mixed/Augmented Reality and Cloud Computing. Indeed, the use of Kiron can lead to several improvements in neurosurgery:

- More accuracy in planning the surgery, given the ability to forecast all anatomical details, in terms of needs during the operation and the predicted time.
- More efficiency for the surgeon, who can concentrate on the operating field without the need of looking away.

[3]https://www.microsoft.com/en-us/hololens

[4]See https://www.docker.com

[5]See https://kubernetes.io

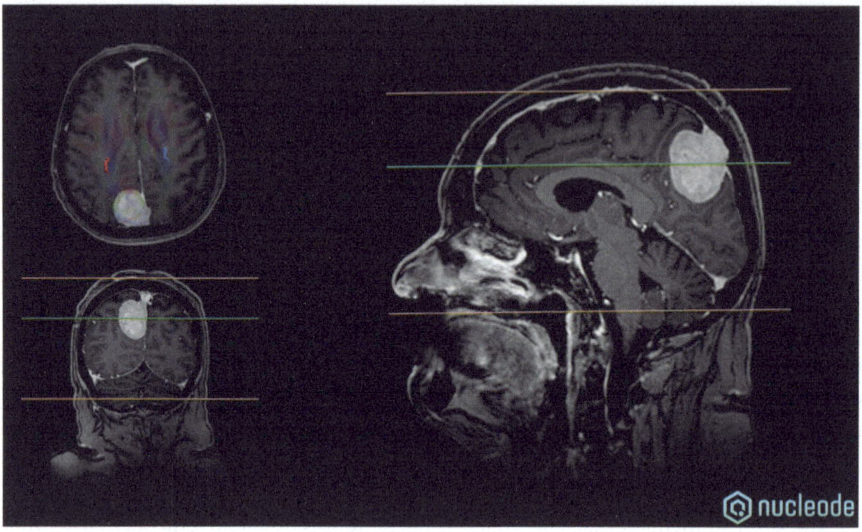

Fig. 2 Kiron scan. Source: Nucleode Srl

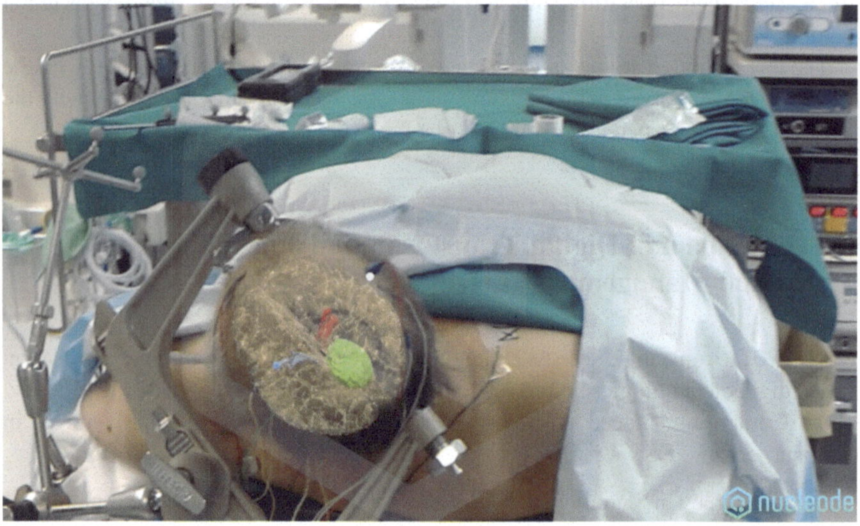

Fig. 3 Kiron in the operatory room. Source: Nucleode Srl

- More data that can be gathered before and after the surgery that can enhance the surgeon's knowledge, as well as the general scientific understanding of neurosurgery.

What is currently happening in healthcare, with the introduction of new digital innovations such as Kiron, can follow the framework of Leif Edvinsson.

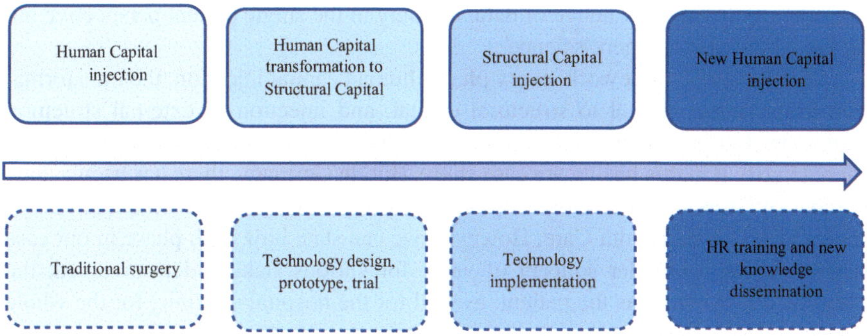

Fig. 4 IC and surgery over time

As explained above, Edvinsson analysed the global growth curve of IC, based on the global scenario and his personal situation as the world's first director of intellectual capital at Skandia AFS (Edvinsson 2000). Edvinsson recognises several phases, which resulted in stock market appreciation shifts. After the first phase of visualisation of the intangibles, phase two concerns a human capital injection, followed up by a third phase in which human capital is transformed into structural capital as a multiplier. The fourth phase is about an external infusion of structural capital.

Kiron was conceived starting from the needs and knowledge of the current stage of human capital, both from an engineering/technological side as well as from a medical perspective. The development of Kiron, from the initial concept to the first project, prototype, and trial, has been possible merging a variety of different actors: both human (doctors, engineers, graphic designers, ...) as well as technical (software and solutions available on the market). The relational capital outside the developer, the company Nucleode, with external doctors and professors, was also crucial to ensure the clinical trial, the measurements, and the validation of the final results.

In this sense, we may see Kiron as the transformation of human capital into a structural capital tool. Once innovative tools as Kiron are included as external devices in healthcare organisations, they require further human capital injections, in terms of new knowledge needed (Fig. 4).

More in detail, the role of the surgeon changes for good. The support of the innovative tool helps to read the clinical situation prior to the surgery. A massive amount of data is collected, so most of the initial guesswork of the physician is replaced by a clearer picture of the clinical condition. Data allows forecasting the time and the resources needed for the operation more accurately. Unpredicted situations will occur less frequently. The surgery itself will end up more comfortably for the surgeon, given the ability to look directly at the affected area, and not on other screens. After the surgery, more data can be collected and analysed. In this sense, the knowledge required by the surgeon will turn more on the experience/guesswork side to the ability to take advantage of data, not only in the single patient perspective but on the whole neurosurgery science.

In Edvinsson's framework, every phase (human capital injection, the transformation from human capital to structural capital, and injection of external structural capital) lead to an increase in the market capitalisation value of the organisations. We cannot verify it in this healthcare case study. But, in Germany, there has been a huge number of cases on Intellectual Capital, also referred to as Wissenskapital, among others with Caritas Health Care. However, we can state how each phase in our case study leads to a broader concept of value for various stakeholders involved: the client/end-user, which is the patient, as well for the hospital or clinic, for the whole society, and for the operator (physician).

More in detail, the innovation allows the patient to get a more accurate preoperational plan and surgery, less linked to the physician's experience and ability. This will lead to a better chance of getting the expected clinical result in terms of healing.

Moreover, the better picture of the initial operational plan can lead to better management of the required resources, both human (e.g. physicians from other hospital departments), as well as technical (correct use and booking of the operating room). This will bring a better cost/benefit value for the healthcare organisation, being it a public or private entity, in terms of efficacy, efficiency, and money spent, with a positive impact on the final outcome (Massaro et al. 2019). In particular, the correct use of the operating room as a key hospital resource brings a better cost/benefit analysis both for the hospital as well as for the patient. Indeed, the clinic can better plan the use of this expensive resource. Coming to the patient, the less he/she needs to stay in the operating room, the better it is, since the probabilities of getting an infection decrease.

For the whole society and science, the extra data collected before, during, and after the surgery can then lead to a better understanding of neurosurgery as a science. Indeed, through the dissemination of results with scientific publications and presentations to medical conferences and congresses data can be useful to any neurosurgeon dealing with the same cases or situations. Moreover, in those economies in which healthcare is mostly paid by the State, hence by the collectivity of citizens, a better use of public resources leads to more financial resources to be spent elsewhere, like for better hospital care or research and development activities.

Last, but not least, innovation tools like Kiron allow the surgeon to better plan his or her activities, reducing the stress of facing unexpected situations (Fig. 5).

The cycle HC injection—HC transformation to SC—SC injection in healthcare can be a repeated process. New technologies and innovation are born from the progress of human capital, which then leads to new structural capital, that requires new skills and changed the way human capital operates. The whole process generates new knowledge and, all in all, more value for the stakeholders.

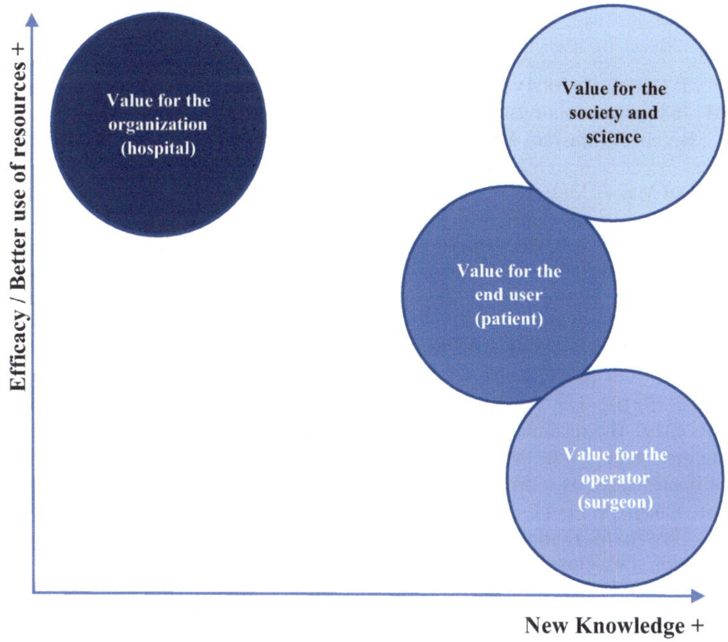

Fig. 5 Technology and healthcare. A value map for stakeholders

5 Conclusion

As stated in the introduction, innovation can lead to possibilities that were previously unknown, leading to progress, bringing extraordinary opportunities for organisations to expand their horizons and knowledge. The strategic introduction and implementation of new innovative technologies point to the need for developing new business models.

Intellectual Capital, defined by its major components of Human Capital, Structural Capital, and Relational Capital, is strongly linked to innovation as well as strategy, as Innovation Capital. Medical treatment in Healthcare is a sector that is mostly affected by new innovative technologies. Analysing the case of Kiron, a new navigation system that can be used in neurosurgery, we identified how intellectual capital evolves in the various steps of digital technologies introduction and implementation in the sector of healthcare. The Innovation Capital dimensions of IC might also expand the model above to Social Capital outcome and Societal Capital Impact. The Science Value adds to Health Value, that adds to Health Value, as well as Societal Value. The Value Galaxy of Intangibles is multiplying long beyond the traditional Market Capital.

References

Abeysekera I, Guthrie J (2004) Human capital reporting in a developing nation. Br Acc Rev 36 (3):251–268. https://doi.org/10.1016/j.bar.2004.03.004

Bagnoli C, Bravin A, Massaro M, Vignotto A (2018) Business model 4.0. Edizioni Ca' Foscari, Venezia

Bagnoli C, Dal Mas F, Massaro M (2019) The 4th industrial revolution and its features. Possible business models and evidence from the field. Int J E-Serv Mob Appl 11:3

Bolton MJ, Stolcis GB (2003) Ties that do not bind: musings on the specious relevance of academic research. Public Adm Rev 63(5):626–630

Bontis N (1998) Intellectual capital: an exploratory study that develops measures and models. Manag Decis 36(2):63–76

Buaron R (1981) New-game strategies. McKinsey Q Spring(Issue 1):24–41

Christensen CM, Bohomer R, Kenagy J (2000) Will disruptive innovations cure health care? Harv Bus Rev 78(5):102–112

Dal Mas F (2019) The relationship between intellectual capital and sustainability: an analysis of practitioner's thought. In: Matos F, Vairinhos V, Selig PM, Edvinsson L (eds) Intellectual capital management as a driver of sustainability: perspectives for organizations and society. Springer, Cham, pp 11–24

Dal Mas F, Massaro M, Lombardi R, Garlatti A (2019a) From output to outcome measures in the public sector: a structured literature review. Int J Organ Anal 27(5):1631–1656

Dal Mas F, Paoloni P, Lombardi R (2019b) Wellbeing of women entrepreneurship and relational capital, a case study in Italy. In: Lepeley MT, Kuschel K, Eijdenberg E, Pouw N (eds) Exploring wellbeing among women in entrepreneurship. A global perspective. Routledge, London, Cap 15, pp 232–243

Drouin S, Kochanowska A, Kersten-Oertel M, Gerard IJ, Zelmann R, Nigris D, Collins DL (2017) IBIS: an OR ready open-source platform for image-guided neurosurgery. Int J Comput Assist Radiol Surg 12(3):363–378

Dumay J, Garanina T (2013) Intellectual capital research: a critical examination of the third stage. J Intellect Cap 14(1):10–25

Edvinsson L (2000) Some perspectives on intangibles and intellectual capital 2000. J Intellect Cap 1 (1):12–16

Edvinsson L (2002) Corporate longitude: what you need to know to navigate the knowledge economy. Pearson Education, London

Edvinsson L, Malone M (1997) Intellectual capital: realizing your company's true value by finding its hidden brainpower. Harper Collins, New York

Enchev Y (2009) Neuronavigation: geneology, reality, and prospects. Neurosurg Focus 27(3):E11

Grafstrom G, Edvinsson L (1996) Accounting for minds. An inspirational guide to intellectual capital. Skandia, Stockholm

Iacopino V, Mascia D, Cicchetti A (2018) Professional networks and the alignment of individual perceptions about medical innovation. Health Care Manag Rev 43(2):92–103

Inoue D, Cho B, Mori M, Kikkawa Y, Amano T, Nakamizo A, Sasaki T (2013) Preliminary study on the clinical application of augmented reality neuronavigation. J Neurol Surg A Cent Eur Neurosurg 74(2):71–76

Lin CY-Y, Edvinsson L (2011) National intellectual capital. A comparison of 40 countries. Springer, New York

Lucas DP (2015) Disruptive transformations in health care: technological innovation and public policy reforms in the hospital industry. Int J Interdiscip Org Stud 9(1):1–22

Mascia D, Di Vincenzo F (2011) Understanding hospital performance: the role of network ties and patterns of competition. Health Care Manag Rev 36(4):327–337

Massaro M, Dumay J, Guthrie J (2014a) On the shoulders of the giants: undertaking a structured literature review (no. 19 November, 2014). PhD workshop. Department of Accounting, University of Waikato, Waikato

Massaro M, Zanin F, Bardy R (2014b) Levers of control and knowledge sharing in alliances among large firms and small firms in the pharmaceutical industry. Manag Cont 2:121–142

Massaro M, Dumay J, Bagnoli C (2017) When the investors speak. Intellectual capital disclosure and the web 2.0. Manag Decis 55(9):1888–1904

Massaro M, Dumay J, Garlatti A, Dal Mas F (2018) Practitioners' views on intellectual capital and sustainability: from a performance-based to a worth-based perspective. J Intellect Cap 19:2. https://doi.org/10.1108/JIC-02-2017-0033

Massaro M, Dumay J, Bagnoli C (2019) Transparency and the rhetorical use of citations to Robert Yin in case study research. Meditari Acc Res 27:44–71. https://doi.org/10.1108/MEDAR-08-2017-0202

Mouritsen J (2006) Problematising intellectual capital research: ostensive versus performative IC. Account Audit Account J 19(6):820–841

Nielsen C, Lund M, Montemari M, Paolone F, Massaro M, Dumay J (2018) Business models: a research overview. Routledge, New York

Oishi M, Fukuda M, Yajima N, Yoshida K, Takahashi M, Hiraishi T, Fujii Y (2013) Interactive presurgical simulation applying advanced 3D imaging and modeling techniques for skull base and deep tumors. J Neurosurg 119(1):1–256

Peng S, Bewley K (2010) Adaptability to fair value accounting in an emerging economy: a case study of China's IFRS convergence. Acc Audit Acc J 23(8):982–1011

Schlegelmilch BB, Diamantopoulos A, Kreuz P (2003) Strategic innovation: the construct, its drivers and its strategic outcomes. J Strateg Mark 11(2):117–132

Secundo G, Massaro M, Dumay JC, Bagnoli C (2018) Intellectual capital management in the fourth stage of IC research: a critical case study in university settings. J Intellect Cap 19(1):157–177

Snowdon A, Schnarr K, Alessi C (2015) Global trends in health-system innovation. In: Singh VK, Lillrank P (eds) Innovations in healthcare management: cost-effective and sustainable solutions. CRC, Boca Raton, FL, pp 11–32

Swanborn P (2010) Case study research: what, why and how? Sage, London

Yin RK (2009) Case study research: design and methods, 4th edn. Sage, Thousand Oaks, CA

ALTUS: A Process-Oriented, Knowledge Governance Maturity Model

Maria-Isabel Sanchez-Segura, Antonio de Amescua Seco, Fuensanta Medina-Dominguez, German-Lenin Dugarte-Peña, and Jose-Arturo Mora-Soto

Abstract In view of the importance of knowledge as a key resource for companies sustainability and improvement, and in view of the existing efforts made to keep organizations informed about the way they should take care of their know-how, this chapter describes ALTUS, a process-oriented, knowledge maturity model, that helps organizations to assess its knowledge maturity level regarding the performance of a set of capabilities that are oriented to improve strategic or business goals through the accomplishment of several specific knowledge governance processes. This orientation through capabilities, processes and strategic/business goals achievement for knowledge governance is auditable, traceable and sustainable along the time.

1 Introduction

We are today immersed in a constantly changing society (Ruiz de Arriaga Ramirez 2011). Value is no longer embodied only in material things, it is present in ideas, design, services or marketing and is driven by continuous improvement and innovation (Kotler et al. 2010). Executives face the difficult challenge of continually improving their company's business value (Dutta 2007). In this context, it is really critical to develop the skills needed for the company to deploy knowledge acquisition, transformation, learning, sharing and reuse (Ruiz de Arriaga Ramirez 2011).

Just as people must renew, replenish and constantly expand their knowledge, companies must improve their ability to learn, adapt and change to ensure survival. Nowadays, companies must innovate or die (Mochas 2015).

M.-I. Sanchez-Segura (✉) · A. de Amescua Seco · F. Medina-Dominguez · G.-L. Dugarte-Peña
Department of Computer Science and Engineering, Universidad Carlos III de Madrid, Madrid, Spain
e-mail: misanche@inf.uc3m.es; amescua@inf.uc3m.es; fmedina@inf.uc3m.es; gdugarte@inf.uc3m.es

J.-A. Mora-Soto
Virtual University Department, Celaya University, Celaya, Mexico
e-mail: jmora@udec.edu.mx

F. Matos et al. (eds.), *Knowledge, People, and Digital Transformation*, Contributions to Management Science, https://doi.org/10.1007/978-3-030-40390-4_10

Since the advent of the knowledge-based economy, the value creation method used by companies has switched from tangible physical assets to intangible knowledge. Therefore, the valuation of intangible assets has become a topic of widespread interest in the future of the economy (Tsai et al. 2012).

The success of leading companies like Amazon, Google, Microsoft or Wal-Mart is based on their intellectual capital. Physical assets such as the distribution of warehouses, office buildings or stores are important but not as important as, for example the knowledge of customers, technologies or markets (Marr 2008).

It is very important, especially for researchers and creditors, to understand the critical factors that affect the company value before making decisions about investments (Tsai et al. 2012). In this respect, knowledge maturity models can help companies to visualize the status of their know-how and how it affects company performance, the achievement of its strategic and/or business goals and, consequently, the digitalization process facing all companies.

The most popular questions concerning knowledge maturity models are:

1. How are they used?
2. How can a company use the information provided by a knowledge management maturity model for its own benefit?
3. How can a knowledge maturity model help an organization to improve?

In the following, we will answer these questions and, at the same time, identify the key features of any knowledge management maturity model.

1. A knowledge management maturity model is a descriptive framework that lists *several capabilities to be fulfilled* in order to guaranty that the company is able to successfully deal with the different knowledge management processes. A *knowledge management process* is a capabilities container that covers the management of all the knowledge related to a specific mission. In order to ascertain a company's knowledge management maturity, *the capabilities must be assessed*, using, for instance, several questions whose responses will determine the level at which the company is performing each capability listed in the knowledge management maturity model. As already mentioned, these capabilities should account for all knowledge management processes. But also, and more importantly, *each capability must be aligned with a generic business or strategic goal*. Thus, when any capability is assessed, it is rated against the achievement of a specific business or strategic goal, on the grounds discussed in point 2 below. In a real case, a specific company may ask to be assessed merely to find out if it is achieving a specific knowledge management process. This is the reason why capabilities are divided by processes. The *knowledge maturity assessment should be supported by an electronic tool* in order to guarantee the traceability of the results of the assessment over the years. All the features highlighted in italics above are the characteristics required to guarantee the applicability and transparency of any knowledge maturity model and, ultimately, the alignment of the results of the assessment with the assessed company's need to improve its strategic or business goals.

2. After the knowledge management maturity assessment, the knowledge management maturity model will offer data about how well the capabilities included in the maturity model are satisfied with respect to the achievement of a specific business or strategic goal. These data must be analyzed in order to define an improvement plan for a specific set of capabilities. By improving capabilities, the aim is to enhance, by transitivity, the strategic or business goal with which the selected capabilities area is aligned in the knowledge maturity model.
3. In the light of the above two points, there is a straightforward answer to Question 3 above. As knowledge management is empirically related to productivity improvement, sustainability and intellectual capital improvement, a company can, by visualizing its knowledge management maturity, decide to improve its maturity by improving a set of capabilities described in the maturity model, whose improvement, if aligned with a specific strategic or business goal, will affect the achievement of the business or strategic goal defined by the company.

We highlighted the main features that a knowledge maturity model must provide above in italics. One of the first things that we realized when examining knowledge management processes is that they must be extended to cover not only the identification, capture, allocation, distribution and reuse of knowledge assets, but also some other processes related to knowledge assets valuation or knowledge assets digital design and development, for example. The traditional view of knowledge management processes does not take these processes into account. Therefore, Sect. 2 will discuss existing knowledge maturity models and how they deal with the above features. In the light of the analysis reported in Sects. 2 and 3 explains our rationale as to why traditional organizational knowledge management processes should be extended and refers to organizational knowledge governance processes. Section 4 describes our proposal of a knowledge governance maturity model called ALTUS. ALTUS was created to cover organizational knowledge governance processes and meet the needs that will, in the future, pose a challenge for knowledge-based companies aware of the importance of their knowledge assets. Finally, Sect. 5 describes the results of using ALTUS to assess seven small- and medium-sized enterprises (SMEs), as well as the opinions of 37 software engineers that used ALTUS to assess the above SMEs. It also summarizes a number of conclusions.

2 Existing Knowledge Maturity Models

A knowledge maturity model defines the stages of maturity that an organization can expect to pass through on its road to improve its overall knowledge-centric practices and processes and, ultimately, business performance (The Knowledge Maturity Compass 2006).

Without practical guidelines for institutionalizing and successfully measuring knowledge management maturity, more and more practitioners question the very concept of knowledge management, arguing that, owing to the high cost in terms of time and commitment and subsequent non-delivery, knowledge management is not worthy of the attention it is receiving (Kruger and Snyman 2007).

One of the most difficult tasks for enterprises is to establish the value of knowledge management (Oliveira and Drebes Pedron 2014). Nevertheless, the question now is: What are knowledge maturity models being used for? We have analyzed several previous works focusing on four issues, which we highlighted in italics in Sect. 1. These four issues are considered essential for a knowledge management maturity model to be useful. The above issues will be used to analyze existing works and are summarized as:

1. Is the model structured as capabilities for assessment, and how will the result provide information about the company with respect to its knowledge maturity?
2. Are the above capabilities aligned with generic strategic or business goals defined by the knowledge maturity model?
3. Is the knowledge maturity model assessment supported by an electronic tool?
4. Is the knowledge maturity model process oriented in the sense that the capabilities are distributed by processes to be performed by the organization?

The knowledge management maturity model (K3M) (WisdomSource Technologies 2019) is a long-term roadmap spread across eight increasingly sophisticated levels for companies to follow in their pursuit of organizational self-actualization. The K3M is progressive insofar as each level depends on the previous layers. However, companies may find that they are competent at one specific level, even though they are still at a rudimentary point in preceding levels.

Although it does not list any, K3M Level 6 is oriented to knowledge processes. However, it is not aligned with the strategic goal, it does not provide any tool for measuring the level that the organization has attained, and it is not oriented to capabilities. Therefore, it does not provide clues about what and how to improve.

The KM Maturity Model Service (KMmm) divides the maturity model into six levels: informal, breakthrough, community, enterprise (KM-oriented processes), managed and optimized (The Knowledge Maturity Compass 2006). It provides a specially designed tool used to gather and evaluate the key factual and perceptual information required to create the customised maturity model. However, the first and third features that we are looking for are not accomplished. Like K3M, KMmm is not aligned with the strategic goal and is not oriented to capabilities.

Some of the questions underlying the knowledge management maturity assessment matrix (KMMAM) by the University of Pretoria are (Kruger and Snyman 2007): Is there a commitment from top management to the establishment of a formal knowledge management function? Does the organization know what constitutes (both tacit and explicit) knowledge resources, where are knowledge resources situated, and why are resources strategic? Is the organization capable of conducting a successful knowledge audit? Is knowledge shared among value chain partners? This maturity assessment consists of seven phases:

- Phase 1: ICT and information management as enablers of knowledge management

- Phase 2: Selection of knowledge management issues
- Phase 3: Formulation of an organization-wide knowledge policy
- Phase 4: Construction of knowledge strategy/strategies
- Phase 5: Formulation of knowledge management strategies
- Phase 6: Ubiquitous knowledge
- Phase 7: The future

The objective of the KMMAM was to determine, through the use of structured questionnaires, the knowledge management maturity in the consulting engineering environment. KMMAM can be said to be oriented to a strategic perspective and that it has a tool, as they propose a questionnaire to enable organizations to test and assess their knowledge management maturity empirically. However, KMMAM does not account for knowledge governance processes, and, once again, it is not oriented to capabilities.

The knowledge management maturity model developed by Oliveira and Drebes Pedron (2014) is based on an analysis of eight knowledge management maturity models previously published in scientific journals. The analysis considers the number of levels, the key factors, how the model is applied and the association of knowledge management with strategic benefits. The proposed model consists of five maturity levels and four key factors and also considers the relationship between the key factors in the KM maturity model and absorptive capacity, innovation and organizational performance. They claim that a KM maturity model should have a complete range of key factors, although the number of key factors should not interfere with its application. They reduced the list of key factors in order to make it easier for organizations to comply with them all. We can conclude that the model is aligned with the strategic goals and is somewhat capability oriented, as a list of key factors is used to identify the attained level. However, there is no tool for measuring attainment or any way of finding out which knowledge governance processes are being covered.

The National University of Singapore proposed a General KM Maturity Model (G-KMMM) (Pee and Kankanhalli 2009). This model defines five levels of maturity: initial, aware, defined, managed and optimizing, which are differentiated in terms of their characteristics related to the people, process and technology aspects of KM. To facilitate the independent validation and practical application of G-KMMM, an accompanying assessment instrument was developed. They claim that the extent to which an organization successfully accomplishes all the key practices characterizing a maturity level is an indicator of the KM maturity of an organization. Thus, a list of practices was created in order to ascertain a company's maturity level. This model is aligned with strategic goals, provides a tool and is capability oriented, as it provides a list of practices to be implemented. However, they do not refer to knowledge governance processes.

Yang and Yu (2013) propose a Knowledge maturity model, based on five maturity levels, knowledge areas and a knowledge management maturity model evaluation, the work is promising, but the proposal is not explained with enough detail to be replicated in other contexts.

Table 1 Summary of the knowledge management maturity models analysis performed

	1. Capability oriented	2. Based on strategic/business goal alignment	3. Provides a tool	4. Alignment with knowledge management processes
K3M (WisdomSource Technologies 2019)				X
Arias-Perez et al. (2016)				X
Oliveira and Drebes Pedron (2014)	X	X		
Yang and Yu (2013)				X
G-KMMM (Pee and Kankanhalli 2009)	X	X	X	
KMMAM (Kruger and Snyman 2007)		X	X	
KMmm (The Knowledge Maturity Compass 2006)			X	X

In the works of Arias-Perez et al. (2016), Buheji and Al-Zayer (2010), Lin et al. (2012), and Serenko et al. (2016) some other knowledge maturity models apart from the above mentioned, have been analyzed, being in common on all of them, the fact that they are aligned with the several knowledge management processes or key areas, the absence of specific capabilities to be reached in order to empower the knowledge capability level, no evidence being aligned with business goals and not providing a support tool.

Table 1 provides a summary of the knowledge maturity models. In the light of the results of the analysis of existing knowledge maturity models against the four essential features required of any knowledge maturity model, we developed a knowledge governance maturity model that satisfies all four established requirements. This model is also auditable, traceable and offers a broader vision of knowledge management processes. Section 3 describes the reasons why knowledge management processes must be extended.

3 Knowledge Governance Processes

From a process perspective, knowledge management is an activity that refers to the identification, capture, allocation, distribution and reuse of knowledge assets.

This perspective of knowledge management is not enough to successfully design and implement the digital perspective of knowledge assets or to assess the knowledge management maturity of a company. It fails to account for the following:

- The processes that can connect the business to the knowledge management mechanism. For this purpose, we propose a set of processes called *knowledge*

Table 2 Knowledge governance processes

Knowledge valuation processes (valuation processes VP)
VP1 Identify strategic/business/process goals, and processes/services for improvement
VP2 Classify intangible strategic/business/process knowledge assets by intellectual capital branches
VP3 Align intangible knowledge assets and strategic/business/process goals
VP4 Assess intangible knowledge assets and intellectual capital
VP5 Define improvement plan (decision-making on assets and capabilities for improvement)
VP6 Measure intangible knowledge asset use
VP7 Measure intangible knowledge asset quality
VP8 Manage intangible knowledge asset configuration (KCM)
VP9 Measure innovation capability
VP10 Assess knowledge governance maturity
Knowledge management processes (management processes MP)
MP1 Identify intangible knowledge assets
MP2 Capture (elicit, develop) knowledge assets
MP3 Allocate (organize) knowledge assets
MP4 Distribute knowledge assets
MP5 Use (maintain) knowledge assets
Knowledge development processes (development processes DP)
DP1 Design knowledge assets
DP2 Implement knowledge assets
DP3 Deploy knowledge assets

valuation processes, used for the identification and assessment of knowledge assets, their connection with company strategic or business goals, their measurement in terms of their use throughout the company, etc.

- The processes for the design, implementation and deployment of the knowledge assets as a digital solution, which we class as *knowledge development processes*.

For these reasons, we claim that the concept of knowledge management should be broadened in order to also embrace:

- Knowledge valuation processes, which are essential for assessing knowledge maturity, identifying and assessing knowledge assets and understanding the evolution of company knowledge.
- Knowledge development processes, which are essential for designing, implementing and deploying a digital solution that supports the digital view of knowledge assets.

With this broader view in mind, we consider that a different dimension, including the valuation and development perspective, should be added to traditional knowledge management. Therefore, we suggest that this broader vision be referred to as *knowledge governance processes*.

Table 2 summarizes and explains the processes covered by the knowledge governance concept.

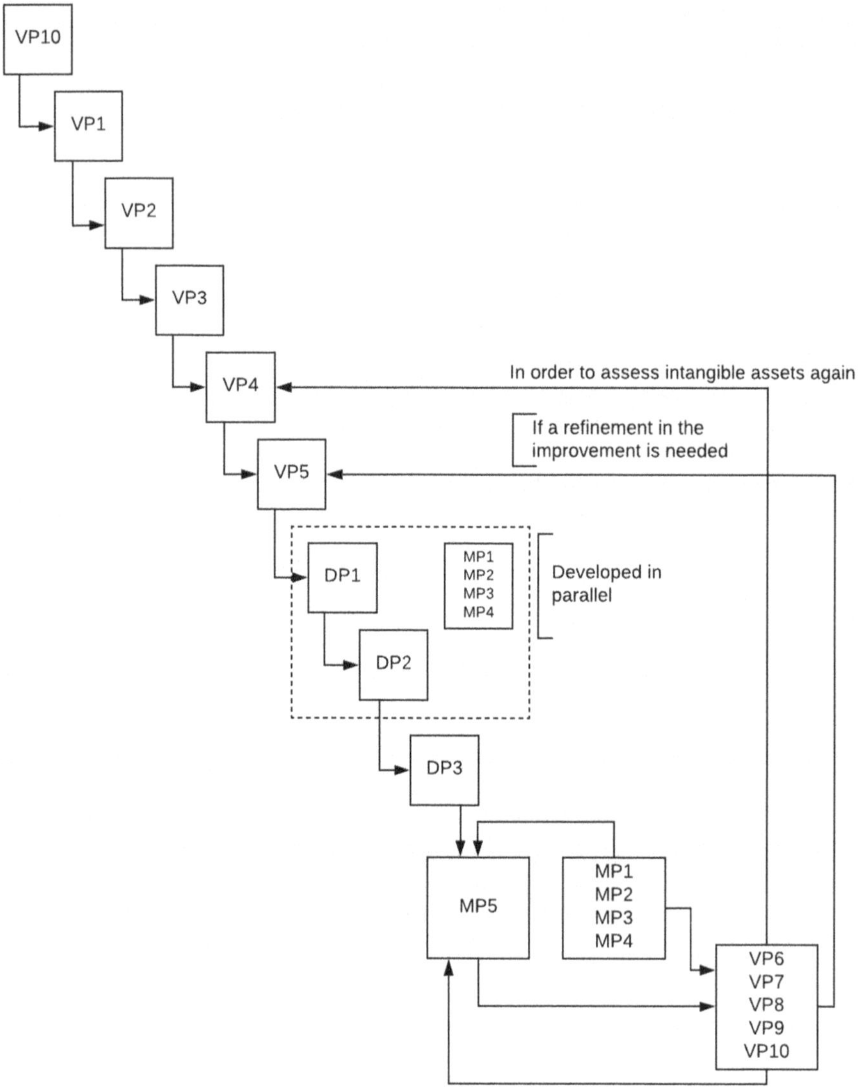

Fig. 1 Knowledge governance processes dependencies

Each company may need to implement or assess just a set of knowledge governance processes. However, the most important thing about the above processes is how they connect with each other. Figure 1 shows the knowledge governance process dependencies.

Next, all knowledge governance processes are explained.

Knowledge Valuation Processes (VP)

- *VP1 Identify strategic/business/process goals, and processes/services for improvement*: The organization has a clear business, strategic or process objectives that it pursues through the improvement of a specific process/service.
- *VP2 Classify intangible strategic/business/process knowledge assets by intellectual capital branches*: Knowledge assets must be classified according to the different types of intellectual capital for two reasons:
  - Because it identifies how each intangible asset produces intellectual capital growth.
  - Because it indicates what part of the company's intellectual capital is being leveraged to achieve the company's specific objectives.
- *VP3 Align intangible knowledge assets and strategic/business/process goals*: The organization aligns the knowledge assets identified for that process/service and the specified objectives.
- *VP4 Assess intangible knowledge assets and intellectual capital*: A mechanism for valuating intangible assets must be provided. This rating will be defined by the impact that each asset has on the achievement of the business and/or strategic objectives selected by the organization.
- *VP5 Define improvement plan (decision-making on assets and capabilities for improvement)*: It is necessary to decide which intangible assets will be improved and which of the capabilities identified in the maturity model will be deployed. They do not necessarily have to be maturity model capabilities that the company does not have, they can be maturity model actions in which the company excels and which it wants to replicate for intangible assets that it does not have.
- *VP6 Measure intangible knowledge asset use*: The company must know what corporate knowledge is being used for, who uses it and when. Therefore, project management, project execution and the use of intangible knowledge assets for project realization have to be connected.
- *VP7 Measure intangible knowledge asset quality*: The company must know how the members of the organization value the knowledge used, for which purpose a scoring system must be established that is as simple as possible so that knowledge can be assessed when it is used.
- *VP8 Manage intangible knowledge asset configuration (KCM)*: It is necessary to save a trace of how knowledge assets are evolving by means of a system for managing the configuration of the above assets.
- *VP9 Measure innovation capacity*: Through the delta of knowledge increase of an organization, it is possible to assess how innovation at this organization has increased. This can be measured by checking how much new knowledge has been applied to new projects.
- *VP10 Assess knowledge governance maturity*
  - An audit (assessment) must be carried out at the beginning and at another point of time during action development to improve the governance of corporate knowledge and ascertain an organization's level of knowledge governance

maturity. This audit will serve to design, together with the intangible assets assessment model, the organizational knowledge process improvement program.
- A mechanism for reporting what knowledge assets are included in each type of intellectual capital, the achieved objectives and the indicators of objective achievement.

Knowledge Management Processes (MP)

- *MP1 Identify intangible knowledge assets*
  - First, it is necessary to identify, together with the process/service expert and the selected assessment technicians, the ten most important knowledge assets for that process/service.
  - If other knowledge assets materialise later on, they must be able to be identified and channelled through to the capture process.
- *MP2 Capture (elicit, develop) knowledge assets*
  - After initial identification, the knowledge assets must be collected using specified elicitation techniques and made available to the organization using mechanisms whereby they can be accessed from any part of the organization at any time. They can be stored in blogs, wikis, patterns, etc.
  - If a knowledge asset is identified at any other time, there must be an appropriate mechanism for its elicitation and creation as above.
- *MP3 Allocate (organize) knowledge assets*: Knowledge assets must be allocated in such a manner that they are accessible to the interested parties at any time and any place, requiring the design of a transactive memory system (TMS). This is decided together with the company and is designed, implemented and deployed by the project consultant.
- *MP4 Distribute knowledge assets*: There must be some mechanism whereby the knowledge assets that are being created are notified to and can be used by the community.
- *MP5 Use (maintain) knowledge assets*: Knowledge must be assessable and used:
  - For individual learning of new knowledge existing in the organization (internalization)
  - For collective learning of new knowledge existing in the organization (socialization)
  - For use in real projects (combination), implying that it is known what knowledge has been used in which projects or what knowledge has been used for which service.

Knowledge Development Processes (DP)

- *DP1 Design knowledge assets*: This process has the mission of designing the digital view of the knowledge assets or knowledge capabilities for improvement.
- *DP2 Implement knowledge assets*: This process has the mission of implementing the digital view of the knowledge assets or knowledge capabilities for improvement.
- *DP3 Deploy knowledge assets*: This process has the mission of deploying the digital solution that supports the knowledge assets or knowledge capabilities for improvement.

Next section describes the ALTUS model.

4 ALTUS: Knowledge Governance Maturity Model Description

The aim of the knowledge governance maturity model (ALTUS[1]) is to lay the groundwork for valuating organizational knowledge, as well as the mechanisms for ensuring its accessibility, usability and learning by all members of the organization (Mora-Soto 2011). It defines the maturity achieved by the organizational knowledge of an institution. At the same time, the organization acquires capabilities for managing its knowledge, and people generate knowledge more efficiently.

The ALTUS model is composed of four maturity levels, each of which is composed of seven architectural levels (configuration, training, operational, proactive, transactive, SP3 valuation and social), and each architectural level is composed of capabilities.

Figure 2 provides an overview of the structure of the ALTUS model.

As can be observed, Fig. 2 shows that the maturity levels are related to architectural levels. Accordingly, the architectural levels define each set of capabilities that the organization must have for its knowledge to reach each maturity level. Each architectural level is supported by a set of technologies. The architectural-level capabilities are related to a set of governance processes and a set of general ALTUS model strategic objectives, and each capability has its respective question/s in order to perform the model assessment.

Next, the Architectural levels are described.

1. Configuration Architectural Level The configuration level defines a set of capabilities that the organization must develop in order to establish the minimum requirements for dealing with changes in the organizational culture, as well as the implementation of the suggested technological tools to support the deployment of

[1]*ALTUS:* Acronym formed with the words in English: assessment, learnability, usability and accessibility, organizational knowledge qualities that are sought through the use of ALTUS.

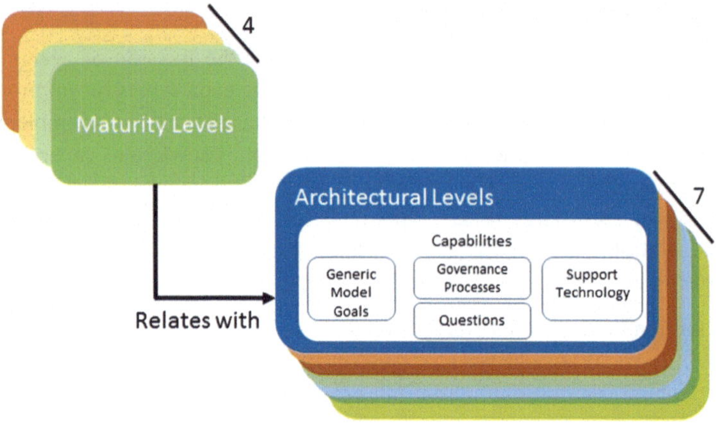

Fig. 2 ALTUS general structure

capabilities of this level within the organization and facilitate the adoption of the practices recommended by this maturity model into the routine work of the members of the organization.

2. Training Architectural Level The training level defines a set of capabilities that specify the mechanisms that must be implemented in the organization to ensure that tacit knowledge about services, products, processes and people is accessible to all members of the organization. Also, it defines the capabilities that an organization must develop so that the process of training its members is enriched by the knowledge that is generated within the organization. Likewise, this level accounts for the definition of mechanisms that help the managers of the organization assess the effectiveness of the training process of its members, as well as the possibility of creating an intelligent training environment where each member of the organization automatically has access to the training resources that best suit their particular learning needs.

3. Operational Architectural Level The purpose of the operational level is to provide the organization with the necessary capabilities to enable its members to access explicit knowledge for reuse in their routine work, as well as for enrichment with new experiences, additional resources or examples of the use of knowledge assets.

4. Proactive Architectural Level The proactive architectural level proposes some of the most innovative capabilities of this model, since it defines a set of capabilities enabling the organization to ensure that its members receive feedback from everything that is being transferred to the repository of collective knowledge and that may be of interest according to the role they play.

5. Transactive Memory Architectural Level To be able to realize its mission of storing all the knowledge of an organization in an explicit, clear and accessible way to promote its sustainable growth, the ALTUS model has to provide the organization with a set of capabilities enabling it to create a repository to store the know-how of its members, as well as everything related to its services, products and processes. To do this, the ALTUS model defines the transactive memory architectural level, which combines theories on transactive memory systems and information technologies to define a series of capabilities enabling an organization to define a repository of organizational knowledge that can store the knowledge relative to the know-how that the members of the organization have about the services, processes and products (Wegner 1987). This constitutes a repository that represents the organizational knowledge as a transactive memory system adapted to the organization's needs, because, despite having a predefined structure, it will contain knowledge that is useful within a specific organization for its members to develop their routine work.

6. Valuation SP3 Architectural Level It has been shown that explicitly storing knowledge per se does not add much value to the organization since it is useless to have a repository that captures an organization's know-how if you do not know what benefits this brings. On this ground, the ALTUS model proposes the SP3 valuation architectural level. SP3 is an acronym for service, process, product and person. This architectural level should satisfy the need to know the benefits and advantages of organizations making the effort to represent their knowledge explicitly. To do this, this architectural level proposes a series of capabilities to monitor the use of knowledge assets, as well as their alignment with the organization's strategic objectives through a balanced scorecard. In addition, this architectural level defines a set of capabilities and technological support tools that can assess the creators of knowledge assets, the actual knowledge, as well as the different components that make up an organization's intellectual capital. Through the combination of assessment techniques and the use of the appropriate technological tools for each organizational element to be evaluated (service, person, processes or product), ALTUS makes a major contribution to the knowledge management, intellectual capital management and valuation areas of the above organizational elements.

7. Social Architectural Level An organization simply would not exist without its members. For this reason, the ALTUS model includes the social architectural level in order to provide the organization with the necessary capabilities to manage how its members interact with each other to create knowledge assets and reuse the explicitly represented knowledge to perform their routine work at individual, workgroup and functional area level. This architectural level also defines the capabilities that an organization must develop to value and recognize people who collaborate with others in the creation and reuse of knowledge to contribute to the achievement of strategic objectives.

Table 3 summarizes the number of existing capabilities by architectural and maturity level.

ALTUS is a capability- and process-oriented model, aligned with strategic goals, focusing on the satisfaction of knowledge governance processes. This model is also supported by a tool that helps in the assessment process.

Table 3 Breakdown of capabilities by architectural levels and maturity levels

	Maturity level (ML)				
Architectural level	ML1	ML2	ML3	ML4	Total
Configuration	7	1	3	1	12
Training	2	2	2	1	7
Operational	1	0	0	0	1
Proactive	2	1	1	4	8
Transactive memory	3	3	0	1	7
SP3 valuation	4	2	3	2	11
Social	1	1	2	1	5
Total capabilities	20	10	11	10	51

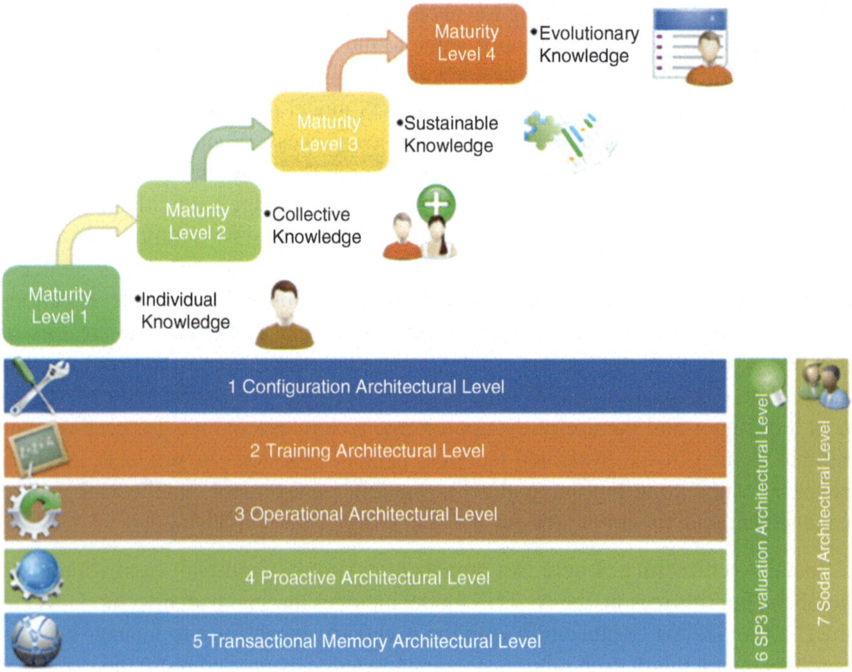

Fig. 3 ALTUS model Maturity and Architectural Levels View

ALTUS model capabilities are guided by the set of generic strategic goals listed below. These goals relate to the different architectural levels:

- Generic goal 1: Improve productivity
- Generic goal 2: Improve competitiveness
- Generic goal 3: Promote innovation
- Generic goal 4: Assess the quality of services, products, processes, and people
- Generic goal 5: Capitalize the organizational knowledge

Table 4 Tabular format used to describe each maturity level

Maturity Level					
Architectural Level	Organization's capability	Assessment Question	Knowledge Governance Process	ALTUS Generic Strategic/business goal	Support technology

As shown in Fig. 3, the maturity and architectural levels coexist at all times. Note that the SP3 Valuation and Social Architectural Levels provide support for the other architectural levels and can interact with each other as the organizational knowledge matures. The achievement of the different ALTUS model maturity levels is staged. This means that it is not necessary to achieve all the capabilities of one level before moving on to achieve the capabilities of the next level.

We use the tabular format shown below in Table 4 to facilitate the description of each maturity level.

In the following sections, each ALTUS model maturity level is described in detail according to the above tabular structure.

Each assessed capability is given a score, which depends on the existing evidence about how well the company achieves the capability. The most commonly used scale for measuring capability performance is the following:

- Excellent—assigned a value of 5: The capability is managed by the company digitally, and the results of this capability are known and used by all the employees that need to do so.
- Good—assigned a value of 4: The capability is managed by the company, albeit not digitally, and the results of this capability are known to all the employees that need to do so.
- Acceptable—assigned a value of 3: The capability is managed by the company, albeit not digitally, and the results of this capability are not known by all the employees that need to do so.
- Poor—assigned a value of 2: The capability is considered by the company, but the necessary instruments for performance are under development.
- Unacceptable—assigned a value of 1: The capability is considered by the company, but no instrument has been designed for its performance.
- Does not exist—assigned a value of 0: The capability is not even considered by the organization.

There are several digital instruments supporting the use of the ALTUS model. The public version of the Excel tool supporting assessment is available at https://promise.sel.inf.uc3m.es/images/files/Altus-Artefacts/ALTUS-template.xlsx, and the document that supports the interview process for assessment purposes is available at https://promise.sel.inf.uc3m.es/images/files/Altus-Artefacts/template-interview-altus.pdf. For more information about the model, do not hesitate to contact the authors.

Maturity Level 1

Explicit and accessible organizational knowledge, mainly for individual use.

At Maturity Level 1, at least 40% of the organizational knowledge necessary for the operation of the organization is accessible to all members of the organization, although it is used primarily individually. At this maturity level, the organization should define mechanisms to monitor how its members use knowledge assets.

On the other hand, at this maturity level, the organization must provide its members with a mechanism to enter new knowledge assets, assess existing assets and receive notifications of modifications or updates of knowledge assets that are of particular interest to them or that they have rated at some point. Likewise, the organization must begin to design its transactive memory system (TMS) and build its repository of organizational knowledge.

To ensure that members of the organization actively participate in the creation of new knowledge assets and encourage the reuse of explicitly represented organizational knowledge, the organization must adopt policies within its bylaws that recognize the value added to the organization by the knowledge assets generated and used by its own members and set up a reward or incentive scheme for people who contribute more actively to the growth of the organization through the creation, use, reuse and valuation of organizational knowledge.

Next, the table below shows an overview of the structure of Maturity Level 1.

Maturity Level 1: Explicit and accessible organizational knowledge mainly for individual use

Architectural level	Organization's capability	Assessment question	Knowledge governance process	ALTUS generic strategic/ business goal	Support technology
Configuration (CONF)	CONF 1: Identification of strategic or business goal	Has your organization defined its strategic/ business goals for this process/service in particular? Do they take into account the importance of KM?	VP1	• Capitalize the organizational knowledge • Assess the quality of services, products, processes and people • Promote innovation Improve productivity	• Wiki
	CONF 2: Identification of process/service for improvement	Which process/service does the organization want to improve?	VP1		
	CONF 3: Classification of process assets as part of the organization's intellectual capital, and alignment of knowledge assets to business/strategic goals	Has your organization identified and classified the process assets for improvement? Have they been aligned with the business/ strategic goals of your organization?	VP2, VP3		
	CONF 4: Knowledge assets created by staff members individually	Does your organization have any mechanism, for creating process assets for this process/service in particular?	MP1, P2		
	CONF 5: Transactive memory system design	Does your organization have a knowledge repository for this process/service in particular? Is it organized and does it have established rules for use?	DP1		
	CONF 6: Design of organizational knowledge network	Has your organization identified formal and informal communication networks for this process/service in particular?	MP3, MP4, DP1		
	CONF 7: Design of an organizational folksonomy	Has your organization taken into account that it has need of a mechanism for classifying its knowledge assets with respect to the labels for later reuse by the members of the organization?	MP3, MP4, DP1		
Training (FORM)	FORM 1: Assurance of knowledge assets accessibility	Do you have any mechanism for knowing what your colleagues know? Which ones?	MP3, MP4, MP5, DP1, DP2, DP3	• Capitalize organizational knowledge Assess the quality of services,	• Wiki with tracking capabilities
	FORM 2: Definition of mechanisms for monitoring self-training	When you take a training course, is the organization aware of your progress? If a	MP1, MP2,		

(continued)

Maturity Level 1: Explicit and accessible organizational knowledge mainly for individual use					
Architectural level	Organization's capability	Assessment question	Knowledge governance process	ALTUS generic strategic/ business goal	Support technology
		person completes a course successfully, does he or she receive a positive or negative appraisal?	MP4, DP1, DP2, DP3	products, processes and people	
Operational (OPER)	OPER 1: Reuse of knowledge assets throughout the project development	When you are developing a project (or service), do you have the possibility of using previous knowledge and experience built up from the development of other projects? How?	MP2, MP5, DP1, DP2, DP3	• Capitalize organizational knowledge • Improve productivity • Promote innovation Improve competitiveness	• Project management tool • Wiki
Proactive (PRO)	PRO 1: Notification of use and assessment of individual knowledge contributions	When you share knowledge with your colleagues, do you feel that it is valued in any way?	MP4, DP1, DP2, DP3	• Assess the quality of services, products, processes and people Promote innovation	Social network with notifications service
	PRO 2: Notification of knowledge asset contribution updates	If there is any resource modification or update that may be significant for you, do you receive the corresponding notifications?	MP4, DP1, DP2, DP3		
SP3 Valuation (VAL)	VAL 1: Assessment of the knowledge provided to the organization by each staff member individually	Personally, do you receive any kind of annual report from the organization in which you are told about your contribution at the level of services, processes or products in which you have participated?	VP4, VP6, VP7	• Assess the quality of services, products, processes and people • Promote innovation • Improve competitiveness. Improve productivity	• Knowledge assets assessment tool • Human capital assessment tool • Human resources valuation tool • Social network with
	VAL 2: Assessment of the importance of knowledge management and improvement plan definition	This is something that should be discussed with senior management. Has the knowledge of government maturity been audited in your organization to ascertain the value that your intangible process assets add to the organization? If so, has a knowledge government capabilities and	VP5, VP10		

(continued)

Maturity Level 1: Explicit and accessible organizational knowledge mainly for individual use

Architectural level	Organization's capability	Assessment question	Knowledge governance process	ALTUS generic strategic/ business goal	Support technology
		intangible process assets improvement plan been established?			assessment service
	VAL 3: Assessment of knowledge assets	When you use a knowledge asset created by someone else, do you have the possibility of giving your opinion about it?	VP4, VP7		
	VAL 4: Assessment of human capital	Does your company have a human intellectual capital assessment mechanism?	VP4		
Social (SOCI)	SOCI 1: Sharing of knowledge assets	Do you have any mechanism for sharing something with the organization or with your colleagues? What?	MP4, MP5	• Capitalize the organizational knowledge • Promote innovation Improve productivity	• Social network with capabilities to share knowledge assets • Wiki
Transactive memory (MEMO)	MEMO 1: Management of individual knowledge contributions	Is there any mechanism in your organization and for this process/service in particular for creating individual knowledge and storing it for later retrieval?	DP1, DP2, DP3	• Improve productivity • Capitalize the organizational knowledge • Assess the quality of services, products, processes and people Promote innovation	• Social network • Transactive memory system • Wiki
	MEMO 2: Mechanisms for assessing individual knowledge contributions	Is there a mechanism in your organization and for this process/service in particular, for valuating individual knowledge?	VP4, VP6, VP7		
	MEMO 3: Mechanisms for following up individual knowledge contributions	Is there a mechanism in your organization and for this process/service in particular for analyzing the growth of or changes in individual knowledge contributions?	VP8, DP1, DP2, DP3		

Maturity Level 2

Explicit and accessible collectively created and used organizational knowledge.

At Maturity Level 2, at least 60% of the organizational knowledge necessary for the operation of the organization must be represented explicitly, and, as in the previous level, it must be accessible to all members of the organization. At this maturity level, the use of knowledge and the creation of new knowledge assets is collective rather than primarily individual. This further enriches the collective memory of the organization stored in the defined transactive memory system, since relationships between knowledge assets can begin to be created once knowledge is used and created collectively, enabling more efficient reuse in project development.

As of this maturity level, the collaboration between the members of the organization is highly relevant, since it is a key factor for evolving the TMS in which more and more organizational knowledge is gradually specified. For this purpose, at this maturity level, the organization must implement mechanisms providing its members with easy access to the knowledge stored in the TMS so that they can then reuse the knowledge and experiences already explicitly represented in the TMS in their routine work.

Another important characteristic of Maturity Level 2 is that the knowledge assets, processes and products are assessed individually and collectively at the level of work or development teams. Likewise, as of this maturity level, the organizational knowledge is enriched with the performance assessment of the members of the organization. This assessment is carried out by co-workers from the same team, group or department. To facilitate the interaction between the members of the organization, a collaborative work protocol must be implemented, supported by tools that facilitate its deployment, for example using a social network.

The next table below shows an overview of the structure of Maturity Level 2.

Maturity Level 2: Explicit and accessible collectively created and used organizational knowledge					
Architectural level	Organization's capability	Assessment question	Knowledge governance process	ALTUS generic strategic/business goal	Support technology
Configuration (CONF)	CONF 8: Creation of collective knowledge assets	Is there any mechanism in your organization and for this process/service in particular for collaboratively creating or sharing knowledge with your colleagues? And what about teams or alike?	MP1, MP2	• Capitalize the organizational knowledge • Assess the quality of services, products, processes and people • Promote innovation • Improve productivity	• Project management tool • Social network • Transactive memory system
Training (FORM)	FORM 3: Definition of mechanism for monitoring group training	Is there any mechanism in your organization and for this process/service in particular for tracking a group of people taking a training course?	VP6, VP8, MP1, MP2, MP3, DP1, DP2, DP3	• Capitalize the organizational knowledge • Improve productivity	• Live learning platform with tracking capabilities • Social network
	FORM 4: Definition of collaborative learning strategy	Is there any mechanism in your organization and for this process/service in particular oriented to courses (or the definition of collective training sessions where a group of people require the same kind of knowledge)?	MP1, P2, DP1, DP2		
Proactive (PRO)	PRO 3: Notification of use and assessment of knowledge assets used in projects	Is there any mechanism in your organization and for this process/service in particular for giving advice, without being asked, about how colleagues used and assessed a specific piece of knowledge shared by an employee?	VP6, VP7, MP3, MP4	• Assess the quality of services, products, processes and people • Promote innovation	• Social network with notifications service

(continued)

Maturity Level 2: Explicit and accessible collectively created and used organizational knowledge					
Architectural level	Organization's capability	Assessment question	Knowledge governance process	ALTUS generic strategic/business goal	Support technology
SP3 Valuation (VAL)	VAL 5: 360° assessment	Is there any mechanism in your organization and for this process/service in particular for superiors, equals and subordinates to rate an employee's knowledge transfer capacity?	VP7	• Assess the quality of services, products, processes and people • Improve competitiveness • Improve productivity	• 360° valuation tool • Technological capital assessment tool • Social network with assessment service
	VAL 6: Assessment of technological capital	Is there any mechanism and for this process/service in particular for valuating the organization's technological capital in your organization?	VP4		
Social (SOCI)	SOCI 2: Creation of group social relations	Is there any mechanism in your organization and for this process/service in particular for creating some sort of active community for building social relationships between employees and reinforcing bonds based on common interests?	MP3, DP1, DP2, DP3	• Promote innovation • Improve productivity	• Social network
Transactive Memory (MEMO)	MEMO 4: Management of group knowledge contributions	Is there any mechanism in your organization and for this process/service in particular for creating and storing knowledge generated through teamwork for later retrieval?	DP1, DP2, DP3	• Capitalize the organizational knowledge • Assess the quality of services, products, processes and people • Improve productivity	• Social network • Transactive memory system • Wiki
	MEMO 5: Management of group knowledge contribution assessments	Is there any mechanism in your organization and for this process/service in particular for assessing the knowledge generated through teamwork?	VP6, VP7		
	MEMO 6: Management of group knowledge contribution follow-ups	Is there any mechanism in your organization and for this process/service in particular for analysing the growth or the knowledge contributions generated by teamwork?	VP8, DP1, DP2, DP3		

Maturity Level 3
Reusable organizational knowledge aligned with the strategic goals and follow-up.

At Maturity Level 3, 80% of the knowledge of an organization must be explicitly represented. Apart from being accessible to all members of the organization, it must be aligned with the strategic objectives of the organization. Likewise, at this maturity level, organizational knowledge must be reusable, and reuse must be guaranteed through knowledge quality control based on checks defined by the organization itself.

Another important quality of organizational knowledge at this level of maturity is that it must be fully traceable. Every time an asset is used, reused, modified, valued, learned or transferred, the organization must provide its TMS with mechanisms that can find out who, how, where (in what project or task) and when a knowledge asset has been used.

Regarding the use of organizational knowledge in project development at Maturity Level 3, there must be an explicit description and assessment of how useful an asset that is reused to support the execution of a project activity or task is. This will help foster innovation within the organization.

As of this level of maturity, cooperation among the members of the organization to create, improve and transfer knowledge assets is more important, and members of the organization that have the spirit and attitude to promote the use of knowledge assets in the organization for its welfare should be selected to play the role of evangelizers and coaches. This rewards people who like to help their peers to grow and improve within the organization for their effort and leadership.

The table below shows the overall structure of Maturity Level 3.

Maturity Level 3: Reusable organizational knowledge aligned with the strategic goals and follow-up					
Architectural level	Organization's capability	Assessment question	Knowledge governance process	ALTUS generic strategic/business goal	Support technology
Configuration (CONF)	CONF 9: Definition of quality controllers	Does any mechanism for collecting any indicator that reflects the quality of a certain product or service assigned to you, any time you work or finish with it, exist in this organization, and in particular for this process/service? These quality parameters are related to the indicator that will be later used for measuring the business or strategic goal scope degree	MP1, MP2	• Assess the quality of services, products, processes and people • Promote innovation • Improve productivity	• Project management tool • Transactive memory system
	CONF 10: Definition of alignment strategy between TMS and the organization's strategic goals	Does any strategy that bets on the processes or services improvement through the knowledge management exist in this organization, and in particular for this process/service?	MP1, MP2		
	CONF 12: Definition of reused knowledge asset improvement protocol	Does any mechanism for feeding back the knowledge assets once they are used by somebody exist in this organization, and in particular for this process/service?	MP1, MP2, DP1, DP2, DP3		
Training (FORM)	FORM 5: Identification of coaches and evangelists	Does any group of people, dependent and held directly by the steering committee of the organization, in charge of looking after and transmitting the organizational knowledge government importance as well as the goals being reached thanks to that government exist in this organization, and in particular for this process/service?	MP1	• Capitalize the organizational knowledge • Assess the quality of services, products, processes and people • Promote innovation • Improve productivity • Improve competitiveness	• Social network with content management service
	FORM 6: Identification of practical examples for training enrichment	Does any mechanism for identifying developed project cases inside of this organization that deserve to be incorporated as use cases at the training courses exist in this organization, and in particular for this process/service?	MP1, MP2, MP3		

(continued)

Maturity Level 3: Reusable organizational knowledge aligned with the strategic goals and follow-up					
Architectural level	Organization's capability	Assessment question	Knowledge governance process	ALTUS generic strategic/business goal	Support technology
Proactive (PRO)	PRO 4: Notification of coaches and evangelists' appraisal	Does any mechanism through which people who act as Coach related to promote the knowledge management are notified their assessments about their role inside the organization exist in this organization, and in particular for this process/service?	MP4	• Assess the quality of services, products, processes and people • Improve productivity • Improve competitiveness	• Social network with notifications service
SP3 Valuation (VAL)	VAL 7: Assessment of structural capital	Does any mechanism for valuing the structural capital of the organization exist in this organization, and in particular for this process/service?	VP4	• Assess the quality of services, products, processes and people • Improve competitiveness	• Social network with external members incorporation service • Structural capital assessment tool • Relational capital assessment tool • Business capital assessment tool • Structural capital assessment tool
	VAL 8: Assessment of relational capital	Does any mechanism for valuing the relational capital of the organization exist in this organization, and in particular for this process/service?	VP4		
	VAL 9: Assessment of business capital	Does any mechanism for valuing the business capital of the organization exist in this organization, and in particular for this process/service?	VP4		
Social (SOCI)	SOCI 3: Recognition of contributions by members of the organization	Does any mechanism through which the members of the organization are recognized their knowledge contributions exist in this organization, and in particular for this process/service?	VP7, VP8, VP9	• Promote innovation • Improve productivity • Improve competitiveness	• Social network with external members incorporation service
	SOCI 4: Recognition of knowledge asset contribution by clients or external contributors	Does any mechanism through which the knowledge contributions for a particular process or service of external clients or collaborators are recognized exist in this organization, and in particular for this process/service?	VP7, VP8, VP9		

Maturity Level 4

Organizational knowledge; evolutive, measurable and accessible in a personalized and intelligent fashion.

At Maturity Level 4, the ideal would be for 100% of organizational knowledge to be explicitly and appropriately represented in the transactive memory system. This, however, is impossible because some (approximately 10%) of the tacit knowledge, which is inherent to each human being and too complex to represent explicitly, will always be locked up inside people's minds (Phillips and Edwards 2008). However, when the knowledge of an organization is rated as having Maturity Level 4, it means that any type of knowledge related to the key processes of an organization that can be represented explicitly must be codified and stored in the transactive memory system and be accessible to any member of the organization that might need it.

At Maturity Level 4, not only does the ALTUS model ensure that most of the organization's knowledge can be represented explicitly, it also always guarantees successful reuse thanks to the quality controllers linked to each knowledge asset. Accordingly, anyone who wants to reuse a knowledge asset will have access before doing so to the diagnosis of the asset they want to use. Therefore, they have decision-making criteria concerning whether or not the asset suits their particular needs. This is one of the most innovative contributions of this knowledge maturity model.

The main feature of Maturity Level 4 is that each knowledge asset is been labelled, catalogued, valued and organized according to its evolution, ensuring the highest maturity level for organizational knowledge. Accordingly, any member of the organization can intelligently access the organizational knowledge stored in the organization's TMS. Intelligently means automatically here. Through the organization's social network, a person will automatically have access to potentially useful knowledge assets by virtue of either the characteristics of their professional profile, the features of the projects they are or have been involved in, or the social networks of which they are members within the organization. Although this type of access to information is currently offered by a wide variety of technological tools, including social networks, content managers or document management systems, the novel aspect of the proposal of this knowledge maturity model lies in the combination of technology and methodology, where any technological tool is always related to a method that describes how this tool should be used to comply at all times with the strategic objectives of the ALTUS model. The table below shows an overview of the structure of Maturity Level 4.

Maturity Level 4: Evolutionary, measurable organizational knowledge that is accessible in a personalized and intelligent fashion					
Architectural level	Organization's capability	Assessment question	Knowledge governance process	Generic ALTUS strategic/business goal	Support technology
Configuration (CONF)	CONF 11: Definition of professiographic profiles	Is there a procedure to define professiographic profiles in your organization and for this process/service in particular?	MP1, MP2	• Assess the quality of services, products, processes and people • Improve competitiveness	• Social network with advanced user profile capabilities
Training (FORM)	FORM 7: Definition of an intelligent training strategy	Is there an intelligent training strategy in your organization and for this process/service in particular?	MP1, MP2	• Capitalize the organizational knowledge • Promote innovation • Improve productivity • Improve competitiveness	• Live learning platform • Transactive memory system • Social network with notifications service and resources intelligent search
Proactive (PRO)	PRO 5: Intelligent retrieval of knowledge for project managers	Is there any mechanism in your organization and for this process/service in particular whereby a project manager regularly receives relevant information on other projects or services that are similar to his or her ongoing projects in order to take advantage of the generated knowledge?	MP4	• Capitalize the organizational knowledge • Assess the quality of services, products, processes and people • Promote innovation • Improve productivity • Improve competitiveness	• Social network with notifications service and resources intelligent search • Transactive memory system • Project management tool with Product Patterns[2] plugin
	PRO 6: Intelligent knowledge retrieval for professional growth	Is there any mechanism in your organization and for this process/service in particular whereby any employee regularly receives knowledge generated inside the company that is potentially useful for his or her professional daily activities?	MP4		
	PRO 7: Intelligent knowledge retrieval for routine work	Is there any mechanism in your organization and for this process/service in particular whereby any employee regularly receives knowledge generated	MP4		

(continued)

Maturity Level 4: Evolutionary, measurable organizational knowledge that is accessible in a personalized and intelligent fashion					
Architectural level	Organization's capability	Assessment question	Knowledge governance process	Generic ALTUS strategic/business goal	Support technology
		inside the company that is potentially useful for his or her routine work?			
	PRO 8: Intelligent knowledge retrieval for decision makers	Is there any mechanism in this organization and for this process/service in particular whereby any employee regularly receives knowledge generated inside the company that is potentially useful for decision making about a particular issue?	MP4		
SP3 Valuation (VAL)	VAL 10: Assessment of transversal organizational social relations	Is there any mechanism in your organization and for this process/service in particular for valuating transversal social relationships?	VP9	• Capitalize the organizational knowledge • Assess the quality of services, products, processes and people • Promote innovation • Improve productivity • Improve competitiveness	• Balance scorecard • Intellectual capital assessment tool • Transversal relationships valuation tool
	VAL 11: Assessment of intellectual capital dynamics	Is there any mechanism in your organization and for this process/service in particular whereby the intellectual capital of the organization can be valuated?	VP4		
Social (SOCI)	SOCI 5: Creation of transversal social networks	Is there any mechanism in your organization and for this process/service in particular whereby networks between people that do not belong to the same area or department can be created?	MP1, MP2, MP3	• Capitalize the organizational knowledge • Promote innovation • Improve productivity • Improve competitiveness	• Social network with intelligent contacts and collaborators service
Transactive Memory (MEMO)	MEMO 7: Management of intelligent information retrieval	Is there any mechanism in your organization and for this process/service in particular for properly retrieving and spreading knowledge of interest to different people that use the process or service?	DP1, DP2, DP3		• Transactive memory system with intelligent search service

[2] See http://productpatternswiki.sel.inf.uc3m.es/mediawiki/index.php/Libreria_de_Patrones_de_Producto

5 Conclusion

After working for a long time in the field of knowledge management, the team presenting this work has proposed a broader way to understand and deploy traditional knowledge management. The missing piece in the perspective of traditional knowledge management, was related to the fact that processes covering knowledge management were not providing mechanisms to knowledge management valuation and development. With this broader vision of knowledge management, we can start talking about "Knowledge Governance", that covers, Knowledge management, valuation and development.

This proposal settles down on four key aspects, and provides a practical solution to be used while analyzing knowledge governance maturity of any organization:

1. ALTUS is process oriented, which means that any organization can decide in which process of knowledge governance to work at each time.
2. ALTUS is business/strategic goal oriented, any action driven to improve knowledge governance is aligned with the company's strategic or business goals.
3. ALTUS is capabilities oriented, so it is easy to understand which capabilities are being well covered and which need to be improved.

ALTUS is supported in an electronic solution that helps during the capability's assessment performance, and the analysis of the data gathered, so the maturity level is easy to visualize as well as the status of each of the model capabilities.

References

Arias-Perez J, Tavera-Mesias J, Castano-Serna D (2016) Building a knowledge management maturity model for a multinational food company from an emerging economy. Prof Inf 25 (1):88–102

Buheji M, Al-Zayer J (2010) Developing a knowledge management maturity model towards government Organisations competitiveness. In: Proceedings of the 7th international conference on intellectual capital, knowledge management and organisational learning, No. 2006, pp 68–78

Dutta S (2007) Recognising the true value of software assets. INSEAD & Micro Focus

Kotler P, Kartajaya H, Setiawan I (2010) Marketing 3.0: from products to customers to the human spirit. Wiley, New York. https://www.wiley.com/en-et/Marketing+3+0%3A+From+Products+to+Customers+to+the+Human+Spirit-p-9780470598825

Kruger CJ, Snyman MMM (2007) Guidelines for assessing the knowledge management maturity of organizations. SA J Inf Manag 9(3). https://doi.org/10.4102/sajim.v9i3.34

Lin C, Wu JC, Yen DC (2012) Exploring barriers to knowledge flow at different knowledge management maturity stages. Inf Manag 49(1):10–23. Elsevier B.V.

Marr B (2008) Impacting future value: how to manage your intellectual capital. The Society of Management Accountants of Canada, The American Institute of Certified Public Accountants and The Chartered Institute of Management Accountants. https://www.journalofaccountancy.com/content/dam/jofa/archive/issues/2008/09/mag-intcapital-eng.pdf

Mochas W (2015) Construyendo una organización inteligente (Organizaciones que aprenden). Universidad Carlos III de Madrid, Spain

Mora-Soto A (2011) Marco Metodológico y Tecnológico para la Gestión del Conocimiento Organizativo que de Soporte al Despliegue de Buenas Prácticas de Ingeniería del Software. Universidad Carlos III de Madrid, Spain

Oliveira MD, Pedron C (2014) Maturity model for knowledge management and strategic benefits. Proc Eur Conf Knowl Manag 2:748–756

Pee LG, Kankanhalli A (2009) A model of organizational knowledge management maturity based on people, process, and technology. J Inf Knowl Manag 8(2):1–21

Phillips JJ, Edwards L (2008) Managing talent retention: an ROI approach. Wiley, New York

Ruiz de Arriaga Ramirez JM (2011) La importancia de la gestión del conocimiento y su impacto en la competitividad de las empresas. Arriaga Asociados, Zaragoza. https://www.arriagaasociados.com/

Serenko A, Bontis N, Hull E (2016) An application of the knowledge management maturity model: the case of credit unions. Knowl Manag Res Pract 14(3):338–352

The Knowledge Maturity Compass (2006) Knowledge optimization services. https://knowledgecompass.com/

Tsai CF, Lu YH, Yen DC (2012) Determinants of intangible assets value: the data mining approach. Knowl Based Syst 31:67–77. Elsevier B.V.

Wegner DM (1987) Transactive memory: a contemporary analysis of the group mind. In: Mullen B, Goethals GR (eds) Theories of group behavior. Springer, New York, NY, pp 185–208

WisdomSource Technologies (2019) K3M: the knowledge management maturity model. http://wisdomsource.com/K3MOverview.pdf

Yang R, Yu Q (2013) Research on knowledge management maturity model: based on the life cycle of the industry. In: 2013 6th International conference on information management, innovation management and industrial engineering (ICIII 2013), vol 3, pp 259–262

Trusting Security When Sharing Knowledge?

Pierre-Emmanuel Arduin, Bako Rajaonah, and Kathia Marçal de Oliveira

Abstract This chapter tackles knowledge sharing by focusing on security and trust issues. Although trust is recognized as important in security issues, few studies on information systems (ISs) deal with both trust and security. Knowledge sharing relies on sense-giving and sense-reading processes which require, encourage, and even create trust within individuals. We argue that individuals are processors of information and interpret information to create their own tacit knowledge.

Recent security reports from organizations have presented that the majority of ISs security threats involve employees within the organizations. Individuals, as well as computers, maybe attacked through social engineering techniques in order to gain their trust. Despite this evidence, most of the work has focused on the control of outsider security threats rather than of insider security threats, particularly when humans are perpetrators.

We propose to study insider threats through a trust factor during the knowledge sharing process. Knowledge sharers may induce insider threats for security due to trust-related attitudes and behaviours. The proposition is twofold with interviews and self-report questionnaires to collect information about the trust, and ontologies to categorize such information. The proposition is then discussed, notably in terms of problems and answers leading to study trust in security when sharing knowledge.

1 Introduction

Web-connected databases and information systems, as well as cloud-based platforms, have become so indispensable to enterprises and many other kinds of organization to support knowledge sharing that managing security issues have become of a priority. Indeed, the security of Web-based systems is a worldwide

P.-E. Arduin (✉)
Université Paris-Dauphine, PSL, CNRS, DRM UMR 7088, Paris, France
e-mail: pierre-emmanuel.arduin@dauphine.psl.eu

B. Rajaonah · K. M. de Oliveira
Université Polytechnique Hauts-de-France, CNRS, LAMIH UMR 8201, Valenciennes, France
e-mail: bako.rajaonah@uphf.fr; kathia.oliveira@uphf.fr

F. Matos et al. (eds.), *Knowledge, People, and Digital Transformation*, Contributions to Management Science, https://doi.org/10.1007/978-3-030-40390-4_11

challenge due to the seriousness of the consequences of security breaches. The media relates almost everyday security issues of Web-based systems. For instance, the BBC News app has a daily updated specific page dedicated to cybersecurity. Taking just the case of information systems (ISs), in the last years, much research and practice have focused on protecting information systems and data from unauthorized access, disclosure, modification, or destruction (Dhillon and Backhouse 2000; Whitman and Mattord 2011). The main idea has been to avoid the access of non-authorized people/software systems that could generate any kind of damage.

Nevertheless, security reports from industry (Kaspersky 2015; Keeney et al. 2005; PwC 2018) show that, contrary to the complex infiltration procedures, the security problems were caused by hacking a specific IS component: the individuals, several times own employees of the organization. Loch et al. (1992) had raised this kind of IS security threat in 1992, distinguishing between insider (internal) and outsider (external) threats, that come from human or natural actions which, in turn, can be accidental and intentional. Individuals may be benevolent, as well as malevolent, particularly through techniques from psychological principles and social engineering (Mitnick and Simon 2011): the attacker gains the trust of the target to persuade him/her of the truthful nature of the information that they are being sent.

Individuals are entry points, as well as computers and digital artefacts are. Organizations have to be aware of such a special feature when considering knowledge sharing: human behaviour is harder to predict and to manage than digital artefacts processing are. However, nowadays, outsider security threats have been widely explored through technological solutions (e.g. cryptography, firewalls), and far less investment is made to control insider threats (Collwill 2009). This chapter proposes to deal with knowledge sharing by focusing on trust and security, which is in an increasingly common context in Web-based society.

Working in this direction involves putting face-to-face technology (analyzing the issues of IS security) and human (as both a user of the IS and a potential attacker against another human via an IS). Dealing with these issues together is innovative and challenging, requiring truly multidisciplinary work that takes social, technological, and management aspects into account. We argue that the individual is a carrier of knowledge and a processor of information. He/she is a component of the Enterprise's Information and Knowledge System (Arduin et al. 2015). Thus, ISs carry information as a source of knowledge. Only individuals can possess genuine knowledge, resulting from their interpretation of information (Tsuchiya 1993). Therefore, individuals' thought processes have to be considered when managing ISs' security (Willison and Warkentin 2013).

As mentioned earlier, we propose to tackle this security issue by considering trust. Section 2 presents the theoretical background. The concept of knowledge sharing is first explained, then the particular problem of insider threats is considered, which is followed by an explanation of that problem through the trust factor. Section 3 proposes to investigate the plausibility of this explanation with regard to the security of knowledge sharing, particularly by considering insider threats. Interviews and self-report questionnaires are presented as techniques to collect information about the perceived trust, whereas ontologies are exposed as a technique to categorize such information about trust. A discussion on identified risks and answers concludes this section. The study presented in this chapter leads to understanding ways of trusting security when sharing knowledge.

2 Theoretical Background

The theoretical background aims at describing the main concepts considered in this chapter. The unifying thread is the relationships between the knowledge sharers, insider threats they may represent for security and their trust. The section details first the concept of knowledge sharing. The issue of insider threats is then explained. Last, an explanation in terms of trust is proposed.

2.1 Knowledge Sharing

Polanyi (1967) was interested in the way in which we endow our discourse with meaning (by speaking or by writing, for example) and in what we attribute meaning to (by listening or by reading, for example). Although they are informal, these actions possess a characteristic model that he calls the structure of tacit knowing: "Both the way we endow our own utterances with meaning and our attribution of meaning to the utterances of others are acts of tacit knowing. They represent sense-giving and sense-reading within the structure of tacit knowing" (Polanyi 1967, p. 301).

Here is a good example on the way Polanyi highlighted knowledge sharing, and particularly tacit knowledge sharing: One morning he saw his son come in and wanted to pass a letter on to him. Remembering that his son only spoke English, he checked the letter and realized that it was in a foreign language. Polanyi was, therefore, conscious of the meaning conveyed by the letter but not the words that had conveyed it. He then explained the contents of the letter to his son in English. This clearly shows that one can (1) possess the meaning of a text without knowing the text itself and (2) put this inarticulate meaning into words. We can, therefore, possess unarticulated knowledge that Polanyi calls tacit knowledge. Polanyi has insisted since 1967 on the fact that: "[. . .] modern positivism has tried to ignore it, on the grounds that tacit knowledge was not accessible to objective observation" (Polanyi 1967, p. 306). As a temporary difficulty, the fact that the language is nothing until there is knowledge of its meaning was ignored at the time, and that still seems to be the case today. There has been an extremely large economic investment in information technology and collaborative tools since the 1970s. Yet, as Landauer (1996) remarked, the productivity of the services who invested in stagnated throughout the world.

The retranscription of the letter that Polanyi offered his son was that of the meaning of the letter as he understood it. Imagine that the letter describes a scene

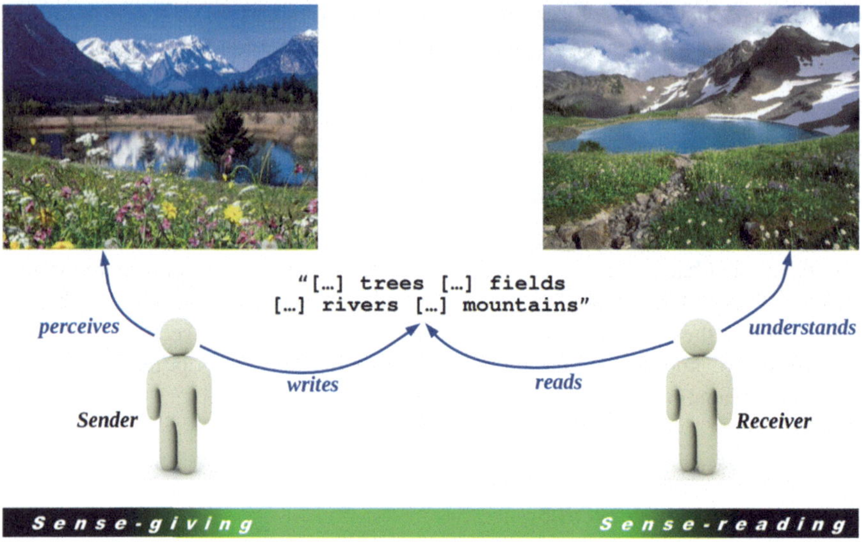

Fig. 1 Tacit knowledge sharing: from sense-giving to sense-reading (Arduin 2018)

that the sender, a traveller, witnessed while he wrote it. Maybe he admired a landscape, a particular instance of trees, fields, rivers, and mountains. When he reported on the scene, he used the general terms "trees", "fields", "rivers", and "mountains", which do not transmit the particular instance that he has witnessed. In doing so, by choosing the words to describe his experience, he has performed a sense-giving process (Fig. 1), he has endowed them with meaning for himself. His lived experience, his perceptions and his tacit knowledge of the place visited have thus been communicated in the form of made explicit knowledge, a letter, whose meaning was tacit.

In receiving the letter and reading it, Polanyi perceives shapes and colours, from which he understands words. Once perceived, the words are forgotten to give way to the meaning attributed to them, which corresponds to a sense-reading process (Fig. 1). He is, therefore, conscious of the meaning of the letter without remembering the text. That is the reason why he forgot that his son, who only spoke English, could not read it.

By communicating his lived experience in a letter, the sender has given meaning to the words, made explicit knowledge, whose meaning is tacit: "[. . .] into a communication which was a piece of explicit knowledge, the meaning of which was tacit. All knowledge falls into one of these two classes: it is either tacit or rooted in tacit knowledge" (Polanyi 1967, p. 314). In this way, all knowledge is either tacit or rooted in tacit knowledge.

Polanyi insists heavily on the "contradiction" of the existence of made explicit knowledge, since, without their tacit coefficients, all words, all formulas, all maps, and all images are simply devoid of meaning. The example that he uses is that of the cyclist who at any time is offsetting his imbalance, by turning the bicycle in a curve with a radius proportional to the square root of its speed divided by the angle of his imbalance. This rule, although made explicit, is useless in learning how to ride a bicycle. Moreover, for someone who does not grasp its tacit meaning, it remains not understood.

However, knowledge sharing raises issues of security, particularly issues of insider threats as individuals are involved as knowledge holders.

2.2 Insider Threats and Security

The main concepts behind IS security are protection of both information and technology against unauthorized access and/or modification (e.g. Dhillon and Backhouse 2000; Whitman and Mattord 2011). The problem is, therefore, to design secure IS, in other words, to design systems such as their users could expect both information and technology to be preserved from unauthorized access and modification. From the perspective of users, IS security is thus a matter of IS trustworthiness: the user's perceptions of IS would influence his/her expectations that his/her data could not be accessed and/or modified by a third other than him/her and authorized people of IS. This is particularly crucial in the case of knowledge sharing, where trust is a common denominator to initiate and perpetuate knowledge sharing processes.

At the beginning of the 1990s, the literature on information systems security had already affirmed that there was "a gap between the use of modern technology and the understanding of the security implications inherent in its use" (Loch et al. 1992, p. 173). The massive arrival of microcomputers was also accompanied by questions regarding the security of interconnected systems where computer science was previously mainframe oriented.

Indeed, the number of technological artefacts has exploded, and this increase has gone hand in hand with the evolution of their various uses (Canohoto et al. 2015). Yesterday, a terminal connected the user to the computer, while today entry points into the information system are multiple, universal, interconnected, and increasingly discreet. Employee's social activity can be supported by social networks and their health maintained using connected watches.

The taxonomy of threats targeting the security of information systems proposed by Loch et al. (1992) presented in Fig. 2 is disturbingly topical, with regard to the four dimensions that make up his angle of analysis: (1) sources, (2) perpetrators, (3) intent, and (4) consequences. It should be recognized that independent of the sources, perpetrators, and intent of an attack, the consequences remain the same: disclosure (of profitable information), modification or destruction (of crucial information), or denial of service (by hindering access to resources). These consequences are covered in the 2013 ISO/IEC 27001 standard: information security management, which defines information security management systems as ensuring the (1) confidentiality, (2) integrity, and (3) availability of information (ISO/IEC 2013).

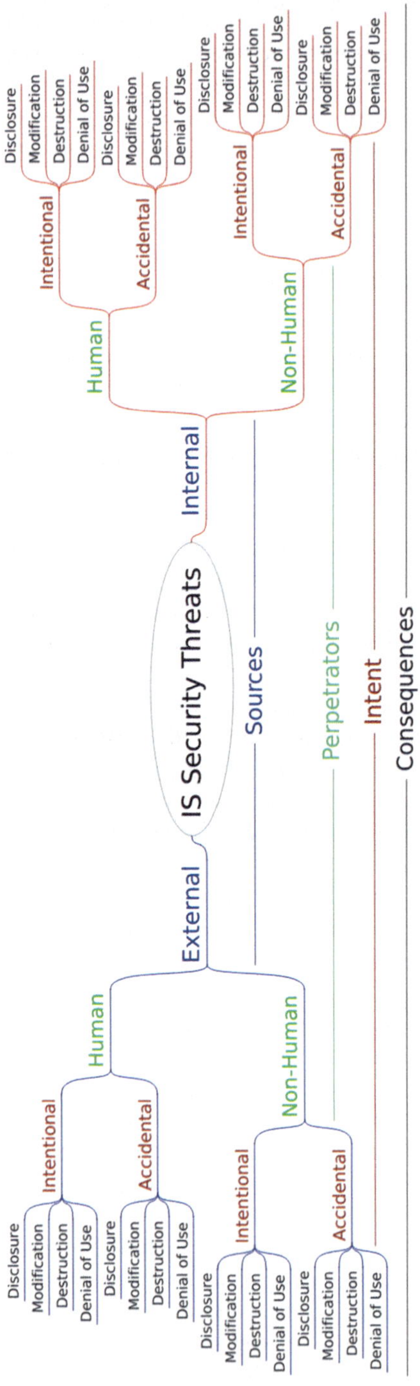

Fig. 2 Taxonomy of IS security threats (inspired from Loch et al. 1992)

A business's firewall constitutes protection against external threats, which appear on the left branch in Fig. 2. Authors such as Willison and Warkentin (2013) represent a part of the literature on information systems security that tends to pay attention to insider threats, more particularly those whose perpetrators are humans with the intention to cause harm (upper right branch in Fig. 2).

For authors such as Arduin (2018), insider threats may be categorized along two dimensions: (1) whether the character of the threat is intentional or not, and (2) whether its character is malicious or not. From the point of view of the employee, who may constitute the entry point into the system, an insider threat can be:

1. Unintentional: Wrong actions taken by an inexperienced or negligent employee, or one manipulated by an attacker; for example an inattentive click, input error, and accidental deletion of sensitive data (Stanton et al. 2005).
2. Intentional and non-malicious: Deliberate actions by an employee who derives a benefit but has no desire to cause harm; for example deferring backups, choosing a weak password, and leaving the door open during a sensitive discussion (Guo et al. 2011).
3. Intentional and malicious: Deliberate actions by an employee with a desire to cause harm; for example divulging sensitive data and introducing malicious software into the computer system (Shropshire 2009).

The study presented in this chapter focuses on the manipulation and social engineering techniques that exploit unintentional insider threats (category 1 above). Even though the attacker is outside the system and the organization, he/she makes an employee, a component of the system, unintentionally facilitate his/her infiltration: the latter has, for example clicked on a link or even opened the door to a self-proclaimed delivery person with a self-proclaimed task. A social engineer is an attacker who targets a legitimate user from whom he/she obtains a direct (rights of access, harmful link visited, etc.) or indirect (vital information, relationship of trust, etc.) means to get into the system (Mitnick and Simon 2011).

As new technological solutions are developed, the exploitation of hardware or software weaknesses becomes more and more difficult. Attackers are then turning toward another component of the system susceptible to attack: the human one. For authors such as Schneier (2000), "Security is a process, not a product". For others such as Mitnick and Simon (2011, p. 14), breaching the human firewall is "easy", requiring no investment, except for occasional telephone calls and involves minimal risk. Every legitimate user constitutes thus an unintentional insider threat to the information system's security.

Individuals are not trained to be suspicious of others. Consequently, they constitute the strongest threat to the security of the information system insofar as any well-prepared individual can win their trust.

2.3 The Question of Trust with Regard to Security

As mentioned earlier, few studies on information systems deal with both trust and security despite the fact that trust is recognized as important in security issues. Trust helps in reducing the perceived complexity of social systems (Luhmann 2000; Möllering 2001). It does exist in situations of uncertainty and, consequently, of risk: a trusting agent is a risk-acceptant agent (Castelfranchi and Falcone 2000). The mechanism of trust is to mentally reduce the occurrence of possible futures (Lewis and Weigert 2012), which provides an illusion of control to the trusting agent and results in a psychological state of expectations (Castelfranchi and Falcone 2000). Trust is a three-part relationship including the trusting agent, the object of trust (i.e., the trusted), and the expectations that relate the trusting agent to the trusted party (Hardin 2001): in a word, A (trusting agent) trusts B (trusted party) to do X (what is expected).

The object of trust can be an individual, a group of individuals, an organization, an institution, or a technology. Whatever the object of trust, trust is an intermediate factor that may guide our attitudes and decision-making processes with regard to this object (Kramer 1999; Lee and See 2004). For instance, the decision to rely or not rely on a technology may be guided by one's level of trust in the technology. Depending on the context reliance on people, organization, technologies, etc. might be appropriate, but it might also be not appropriate: it is the concept of trust calibration described by Muir (1987) who is one of the firsts who studied trust in machines.

Trust calibration requires the understanding of the context and of how much the trusted parties will be able to fulfil or not fulfil what is expected from them in that context, that is how much they could be trusted or distrusted. Experimental studies have shown that trust could be considered as a continuous variable opposing trust and distrust (e.g. Jian et al. 2000). The level of trust (or distrust) would depend on the trusting agent's goals, beliefs, and assessments, which constitute the dimensions of trust, or what makes trust level changing (e.g. Hoffman et al. 2013). These dimensions, viewed from the perspective of the trusting-agents, are their "good reasons" to trust or distrust (Möllering 2001).

As for the context of this chapter, that is to say, considering ISs in the context of knowledge sharing, trusting agents and trusted parties are multiple and various, and the same is thus true regarding expectations (Fig. 3).

Taking the example of an organization which activities go through an IS, Fig. 2 shows that each part of the organization is responsible for IS security and has good reasons to be confident, at different levels. Let us focus on the organization's members who interest us as potential insider threats: they are expected to behave in a responsible way by both the organization's managers and the IS administrators. In return, the members have expectations toward the information system and their administrators. In a word, they trust both the IS and its administrators. In fact, they also trust the other organization's members, themselves and, perhaps, the attackers,

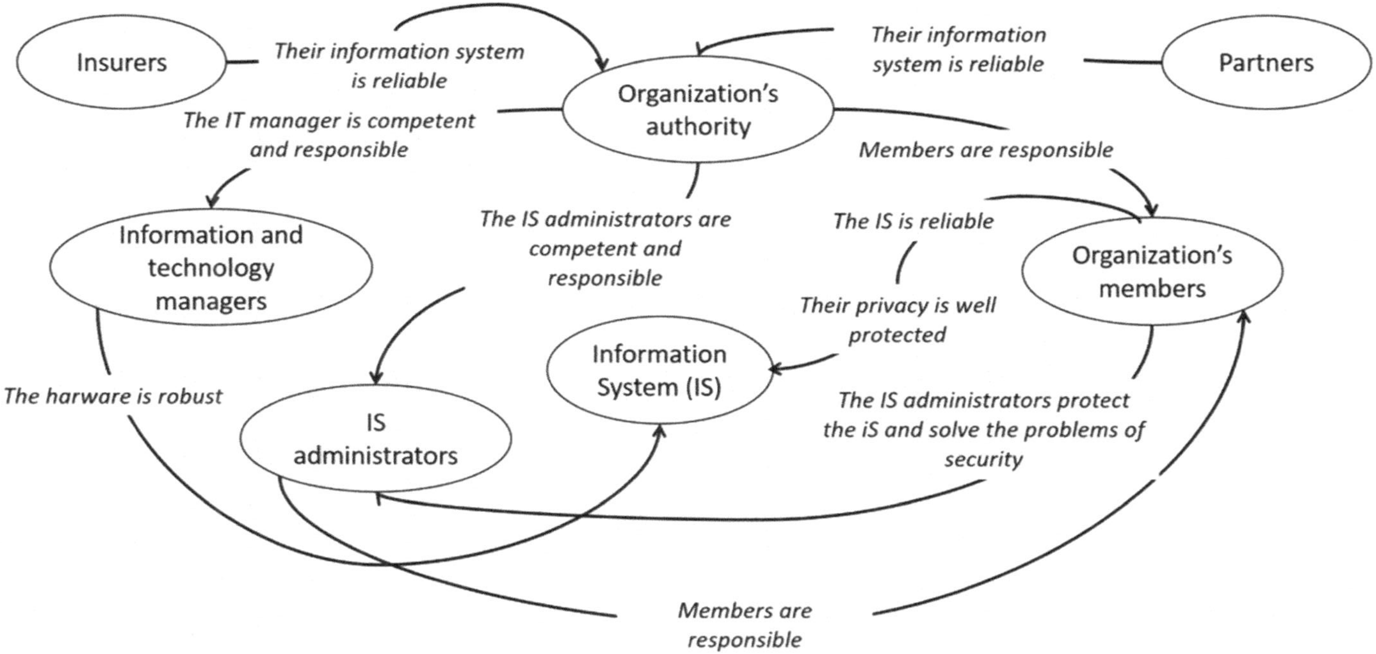

Fig. 3 The multiplicity of trusting agents, trusted parties, and expectations with regard to an organization's information system (adapted from Rajaonah 2017, p. 117)

at least they may believe the attackers would spare them (but not the others), who knows!

The main hypothesis could, therefore, be that users of ISs may be intentionally harmful because their trust in technology, people, and themselves is not well calibrated, as well as, corollary, they are too much optimistic.

Let us review some results in the field of psychology, which could justify that hypothesis.

(a) Optimism. People tend to be naturally toward optimistic, which is namely the bias of unrealistic optimism: Weinstein (1980) shows that people tend to believe that positive events are more likely to happen to them than to others, and that negative events are less likely to happen to them than to others. That is true in the situation of risk in which people tend to believe that they are less exposed to risk than others are, which has consequences on their decisions and behaviours (e.g. Lench and Bench 2012; Slovic et al. 1984). It can be thus supposed that their optimism leads them to be excessively trustful with regard to security, which includes attackers: in their natural optimism, individuals may fail to consider that they could be a target for attackers.
(b) Lack of awareness and knowledge. Optimistic bias could be partly explained by a lack of awareness and/or knowledge about objective risks. Sasse and Flechais (2005) notice that organizations' members tend to lack of understanding of information security issues and of how their behaviours could be a threat against security. As shown in the EY's Global Information Security Survey 2015 (EY 2015), employees are often careless and unaware of cybersecurity. It is thus a fact that those people are not aware that they are potentially harmful to the organization's information security. It can be then assumed that the lack of awareness and knowledge contributes to induce excessive optimism and trust with regard to security.
(c) Self-confidence and illusion of control. The illusion of control had been described in the 1970s as being "an expectancy of a personal success probability inappropriately higher than the objective probability would warrant" (Langer 1975, p. 311). More simply, the illusion of control is the tendency to believe that we have the ability to control events (who has never blown on the dice before throwing them?). Self-efficacy is a closely related concept: perceived self-efficacy is the people's belief in their efficacy to influence events that affect their lives (Bandura 1997). There is, therefore, a tendency for people to be naturally confident in their own abilities to master the situation. Despite their lack of awareness and knowledge, it can be assumed that organizations' members are over-confident in their skills to deal with information security, and that may also be true concerning that personal data (Akhter 2014). It can also be assumed that their over-confidence leads them to minimize security issues, or even believe that attackers could not reach them.
(d) Responsibility. Organizations' employees tend to believe that security is the matter of the others (e.g. Hadlington 2018). In other words, they do not consider cybersecurity as a shared issue. It can thus be assumed that they prefer being

excessively trustful towards organizations' authorities and IS's administrators than questioning their own attitudes and behaviours.

Optimistic bias, lack of awareness and knowledge, the illusion of control, and misplaced responsibility could be good reasons for ISs users to be excessively trustful regarding security and then constitute insider threats. We propose an approach that would categorize these users through an analysis of *their* good reasons.

3 Proposition: Studying Insider Threats with the Factor of Trust

The objective of this section is to propose to investigate the plausibility of explaining insider threats with the factor of trust. This proposition consists in (1) collecting information about trust, attitudes, and behaviours of knowledge sharers, and (2) categorizing this information into meaningful units that could be related to different levels of insider threats. The section begins with the techniques of interview and questionnaire used in social sciences and then explains the technique of ontology used in computer sciences.

3.1 Interviews and Self-Report Questionnaires to Collect Information About Trust

We propose to start by gathering information from the three-part circle of ISs security from the perspective of the users' trust, namely, the organization' authority, the IS administrators, and the simple users (not experts). The techniques used will be interviews and self-report questionnaires.

Interviews are used to collect focused and qualitative data and are particularly relevant to obtain information about participants' experiences and viewpoints (Turner 2010). This author distinguishes (a) the informal conversational interviews that lack of structure allows interviews to be flexible, (b) the general interview guide approach in which questions may be adapted to the respondents during the interview in order to collect the desired information, and (c) the standardized open-ended interviews that focus the answers on specific questions.

As for self-report questionnaires, they could be used to gather both qualitative and quantitative data. They are perfect to gather opinions and measure attitudes (Grawitz 1993). The main advantage of closed questionnaires is that they are economic in the sense that the same questionnaire can be completed by thousands of people. Open questions allow to collect in-depth answers because answers are not constrained, but their analysis is rather complex because of the heterogeneity of the collected information. Closed questions structure the answers with preset responses, which facilitate data analysis, especially when there are hundreds or thousands of participants. Another advantage of closed questions is that they can provide quantitative information through ordinal data.

We propose to use standardized open-ended interviews and self-report questionnaires based on closed questions. The techniques used depend on the kind of information which we desire, and thus on the targeted respondents in one or more organization(s). The participation of end users of an organization's information system is, therefore, the main prerequisite.

Interviews, the first step, are used to collect information from authorities and administrators in the form of face-to-face open-ended interviews focused on the organization members' attitudes and behaviours concerning information security from the experience and viewpoints of authorities and administrators. The interviews could be carried out individually or with a staff of more than one individual (it is then similar to a focus group). Preliminary questions that would be the same for each respondent would be prepared, but the responses will be open to not constrain the respondents. The main questions will be related to the basic rules that are communicated to the users and the means of communication; the users' self-reported behaviours and underlying attitudes; their trust in the users; their categorization of the users, as well as the different levels of the user's harmfulness; etc. The data analysis will be performed by at least two researchers to avoid biases of interpretation. The results will be used to build the questionnaire survey dedicated to the users.

The next step (self-report questionnaires) aims to collect information from the organization's non-expert members (i.e., neither technicians nor engineers working on the organization's IS) in the form of a closed questionnaire survey. Apart from the demographics, each question will be evaluated using the visual analogical scale (VAS) in order to get both qualitative and quantitative information. For example, see Muir and Moray (1996) who used 100 mm scales to measure self-reported trust in automated systems. The VAS relies on the premise that, in our case, the variables investigated through the questionnaire's items are continuous variables, which is the case for attitudes that can thus be directly measured. Consequently, the use of such a scale will enable to carry out correlation analysis in order to relate users' level of trust to the strength of their good reasons to trust or distrust, as well as to carry out statistical inference analyses if necessary. Even though the questionnaire will be built according to the information collected at the previous step, the items will necessarily investigate the users' opinions, attitudes, and behaviours toward information security and data privacy, as well as their related level of self-confidence, their perceptions of cyber-risk, their awareness and knowledge about cybersecurity, etc. Clustering analysis will be carried out complementary to the correlation analysis in order to provide information for the development of the ontology that takes the categorization of the users accordingly to their degree of harmfulness into account.

3.2 Ontologies to Categorize Information About Trust

Ontology is a description of entities and their properties, relationships, and constraints expressed via axioms (Grüninger and Fox 1995). Domain ontologies (Guarino 1998) express conceptualizations that are specific for a particular domain (e.g. transportation, family organization, risks management). They put constraints on the structure and contents of domain knowledge. For instance, when talking about family, one can say that a child must have at least a parent.

Ontologies may serve to various purposes in the context of knowledge management (Anquetil et al. 2007):

- Reference on a domain—Made explicit knowledge serves as a reference to which people, looking for detailed information on the domain modelled, may use.
- Classification framework—The concepts made explicit in an ontology are a good way to categorize information on the domain modelled. Indication of synonyms in the ontology helps to avoid duplicate classification. Other relations among the concepts of the ontology help one browsing it and finding the information one is looking for.
- Interlingua—Tools and/or experts wishing to share information on the domain modelled, may use the ontology as a common base to resolve differing terminologies.

Several works on ontology about security and trust can be found in the literature. We quote, for instance, the proposition of Viljanen (2005), Huang and Fox (2006), and Fenz and Ekelhart (2009).

Viljanen (2005) analyzed 13 trust models to identify the main features of trust considered in which one of them. As a result, they assumed that the union of these features across all models provides a list of trust input factors. These factors were, in turn, organized in an initial ontology. This initial ontology considers only concepts, and no axiom was defined.

Huang and Fox (2006) also defined an ontology, but focused on transitivity issuers. They discuss that the use of web application implies the need for trust between entities (sometimes unfamiliar or unknown) that interacts with each other. They argue that social networks have been proposed as a remedy to assure trust in the web; however, as a consequence, trust needs to be transitive. They proposed, therefore, a formal ontology that explicit the semantics for trust transitivity.

Fenz and Ekelhart (2009) have proposed a large ontology that organizes the knowledge about information security. Their goal is to support and enhance risk management approaches. To that end, they reuse some known taxonomies in the domain of security and telecommunication.

All these works deal with the concepts of trust and security separately in ontology models. Developing an ontology using Protégé,[1] for example relies on basic steps that are described below from Noy and McGuinness (2010):

---

[1] https://protege.stanford.edu

(a) Determining the domain and scope of the ontology through basic questions is first required:

1. What is the domain covered by the ontology? A domain is the representation of a part of the reality. Here, the objective is to represent the role of organizational members' trust in IS's security threats. The domain will thus cover IS security and an individual's trust in organizations.
2. What is the use of the ontology? The ontology will allow the researchers to categorize the users of an organization's IS in terms of their potentiality to be insider threats; the ontology will be thus useful to the IS's administrators, technicians, and engineers to design countermeasures and develop targeted information to the organization's members.
3. For what questions the information in the ontology should provide answers? These questions could be about the good reasons of organizations' member to trust or distrust their organization's IS, other Internet-connected systems, their colleagues, and the IS's managers, but also about their perceptions of cyber-risk; their level of awareness, knowledge, and practice, as well as their level of self-confidence, concerning their skills regarding cybersecurity.
4. What are the competency questions, that is that the ontology should be able to answer? The competency questions will be defined from the answers to the interviews and self-report questionnaires. Nevertheless, the ontology should be able to provide information about the relevant dimensions of the trust of IS's users in terms of cybersecurity, as well as the relationships between these dimensions and the potentiality of the users to be insider threats.

(b) Considering reusing other ontologies could be useful: A state of the art of existing ontologies related to the domains of cybersecurity (e.g. Oltramari et al. 2015) and of trust (e.g. Viljanen 2005) will be necessarily carried out, even before defining the competency questions in order to make sure that the proposed ontology will be useful for the purpose and/or even enrich the existing ones.
(c) Defining the important terms of the ontology, as well as the related concepts: This needs expert knowledge about knowledge sharing, information system, trust, and psychology (considering that being or not being trustful is a matter of cognitive and social psychology). The terms and related concepts should be cover those of the questions defined in the first step, as well as of their expected responses.
(d) Defining classes (or concepts) and arranging them in a taxonomic hierarchy: The objective of the ontology is to categorize organization's users in order to provide appropriate information and countermeasures to potential insider threats. We can rely on the bottom-up development process described in Noy and McGuinness (2010) by starting from the results of the analyses of correlation and clustering, that is to say from the categories of users related to the degrees of their harmfulness to finish at the level of the most general concepts.

(e) The next steps before developing the ontology are to define the properties of classes and sets of properties (slots), as well as the values of the properties. Such properties may be defined from the clusters obtained during the previous step.

In doing so, developing an ontology creates knowledge. In our case, trust, insider threats, and security will contribute to the ontology. Information about trust collected through interviews and self-report questionnaires will answer and refine the competency questions raised during ontology definition. Some success indicators are the number of respondents who will accept to be interviewed and the number of respondents in the survey. Such indicators, as well as identified risks, are now discussed.

3.3 *Discussion*

Although it seems obvious that trust and security are two concepts that are intrinsically associated, since the trust that a user has in a system depends, among other factors, on the security that it provides, explicitly associating these concepts is not trivial and very challenging. It requires an analysis from different points of view (social, psychological, managerial, and technical), implying a multidisciplinary team. It is also challenging to define an ontological model that represents the theory on the subject but also the contexts and intents of knowledge sharers. Focusing the study on insider threats leads to deal with probably untapped issues in the case of knowledge sharing.

Nevertheless, based on our goals and on the chosen method, we identify the following problems that may occur to carry out the investigation study:

(a) Conflict relating to intellectual property, regarding access and use of research results—This risk may appear if several institutions participate in the study. To mitigate this risk, we recommend to predefine types of protection and exploitation of results that will be formally signed by all participants in an intellectual property agreement at the beginning of the project. In the case of students integrating the project, we recommend that they also are asked to sign this agreement.
(b) Risk related to data collection (not secure, lost, unverified)—Interviews and self-report questionnaires to collect information about trust are planned. The results of these surveys will be used in the ontology definition. Survey data may risk of being accessed and modified, lost or unverified to assure its provenance and correctness of the collection procedures. To mitigate this risk, we recommend the use for the survey of a well-known platform from one of the partners.
(c) Breach of confidentiality—This risk is related to the need for validation of the study with real cases from industry. A formal agreement of confidentiality has to be signed by the industry and the consortium representatives. In this agreement, it will be clearly defined what can be disclosed or not about the study carried out.

As the reader may understand, this chapter focuses not only on knowledge sharing, which already is a sensitive field of study, but also on trust, insider threats and security. We have observed within industrial fields that it is extremely hard to obtain access to the research material needed for such a study, i.e. knowledge sharers accepting any interview or self-report questionnaire. We are currently experiencing ethnographic workplace study in the sense of Jordan (1996) to mitigate such a reserve from industrial partners.

4 Conclusion

Nowadays, hacking digital artefacts supporting ISs is more a militarist and intellectual exercise than an optimized crime. Through procedures, code fragments, and infrastructures with known, managed, and rational behaviours, the digital part of ISs has been secured and may now be trustworthy. Moreover, ISs also contain a human part leading us to focus on a certain category of threats that are no longer outside organizations; their firewalls being efficient, threats do no longer target digital artefacts and computers which have become too safe. In this chapter, we argued that threats might be human and inside organizations and particularly during knowledge sharing processes. In other words, we defend that the biggest threat to an organization's IS does not come from outside. It is often due to internal factors, whether intentionally or not. Organizations will be, are, and/or have already been confronted with attacks coming from their own employees, users of their information system. Attacked organizations are not always aware of having been attacked, and when they are aware of having been attacked, they do not always report it. Among these internal factors, which are unfortunately exploited by hackers to carry out attacks, one can mention the lack of awareness among knowledge sharers of certain practices. For example, to override increasingly effective security systems against external attacks, new methods of attacks based on social engineering are more and more being implemented. They use the internal staff of an organization as an attack vector. One can also mention the uncontrolled use of access rights and privileges that are sometimes attributed in little rigorous to certain knowledge sharers who thus become potential vectors of attacks against the IS security.

These attacks use all means contributing to the functioning of the organization, including e-mail, smartphones/tablets, and social media. As a consequence, these attacks deal with several issues: social (e.g. interrelationship among employees and their managers), economic (e.g. financial loss), regulatory (e.g. non-respect or non-existence of adequate policies of the organization), and industrial (e.g. security of industry objectives).

In order to defend against attacks inherent to the human factor, and from the technical point of view, one needs to identify the vectors, the attack surfaces, the agents used to perpetrate these attacks and the possible internal attackers. We argue that cognitive processes, as well as organizational contexts, influence the ways security may be trusted during knowledge sharing processes.

References

Akhter SH (2014) Privacy concern and online transactions: the impact of Internet self-efficacy and Internet involvement. J Consum Mark 31(2):118–125

Anquetil N, Oliveira KM, De Souza KD, Dias M (2007) Software maintenance seen as a knowledge management issue. Inf Softw Technol 49(5):515–529

Arduin P-E (2018) Insider threats. Wiley-ISTE, Hoboken, NJ

Arduin P-E, Grundstein M, Rosenthal-Sabroux C (2015) Information and knowledge system. Wiley-ISTE, Hoboken, NJ

Bandura A (1997) Perceived self-efficacy: the exercise of control. W.H. Freeman/Times Books/ Henry Holt, New York, NY

Canohoto AI, Dibb S, Simkin L, Quinn L, Analogbei M (2015) Preparing for the future—how managers perceive, interpret and assess the impact of digital technologies for business. In: Proceedings of the 48th Hawaii international conference on system sciences

Castelfranchi C, Falcone R (2000) Trust is much more than subjective probability: mental components and sources of trust. In: Sprague RH (ed) Proceedings of the 33rd annual Hawaii international conference on system sciences, 7 January 2000, Maui, HI. IEEE, Piscataway, NJ

Collwill C (2009) Human-factors in information security: the insider-threat—who can we trust these days? Inf Secur Tech Rep 14:186–196

Dhillon G, Backhouse J (2000) Technical opinion: information system security management in the new millennium. Commun ACM 43(7):125–128

EY (2015) Creating trust in the digital world. Global Information Security Survey (GISS) 2015. https://www.ey.com/Publication/vwLUAssets/ey-global-information-security-survey-2015/$FILE/ey-global-information-security-survey-2015.pdf. Accessed 6 May 2019

Fenz S, Ekelhart A (2009) Formalizing information security knowledge. In: Proceedings of the 4th international symposium on information, computer, and communications security, pp 183–194

Grawitz M (1993) Méthodes des sciences sociales [Methods in social sciences], 9th éd. Dalloz, Paris

Grüninger M, Fox MS (1995) Methodology for the design and evaluation of ontologies, technical report. University of Toronto, Toronto

Guarino N (ed) (1998) Formal ontology in information systems. In: Proceedings of FOIS'98, Trento

Guo KH, Yuan Y, Archer NP, Connelly CE (2011) Understanding non-malicious security violations in the workplace: a composite behavior model. J Manag Inf Syst 28(2):203–236

Hadlington L (2018) The 'human factor' in cybersecurity: exploring the accidental insider. In: McAlaney J, Frumkin LA, Benson V (eds) Psychological and behavioral examinations in cyber security. IGI Global, Hershey, PA, pp 46–63

Hardin R (2001) Conceptions and explanations of trust. In: Cook KS (ed) Trust in society. Russell Sage Foundation, New York, pp 3–39

Hoffman RR, Johnson M, Bradshaw JM, Underbrink A (2013) Trust in automation. IEEE Intell Syst 28(1):84–88

Huang J, Fox MS (2006) An ontology of trust—formal semantics and transitivity. ICEC 6:259–270

ISO/IEC (2013) ISO/IEC 27001, information security management. Technical report

Jian JY, Bisantz AM, Drury CG (2000) Foundations for an empirically determined scale of trust in automated systems. Int J Cogn Ergon 4(1):53–71

Jordan B (1996) The design of computer-supported cooperative work and groupware systems. In: Ethnographic workplace studies and computer supported cooperative work. Elsevier Science, North Holland, pp 17–42

Kaspersky (2015) Carbanak APT—the great bank robbery, Kaspersky Lab Report, February 2015. https://securelist.com/files/2015/02/Carbanak_APT_eng.pdf

Keeney M, Kowalski E, Cappelli D, Moore A, Shimeall T, Rogers S (2005) Insider threat study: computer systems sabotage in critical infrastructure sectors. CERT, Software Engineering Institute, Carnegie Mellon University

Kramer RM (1999) Trust and distrust in organizations: emerging perspectives, enduring questions. Annu Rev Psychol 50(1):568–598

Landauer TK (1996) The trouble with computers: usefulness, usability, and productivity. MIT Press, Cambridge, MA

Langer EJ (1975) The illusion of control. J Pers Soc Psychol 32(2):311–328

Lee JD, See KA (2004) Trust in automation: designing for appropriate reliance. Hum Factors 46 (1):50–80

Lench HC, Bench SW (2012) Automatic optimism: why people assume their futures will be bright. Soc Personal Psychol Compass 6(4):347–360

Lewis JD, Weigert AJ (2012) The social dynamics of trust: theoretical and empirical research, 1985–2012. Soc Forces 91(1):25–31

Loch K, Carr H, Warkentin M (1992) Threats to information systems: today's reality, yesterday's understanding. MIS Q 16(2):173–186

Luhmann N (2000) Familiarity, confidence, trust: problems and alternatives. In: Gambetta D (ed) Trust: making and breaking cooperative relations. Department of Sociology, University of Oxford, pp 94–107. http://www.sociology.ox.ac.uk/papers/luhmann94-107.pdf. Accessed 6 May 2019

Mitnick KD, Simon WL (2011) The art of deception: controlling the human element of security. Wiley, Indianapolis, IN

Möllering G (2001) The nature of trust: from Georg Simmel to a theory of expectation, interpretation and suspension. Sociology 35(2):403–420

Muir BM (1987) Trust between humans and machines, and the design of decision aids. Int J Man Mach Stud 27(5–6):527–539

Muir BM, Moray N (1996) Trust in automation. Part II. Experimental studies of trust and human intervention in a process control simulation. *Ergonomics* 39(3):429–460

Noy NF, McGuinness DL (2010) Ontology development 101: a guide to creating your first ontology. University Stanford, Stanford, CA. https://protege.stanford.edu/publications/ontology_development/ontology101.pdf. Accessed 6 May 2019

Oltramari A, Henshel D, Cains M, Hoffman B (2015) Towards a human factors ontology for cyber security. In: Proceedings of tenth international conference on semantic technology for intelligence, defense, and security, 18–20 November 2015, Fairfax, VA, pp 26–33. http://ceur-ws.org/Vol-1523/STIDS_2015_T04_Oltramari_etal.pdf. Accessed 6 May 2019

Polanyi M (1967) Sense-giving and sense-reading. Philosophy 42(162):301–325

PwC (2018) The global state of information security® survey 2018—strengthening digital society against cyber shocks. PriceWaterhouseCoopers report

Rajaonah B (2017) A view of trust and information system security under the perspective of critical infrastructure protection. Ing Syst Inf 22(1):109–133

Sasse MA, Flechais I (2005) Usable security: why do we need it? How do we get it? In: Cranor L, Garfinkel S (eds) Security and usability: designing secure systems that people can use. O'ReillyMedia, Sebastopol, CA, pp 13–30

Schneier B (2000) The process of security. Inform Secur 3(4):32

Shropshire J (2009) A canonical analysis of intentional information security breaches by insiders. Inf Manag Comput Secur 17(4):296–310

Slovic P, Fischhoff B, Lichtenstein S (1984) Behavioral decision theory perspectives on risk and safety. Acta Psychol 56(1–3):183–203

Stanton JM, Stam KR, Mastrangelo P, Jolton J (2005) Analysis of end user security behaviors. Comput Secur 24(2):124–133

Tsuchiya S (1993) Improving knowledge creation ability through organizational learning. In: ISMICK 1993: proceedings of the international symposium on the management of industrial and corporate knowledge, pp 87–95

Turner DW (2010) Qualitative interview design: a practical guide for novice investigators. Qual Rep 15(3):754–760

Viljanen L (2005) Towards an ontology of trust. In: Katsikas S, López J, Pernul G (eds) Trust, privacy, and security in digital business. TrustBus 2005. Lecture Notes in Computer Science, 3592. Springer, Berlin, pp 175–184

Weinstein ND (1980) Unrealistic optimism about future life events. J Pers Soc Psychol 39 (5):806–820

Whitman ME, Mattord HJ (2011) Principles of information security, 4th edn. Cengage Learning, Mason, OH

Willison R, Warkentin M (2013) Beyond deterrence: an expanded view of employee computer abuse. MIS Q 37:1–20

Sustainable Corporate Development: A Resource-Oriented Approach

Ronald Orth, Holger Kohl, and Mila Galeitzke

Abstract Sustainable corporate development can be understood as a strategy that respects not only economic goals but also environmental and social aspects, weigh against each other and thus, ensures the long-term business success. The number of enterprises that are oriented towards corporate sustainability has increased in recent years, but the implementation still encounters a variety of limits. The goal of this chapter is the development of an integrated approach to foster sustainable development on the corporate level. In this context, not only tangible resources (e.g. raw material, energy or machines) but in particular intangible resources (e.g. expertise and professional competence of the employees, corporate culture or relations with stakeholders) are considered key success factors for a sustainable corporate development. For its application, the integrated approach provides a set of instruments and procedures, which can be used for the purpose of analysis, planning, controlling and reporting of sustainable corporate development.

1 Introduction

Against the background of current societal challenges, such as the increase in the world population, globalisation, climate change and digital transformation, the principle of sustainability is widely respected in the public, political and economic spheres. In a recently published reflection paper, the EU Commission calls the UN's Sustainable Development Goals (SDGs) a compass. With the help of these goals, Europe should be able to achieve strong economic growth in the future. Business success is to be achieved through innovations in sustainability and the transformation of companies or even entire sectors. Complex environmental

R. Orth (✉) · M. Galeitzke
Fraunhofer Institute for Production Systems and Design Technology, Berlin, Germany
e-mail: ronald.orth@ipk.fraunhofer.de; mila.galeitzke@ipk.fraunhofer.de

H. Kohl
Technical University Berlin, Berlin, Germany
e-mail: holger.kohl@tu-berlin.de

F. Matos et al. (eds.), *Knowledge, People, and Digital Transformation*, Contributions to Management Science, https://doi.org/10.1007/978-3-030-40390-4_12

challenges require new technologies and new business solutions (European Commission [EC] 2019).

The number of companies oriented towards sustainability principles has increased continuously in recent years. Studies have identified different drivers for this dynamic. These include, for example changing customer requirements, employee expectations and legal framework conditions as well as increasing environmental responsibility (Berns et al. 2009; UN Global Compact and Accenture 2013). Sustainable management also increases social acceptance, secures the (social) status of the company among relevant stakeholders and is increasingly incorporated into the financial valuation of the company by the capital market (Eccles et al. 2010; International Integrated Reporting Council [IIRC] 2013).

Sustainable corporate development aims to secure the long-term existence of a company under a set of requirements for this existence. The path of sustainable corporate development must be defined specifically for each company. Against the background of the respective framework conditions, business processes and value drivers, it is necessary to determine the success factors relevant to sustainability and to show how these can be measured and controlled. The principal assumption here is that an effective and efficient use of resources is key to improving the sustainability performance of companies. In addition to the careful use of tangible resources (e.g. raw materials, energy and machines), intangible resources (e.g. knowledge and skills of employees, trust or innovation capabilities) in particular are regarded as central success factors for the implementation of sustainable development.

In order to act sustainably, companies must be aware of their strengths and weaknesses and derive targeted options for action from them. This requires a transparent assessment of financial and non-financial issues. The approach provides pragmatic decision-making support for management and instruments, techniques and procedures that can be used to enhance corporate management systems, taking economic, environmental and social objectives into account. The approach also supports corporate reporting, in particular, to meet the increased information needs of different stakeholder groups. For this reason, the approach also aims to link the internal management of the company with its external communication.

2 Basic Principles of Sustainable Management

Sustainable development at the societal level can only be achieved if companies make a corresponding contribution at the firm level: Companies provide jobs and determine an essential part of the quality of life through working conditions. Furthermore, they have a considerable influence on the natural environment and contribute significantly to the economic growth of an economy (Promberger et al. 2006).

The activities of companies that contribute to implementing the sustainability principle at the corporate level are discussed under the term “sustainable management". The Verein Deutscher Ingenieure (VDI) Guideline 4070 defines the term as a "type of management with the goal of developing economic success while maintaining environmental sustainability and encouraging social justice, to be practised and improved upon over the long term". The three dimensions of sustainable management and their relation to each other are outlined below (Verein Deutscher Ingenieure [VDI] 2016, p. 4).

Economic Dimension From an economic perspective, the primary entrepreneurial task is to achieve the most positive economic results possible, the consideration of which is particularly rooted in classical business administration thinking (Schaltegger 2013). In the sense of sustainable economic development at the company level, the objectives of action are to secure the long-term existence of the company, to maintain competitiveness and innovation, and to achieve healthy growth with appropriate surpluses (Drenk 2009). Efficient use of energy and raw materials can, for example help to reduce production costs and thus improve the company's revenue situation. However, also, the reduction of company risks (e.g. by avoiding environmental pollution and child labour) can help to avoid potential economic disadvantages (Kölle 2008). Furthermore, sustainable products and services open up the possibility of developing new customers or business fields (Cocca and Meiren 2013).

Environmental Dimension At the company level, "environmental effectiveness" is the central benchmark for assessing how well a company meets the environmental sustainability criteria. In addition to reducing the use of energy, water and materials, this also includes the development and implementation of technical innovations that reduce the use of resources or lead to greater use of renewable resources (Kölle 2008). Further fields of action in the environmental dimension of sustainability include minimising risks for people and the environment (e.g. through sustainable product design), responsible handling of ecosystems and the environmental compatibility of products and processes (e.g. by installing filter systems) (Drenk 2009).

Social Dimension The social sustainability perspective emphasises that companies are an essential part of the society. It applies to companies in the way that they fulfil their social responsibility in particular if they reduce the socially undesirable effects of their actions and promote positive social effects (Schröder 2011). Companies should take into account the needs of internal and external stakeholder groups that are in contact with the organisation (Deutsches Institut für Normung [DIN] 2011). The internal perspective of the social sustainability dimension includes, in particular, the following fields of action (Drenk 2009): providing and securing jobs, promoting occupational safety and health and involving employees in company decisions. Furthermore, equal rights, employee-friendly working models, the compatibility of family and career as well as the promotion of training and education are counted among this internal perspective. Central elements of the external perspective of the social sustainability dimension are, for example cooperation with stakeholders, an open information policy and compliance (Schaltegger 2013).

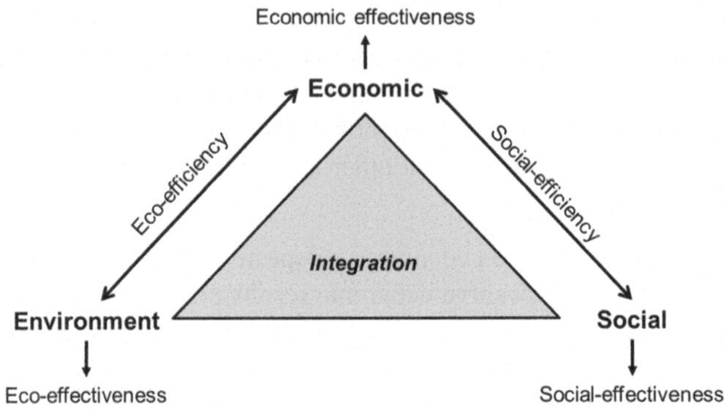

Fig. 1 The sustainability challenges for companies (based on Schaltegger et al. 2007, modified)

Integration Challenges of Sustainable Management At the centre of a holistic understanding of sustainability on an operational level is a company's ability to meet economic, environmental and social performance criteria in order to secure its long-term success. A closer look reveals that the three dimensions influence each other. These interdependencies must be taken into account in decision-making processes and weighed up against each other (Fig. 1). In this process, companies are exposed to potential conflicts of objectives: On the one hand, the aim is to increase the effectiveness in the individual dimensions; on the other hand, the dimensions must not be viewed in isolation from each other (Schaltegger et al. 2007).

In this context, effectiveness aims at the absolute reduction or minimisation of negative environmental, economic and social impact of the company (Schaltegger et al. 2007) or increasing the positive effects, respectively. Consequently, effectiveness constitutes the normative requirement to adapt or develop strategies and objectives (Stahlmann and Clausen 1999). At the level of this content-related integration perspective, the consideration of eco- and social efficiency represents a possibility to shed more light on the interrelationships between the sustainability dimensions. These efficiency criteria describe the relationships between the use of resources and the result or degree to which objectives have been achieved (Onischka et al. 2011). Eco-efficiency refers to the economic value added in relation to the ecological impact that results from the production of products or services (e.g. the amount of energy consumed). It is defined as the relationship between economic, monetary units, and a physical (environmental) quantity (Schaltegger et al. 2007). The same applies to social-efficiency, which describes the relationship between social benefit or harm (e.g. number of accidents at work or sick days) and the value added by an organisation. The following formulas use examples to show how eco- and social efficiency can be calculated. Measures that improve the relationship between monetary value added and ecological or social impacts contribute to increasing eco- or social efficiency (Kaldschmidt 2009; Onischka et al. 2011).

$$\text{eco}-\text{efficiency}=\frac{\text{Economic value of a product or service (e.g.added value in €)}}{\text{Influence or impact on the environment (e.g.energy used in kWh)}}$$

$$\text{social}-\text{efficiency}=\frac{\text{Economic value of a product or service (e.g.added value in €)}}{\text{Influence or impact on society (e.g.number of accidents at work)}}$$

In addition to the content-related integration challenge described above, i.e. the simultaneous consideration of the requirements described with regard to effectiveness and efficiency in the three sustainability dimensions, there is a further challenge at the instrumental level. This instrumental-related integration challenge consists in embedding environmental and social management methodically into the traditional economic-oriented management system. Schaltegger et al. (2007) see this as the central goal of sustainable development at the company level, i.e. the coordinated consideration of all challenges and the merging of conventional management with the management of sustainability aspects to form an integrative sustainability management.

3 Reference Model for Sustainable Corporate Development

The above-outlined concept of the three dimensions is often used to describe sustainable management in an organisational context. At the centre of this holistic understanding of sustainability is the ability of companies to meet economic, environmental and social performance criteria.

In this chapter, companies are seen as resource-dependent systems (Pfeffer and Salancik 2003). In order to ensure the long-term existence of the company, securing resources is a central task of sustainable corporate development. As a result, it is necessary to systematically manage the resource base and invest in its preservation (Müller-Christ 2010). Resources are means of action that are used or can be used to achieve objectives (Verein Deutscher Ingenieure [VDI] 2014). While the resource perspective thus spans the design framework at the company level, the sustainability concept provides the corresponding yardstick and criteria for assessing the handling of tangible and intangible resources.

Against this background, the Sustainable Corporate Development (SCD) reference model follows the logic of the system-oriented models and distinguishes between an internal and an external perspective with a permeable system–environment boundary. As shown in Fig. 2, the model describes three central elements of sustainable enterprise development and their interaction. Accordingly, resources are used within business processes to achieve results.

The basic assumptions and main elements of the SCD reference model are outlined below.

System–Environment Relationship Companies are to be understood as open systems that are in a permanent exchange of resources with their external

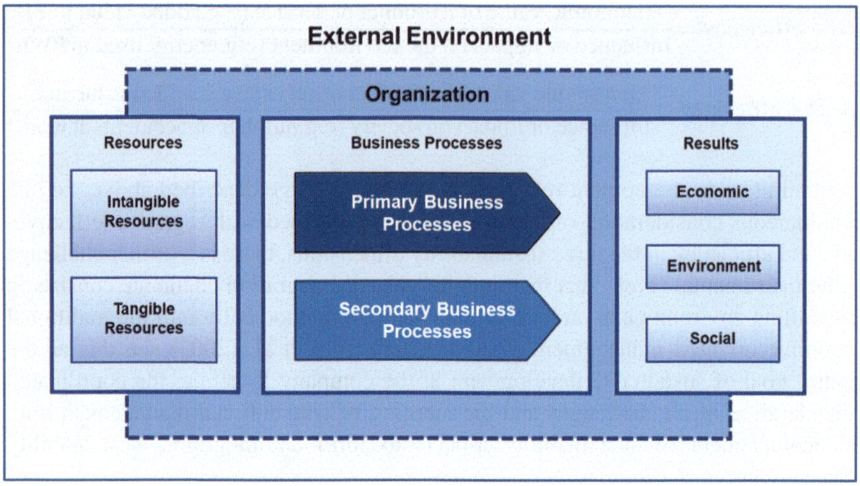

Fig. 2 Fraunhofer reference model for sustainable corporate development

environment. They must secure their inflow of resources from the environment and at the same time, make sensible use of them within their business operations. Due to the permeable system–environment boundary, there are further interfaces to the external environment on the company results side. Organisations are, therefore, integrated into a socio-economic context in which the use or management of resources simultaneously influences their own and society's resource base.

Resources Based on the SCD reference model, the resources used by the company to create value can be divided into tangible and intangible resources. The resources are differentiated on the basis of six types of capital.[1] For the classification of tangible resources, a distinction is made between the dimensions of financial capital, manufactured capital and natural capital. Intangible resources are divided into human, structural and relational capital. From the perspective of the resource-based view of the firm, it is the intangible resources in particular that create lasting competitive advantages for companies (Peteraf 1993; Wernerfelt 1984). These resources have a company-specific component, cannot usually be obtained via the classic factor markets (e.g. capital or raw materials market) and can, therefore, be only built up internally by companies (Barney 1991).

Business Processes In order for organisations to be able to act effectively, different tasks must be linked to one another and merged across functions. According to ISO 9000, a group of activities that uses resources to enable input to be converted into

[1]Various concepts are used in the sustainability literature to operationalize the concept of resources at company level. Some authors use so-called capital approaches (e.g. IIRC 2013; SIGMA 2003; White 2010). Also in the discussion about intellectual capital, intangible resources in particular are divided into different types of capital (e.g. Alwert et al. 2013; Edvinsson and Malone 1997).

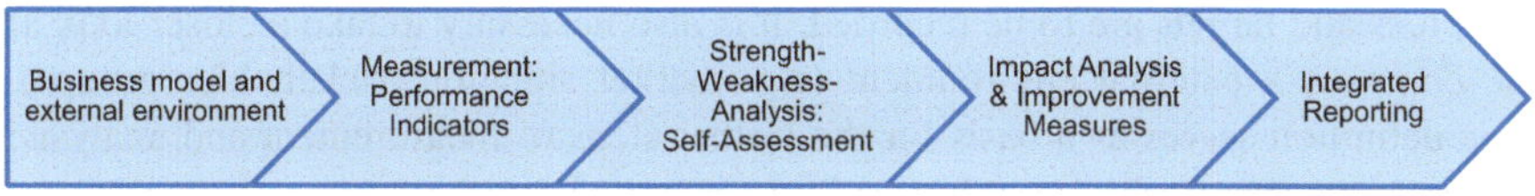

Fig. 3 Procedure model: process and instruments for fostering corporate sustainability

results is understood as a process (Deutsches Institut für Normung [DIN] 2015). In the context of this work, a distinction is made between primary and secondary business processes based on Schmelzer and Sesselmann (2013). Primary business processes serve the operational production of goods and services and form the foundation of a company's value creation. Secondary business processes serve to control and support primary business processes (ibid.).

Results (Sustainability Performance) Results are achieved through the use of resources in processes (DIN 2015). In accordance with the understanding of sustainable management presented in Sect. 2, the following three perspectives are used to measure the company's sustainability performance: (1) Economic perspective (financial results), (2) Environmental perspective (environmental impact) and (3) Social perspective (employee-related and social results). It is also important for companies to set targets or specifications in the individual perspectives. Interactions between the dimensions must be considered as well (Socio-Efficiency and Eco-Efficiency).

4 Implementation Procedure

The reference model outlined above is supplemented by a procedure model. This procedure model aims at providing clear assistance to companies in their sustainable corporate development and describes the most important steps of the application (Fig. 3). Along with the individual steps of the procedure model, appropriate instruments are provided that can be used for the analysis, planning, control and reporting of sustainable corporate development. Companies can use the instruments to expand existing management systems or to set up an independent management system for sustainable corporate development.

The five respective steps of the procedure model for the fostering of a sustainable corporate development are described in the following sections.

4.1 Business Model and External Environment

The path of sustainable corporate development must be specified for each company against the background of its internal and external framework conditions. The aim of the first step is to capture the company-specific initial situation. First, the goals and strategy of the company are to be described, and the central business processes, resources and targets are to be recorded. It is also necessary to take a closer look at the company's external environment (e.g. market situation, stakeholder groups). This definition serves as a basis for the further steps of measurement and analysis. Furthermore, the results are to be used for integrated reporting.

Regarding the capture, guiding questions for the determination of the business model and the external environment are provided along with the relevant elements of the SCD reference model.

Organisational Overview and Corporate Objectives

Selected data must be documented for an initial classification of the company. Here it is also necessary to specify the purpose, objectives and central values of the company. The following guiding questions can be used for this purpose:

- What is the self-conception of our company (e.g. vision, mission)?
- Which central values guide our actions?
- What goals do we want to achieve in the short, medium and long term in the areas of the economy, environment and social affairs?

External Environment and Stakeholders

The external environment of the organisation consists of the task environment and the macro environment. This gives rise to opportunities and risks that have an impact on the development of the company. In this context, it is important to identify relevant stakeholders of the company and to assess their expectations.

For a more detailed description of the task environment, the following key questions must be answered from the point of view of the company—taking risks and opportunities into account:

- What are the current developments in the business environment (value chain, industry trends)?
- What is the situation in the sales markets (customer perspective)?
- What is the situation on the procurement markets like (supplier perspective)?

Guiding questions regarding the description of the macro-environment of the company are:

- What political framework conditions need to be taken into account?
- Which laws, regulations and requirements must be observed (legal aspects and liability risks)?
- Which environmental aspects have to be considered (e.g. emissions, waste)?
- What does the social environment look like (employees and labour market, regional environment, society)?

Business Processes

Business processes are derived from corporate objectives (Hammer and Champy 2003). They form the basis of a company's economic activities and at the same time represent the starting point for the use and transformation of resources. An essential part of the description of the business model is, therefore, to characterise the value-adding processes of the company more precisely. For this purpose, the following key questions regarding business processes must be answered:

Table 1 Examples of a company's primary and secondary business processes

Type	Exemplary business processes	Example of an enterprise-specific short description of a business process
Primary business processes	Research and development, production, marketing and sales, service	*Service process:* The service process includes the installation and maintenance of systems, operator training, spare parts business and the processing of customer complaints
Secondary business processes	Strategic planning, procurement, controlling, HR management, ICT	*HR management process:* The HR management process comprises the planning, procurement, support, qualification and release of personnel

- Which business processes are there in our company?
- What are our central value-added processes?
- What are the central results of our value-added processes in terms of products and services on the market?

Against this background, the business processes must be described in a company-specific way. Table 1 shows examples of selected business processes based on the classification of the SCD reference model, and, therefore, a distinction is made between primary and secondary business processes.

Sustainability Performance

In order to measure the company's sustainability performance, result variables are considered on the basis of economic, environmental and social aspects. The guiding questions listed below help to concretise these result variables within the framework of the company-specific description of the business model:

- How do we measure the economic, environmental and social performance of our company?
- Where in our company are dependencies between the three dimensions of sustainability?
- What results must we ensure in the short, medium and long term in order to achieve our overarching goals and to safeguard the company's ability to survive?

Table 2 provides an overview of how corporate performance can be measured in the three sustainability dimensions based on selected financial and non-financial indicators.

Resources

Companies use resources within business operations. These resources can be raw materials such as energy and water, but also intangible resources such as qualified employees or good customer relations. This step is, therefore, about identifying and describing the critical resources that are used within the company's value creation activities.

The reference model distinguishes between tangible and intangible resources and differentiates between them on the basis of six types of capital. Regarding the company-specific selection and description of respective factors, the following key questions are used for the respective capital types:

Table 2 Examples of indicators for measuring sustainability performance

Dimension	Exemplary performance indicators
Economy	Key figures for measuring economic effectiveness, e.g. profit, profitability, growth, and costs
Environment	Key figures for measuring environmental effectiveness (e.g. emissions and waste) and eco-efficiency (e.g. energy consumption in relation to value creation)
Social	Key figures to measure social effectiveness (e.g. sickness absence, fluctuation, newly created jobs) and socio-efficiency (e.g. share of training expenditure in relation to sales)

- Manufactured capital (MC): What infrastructure, technologies and equipment do we need to achieve our business goals?
- Financial capital (FC): What financial resources (e.g. capital resources, liquidity) do we need to achieve our goals?
- Natural capital (NC): What natural resources are available to us and to what extent do we need them to achieve our defined goals?
- Human capital (HC): What skills, competences and characteristics of employees are relevant to achieving our goals?
- Structural capital (SC): What internal structures and processes for efficient collaboration do we need to achieve our goals?
- Relational capital (RC): Which relationships with external reference groups are important for achieving our corporate goals?

Table 3 shows an example of how resources can be described in a company-specific perspective. It distinguishes between four levels in accordance with the operationalisation of the concept of resources described above: Resources are differentiated on the basis of the six types of capital. These types of capital are

Table 3 Differentiation of tangible and intangible resources on the basis of types of capital and factors

Resources	Capital type	Factors	Indicators
Tangible resources	Financial capital	Capital structure, asset structure; liquid funds, equities or bonds	To be selected and surveyed on a company-specific basis
	Manufactured capital	Equipment, machines, inventories and stocks, infrastructure	
	Natural capital	Energy, water, soil	
Intangible resources	Human capital	Professional competence, social competence, employee motivation, leadership competence	
	Structural capital	Innovation, knowledge transfer, corporate culture, information technology, management instruments	
	Relational capital	Customer relationships, supplier relationships, relationships with investors, relationships with the public, relationships with cooperative partners	

assigned factors for which indicators need to be selected and collected at the company-specific level.

4.2 *Measurement: Performance Indicators*

The aim of the second step is to determine the status quo of sustainable corporate development. Financial and non-financial aspects of value creation must be taken into account. Based on the SCD reference model, a key figure catalogue is provided. The catalogue can be used as a basis for the company-specific analysis whereby the resource and performance perspective is taken into account.[2]

At the enterprise level, these key figures perform different functions. They can be used as targets and therefore, as a control measure. Key figures can also be used as a medium for comparison, communication or presentation (Küpper 2005).

Key Figures for Measuring the Resource Base Resources are divided into tangible and intangible resources according to the SCD reference model. For further differentiation, the key figures are assigned to the six types of capital. Table 4 shows selected examples of indicators for measuring the use of resources.

Key Figures for Measuring the Sustainability Performance This section describes selected key figures that make it possible to measure corporate performance in the three dimensions of sustainability (Table 5). In doing so, interrelations between the dimensions are also considered, i.e. in addition to eco- and social-effectiveness, the areas of eco- and social-efficiency are also specifically considered (see Sect. 2).

The catalogue described above supports companies in measuring sustainable corporate development and provides financial and non-financial key figures as well as their specific calculation rules. The indicators have a documentation and information function by providing and communicating data for operational decisions. In addition to being used for internal management purposes, the indicators can also be used for external corporate reporting. Figure 4 shows selected indicators for the human capital dimension. In addition to the age structure of the workforce (age distribution), the qualification profile of the workforce is also visualised in the upper part of the illustration. In the section below, further key figures are displayed for the description of the human capital (e.g. average age, length of service). In addition to the values from the current period, values from previous periods are also displayed

[2]For the development of the performance indicator catalogue to promote sustainable corporate development, several KPI collections (e.g. Alwert et al. 2013; Global Reporting Initiative [GRI] 2013; Kaldschmidt 2009; Kohl 2007; VDI 2016) were analysed and evaluated systematically. Based on interim results, expert surveys were conducted among company representatives and scientists from various disciplines in order to prioritise particularly meaningful indicators. Selected results have been incorporated into the catalogue of indicators presented here. For more details on the process and for a more detailed list of indicators see Orth (2016).

Table 4 Key figures for measuring the resource base

Indicator (unit)	Calculation
Financial capital	
Equity-to-asset ratio (%)	(Equity capital/total assets) × 100
Debt-to-equity ratio (%)	(Short-term loans + long-term loans)/equity capital × 100
Acid test (%)	(Trade debtors + cash in bank and in hand + other current assets)/(trade creditors + other current liabilities + short-term loans) × 100
Manufactured capital	
Rate of investment (%)	(Capital investments/total turnover) × 100
Scrap rate (%)	(Rejects/volume produced)
Stock turnover (#)	Direct material costs/inventories
Natural capital	
Energy consumption (kWh)	Total electricity consumption in the year under review
Freshwater consumption (m^3)	Total freshwater consumption in the year under review
Share of renewable sources of energy (%)	Share of renewable energies in total energy consumption
Share of capital investment in environmental protection measures (%)	Environmental protection investments/investments × 100
Human capital	
Number of employees (#)	Number of employees incl. apprentices in FTE
Years with the company (a)	Average length of service = total length of service/total number of employees (without apprentices)
Number of executives (#)	Number of employees in executive positions
Age distribution (%)	Number of employees per group/total number of employees (in the groups: Employees <25 years, 25–35 years, 36–45 years, 46–67 years, >67 years
Structural capital	
Ratio of employees to managers (#)	Number of employees/number of executives
R&D intensity (%)	R&D expenses/total turnover × 100
ICT expenses per employee (€)	Expenses for information and communication technology/number of employees
Valid patents (#)	Number of patents with current validity
Relational capital	
Number of current customers (#)	Number of different customers with order in the current year (completed, ongoing, launched)
Complaints per customer (#)	Number of customer complaints/total number of customers
Number of current suppliers (#)	Number of different suppliers with purchase orders in the current year (completed, ongoing, launched)
Delivery quality of suppliers (%)	Value of deliveries subject to complaint/direct material costs × 100

Table 5 Key figures for measuring sustainability results

Indicator (unit)	Calculation
Economic sustainability	
Return on sales (%)	Profit before taxes/sales × 100
Return on Investment (ROI) (%)	Profit/total capital
Value added as a percentage of turnover (%)	(Total sales – direct material costs)/total sales × 100
Sales growth (%)	Sales growth compared to previous year
Environmental sustainability	
Waste volume (t)	Total of all types of waste in the reporting year
CO_2 emission (t)	Total CO_2 emissions in the reporting year
Energy consumption in relation to value added (€/kWh)	(Total sales – direct material costs)/energy consumption in kWh
Environmental expenditure in relation to total expenditure (%)	Expenses for environmental protection/total expenses × 100
Social sustainability	
Accident coefficient (#)	Number of occupational accidents/number of employees
Sick rate (#)	Number of days absent/number of employees
Employee fluctuation rate (%)	Number of employees who left the company/number of employees × 100
Intensity of training and further education (%)	Expenses for training and further education/turnover × 100

here. This makes it easy to identify developments and trends that can be used for decision-making.

4.3 Strength and Weakness Analysis (Self-Assessment)

The aim of the third step is to determine the status quo of sustainable corporate development. For this purpose, strengths and weaknesses related to the resource base, business processes and results of the company are to be identified, and corresponding fields of action are to be derived.

A self-assessment procedure is used for this analysis step, allowing companies to involve employees in the process of sustainable corporate development. The dialogue-oriented workshop procedure serves to evaluate the factors (e.g. professional competence, corporate culture or technical infrastructure) defined in the context of the description of the business model.

The company-specific objectives defined in step one are used as a reference point for the status quo diagnosis. Against this background, the workshop team evaluates the selected factors according to the dimensions quantity, quality and systematic. The evaluation is based on a percentage scale divided into four central levels:

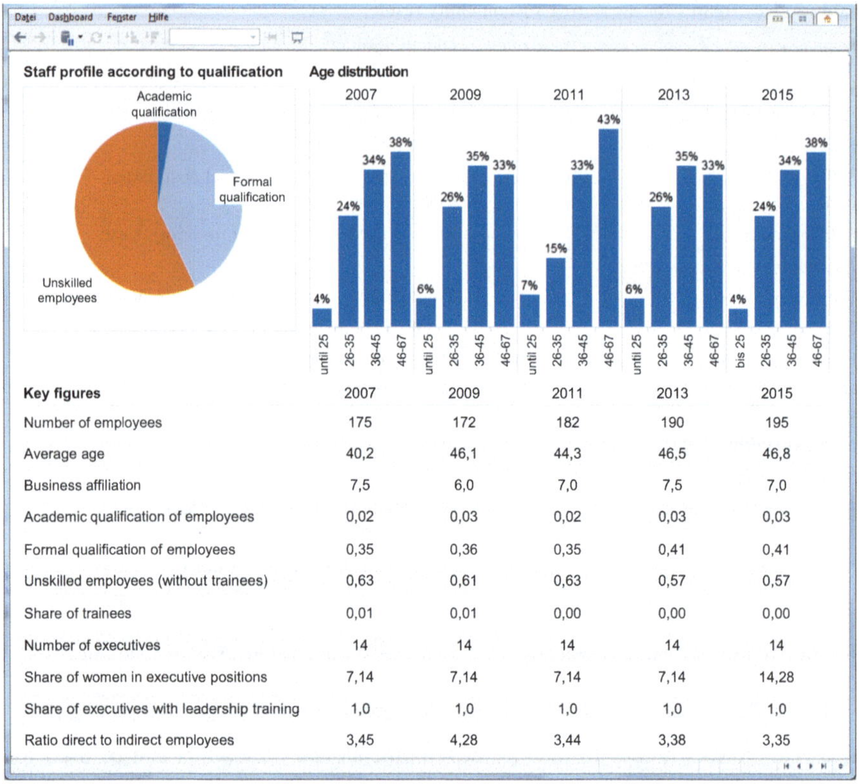

Key figures	2007	2009	2011	2013	2015
Number of employees	175	172	182	190	195
Average age	40,2	46,1	44,3	46,5	46,8
Business affiliation	7,5	6,0	7,0	7,5	7,0
Academic qualification of employees	0,02	0,03	0,02	0,03	0,03
Formal qualification of employees	0,35	0,36	0,35	0,41	0,41
Unskilled employees (without trainees)	0,63	0,61	0,63	0,57	0,57
Share of trainees	0,01	0,01	0,00	0,00	0,00
Number of executives	14	14	14	14	14
Share of women in executive positions	7,14	7,14	7,14	7,14	14,28
Share of executives with leadership training	1,0	1,0	1,0	1,0	1,0
Ratio direct to indirect employees	3,45	4,28	3,44	3,38	3,35

Fig. 4 Presentation of selected employee key figures over time

- 0% = the quantity, quality or systematics are not sufficient
- 30% = ... partly sufficient
- 60% = ... mostly sufficient
- 90+ % = ... always sufficient

The results of this step can be visualised in the form of a bar chart. Figure 5 provides an overview of the company's relational capital by summarising the evaluation of the relevant external stakeholder relationships. The actual values of the evaluation dimensions quantity, quality and systematic (QQS) are visualised graphically, whereby the bar length corresponds to the percentages from the evaluation. The QQS diagram can be used to identify the factors and assessment dimensions for which there is potential for optimisation.

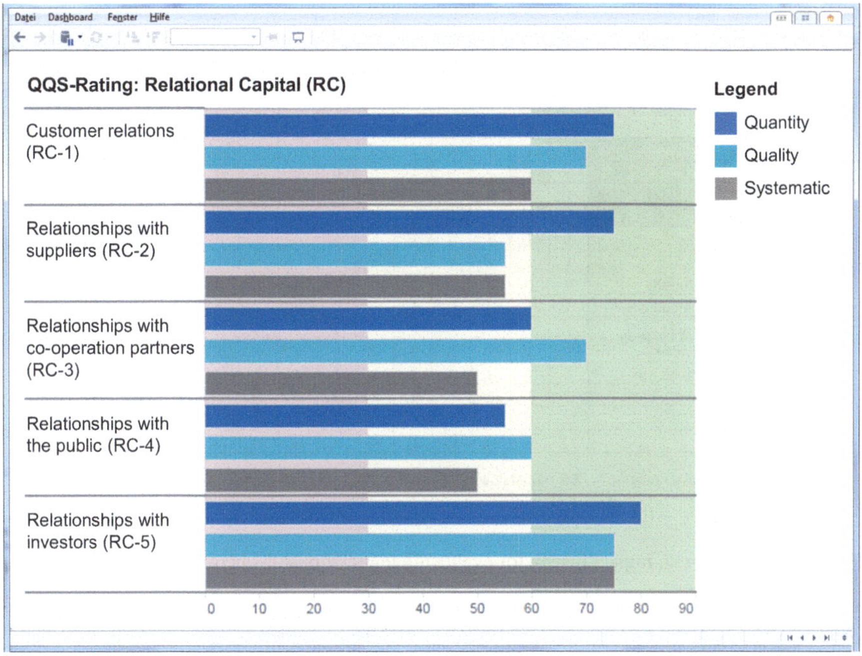

Fig. 5 QQS bar chart relational capital

4.4 *Impact Analysis and Improvement Measures*

Since corporate development is to be understood as a dynamic process that can be actively influenced, the approach supports the handling of complex interrelationships in companies and to illustrate conflicts of objectives between the sustainability dimensions.

Based on the analysis results from step two and step three, the aim of this step is to analyse the interrelations between the factors of sustainable corporate development, to derive appropriate optimisation measures for the identified fields of action, to align them with the corporate objectives and to plan their implementation. For this purpose, the sensitivity analysis, according to Vester (2015) is used. It makes it possible to analyse interactions between the factors of the SCD reference model. This allows statements to be made on the influence and controllability of the factors to be taken into account in the planning and implementation of measures.

The cause–effect relationships are recorded using a matrix in which the influence of each factor on all other factors is evaluated. For each factor, the question is answered how strongly the change in the factor under consideration (cause) affects another factor (effect). A four-point scale is used to evaluate the cause–effect relationships:

Datei Dashboard Fenster Hilfe

Impact Analysis: Impact of factors (rows) on other factors (columns)

Cause		BP-1	BP-2	BP-3	BP-4	SR-1	SR-2	SR-3	HC-1	HC-2	HC-3	HC-4	SC-1	...	Active sum
BP-1	Engineering and Construction	x	1	1	0	2	0	0	0	1	0	1	1	...	17
BP-2	Marketing and Sales	3	x	2	0	1	0	0	0	1	0	0	1	...	13
BP-3	Production	1	1	x	0	2	1	2	0	2	0	1	2	...	27
BP-4	Support Processes	0	0	0	x	1	1	2	0	1	0	2	2	...	21
SR-1	Economic Results	1	1	1	1	x	1	2	0	2	0	0	1	...	26
SR-2	Social Results	1	1	2	1	1	x	1	1	2	1	0	1	...	19
SR-3	Environmental Results	0	0	1	0	1	0	x	0	1	0	0	1	...	14
HC-1	Professional Competence	1	1	2	0	1	2	0	x	2	2	1	1	...	27
HC-2	Social Competence	2	1	1	0	2	2	1	2	x	2	1	2	...	24
HC-3	Employee Motivation	1	1	2	0	1	2	0	2	2	x	2	2	...	24
HC-4	Leadership Competence	2	1	2	1	1	1	2	1	2	2	x	0	...	25
SC-1	Corporate Culture	2	1	2	2	2	2	2	2	3	1	1	x	...	38
...	...	...	...	...	...	...	...	...	...	...	...	...	...	x	...
	Passive sum	22	18	34	13	31	18	25	12	30	18	15	29	12	

Legend: BP = Business Process • SR = Sustainability Result • HC = Human Capital • SC = Structural Capital

Fig. 6 Extract from an impact matrix for evaluating the relationships between the factors

- 0 = No effect
- 1 = Weak effect (under-proportional)
- 2 = Average effect (proportional)
- 3 = Strong effect (disproportionate)

As a result, the user receives a comprehensive effect structure of the organisation. Figure 6 shows the section of a completed impact matrix according to the above scale. In addition to the direct effect between the individual factors, a column and row sum can also be determined for each factor. In line by line analysis, the active sum for each factor is shown, which represents the influence of one factor on all other factors. A high active sum signals a high influence in the system, i.e. changes in such a factor cause a strong change in the system (Alwert et al. 2013).

In addition, the time-related dimension can also be examined more closely within the impact analysis. Analogous to the determination of the strength of the effect, the period of effect, i.e. the time delay until an effect occurs with a factor, is determined here on the basis of a four-stage scale. A distinction is made between immediate, short-, medium- and long-term effects.

Combination of Impact Analysis and Diagnosis of Strengths and Weaknesses
The self-assessment procedure described in step 3 serves, in particular, to assess the status quo of sustainable corporate development. The impact analysis, on the other hand, aims to record the dependencies of the factors and to present correlations transparently. The results of the impact analysis can be combined with the results of the strengths and weaknesses analysis. These results in further evaluation options can be visualised in corresponding portfolio representations. This visual representation summarises the results of the two methods described above in one picture and thus provides an overview of prioritising fields of action.

Fig. 7 Management portfolio for sustainable corporate development

The management portfolio illustrates the development potential of the factors using two dimensions and distinguishes between four quadrants (Fig. 7). The abscissa depicts the mean value of the QQS assessment for each factor, which shows the improvement potential of a factor. The further to the left, a factor is, the worse its assessment is and the greater its improvement potential. On the ordinate, the influence weight of the influence factor, i.e. the impact strength on the overall system, is indicated. The influence weight is calculated on the basis of the relative active sum of the respective factor. In this case, the higher a factor is located in the portfolio, the greater its influence on the sustainable development of the company.

Depending on the position of the factors, these are to be treated differently. Four basic recommendations for actions can be derived from the quadrants of the management portfolio (Mertins et al. 2016):

- **Stabilise** (top right): Factors in this field have a high influence weight on the overall system and a high average rating. These factors are, therefore, the strengths of a company that needs to be maintained at a high level.
- **No need for action** (bottom right): Factors in this quadrant are currently well developed. However, since their relevance for sustainable corporate success is not of central importance, there is no acute need for action.
- **Analyse** (bottom left): Factors in this field are of secondary importance for the achievement of corporate goals and at the same time are rated less highly. Due to their potential for improvement, however, they should be analysed and observed more closely, as they may have indirect effects on other factors.
- **Develop** (top left): These factors receive special attention because they are highly relevant and at the same time, relatively poorly assessed. They thus have the highest intervention potential, i.e. relatively small improvements can achieve relatively large results (leverage effect).

Once the fields of action have been prioritised, appropriate measures need to be developed. At this point, the consideration of interdependencies again makes a valuable contribution. For this purpose, the results from the impact matrix are transferred to impact networks. The impact networks are used to visualise the dynamic relationships and interactions between resources, processes and sustainability results. Based on this modelling of dependencies, possible future effects can be better estimated. The representation of time delays and generators (control loops of two or more factors that influence each other) makes it possible to identify factors and mechanisms that affect value creation in the short, medium and long term. Figure 8 shows an example of a generator that combines factors of human and structural capital with economic and social business success and can set self-reinforcing processes in motion. For example, broad-based employee training aimed at improving the technical skills of employees (HC-2) in production can have a positive impact on the generator shown in the figure.

4.5 Integrated Reporting

The SCD procedure also supports corporate reporting, in particular, to meet the increased information needs of stakeholders from the company's external environment. The aim of this last phase is to prepare the results of the previous steps for reporting purposes. Depending on the addressee, the information on the company's sustainability performance must be compiled according to the target group. To this end, recommendations are formulated for content elements as well as reporting principles to be taken into account.[3]

[3]For developing the principles and content elements of the integrated reporting approach outlined in this chapter, different guidelines for non-financial reporting have been analysed (e.g. Alwert et al. 2013; Gebauer and Westermann 2012; GRI 2013; IIRC 2013). For more details see Orth (2016).

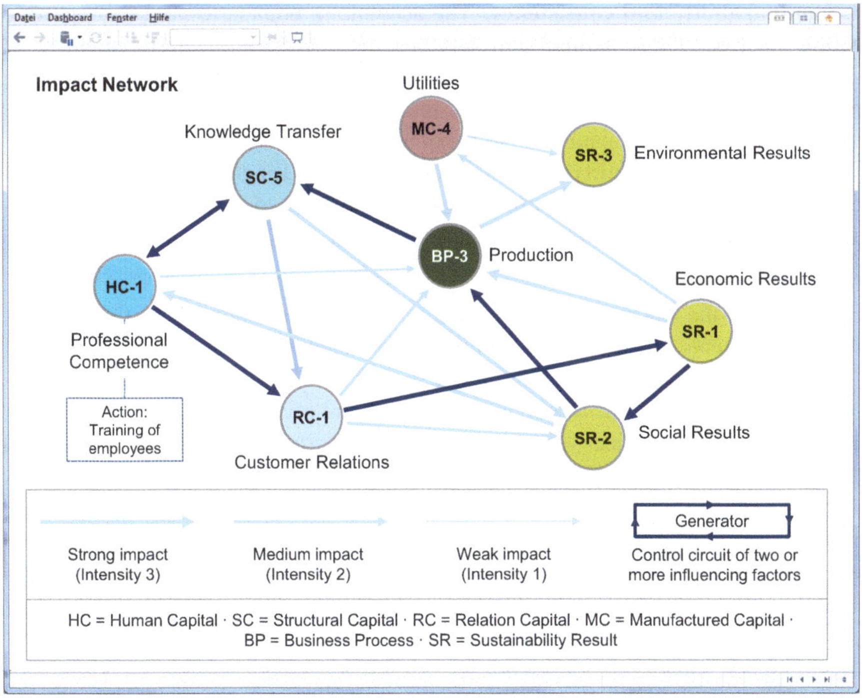

Fig. 8 Impact network with generator and planning of measures

Reporting Principles

The reporting principles serve in particular to ensure the quality and meaningfulness of the report. The five key reporting principles are explained below:

Materiality: The report should concisely present all necessary and sufficient information for the assessment of short-, medium- and long-term value creation. It should also explain the criteria and process for determining the materiality of content.

Completeness: The information should be correct, open and complete. The planned and (possibly) not achieved performance in connection with the business strategy must be presented. Both positive and negative aspects, e.g. with regard to capital types or corporate performance, must be taken into account to a sufficient extent and backed up with comprehensible data. Conflicts of objectives must also be described in the report. The integration of external perspectives into the report is desirable.

Connectivity: The report should make connections and interactions of essential financial and non-financial factors—related to the past, present and future—visible and comprehensible for the reader.

Comparability and consistency: The accounting boundaries and the reporting period must be clearly defined. Furthermore, the data basis of the report must be specified, and a comparison of the results over different reporting periods must be made possible. In addition to company-specific consistency and consistency, comparisons with other companies should also be made possible.

Communicative quality: The structure, text and design of the report should convey a clear picture of the company's sustainability performance and challenges and ensure rapid access to the essential information.

Content Elements

In addition to the reporting principles outlined above, the following section outlines the main contents that are to be listed in an integrated report:

Organisational overview: The report should describe the purpose of the company and the main business activities, products and services as well as the central values and strategic objectives of the company. Information on the general conditions must also be provided. This includes, for example information on locations, sales, employee and management structure and ownership.

External environment: The description of the external environment should include the relevant aspects of the current market situation of the company as well as the external framework conditions (e.g. technological, legal and social aspects). In addition, the relationships with relevant external stakeholder groups must be described and named in the report.

Business model: When describing the business model, the value-determining drivers of the business activity and success factors of the company's value creation must be concretised. To this end, the key resources used as input for value creation must be presented in the report.

Performance: Against the background of the company-specific goals, the sustainable company performance should be presented within the framework of the report with the help of quantitative and qualitative information. This includes key performance indicators as well as (positive and negative) effects on the organisation's resources.

Measures and outlook: The report should describe which measures and programs the company is taking or intends to take to respond to identified challenges. It will also report on the status of ongoing and recently completed actions. This will help to show the company's position for future challenges and opportunities.

Procedure for Selecting and Compiling Report Contents

The recommendations and principles described above must be taken into account when selecting and compiling the content of the report. Table 6 illustrates how the results from the preceding steps are meaningfully structured and integrated into the report. In this context, it is shown how the SCD instruments are used to generate the corresponding report content and how this also contributes to fulfilling the formulated reporting principles.

Table 6 Content elements and principles for integrated reporting

Content elements	Origin of the report contents based on the SCD procedure model	Reference to the reporting principles
Organisational overview	Step 1 provides the basic content for describing the organisational overview, the external environment and the business model. In this way, the accounting limits are clearly defined and, in particular, the principle of comparability and consistency is taken into account	*Comparability and consistency*
External environment		
Business model		
Performance	On the basis of strength–weakness analyses (step 3) positive and negative facts are determined and deposited by meaningful characteristic numbers (step 2). Thus a contribution is made to the principle of completeness	*Completeness*
	The principle of comparability and consistency is supported by the definition and documentation of the factors and key figures as well as their calculation and evaluation bases (step 2)	*Comparability and consistency*
	By using the impact matrix, factors are identified that have a significant influence on the overall system (step 4). Thus a selection of essential report contents is supported	*Materiality*
	In addition to the determination of the strength of action, sensitivity analysis can also be used to determine periods of action. In this way, aspects of short-, medium- and long-term value creation can be presented, and the principle of materiality promoted	*Materiality*
	The use of sensitivity analysis illustrates interactions between the relevant influencing variables, results and success factors. This clarifies correlations between key financial and non-financial performance parameters and thus takes the principle of connectivity into account	*Connectivity*
	Cause–effect correlations can be investigated and conflicting objectives can be uncovered using cross impact maps. Their presentation in the report promotes compliance with the principle of completeness	*Completeness*
Measures and outlook	Based on the analysis of interdependencies, measures are derived for the identified fields of action (step 4) and presented in the report. This provides sufficient information for assessing short-, medium- and long-term value creation	*Materiality*

5 Summary and Outlook

Sustainable management combines economic success with demands for environmental compatibility and social responsibility. Companies face the challenge of balancing the three dimensions of sustainability and integrating them into the conventional management system. Against this background, a conceptual framework was developed with the SCD reference model, which describes the essential elements of the approach and explains their interrelationships. The SCD reference model is complemented by the SCD procedure model, which describes the most important steps for the implementation of sustainable corporate development. The procedure model distinguishes between four central steps. Instruments for the analysis, planning, control and reporting of sustainable corporate development are provided along with the steps of the procedure model. Companies can use these instruments to expand existing management systems or to set up an independent management system for sustainable corporate development.

The application of the SCD approach and the use of the instruments provides companies with the following benefits:

- Analysis of the company's resource base and sustainability performance in relation to corporate objectives.
- Quantitative measurement of the resource base and sustainability performance using financial and non-financial performance indicators.
- Qualitative sustainability assessment using workshop-based self-assessment procedures (strengths/weaknesses analysis).
- Analysis of interdependencies between resources, processes and sustainability results.
- Derivation and prioritisation of fields of action, development goals and measures to promote sustainable corporate development and monitoring of implementation success.
- Integrated perspective—linking internal management and external reporting.

At this point, however, it should be noted that the method presented here for promoting sustainable corporate development has its limits. This opens up the potential for further research and development activities.

Although the approach respects the fundamental relevance of the external environment for successful sustainable corporate development, activities within the organisation are considered in particular. This limitation of the system boundary could be extended by considering more upstream and downstream stages of the value chain.

In the context of the chapter, a catalogue of key figures was presented, which helps to measure tangible and intangible resources as well as sustainability performance at the company level. An added value for the performance indicator analysis can arise if comparative data is available from other companies that produce similar goods and operate in a similar context (benchmarking). Benchmarking concepts aim in particular to take greater account of non-financial aspects of human capital and to use indicators to measure social and environmental sustainability appear desirable.

As part of the contribution, a controlling and reporting instrument was developed for anchoring sustainability aspects in the conventional management system. Further research efforts should increasingly focus on questions of external reporting and the user groups addressed with it. A recent GRI study on future trends in sustainability reporting up to 2025 shows that reporting formats, platforms and technologies will shift in the digital age: "One thing is clear: the future will be increasingly dominated by digital data, which can be tagged to provide easy access and enable analysis" (Global Reporting Initiative [GRI] 2015, p. 9).

References

Alwert K, Bornemann M, Will M, Wuscher S (2013) Wissensbilanz—Made in Germany. Leitfaden 2.0 zur Erstellung einer Wissensbilanz. Bundesministerium für Wirtschaft und Technologie, Berlin

Barney JB (1991) Firm resources and sustained competitive advantage. J Manag 17(1):99–120

Berns M, Townend A, Khayat Z, Balagopal B, Reeves M, Hopkins MS, Kruschwitz N (2009) Sustainability and competitive advantage. MIT Sloan Manag Rev 51(1):19–26

Cocca S, Meiren T (2013) Green Services – Studie zu Trends und Perspektiven nachhaltiger Dienstleistungsangebote. 2. überarbeitete Auflage. Fraunhofer, Stuttgart

Deutsches Institut für Normung (2011) Leitfaden zur gesellschaftlichen Verantwortung (ISO 26000:2010). English edition: Guidance on social responsibility (ISO 26000:2010). Beuth, Berlin

Deutsches Institut für Normung (2015) Quality management systems—fundamentals and vocabulary (ISO 9000:2015). German and English version EN ISO 9000:2015. Beuth, Berlin

Drenk D (2009) Nachhaltiges Wirtschaften bei kleinen und mittleren Unternehmen. Eine Untersuchung der ökonomischen und sozialen Effekte von ÖKOPROFIT-Unternehmen. Dissertation, TU Dortmund, Kovač, Hamburg

Eccles RG, Cheng B, Saltzman D (eds) (2010) The landscape of integrated reporting. Reflections and next steps. Harvard Business School, Cambridge, MA

EC European Commission (2019) Reflection paper—towards a sustainable Europe by 2030. European Union, 2019. Retrieved from https://ec.europa.eu/commission/sites/beta-political/files/factsheets_sustainable_europe_012019_v3.pdf

Edvinsson L, Malone T (1997) Intellectual capital. Harper, New York

Gebauer J, Westermann U (2012) IÖW/future-Ranking der Nachhaltigkeitsberichte deutscher KMU 2011: Ergebnisse und Trends. Münster, Berlin

Global Reporting Initiative (2013) G4 sustainability reporting guidelines. Reporting principles and standard disclosures. https://www.globalreporting.org/resourcelibrary/GRIG4-Part1-Reporting-Principles-and-Standard-Disclosures.pdf. Accessed 22 Apr 2016

Global Reporting Initiative (2015) Sustainability and reporting trends in 2025—preparing for the future. GRI's reporting 2025 projects: first analysis paper, May 2015. Retrieved from https://www.globalreporting.org/resourcelibrary/sustainability-and-reporting-trends-in-2025-1.pdf

Hammer M, Champy J (2003) Business Reengineering. Die Radikalkur für das Unternehmen. 7. Auflage. Campus, Frankfurt/Main

International Integrated Reporting Council (2013) International <IR> Framework. Retrieved from http://integratedreporting.org/resource/international-ir-framework/

Kaldschmidt S (2009) Benchmarking zur Messung und Steigerung der Nachhaltigkeit. In Mertins K, Kohl H (eds) Benchmarking. Leitfaden für den Vergleich mit den Besten. 2. Auflage. Symposion, Düsseldorf, pp 209–236

Kohl H (2007) Integriertes Benchmarking für kleine und mittlere Unternehmen. Dissertation, Technische Universität Berlin. IRB, Berlin

Kölle A (2008) Risikomanagement als strategisches Instrument zum nachhaltigen Wirtschaften. Dargestellt am Beispiel der Ernährungsbranche. Dissertation, Kovač, Hamburg

Küpper H-U (2005) Controlling. Konzeption, Aufgaben, Instrumente. 4. Auflage. Schäffer-Poeschel, Stuttgart

Mertins K, Will M, Orth R (2016) Die Wissensbilanz. In: Kohl H, Mertins K, Seidel H (eds) Wissensmanagement im Mittelstand. Grundlagen—Lösungen—Praxisbeispiele. Springer, Berlin, pp 91–99

Müller-Christ G (2010) Nachhaltiges Management. Einführung in Ressourcenorientierung und widersprüchliche Managementrationalitäten. Nomos, Baden-Baden

Onischka M, Ritthoff M, Liedtke C (2011) Instrumentenwegweiser zur Steigerung der Ressourceneffizienz. Praxishandbuch des Umwelt- und Nachhaltigkeitscontrollings für KMU. 2. Auflage. Books on Demand, Norderstedt

Orth R (2016) Nachhaltige Unternehmensentwicklung aus ressourcenorientierter Perspektive: Integrierte Methode zur Bewertung, Steuerung und Berichterstattung für kleine und mittlere Unternehmen. Dissertation, TU Berlin. Fraunhofer, Stuttgart

Peteraf MA (1993) The cornerstones of competitive advantage: a resource-based view. Strat Manag J 14(3):179–191

Pfeffer J, Salancik GR (2003) The external control of organizations: a resource dependence perspective, Stanford Business Books. Stanford University Press, Stanford, CA

Promberger K, Spiess H, Kössler W (2006) Unternehmen und Nachhaltigkeit. Eine management-orientierte Einführung in die Grundlagen nachhaltigen Wirtschaftens. Linde, Wien

Schaltegger S (2013) Messung und Steuerung unternehmerischer Nachhaltigkeit. In: Rogall H, Binswanger HC, Ekardt F, Grothe A, Hasenclever W-D, Hauchler I (eds) 3. Jahrbuch Nachhaltige Ökonomie. Im Brennpunkt: Nachhaltigkeitsmanagement. Metropolis, Marburg, pp 285–305

Schaltegger S, Herzig C, Kleiber O, Klinke T, Meyer J-A (2007) Nachhaltigkeitsmanagement in Unternehmen. Von der Idee zur Praxis: Managementansätze zur Umsetzung von Corporate Social Responsibility und Corporate Sustainability. Centre for Sustainability Management (CSM), Lüneburg

Schmelzer HJ, Sesselmann W (2013) Geschäftsprozessmanagement in der Praxis. Kunden zufrieden stellen—Produktivität steigern—Wert erhöhen. 8. überarbeitete und erweiterte Auflage. Hanser, München

Schröder RW (2011) Integration der Nachhaltigkeit in Performance Measurement-Systeme von kleinen und mittelständischen Unternehmen. In: Meyer J-A (Hg.) Nachhaltigkeit in kleinen und mittleren Unternehmen. Jahrbuch der KMU-Forschung und -Praxis 2011. Lohmar, Eul, S 225–243

SIGMA (2003) Sigma guidelines—putting sustainable development into practice: a guide for organisations. http://www.projectsigma.co.uk/Guidelines/SigmaGuidelines.pdf. Accessed 29 Apr 2017

Stahlmann V, Clausen J (1999) Öko-Effizienz und Öko-Effektivität. In: Ökologisches Wirtschaften 3/1999. IÖW and oekom, Berlin

UN Global Compact, Accenture (2013) The UN Global Compact-Accenture CEO study on sustainability 2013. Architects of a better world

Verein Deutscher Ingenieure (2014) Resource efficiency—methodical principles and strategies. VDI 4800 Blatt 1:2014-07. Beuth, Berlin

Verein Deutscher Ingenieure (2016) Sustainable management in small and medium-sized enterprises. Guidance notes for sustainable management. VDI Richtlinie 4070, Part 1. Beuth, Berlin

Vester F (2015) Die Kunst vernetzt zu denken. Ideen und Werkzeuge für einen neuen Umgang mit Komplexität. Der neue Bericht an den Club of Rome. 10. Auflage. DTV, München

Wernerfelt B (1984) A resource-based view of the firm. Strateg Manag J 5:171–180

White AL (2010) The five capitals of integrated reporting: toward a holistic architecture for corporate disclosure. In: Eccles RG, Cheng B, Saltzman D (eds) The landscape of integrated reporting. Reflections and next steps. Harvard Business School, Cambridge, MA, pp 29–32

KM 3.0: Knowledge Management Computing Under Digital Economy

Xuyan Wang, Xi Zhang, Hui Xiong, and Patricia Ordóñez de Pablos

Knowledge will replace land, labor, capital and machine equipment, becoming the most important production factor.
Peter Drucker

Abstract As an emerging discipline that studies the basic laws of knowledge innovation activities, knowledge management (KM) has been developed for over 20 years. The development process of KM has experienced KM 1.0 era and KM 2.0 era. In recent years, with the digital transformation of the global economy and reverse globalization trends, some unprecedented features and phenomenon are emerging in knowledge innovation activities. That is, KM has entered into 3.0 era. In this chapter, we will review KM 1.0 and KM 2.0, and describe some of the characteristics and future challenges of the upcoming KM 3.0. We hope that this review will provide guidance for future research in the KM area.

1 Introduction

Nowadays, our world is transferring to knowledge and digital economic era, for knowledge is recognized as the most important power to promote the development of the world economy. As an emerging discipline that studies the basic laws of knowledge innovation activities, knowledge management (KM) has been developed for over 20 years. Nowadays, KM is well accepted by global organizations as it can

X. Wang · X. Zhang (✉)
College of Management and Economics, Tianjin University, Tianjin, China
e-mail: wangxuyan@tju.edu.cn; jackyzhang@tju.edu.cn

H. Xiong
Rutgers Business School, Rutgers University, Camden, NJ, USA
e-mail: hxiong@rutgers.edu

P. O. de Pablos
Department of Business Administration, University of Oviedo, Oviedo, Spain
e-mail: patriop@uniovi.es

F. Matos et al. (eds.), *Knowledge, People, and Digital Transformation*, Contributions to Management Science, https://doi.org/10.1007/978-3-030-40390-4_13

be used to explore the mechanisms of knowledge activities intra- or inter- organizations, and to help manage organizational knowledge systematically (Alavi and Leidner 2001; Darr et al. 1995). The development process of KM can be divided into three stages: KM 1.0, KM 2.0, and KM 3.0.

KM 1.0 focuses on the understanding, exploration, and theoretical construction of the nature of knowledge within organizations. The aims of studying KM in this stage are promoting the management of organizational internal knowledge resources, and facilitating knowledge creation process within the organizations (Nonaka 1994). The representative research was from Ikujiro Nonaka in 1994, who studied the knowledge creation process of Toyota Motor Corporation in Japan and published the research findings in *Organization Science* (Nonaka 1994). And then in 1995, Nonaka and Takeuchi published "The knowledge-creating Company: How Japanese Companies Create the Dynamic of Innovation," which is regarded as one of core literature in KM 1.0 (Nonaka and Takeuchi 1995). With his great contributions, Nonaka was recognized as one of the most influential KM researchers in the world. He studied Japanese manufacturing enterprise management practice, struggled to explore excellence enterprise KM idea, and constructed the model of organizational knowledge creation in theory.

With the development of Internet and globalization tendency from 2000, knowledge management (KM) not only focuses on managing knowledge within organizations but also leveraging global knowledge outside by using Internet technologies (Bell and Loane 2010; Pan and Leidner 2003). Thus, KM 2.0 era is described as global knowledge transfer period. With the deepening of economic globalization, the globalization model had become one of the most important modes in the development of enterprises. Accordingly, the global and distributed research and development (R&D) centers rose. For example, Microsoft and Huawei had set up dozens of R&D centers in the world. Global companies began to establish e-platforms (e.g., electronic repositories, electronic knowledge networks, or knowledge markets) to facilitate knowledge transfer and collaboration among partners in this period (Bell and Loane 2010). In the KM 2.0 era, how to improve the efficiency of global knowledge transfer and cooperation through Internet-based platforms become the focus of researchers.

In recent years, with the digital transformation of the global economy and reverse globalization trends, some unprecedented features and phenomenon are emerging in knowledge innovation activities (Sharma et al. 2008). That is, KM has entered into 3.0 era. In this new era, the global market competition is becoming fierce seriously. Compared with 2.0 era, the critical issue changed from "how to facilitate knowledge transfer from two fixed partners" to "how to find high potential and valuable partners from numerous emerging SMEs and individuals," and "how to establish an agile and dynamic knowledge sharing model with numerous and temporal partners." In KM 3.0 era, only enterprises obtain new knowledge constantly to produce value, they may catch up with other fast-speed innovation competitors. Thus, enterprises became brought open innovation model, big data mining technologies, and artificial intelligence (AI) to find high potential collaborators, facilitate agile knowledge sharing, and promote data-driven knowledge creation process (Shollo and Galliers 2016).

In this new era, enterprise knowledge management faces new opportunities and challenges in the near future. For example, with the development of big data and cloud computing, the storage of knowledge and structuring of communication data is no longer the critical difficulty and the focus in organizational knowledge management. However, the main concern in the era of KM 3.0 is how to transform big data into knowledge, how to exploit knowledge with AI, and how to managing knowledge effectively under the background of global economic transformation (Erickson and Rothberg 2014; Kabir and Carayannis 2013).

In the following, this chapter will review KM 1.0 and KM 2.0. Then, we will describe the characteristics and future challenges of KM 3.0.

2 KM 1.0: Knowledge Transferring Within the Organization

With the coming of knowledge economics, the organization's internal knowledge becomes more and more important resources for the organizations (Alavi and Leidner 2001). In this period, knowledge management (KM) was promoted and well adapted by researchers and practitioners as a discipline that studies the process of acquiring, creating, sharing, integrating, recording, accessing, updating, and innovating knowledge to enhance organizational efficiency and innovation (Charband and Navimipour 2016; Nelson and Cooprider 1996).

According to KM theory, knowledge can be divided into explicit and tacit knowledge according to whether the knowledge can be clearly expressed and effectively transferred (Nonaka and Takeuchi 1995; Reber 1967). Explicit knowledge refers to knowledge that can be easily transmitted through language, or words, while tacit knowledge represents difficult-to-express knowledge that is difficult to spread. Tacit knowledge and explicit knowledge can be transformed into each other. In an organization, the number of tacit knowledge is much more than explicit knowledge (Leonard 1995). Thus, how to make tacit knowledge more explicit is one of the core issues in knowledge management research in this period (Nonaka and Takeuchi 1995). For the evolution process of tacit knowledge and explicit knowledge, SECI model is recognized as the most effective model to describe the evolution process of knowledge within organizations (Nilmanat 2011).

SECI theory divides the whole process of knowledge evolution into four parts according to the starting state and ending state of knowledge transformation (Nonaka 1994): socialization, externalization, combination, and internalization. Socialization is the process of tacit knowledge diffusion, in which experiences are shared and learned from each other. People obtain new tacit knowledge mainly from observation, imitation, and practice, rather than by language. Externalization is the process of expressing tacit knowledge. Such tacit knowledge (like ideas in mind) can be expressed as a concept that is easy to understand through metaphor. For example, designing environmentally friendly products to make consumers feel close to nature. Combination is the process of explicit knowledge integration. Through sorting, readjusting, and integration, knowledge is captured in the explicit knowledge form. Internalization is the process of assimilating into tacit knowledge through the understanding and diffusion of explicit knowledge, which has certain similarities with the traditional concept of "learning."

Knowledge created through the SECI process can trigger a new knowledge creation process, extending the organization horizontally and vertically (Nonaka 1994). This is a dynamic process that begins at the individual level and continues to expand across interactive communities across departments, and even organizational boundaries. Organizational knowledge creation is a dynamic process, constantly improving itself.

Another critical concept of KM1.0 is knowledge asset. According to the theory of KM proposed by Nonaka, the process of knowledge creation occurs in Ba, and this Ba can exist as an entity or as a virtual one (Nonaka and Konno 1998). And knowledge will form knowledge assets and solidify knowledge in the process of creation and transformation (Nonaka and Takeuchi 1995). The foundation of the knowledge creation process is knowledge assets. Researchers define assets as company-specific resources that are essential to creating value for the company (Marr et al. 2004). Knowledge assets are the input, output and adjustment factors of the knowledge creation (Nonaka et al. 2000).

3 KM 2.0: Knowledge Transferring Across the Organizations

In the context of globalization, the focus of KM 2.0 shifts from knowledge transfer within the organization to interorganizational knowledge transfer (Rottman 2008). Many companies began to expand global markets and overseas R&D laboratories were set up due to economic globalization (Kumar 2001). Gaining value and benefit from the conversion of knowledge between overseas subsidiaries and parent companies was what stockholders hope to see. An obvious feature of this stage was the rise of multinational companies and internalization of R&D centers (D'Agostino and Santangelo 2012).

In the KM2.0 era, companies were keen to find partners on a global scale. That means, multinational companies do not consider overseas countries only as of the production and manufacturing bases, but also partners for knowledge transfer or collaborative R&D (Kumar 2001). In order to meet the needs of the local market, some multinational companies want to set up overseas R&D centers to develop products for local market features. They even hire local technical talents to meet the needs of teams. In addition, based on the development of web 2.0 technologies (e.g., instant messenger, VoIP, or other social media technologies), numerous companies started using IT tools to improve knowledge transfer across organizations. For example, global knowledge management systems (KMS) or virtual teams-based collaborations are constantly being improved to facilitate knowledge transfer between global business partners (Sherif et al. 2006).

4 The Coming of KM 3.0 Era: Big Data-Driven Knowledge Management

KM 3.0 emerged with big data era. With the development of big data (BD) and artificial intelligence (AI) technologies, how to improve the abilities to acquire and utilize knowledge from huge unstructured data has become a hot topic (Jin et al. 2015). Many enterprises are paying attention to and discussing BD/AI technologies and believe that such abilities will become an important and indispensable competitive edge. KM 3.0 era can also be called the stage of big data-driven KM, in which knowledge innovation through data becomes the key to knowledge management (Kabir and Carayannis 2013). Besides, AI and other technologies will become important support in the process of knowledge management (Ordóñez de Pablos and Lytras 2018). With help of the big data mining technologies, knowledge management is combined with many fields, extending the boundary of organizational knowledge, focusing on the deep mining and micro mechanisms of the knowledge creation process, so as to help enterprises improve their ability of knowledge absorption and create more benefits (Provost and Fawcett 2013). In this section, we will discuss the characteristics and challenges of KM 3.0.

5 Uncertain: The Characteristics of KM 3.0 Era

5.1 The Process of Knowledge Creation Is Uncertain

In the era of KM 3.0, IBM, Google, and other top international high-tech companies are facing the "dilemma of innovation" in research and development, that is, the knowledge to be used is no longer ready-made, but rather in-depth exploration and discovery. The demand for knowledge management has changed from "sharing management of existing knowledge resources" to "predicting management of complex knowledge creation" (Acharya et al. 2018).

5.2 The Platform for Knowledge Acquisition Is Uncertain

"Reverse globalization" has made it difficult for large companies to transfer knowledge globally (Anand 2015). In recent years, the reverse globalization trend of global economic development has blocked the knowledge transfer among large global companies during the knowledge management 2.0 period. Knowledge-based innovation activities in developing countries represented by China will rely more on open innovation models such as crowdsourcing (Cassiman and Valentini 2016). The key issue of KM 3.0 is also transforming to "how to intelligently and accurately find high-value partners from millions of micro-innovators distributed around the world," rather than "how to improve the efficiency of knowledge transfer between fixed partners with big companies."

5.3 The Cooperation Mechanisms and Partners of Knowledge Are Uncertain

Compared with large enterprises, small and micro enterprises (SMEs) are not mature enough at all. They may be imperfect in management and talents. And most importantly, there is not enough money for them. Therefore, these enterprises are facing great obstacles in the application of information technology. According to statistics, there are more than 40 million SMEs in China, and the proportion of informatization is less than 10%.[1] Due to the lack of information support, most of SMEs are difficult to identify knowledge partners, which hinders further development of them greatly. Thus, how to establish an agile knowledge sharing model from these SMEs' and high potential talents by using low-cost technologies (e.g., cloud computing) becomes a critical issue in the KM 3.0 era.

5.4 The Rise of Big Data Technology: Digital Transformation

Digital transformation is an effective response strategy for enterprises to face the economic slowdown, intensified industry competition, and increasingly personalized customer demand (Bharadwaj et al. 2013; Khanagha et al. 2014). Digital transformation is essentially a business transformation, a prerequisite, and an insurmountable stage of intelligence. It is a critical way for enterprises to reshape their core competitiveness in the big data era. At present, the world has entered a new era of digital transformation, and some large and leading enterprises (e.g., IBM, Microsoft,

[1]See: https://www.qianzhan.com/analyst/detail/220/190219-23e2fab7.html

and Huawei[2]) in the world start to establish big data analyzing capabilities to ensure their knowledge advantages in R&D. Especially, with the application of new technologies such as 5G technology, big data, and AI technologies will drive a more agile KM model in developing a new product (Khan and Vorley 2017).

In summary, KM 3.0 can be defined as "highly interactive, highly forward-looking intelligent knowledge management driven by big data and AI technologies."

6 The Challenges and Agenda of KM 3.0

6.1 New Knowledge Management Computing Theories Should Be Built

In the digital transforming era, the forms and speed of knowledge appear very different from the past. The past knowledge creation theory is likely to be unable to explain the knowledge phenomenon in the existing environment, for example, how to accurately predict knowledge creation process and establish an agile KM model. Therefore, combined with some big data-based theories, future research should explore the issues on the forms and theoretical mechanisms of knowledge creation and innovation in the digital environment deeply.

6.2 Difficulties in Analysing Multisource and Unstructured Data

The social media industry is a typical representative of comprehensive digital business. Social networks (Twitter, WeChat), mobile networks, and other smart tools are generating huge amounts of data. The Internet information explosion has caused the scarcity of truly valuable information. In digital environments, people's demands for spiritual consumptions is increasing substantially, leading to a great thirst for knowledge. The developed Internet makes a variety of open knowledge platforms develop rapidly, such as Quora (the United States) and Zhihu (China) (Zhao et al. 2018). Furthermore, with the development of 5G technologies, there are more sensor-based data will be generated in the business processes.

The data generated from these platforms are characterized by massive and multiple types, such as web pages, voice, video, sensor-based data, and so on. So there is an urgent need for knowledge management computing technologies, such as

[2]See: http://www.xinhuanet.com/tech/2017-07/09/c_1121288471.html

AI algorithms, big data (BD) processing platforms, and new data processing techniques to process BD in real time, and to mine the hidden knowledge in huge amounts of data.

6.3 The Concept of Knowledge Needs to Be Revisited

Due to the rapid change of the environment, people's understanding of knowledge needs to change from the past. Based on large amount of data in the digital environment and rich knowledge interaction, the main bodies, actions, and processes of different knowledge activities (e.g., knowledge exchange and knowledge sharing) are changed from the past (Provost and Fawcett 2013). Researchers and practitioners should understand and explore the behavioral law of individuals in new environments, then gaining process model of knowledge creation in digital environments.

Based on the characteristics of the digital environment, different mechanism changes may occur for different knowledge activities. Through the rich data of digital platforms, the impact of different activities, different enterprise characteristics, different platform characteristics, and even different industry characteristics on the knowledge creation process should be explored. For innovative enterprises such as high-tech enterprises, they should take knowledge innovation urgently as the core competitiveness. And from the perspective of knowledge innovation, they need to consider their own characteristics to make innovation decisions. With the help of intelligent technologies and KM computing, the knowledge links may change from "information-knowledge" to "knowledge-wisdom."

7 Conclusion

This chapter reviews the knowledge characteristics of the knowledge management era 1.0 and the knowledge management 2.0 era, and describes some of the characteristics and future challenges of the upcoming knowledge management 3.0 era. Figure 1 shows the characteristics of several knowledge management eras. Figure 2 summarizes the future challenges of the KM 3.0 era. The KM 3.0 era is still in its infancy based on technologies such as big data and AI, and many aspects are not fully understood. We hope that this review will promote research in this area and provide guidance for future research. The work was supported by National Natural Science Foundation of China (No. 71722005, 71571133, 71790594, 71790590, 91746301), and Tianjin Natural Science Foundation (No. 18JCJQJC45900).

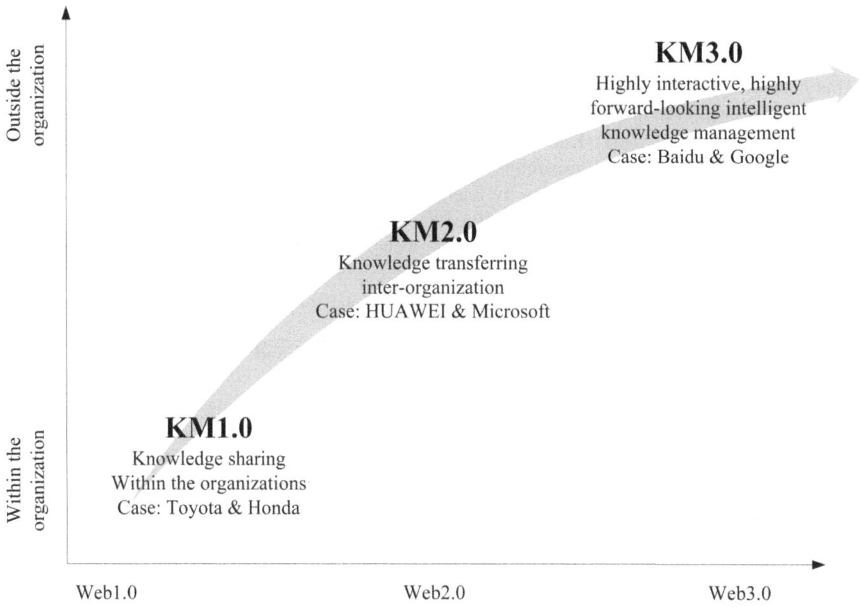

Fig. 1 The characteristics of KM 1.0, KM 2.0, and KM 3.0 (Source: Adapted from Labrecque et al. 2013)

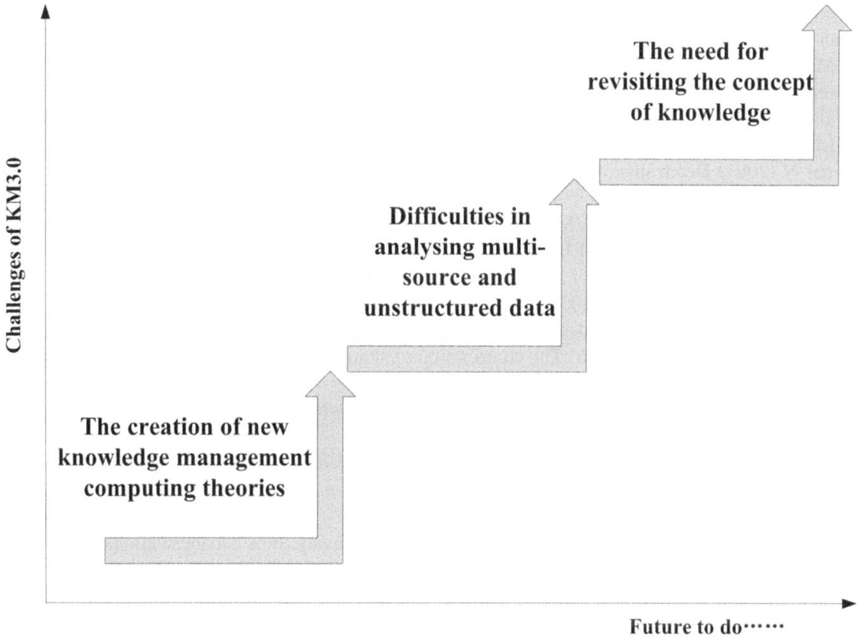

Fig. 2 The challenges and agenda of KM 3.0 (Source: The authors)

References

Acharya A, Singh SK, Pereira V, Singh P (2018) Big data, knowledge co-creation and decision making in fashion industry. Int J Inf Manag 42:90–101

Alavi M, Leidner DE (2001) Knowledge management and knowledge management systems: conceptual foundations and research issues. MIS Q 25(1):107–136

Anand B (2015) Reverse globalization by internationalization of SME's: opportunities and challenges ahead. Procedia Soc Behav Sci 195:1003–1011

Bell J, Loane S (2010) 'New-wave' global firms: web 2.0 and SME internationalisation. J Mark Manag 26(3–4):213–229

Bharadwaj A, El Sawy OA, Pavlou PA, Venkatraman N (2013) Digital business strategy: toward a next generation of insights. MIS Q 37(2):471–482

Cassiman B, Valentini G (2016) Open innovation: are inbound and outbound knowledge flows really complementary? Strateg Manag J 37(6):1034–1046

Charband Y, Navimipour NJ (2016) Online knowledge sharing mechanisms: a systematic review of the state of the art literature and recommendations for future research. Inf Syst Front 18 (6):1131–1151

D'Agostino LM, Santangelo GD (2012) Do overseas R&D laboratories in emerging markets contribute to home knowledge creation? Manag Int Rev 52(2):251–273

Darr ED, Argote L, Epple D (1995) The acquisition, transfer, and depreciation of knowledge in service organizations: productivity in franchises. Manag Sci 41(11):1750–1762

Erickson S, Rothberg H (2014) Big data and knowledge management: establishing a conceptual foundation. Electron J Knowl Manag 12(2):101

Jin X, Wah BW, Cheng X, Wang Y (2015) Significance and challenges of big data research. Big Data Res 2(2):59–64

Kabir N, Carayannis E (2013) Big data, tacit knowledge and organizational competitiveness. Paper presented at the proceedings of the 10th international conference on intellectual capital, Knowledge Management and Organisational Learning: ICICKM

Khan Z, Vorley T (2017) Big data text analytics: an enabler of knowledge management. J Knowl Manag 21(1):18–34

Khanagha S, Volberda H, Oshri I (2014) Business model renewal and ambidexterity: structural alteration and strategy formation process during transition to a C loud business model. R&D Manag 44(3):322–340

Kumar N (2001) Determinants of location of overseas R&D activity of multinational enterprises: the case of US and Japanese corporations. Res Policy 30(1):159–174

Labrecque LI, vor dem Esche J, Mathwick C, Novak TP, Hofacker CF (2013) Consumer power: evolution in the digital age. J Interact Mark 27(4):257–269

Leonard D (1995) Wellsprings of knowledge. Harvard Business School Press, Boston

Marr B, Schiuma G, Neely A (2004) Intellectual capital – defining key performance indicators for organizational knowledge assets. Bus Process Manag J 10(5):551–569

Nelson KM, Cooprider JG (1996) The contribution of shared knowledge to IS group performance. MIS Q 20(4):409–432

Nilmanat R (2011) Investigating image usage and tacit knowledge sharing in online communities. Int J Innov Learn 10(4):350–364

Nonaka I (1994) A dynamic theory of organizational knowledge creation. Organ Sci 5(1):14–37

Nonaka I, Konno N (1998) The concept of "Ba": building a foundation for knowledge creation. Calif Manag Rev 40(3):40–54

Nonaka I, Takeuchi H (1995) The knowledge-creating company: how Japanese companies create the dynamics of innovation. Oxford University Press, New York

Nonaka I, Toyama R, Konno N (2000) SECI, Ba and leadership: a unified model of dynamic knowledge creation. Long Range Plan 33(1):5–34

Ordóñez de Pablos P, Lytras M (2018) Knowledge management, innovation and big data: implications for sustainability, policy making and competitiveness. Sustainability 10(6):2073

Pan SL, Leidner DE (2003) Bridging communities of practice with information technology in pursuit of global knowledge sharing. J Strateg Inf Syst 12(1):71–88
Provost F, Fawcett T (2013) Data science and its relationship to big data and data-driven decision making. Big Data 1(1):51–59
Reber AS (1967) Implicit learning of artificial grammars. J Verbal Learn Verbal Behav 6 (6):855–863
Rottman JW (2008) Successful knowledge transfer within offshore supplier networks: a case study exploring social capital in strategic alliances. J Inf Technol 23(1):31–43
Sharma RS, Carrillo FJ, Ng EWJ, Dharmawirya M, Keong Lee C (2008) Beyond the digital divide: a conceptual framework for analyzing knowledge societies. J Knowl Manag 12(5):151–164
Sherif K, Hoffman J, Thomas B (2006) Can technology build organizational social capital? The case of a global IT consulting firm. Inf Manag 43(7):795–804
Shollo A, Galliers RD (2016) Towards an understanding of the role of business intelligence systems in organisational knowing. Inf Syst J 26(4):339–367
Zhao Y, Liu Z, Song S (2018) Why should I pay for the knowledge in Social Q&A Platforms? Paper presented at the International Conference on Information

Key Competencies for Digital Transformation in Workplace

Inês Faina and Filomena Almeida

Abstract There is evidence that artificial intelligence and automation will affect and be present in portions of almost all jobs, either in a greater or lesser degree. Notwithstanding, these digital transformations will eliminate very few jobs and occupations over the next decades. Taking this into account, this research intends to identify which competencies are more valuable for workers who work in a technological workplace, by the employers' perspective. It means this research will explore, listening to employers' opinion, which competencies are the ones that make a worker lead and responds positively to a digital implementation in their workplace. Results were gathered through a Delphi study, within a panel of six experts in the human resources for the technological industries field. It is finding that employers consider adaptability and creativity as the most important competencies for technological work. In addition, informatic competencies were less valuable by employers while considering the importance of workers dealing with digital transformations in workplaces.

1 Introduction

It is now clear the evidence of the impact of automation and artificial intelligence in almost all jobs and functions of the current job market, as well as the urgency to understand the phenomena and to act within that. This conviction conducts academic and business worlds to concern about that, analyzing and taking conclusions about the next decades regarding workplace and workers' capacities to deal with that. It seems crucial to understand the phenomena before it grows unduly and uncontrolled.

There are also companies that need to clarify and help their own employees understanding the impact of automation in their workplace. This help seems to be important since the impact and relevance of the increasing automation in production

I. Faina (✉) · F. Almeida
ISCTE - IUL Business School, Lisbon, Portugal
e-mail: ines_raquel_faina@iscte-iul.pt; filomena.almeida@iscte-iul.pt

F. Matos et al. (eds.), *Knowledge, People, and Digital Transformation*, Contributions to Management Science, https://doi.org/10.1007/978-3-030-40390-4_14

and services is yet seen for many as a cause of aggregate unemployment, causing fear and negative feelings.

Companies, mostly managers and decision makers, should face this problem not in a negative but in a positive perspective, considering this not as a question *robot* versus *people* (which sees digital, robotics, and artificial intelligence as a way of stealing jobs and functions of humans—where the first ones, robots, are collectors of the people's jobs) but the question of which competencies should an employee have or should develop to make himself as an adaptable employee, who has a positive reaction to a technological or digital change in his/her functions or even in his/her workplace.

As important to understand this problem of robotic, technological implementation and its presence in companies, is to understand which competencies are considered important for employees who face these digital transformations.

In order to define the key competencies for an employee with digital transformation in his/her workplace, which means competencies that make the worker leads and respond positively to a digital transformation in their workplace, it was developed a Delphi study through a sample of Portuguese employers. During this chapter, it will be possible to understand which competencies are more valuable for employers within employees who deal with technological and robotic presence in their workplace.

2 Historical Review of Competencies

For the past decades, employee's competencies have played an important role within both the labor market and the academical literature. Realizing the importance of certain characteristics of the employees, companies, employers, and academics have further look to these characteristics.

Furthermore, competencies have attracted much attention in practical and theoretical fields. Quoting Dubois (1998), Rothwell and Lindholm (1999) say "there is growing interest in competencies in medium-sized and smaller organizations."

In the year of 1973, David McClelland, Professor of Psychology at Harvard University, wrote his paper, the "*Testing for Competence Rather than Intelligence*," (McClelland 1973) stirring the field of industrial psychology. McClelland "defined 'Competence' as 'a personal trait or set of habits that leads to more effective or superior job performance'" (Chouhan and Srivastava 2014).

The McClelland work was majority focused on the application on the education sector, Boyatzis was responsible for the business perspective of competence (Boyatzis 2008). In his book "The Competent Manager," Boyatzis (1982) defines competency as "an underlying characteristic of a person which results in effective and/or superior performance in a job."

Many definitions of the term "competency" have risen over the last years. According to Chouhan and Srivastava (2014), the definition that is most preferred is that "Competencies include the collection of success factors necessary for achieving important results in a specific job or work role in a particular organization."

As Le Deist and Winterton (2005) say, in their "What Is Competence?" publication, "the concept of competence or competency (. . .) dominated the management strategy literature of the 1990s, which emphasized 'core competence' as a key organizational resource that could be exploited to gain competitive advantage."

Teodorescu (2006) devoted herself to understand not only the distinction, but also the approximation, of both concepts: competence and competency, analyzing information resulted from Dubois (1998) research.

According to Dubois (1998), competencies (plural for competency) are "those characteristics—knowledge, skills, mindsets, thought patterns, and the like—that when used whether singularly or in various combinations, result in successful performance." For this chapter, as for the research here presented, it was adopted this definition proposed by Dubois.

According to Blázquez et al. (2018), more attention to noncognitive skills and competencies starts by the fact that the switch from university to work has become a crucial phase in graduates' lives. Due to that, it is important to know which competencies will enable these newly graduates to the benefit of gifted job chances. Additionally, authors refer to know these competencies are crucial not only from the perspective of the individual but also from the point of view of education policy.

These authors consider there are two main topics within the studies on this topic, first group observes the correlation between labor market outcomes and skills depending on their cognitive or noncognitive nature, second one emphasis the specific competencies regardless of whether they are cognitive or non-cognitive.

These authors distinct skills into cognitive (measured by objectives tests) and non-cognitive (harder to measure, analyzed by means of self-reported information). Authors' definition of competencies by type (cognitive or non-cognitive) is presented in Table 1.

Throughout the literature available, one can notice that some authors refer competencies transversal and transferable across not only jobs, but also personal situations (Baxter and Young 1982; Teijeiro et al. 2013) while others distinct specific technical skills by occupation, task, or job.

3 Digital Transformation and Competencies

It is also important to analyze literature regarding digital transformation in order to better understand its connection with key competencies of employees.

In this scope, recognizing the change technology creates in an organization, including its people, procedures, and culture, Ghani and Jayabalan (2000) developed a framework analyzing the technology implementation effect on a company. According to these authors, technology implementation occurs through structural mechanisms that are designed in pursuance of manufacturing objectives. The framework, showed in Fig. 1, describes a firm's technology as an endogenous variable,

Table 1 Competencies by type, by Blásquez et al. (2018)

Cognitive competencies	Alertness to new opportunities
	Ability to come up with new ideas and solutions
	Willingness to question your own and others' ideas
	Ability to write reports, memos, or documents
	Analytical thinking
	Ability to rapidly acquire new knowledge
	Knowledge of other fields or disciplines
	Mastery of your own field or discipline
	Ability to use computers and the Internet
	Ability to write and speak in a foreign language
Noncognitive competencies	Ability to mobilize the capacities of others
	Ability to make your meaning clear to others
	Ability to assert your authority
	Ability to negotiate effectively
	Ability to perform well under pressure
	Ability to coordinate activities
	Ability to use time efficiently
	Ability to work productively with others
	Ability to present products, ideas, or reports to an audience

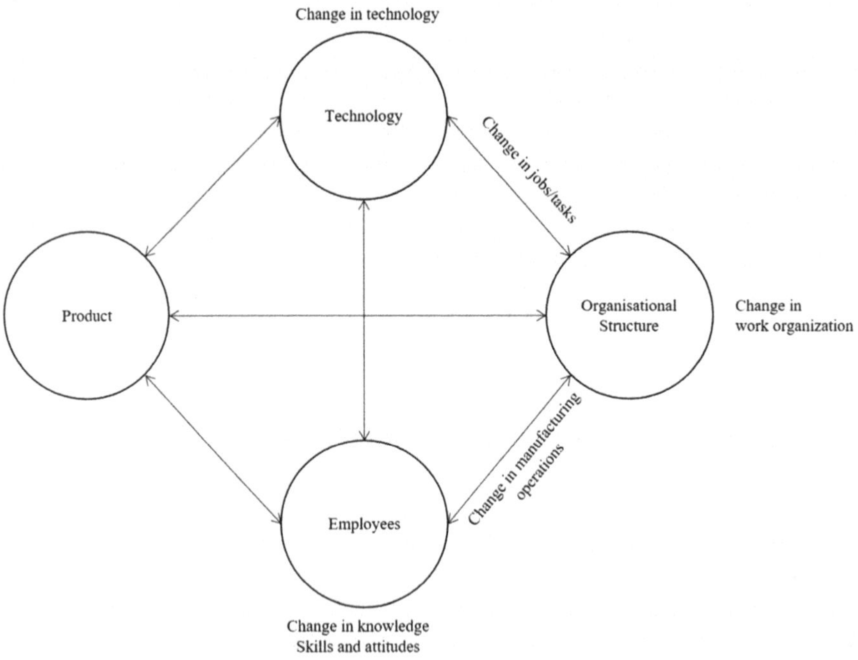

Fig. 1 Adapted from the conceptual framework by Ghani and Jayabalan (2000)

following the evolutionary models, that undergoes frequent adaptations to remain technically competitive.

Ghani and Jayabalan (2000), also state that, when there is an implementation of new technologies, total productivity at first falls because of the natural response of employees resistance to accepting new technology. Notwithstanding, as workers familiarize to new technology, their acceptance rate improves and their attitudes toward new technology become more positive.

Knowing there are differences between humans and robots, Jarrahi (2018) proposes two ways to build a partnership between them. First, this author suggests specializing each one of the intervenients in different aspects, namely:

> AI is likely to be well positioned to tackle complexity issues (using analytical approaches). Humans can focus more on uncertainty and equivocality, using more creative and intuitive approaches. (Jarrahi 2018)

Secondly, Jarrahi (2018) presents that the most complex decisions are likely to involve marks of uncertainty and equivocality, which induces and requires human involvement, the author adds that “therefore, humans and AI will play a combined role in almost all complex decision making.”

When facing these digital transformations, it is crucial to understand how employees’ reactions can occur. Wittig (2012) refers that “the line in employees” reactions to organizational change between resistance and acceptance is often blurred. So, according to this, as change initiatives are not static, and factors continually occur affect employee’s reactions, employees’ reactions are consistently fluctuating and never stagnant.

4 Employers Opinion

In order to understand and take conclusions regarding the key competencies for an employee to deal with digital transformation in his/her workplace, a Delphi method was proceeded.

Mitroff and Turoff (2002) defined Delphi method as a method for structuring a group communication process so that the process is effective in allowing a group of individuals, as a whole to deal with a complex problem. This method, as a technique, allows the gather of opinion and/or judgments of experts and practitioners regarding complex matters where precise information or consensus, of both practitioners or academics, is not available.

More than a technique to achieve consensus and to understand what is really going on regarding the topic studied, Delphi method is also able to produce and develop trends and needs in and for the atmosphere it was created for, in this specific research, the competencies needed for an employee who has technologies, automation, or robotic in their workplace.

The application of the Delphi method, in the scope of the research developed and presented within this thesis, went through several phases, by the application of three rounds.

Firstly, it was necessary to identify a panel of experts, determining the willingness of individuals to serve on the panel. Every possible was asked to be part of this research by email. It was gathered with a panel six members.

Considering that the outcome of a Delphi research is as valid as the opinion of the experts who made up the panel, the definition of the Delphi panel assumes great importance in which concerns to have a great output from the research process.

In what concerns to the design of the Delphi panel, and defining which experts invite to participate, it is important to avoid the "representativeness" criteria. Avella (2016) refers that "choosing a representative sample is something typically sought out in quantitative studies so the results can accurately portray the total population," therefore, for a Delphi study, representation is not a quality to fulfil imperatively, but expertise is.

During the process of expert selection, it was considered critical characteristics to the execution of the Delphi method in an accurate and adequate way, namely: anonymity, feedback, and panel membership.

Anonymity is important because keeping panel members isolated from each other allows each individual freedom of expression without outside pressure or influence (Avella 2016).

During this research, only the researcher contacted each member of the panel, in order to have their participation in each round.

Regarding the characteristic of feedback, knowing the process of a Delphi study, which consists of achieving consensus by a communication process, this characteristic is crucial for good results. During the time of this Delphi study, contacts between the researcher and the members of the panel were consistent and frequent, always by email.

Selecting individuals who meet expertise qualifications for panel membership is critical and cannot be overstressed. In this scope, it is important to notice that the six members of the panel have tenure in the field of Human Resources comprehended between 14 and 28 years.

In this scope, it is important to refer the panel for this research is composed of the following members:

- HR Director of an aviation group, with about 11,000 workers around the world.
- General Director of a company within the pharmaceutical industry, with about 35 workers.
- HR consultant, with an important focus in behavioral training.
- HR Director of a delivery company, inside a group of delivering experts across Europe, with about 800 workers all over Portugal.
- Senior HR Specialist in development in a company within the automotive industry, with about 6,000 workers.
- HR Responsible in a regulatory public agency with about 400 workers.

Furthermore, according to Akins et al. (2005), certain criteria apply to membership on all Delphi Panels, specifically interest, time, and written communication.

So, in what concerns to interest as a criterion to membership on Delphi Panels, it is worthy of relevance that the participants express interest in the topic and a willingness to contribute to the research inference.

On the other hand, regarding time, it was carefully explained to the experts, at the beginning of the research, even before they accept to participate, the needed time to be in the process so that they can be aware of this.

Lastly, the language of the surveys and panel rounds was consensual within the panel members, and it was "the one native language most prevalent among panel members or one based on a specific requirement for a language in which panel members shared fluency" (Avella 2016).

Having the panel defined, it was important to design and construct the instrument to the data collection, a questionnaire.

After the building of a provisional questionnaire, a pilot test was conducted. Five individuals participated in the pilot test, resulting in a group of changes to the provisional questionnaire, with detailed feedback regarding their perception of the questionnaire.

Considering feedback provided, it was built a final questionnaire, presented in Annex A, constituted by four parts, each one with a specific objective for the research. Part I of the questionnaire intends to gather information regarding the experts' characterization.

The second part of the questionnaire aims to know in what way experts consider important each competency, used competencies proposed by Blázquez et al. (2018), for an employee in a company with the presence of robots or technology in its workplace.

Regarding Part III of the questionnaire, it faces experts with a situation (presented in Fig. 1) and two workers' profiles. It is presented professional, academic, and personal paths for both workers, and it is asked which competencies experts identify in each one of the profiles presented, as well as which worker do they think will have a more positive reaction to a technological or robotic intervention or change in their workplace. Through this part of the questionnaire, it will be possible to identify which competencies experts consider more valuable for a worker in a situation of robotic presence or implementation.

In this scope, it was proposed to experts to classify who has more developed each one of the following competencies: Creativity; Informatic Knowledge; Resilience; Computer Skills; Autonomy; and Self-development.

Last part intends to explore experts' opinions, giving them the possibility to fulfil six spaces, ordering, by importance, six competencies considered valuable and essential to workers in the presence of technology or robotic in their workplace.

This questionnaire was applied through three rounds to all the initial members of the panel.

For each round of the method, the following steps were conducted:

1. Gathering of the individual experts' opinions through an online questionnaire—Annex B.

2. Analyzing data gathered from the panel.
3. Compiling information and sending the questionnaire to each panel member for their review.

Through the answers to the first round of this Delphi study, it was possible to conclude that, according to the panel of experts, the more important competencies, and the ones which reunite more consensus, for an employee with technology or robots in the workplace, were *Ability to rapidly acquire new knowledge*, *Alertness to new opportunities* and *Ability to use computers and the Internet*. In a global perspective, in the experts' opinion, the less valuable competencies for an employee, who has technology or robots in the workplace, are *Ability to negotiate effectively*, *Knowledge of other fields or disciplines* and *Mastery of your own field or discipline*.

Concerning the situation presented in Part III of the Questionnaire, experts well-thought the following:

- Expert 01—Considered worker B, the one with a more positive reaction to a technological change and robot implementation. Simultaneously, considered that worker B has Creativity, Resilience, Autonomy, and Self-development more developed.
- Expert 02—Considered worker A the one with a more positive reaction to a technological change and robot implementation. Simultaneously, considered that worker B has Informatic Knowledge, Resilience, Computer Skills, Autonomy, and Self-development more developed. This expert also proposed Flexibility and Adaptability as competencies developed by worker A.
- Expert 03—Considered worker B, the one with a more positive reaction to a technological change and robot implementation. Simultaneously, considered that worker B has Creativity, Informatic Knowledge, Computer Skills, and Autonomy more developed.
- Expert 04—Considered worker A the one with a more positive reaction to a technological change and robot implementation. Simultaneously, considered that worker B has Informatic Knowledge, Resilience, Computer Skills, Autonomy, and Self-development more developed.
- Expert 05—Considered worker B, the one with a more positive reaction to a technological change and robot implementation. Simultaneously, considered that worker B has Creativity, Informatic Knowledge, Computer Skills, Autonomy, and Self-development more developed.
- Expert 06—Considered worker B, the one with a more positive reaction to a technological change and robot implementation. Simultaneously, considered that worker B has Creativity, Informatic Knowledge, Resilience, Computer Skills, Autonomy, and Self-development more developed.

Regarding Part IV, results found out for this first round are presented in Table 2. In this scope, it is important to consider the information presented in Table 2 is exactly the information provided by experts.

Table 2 First round—Answers to Part IV

	Expert 01	Expert 02	Expert 03	Expert 04	Expert 05	Expert 06
1st	Innovation	Adaptability to new situations	Adaptability	Ability to continuously learn	Innovation and changeability	Proactivity
2nd	Opening for change	Critical analysis	Adaptability to change/ creativity	Teamwork	Creativity	Communication
3rd	Resilience	Resilience	Resilience	Adaptability	Adaptability	Opening for change
4th	Self-examination	Adaptability	Ability to learn	Creativity	Ability to work with informatic tools	Logical thinking
5th		Decision-making	Analysis capacity	Technological knowledge		Analytical capability
6th		Stress resistance	Orientation to continuous improvement	Resilience		Creativity

Imagine a situation of a company acting in the field of the automotive components industry. There will be a change in the production line, it will be introduced in it a robot which will solve an identified problem. This robot will contribute to a higher productivity of the factory, producing more components per minute, with the same number of employees.

Consider that Employee A and Employee B are employees in this specific factory sector and will be impacted by this new robot. They will need to learn to use the robot and to solve possible problems that can occur.

Personal and professional profile of both employees are the following:

Employee A – did not finish high school; started working in automotive industry in his/her first work; never change his/her job or employer; he/she belong to a scoop troup for 7 years, having been responsible for the organization of the main events of the group; use the internet and computer to interact with his/her family and friends; he/she has 2 kids and is raising them alone because their other parent disappear; his/her children are happy and successful young people.

Employee B – frequented 3 art courses in high school; finished high school; have changed job for four times during his/her career path because he/she was unsatisfied with his/her functions; do not use his/her computer; his/her hobby is painting and baking; has no kids or pets; often attends to workshops in his/her area of interest.

Fig. 2 Questionnaire Part III

At this stage of the research, it was not any kind of speech revision or change in the language used. As in all following rounds, all experts receive a report with the results found out within this first round.

The second round of this Delphi study was performed with five experts, who consider the more important competencies, with more consensus, *Alertness to new opportunities*, *Willingness to question your own and others' ideas* and *Ability to mobilize the capacities of others*. For the experts, the more valuable competencies for an employee who has technology or robots in the workplace are *Alertness to new opportunities*, *Ability to come up with new ideas and solutions*, *Willingness to question your own and others' ideas*, *Ability to rapidly acquire new knowledge* and *Ability to use computers and the Internet*. On the other hand, experts consider as the less valuable competency for an employee who has technology or robots in the workplace the *Ability to negotiate effectively*.

When faced with the situation presented in Part III of the Questionnaire (see Fig. 2), experts considered the following:

- Expert 02—Considered worker A the one with a more positive reaction to a technological change and robot implementation. Simultaneously, considered that worker A has Creativity, Informatic Knowledge, Resilience, Autonomy, and Self-development more developed. For this round, this expert did not propose more competencies than the proposed ones.
- Expert 03—Considered worker B, the one with a more positive reaction to a technological change and robot implementation. Simultaneously, considered that worker B has Creativity, Informatic Knowledge, Resilience, Computer Skills, and self-development more developed.

Table 3 Answers to Part IV—Second round

	Expert 02	Expert 03	Expert 04	Expert 05	Expert 06
1st	Change management	Adaptability	Opening for change	Innovation and changeability	Proactivity
2nd	Resilience	Adaptability to change	Ability to continuously learn	Creativity	Communication
3rd	Stress resistance	Self-learning	Analytical thinking	Adaptability	Opening for change
4th	Organization of the work	Orientation to continuous improvement	Teamwork	Ability to work with informatic tools	Logical thinking
5th	Time management		Resilience		Analytical capability
6th	Creativity		Positiveness		Creativity

- Expert 04—Considered worker A the one with a more positive reaction to a technological change and robot implementation. Simultaneously, considered that worker B has Informatic Knowledge, Resilience, Computer Skills, Autonomy, and Self-development more developed.
- Expert 05—Considered worker B, the one with a more positive reaction to a technological change and robot implementation. Simultaneously, considered that worker B has Creativity, Informatic Knowledge, Computer Skills, Autonomy, and Self-development more developed.
- Expert 06—Considered worker B, the one with a more positive reaction to a technological change and robot implementation. Simultaneously, considered that worker B has Creativity, Informatic Knowledge, Resilience, Computer Skills, Autonomy, and Self-development more developed.

Results found out in Part IV of the questionnaire, for this second round, are presented in Table 3. At the end of the data analysis, experts received a report with the outcomes from this round, accessible in Annex C.

In the third round of this Delphi study, four experts have participated. Through their answers, it is possible to observe three competencies reach a consensus regarding the level of importance for an employee with digital transformations in the workplace: *Knowledge of other fields or disciplines*; *Ability to perform well under pressure*; *Ability to coordinate activities*. Each one of these competencies was considered by all the experts as Very Important to an employee who deals with technology in the workplace.

Additionally, it is possible to conclude that, according to the panel of experts, the more important competencies for an employee with technology or robots in the workplace, the ones which were listed only as Very Important or Extremely Important, apart the ones considered only as Extremely Important, were: *Ability to come up with new ideas and solutions, Willingness to question your own and others' ideas, Analytical thinking, Ability to rapidly acquire new knowledge, Mastery of your own field or discipline, Ability to use computers and the Internet, Ability to write and speak in a foreign language, Ability to make your meaning clear to others* and *Ability to assert your authority.*

In a global perspective, according to the experts' opinion, the more valuable competency, it means the competency listed by more experts (three in a total of four experts) as Extremely Important, is *Mastery of your own field or discipline.*

In the experts' opinion, the less valuable competencies, within the ones presented to the experts, are *Ability to negotiate effectively* and *Ability to write reports, memos, or documents.*

For the situation presented in Part III of the Questionnaire, experts stated the following:

- Expert 02—Considered worker A the one with a more positive reaction to a technological change and robot implementation. Simultaneously, considered that worker A has Creativity, Informatic Knowledge, Resilience, Computer Skills, Autonomy, and Self-development more developed. For this round, this expert also proposed that worker A has developed the ability to work under pressure and also the ability to work in a team.
- Expert 03—Considered worker B, the one with a more positive reaction to a technological change and robot implementation. Simultaneously, considered that worker B has Creativity, Informatic Knowledge, Computer Skills, and Self-Development more developed.
- Expert 05—Considered worker B, the one with a more positive reaction to a technological change and robot implementation. Simultaneously, considered that worker B has Creativity, Informatic Knowledge, Computer Skills, Autonomy, and Self-development more developed.
- Expert 06—Considered worker B, the one with a more positive reaction to a technological change and robot implementation. Simultaneously, considered that worker B has Creativity, Informatic Knowledge, Resilience, Computer Skills, Autonomy, and Self-development more developed.

When questioned regarding the competencies not mentioned that could be important for a positive reaction to the technological implementation described, experts also proposed adaptability to change (expert 02), problem solving (expert 02 and expert 03), decision-making capability (expert 02), technical knowledge for the software/equipment (expert 03), process management (expert 03), orientation to continuous improvement (expert 03), quality focus (expert 03), adaptability (expert 05), continuous learning (expert 05), constructive feedback (expert 05), and strategic behavior (expert 05).

Regarding Part IV of the questionnaire, results found out for this third round are presented in Table 4. In this scope, it is important to consider that the information presented in Table 4 is exactly the information provided by experts; no changes were made in the speech used by them.

At the end of these three rounds, experts were presented with a report stating the results found out, presented in Annex D.

Table 4 Answers to Part IV—Third round

	Expert 02	Expert 03	Expert 05	Expert 06
1st	Adaptability to new situations	Adaptability to change	Innovation and changeability	Proactivity
2nd	Adaptability	Adaptability	Creativity	Communication
3rd	Resilience	Self-learning	Adaptability	Opening for change
4th	Capability to work under pressure	Problem solving	Ability to work with informatic tools	Logical thinking
5th	Self-esteem			Analytical capability
6th	New challenges appetite			Creativity

5 Findings and Conclusions

The results gathered through the Delphi study performed, allows to understand which competencies are valuable for an employee who deals with robots, technology, or digital transformations in his/her workplace, from the perspective of the employers.

It is important to notice the questionnaire was passed throughout experts in their mother language, Portuguese, so that they can feel more comfortable reading and writing. All proposed competencies were written in Portuguese by the experts, with no guidelines or support. So, it seems to be natural that the results show different competencies, notwithstanding the different possibility competencies, presented by different experts and their perceptions, have the same meaning at the end of the research.

In order to adequate this speech differences, all competencies were reviewed and aligned in a group of a major, and more standardized, competencies, as it will be shown.

For the first round, it was proposed a total of 32 competencies by six experts, in the second round, it was proposed a total of 26 competencies by five experts, and within the last round, the third one, it was proposed a total of 20 competencies by four experts.

After the revision of the competencies proposed, only in a perspective of language and differences of speech, it is possible to conclude that it was proposed a total of 82 different competencies. So, according to a deep revision of each one of these competencies, reviewing and standardizing the way they were exposed and written by experts, it results in a group of 29 different competencies, presented in Table 5.

In a more detailed revision of the gathered data, it seems relevant to analyze the predominance of some competencies, which will be important to take conclusions from the research developed.

Within this scope, it will be analyze the reference, through the three rounds, to Resilience, Adaptability, Informatic Competencies, Learning Skills, and Creativity.

Table 5 Answers to Part IV—Third round

Competency	Number of times referred through the Delphi study
Adaptability	10
Creativity	9
Resilience	7
Innovation ability	5
Opening for change	5
Analytical capability	4
Ability to work with informatic tools	4
Learning capability	3
Proactivity	3
Communication	3
Logical thinking	3
Adaptability to change	3
Stress resistance	2
Team work	2
Self-learning	2
Self-examination	1
Decision maker	1
Orientation to continuous improvement	1
Change management	1
Organization of the work	1
Time management	1
Analytical thinking	1
Positiveness	1
Capability to work under pressure	1
Self-esteem	1
New challenges appetite	1
Problem solving	1

These competencies were chosen to the deepest analysis based on, not only the number of times it was referred by experts, but also on the existing literature and the researcher's understanding of the subject.

Additionally, for easier analysis, it was considered Informatic Competencies as the *Ability to work with informatic tools* proposed four times within the Delphi study.

According to the information gathered and displayed in Table 6, it is possible to understand the percentage of experts who refer each competency, as well as the weighted average of reference by the experts for listed competencies. The weighted average is computed as follows:

$$\bar{x} = \frac{\text{Sum of number of competency references in each round}}{\text{Total number of experts participating in all rounds}}$$

Table 6 Percentage of reference by experts through the Delphi study

	1st Round	2nd Round	3rd Round	
	Six experts (%)	Five experts (%)	Four experts (%)	Weighted average percentage of reference (%)
Resilience	66.7	40.0	25.0	**46.7**
Adaptability	66.7	60.0	75.0	**66.7**
Informatic competencies	33.3	20.0	25.0	**26.7**
Learning skills	33.3	40.0	25.0	**33.3**
Creativity	66.7	60.0	50.0	**60.0**

Bold values indicates the most referenced competencies, in average, through the three rounds

In this scope, on average, the most referenced competencies were *Adaptability* and *Creativity* with 66.7 and 60.0%, respectively. The less referred was *Informatic Competencies* with 26.7% of references.

The intent of this research is to find out which competencies are considered more valuable for a positive reaction of employees when dealing with digital transformations in their workplace, by the employers' perspective, and perception of the topic.

From the Delphi study performed, it results that a reaction of an employee to digital transformations in his/her workplace is impacted by two big groups of competencies: Informatic Skills (which are constructed based on two different topics—informatics knowledge and computer skills) and Personal Competencies (based on the competencies proposed by experts, namely *Adaptability*, *Resilience*, *Creativity,* and *Learning Skills*).

In a consensual way, at the end of the research process, respondents consider that, for a more positive reaction to digital transformations in workplaces, employees should have, or be able to develop, competencies like *Adaptability* and *Creativity*. Employers expect that a worker use competencies, mostly transversal to other fields, in order to better know how to manage and handle with technological or robotic tools.

6 Limitations and Future Work

The initially stated overarching aim of this research was to identify competencies employers consider important for a worker to deal with digital transformations in the scope of his/her workplace. While recognizing limitations, it is possible to identify how critical it is to identify a panel of experts to represent companies who employ workers to deal with technology or robotic continually. Even so, the gathered panel for the Delphi study pursued was highly satisfactory in terms of quality. However, it can be identified as difficulty, the constant feedback needed to the experts in order to maintain the number of participants in each round. Although there were a constant feedback and contact with experts, two of them eventually did not fulfil all rounds of the study. Regarding this limitation, it is worth to refer also the need for time to have consistent participation from the experts: this consists of a limitation for the experts and, consequently, for the research.

Recommendations for future research also go through the importance to define consistent strategies to develop the more needed competencies within the job market, in order to cope with challenges promoted by the presence of technology, robots, and digital in the current workplaces.

References

Akins R, Tolson H, Cole B (2005) Stability of response characteristics of a Delphi panel: application of bootstrap data expansion. BMC Med Res Methodol 5:37. https://doi.org/10.1186/1471-2288-5-37

Avella JR (2016) Delphi panels: research design, procedures, advantages, and challenges. Int J Dr Stud 11(11):305–321

Baxter MB, Young JL (1982) What do employers expect from high school graduates? NASSP Bull 66(458):93–98

Blázquez M, Herrarte A, Llorente-Heras R (2018) Competencies, occupational status, and earnings among European university graduates. Econ Educ Rev 62:16–34. https://doi.org/10.1016/j.econedurev.2017.10.006

Boyatzis RE (1982) The competent manager: a model for effective performance. Wiley, New York

Boyatzis RE (2008) Competencies in the 21st century. J Manag Dev 27(1):5–12. https://doi.org/10.1108/02621710810840730

Chouhan VS, Srivastava S (2014) Understanding competencies and competency modeling - a literature survey. IOSR J Bus Manag 16(1):14–22. https://doi.org/10.9790/487X-16111422

Dubois DD (1998) *The competency casebook: twelve studies in competency-based performance improvement*. HRD Press, Amherst, MA

Ghani KA, Jayabalan V (2000) Advanced manufacturing technology and planned organizational change. J High Technol Managem Res 11(1):1–18

Jarrahi MH (2018) Artificial intelligence and the future of work: human-AI symbiosis in organizational decision making. Bus Horiz 61(4):577–586. https://doi.org/10.1016/j.bushor.2018.03.007

Le Deist FD, Winterton J (2005) What is competence? Hum Resour Dev Int 8(1):27–46. https://doi.org/10.1080/1367886042000338227

McClelland DC (1973) Testing for competence rather than for 'intelligence'. Am Psychol 28(1):1–14. https://doi.org/10.1037/h0034092

Mitroff I, Turoff M (2002) Philosophical and methodological foundations of Delphi. In: Linstone HA, Turoff M (eds) The Delphi method: techniques and applications. Addison Wesley, New York, pp 17–34

Rothwell WJ, Lindholm JE (1999) Competency identification, modelling and assessment in the USA. Int J Train Dev 3(2):90–105. https://doi.org/10.1111/1468-2419.00069

Teijeiro M, Rungo P, Freire MJ (2013) Graduate competencies and employability: the impact of matching firms needs and personal attainments. Econ Educ Rev 34:286–295. https://doi.org/10.1016/j.econedurev.2013.01.003

Teodorescu T (2006) Competence versus competency: what is the difference? Perform Improv 45(10):27–30. https://doi.org/10.1002/pfi.4930451027

Wittig C (2012) Employees' reactions to organizational change. OD Pract 44(2):23–29

The Ungoverned Space of Cyber: Protecting Your Intangibles

Linus Owman

Abstract Organisations need to have an updated strategic understanding of information security to safeguard their intangible assets (such as intellectual property, talents and skills, privacy data). This understanding should not be limited to the organisation per se, but should include the whole organisational universe. The return of geopolitics, coupled with the fact that the space of cyber is largely ungoverned poses new and significant challenges. The rising plethora of regulations in the digital domain aim to restore public trust in a digitised society, at the same time as the general distrust in both institutions and technology is on the rise. In this context, technology is never objective, but any application of technology will, by necessity, counter or reinforce one of the two main information paradigms that are developing.

1 Introduction

In a digitised world, intangibles have become a key strategic asset for any organisation. As the "digital age" is a result from gradual developments over the course of the last decade, not all organisations have risen to the challenge this development poses, and in some cases, the need for an updated strategic understanding is now acute. In order to safeguard intangibles, organisations need to broaden their understanding of both intangibles and digital protection. The protection of intangibles is not a matter of IT, but a matter of information security, which as a term is broader and includes all kinds of data/information, both digital and physical, structured as well as unstructured. Legal measures that operate outside of the largely ungoverned domain of cyber will not suffice.

In this chapter, we will begin by understanding how and why intangibles have become important to the organisational strategic core, as well as providing examples of what they are. We will then move on to provide a backdrop as to how this development came about, taking changes in the surrounding world as our point of

L. Owman (✉)
PwC, Stockholm, Sweden

The New Club of Paris, Vienna, Austria

F. Matos et al. (eds.), *Knowledge, People, and Digital Transformation*, Contributions to Management Science, https://doi.org/10.1007/978-3-030-40390-4_15

analytical departure, highlighting changes and drivers behind this development. From this, we move on to discuss the ungoverned space of cyber and how its lack of governance poses a new and important challenge to organisations. We also look at some of the responses from governments to the challenge of an ungoverned cyber space, resulting in the formation of new global paradigms in the view of data and information handling.

2 The Intangibles: The New Crown Jewels

In the digital age, it has become evident that the intangible assets of organisations and corporations have become the main strategic assets, not least in terms of market value. Financial capital is now just a means to an end, i.e. company growth, investment in the future capital of knowledge, or simply filling the corporate coffers for the next financial downturn. At the same time, the protection of intangible assets is faltering, and the ability for organisations to map, understand and classify their intangibles is, at best, low. Further, the organisational understanding of the risk landscape tends to focus mainly on regulatory compliance.

In order for organisations to become more risk-conscious and resilient to attacks and disruption in digital services, that are more than likely to hit their intangibles as well, there is a need for a better strategic understanding of where the intangibles are, what they are, how they relate to organisational strategy, and how to protect them.

Many companies, especially in the R&D domain, are naturally protective about their *intellectual property* (*IP*), regarding it as a key asset for the company's longevity. At the same time, the protection of IP is oftentimes concentrated to the judicial domain with patents, contracts and legal measures to protect it from piracy or theft. But even though these measures are not uncalled for or unimportant, they are not enough to enable the organisation to bolster its strategic understanding and ability to protect from theft or corruption of intangibles. Thus, there is a need for *information security* based upon a coherent strategy, and having internal policies in place may not be enough. In some cases, the digital policies of the organisation are far from addressing the core goal of the organisation; for example protecting the IP produced. Rather, the policies address business-as-usual and end-user behaviour, without the employees understanding the link between the corporate security culture and the overarching end to protect IP.

Other intangible assets are the *talents and skills* within the company (often referred to as human capital). Recruitment processes, skills sought and talent retention policies are core competitive advantages in the war for talent. But at times, this critical data is held in a less protective environment than data, which is more directly related to the core production processes. Adjacent to this type of data is the *personal data*, which is sometimes sensitive (including, amongst other things, information about sexual orientation, union membership, religious beliefs and health status). In times when socially engineered attacks and spear-phishing campaigns are commonplace, leaked data of this kind may embolden an adversary to target-specific individuals, for example posing as a healthcare provider in an ongoing treatment in order to obtain login credentials to the corporate intranet.

But vulnerabilities relating to intangibles are not only confined to the organisation per se, but needs to be addressed from a broader standpoint; that of the corporate universe. In a world where many organisations operate in transnational markets, or with vendors whose service delivery—or call centres are located within another jurisdiction (such as a European company outsourcing its support function to India)—there are crucial vulnerabilities to consider. For companies outsourcing digital services to other jurisdictions, there is a need for a less naïve outlook on what outsourcing could strategically mean for the company from a threat perspective, not to mention from a national security perspective. For example, recently introduced regulations in both China and India means that the state governments of these territories have the legal right to access the data of local companies, regardless of whether the data they store or the services they provide are done for a company located elsewhere.[1] New provisions made to China's Cybersecurity Law last November gives state agencies the legal authority to remotely conduct penetration testing on any Internet-related business operating in China, and even copy and later share any data government officials find on inspected systems (Cimpanu 2019). For a company that provides services or products in the cybersecurity domain, or whose client is a governmental authority in another territory, there are clearly security implications to consider.

Further, in order to safeguard the security standards set up by the organisation, the subcontractors and the logistical support firms, as well as the producers of goods and services for the parent company, need to have the same level of protection, and be under the same scrutiny, as the parent company, since a breach in the supply chain many not only cost money, but also potential IP loss, illegal access to data and in the end a decline in consumer (or citizen) trust. The digital world means that organisational protection is only as strong as the weakest link in the digital chain to which the organisation belongs. Too often, this is an overlooked aspect and examples on where faltering security on subcontractor level has had real repercussions for the parent company are legion.

3 The World in Flux: New Challenges to the Protection of Intangibles

As we have seen above, the challenges for companies on the protection of corporate data and intangibles, wherever they are located, are paramount. In order to understand these challenges, and to enable the organisation to make strategic decisions for protection, there is a need to understand the corporate universe or, simply, the surrounding world. The complexity to navigate the world in the post Cold War

[1] See: https://www.indiatoday.in/india/story/government-snooping-order-1414231-2018-12-21

World is immense. The return of geopolitics, the ungoverned space of cyber, tensions between new paradigms of information and hybrid warfare (explored below) are just a few examples of phenomena on the strategic horizon in the digital landscape, but also phenomena that cannot be easily ignored by organisations striving for stability, predictability, investor trust, and long-term growth.

3.1 The Return of Geopolitics

It would be fair to say that global instability is on the rise with countries facing levels of internal political disruption and external turmoil rarely seen since the end of the Cold War. Significant changes to economics and societies of (primarily) the West driven by globalisation, technological disruption and new forms of communication are altering the global balance of power and undermining some of the fundamental pillars of the old order. The globalisation trend of the last 20 years has resulted in an interconnected world. This has been further underscored by the coming of the Internet and (later) the digital revolution, which has been disrupting markets and business models, flattening the competitive landscape and empowering anyone with an Internet connection to start a business, to broadcast messages and to promote activism, etc. The international system of states is moving from a more or less uni- or bipolar world, with one or two relative superpowers, to a multipolar world, where news superpowers challenge the status quo. As the tables are turning, other states (sometimes more aggressively than before) seek to safeguard or promote their national interests in a variety of spheres. This process includes renegotiation of trade deals, military alliances, tariffs, etc., as well as exploring the ways to increase influence through the space of cyber.

A changing international environment presents both business security opportunities and challenges, depending on perspective. Through technology, states and other agents are able to exert power in new ways. Social media campaigns to nudge the electorate in a foreign country in a favourable direction is one example. Deep cyberattacks to disturb or disrupt national services in the areas of energy, water, communications, or other systems of critical infrastructure are now commonplace and underscores the previously made argument for supply chain protection. Hybrid warfare, as opposed to conventional military warfare, has become part of everyday activities of states and other agents, where information or disinformation ("fake news" or "alternative facts") has become weaponised.[2]

The military alliance of NATO recently added cyberspace as the fourth defence line (air, land, sea, cyber) (Stoltenberg 2018). At the same time, the tax base in many

[2]As a point for further reflection, the ability to respond decisively to these attacks has further been weakened by the philosophical victories of the postmodern worldview, where concepts such as "truth" have been deconstructed to anything which is true for the individual. "Alternative facts", no matter how factually untrue they are, is just another version of the truth. Unfortunately, this has become a severe weakness in the ability of states and organizations to take action.

countries is shrinking because of declining birth rates or because of lack of re-/upskilling programmes for the unemployed. With the ongoing wave of industrial disruption via automation, sometimes referred to as the 4IR, this challenge will become even more essential. For a good overview, see Probst and Scharff (2018).

Countries are responding to these changes in the international system by seeking to exploit the temporal disorder they have created. More broadly countries, particularly the United States, are reverting to the use of international sanctions to pressure their adversaries as they look to secure their interests. Domestically, the national or social identity (for good or bad) is challenged by a multitude of competing and overlapping identities. The social contract between the individual and the state is now undergoing a renegotiation phase, where the influx of globalisation, identity and technology are in play, but so far it seems not many nations have identified the challenge this will have on the functions of the welfare state in the coming years. This is primarily a challenge for Western welfare states, but also for the post WWII world order. Another way of wording the current trends could be in the language of Adrian Wooldridge of *The Economist*, telling the tale of *three demons* unleashed from their prisons now roaming about the world, making old solutions dysfunctional and creating new realities; "the rise of inequality", "the return of the disposable worker" and "the rise of identity politics" (Wooldridge 2015). The rise of inequality alludes to the same mechanisms as identified by the World Economic Forum and others in terms of wealth disparity. The disposable worker alludes to automation and the shift in economic power to the East. The rise of identity politics alludes to the rise of identity as a mobilising marker of collectives, regardless of whether this is religious, nationalist or gender-based, in a "post truth" setting, making public conversation about these challenges polarised.

Regardless of how you choose to combine the identified trends, drivers and/or risks above into a coherent whole, the matter of security or securing intangibles is present both directly or indirectly in nearly all of them, simply because there is an intangible and often digital aspect to nearly all of them. For example, ageing populations will mean more health-related scientific data and medical records. Shifting power relations will mean more state agents acting in the grey zone of cyber espionage to increase their influence. And changing climate means, very concrete, that data centres must be protected against flooding, tidal waves, heat waves and social unrest. No corporate board worthy of its strategic salt can afford to ignore these.

4 The Ungoverned Space of Cyber

The World Economic Forum has listed a set of trends that point to risk, security and intangibles in their Global Risks Report 2020, where "information infrastructure breakdown" and "cyberattacks" are mentioned as two of them (World Economic Forum 2020). At the same time, as the dependency on cyber solutions is on the rise, the domain of cyber is largely ungoverned and operated without broadly accepted norms (Wheeler 2018). Cross-national agreements are limited to security frameworks and risk models and to a few cases of multilateral cooperation on government levels in terms of cyber defence.[3] Apart from this, there is little or no governmental protection for private companies operating in this domain. So, whilst the international system of states is still guided by diplomatic agreements and channels for communication and (at best) consensus-seeking efforts, in a somewhat orderly (albeit nowadays less predictable) fashion, the domain of cyber is largely ungoverned and in an almost Hobbesian state of "war of all against all", *bellum omnium contra omnes* (Hobbes 2005). This adds to insecurity, as each agent/organisation/governmental body thereby literally needs to provide for its own full defence against all kinds of threats, thwarted by all kinds of agents. On a national level, there is currently little or no national cyber defence in place, and the national aspect of this is aimed at defending critical functions and infrastructure owned by the government, unlike in the territorial domain where defence of borders means a safe haven for all organisations within them.

The lack of international governance further means that this has become the main opportunity space for indirect and informal foreign policy interest promotion and influence. And not only for states; organised crime and terrorist groups are agents who are continuously increasing their reach in order to find new ways of financing their activities. For example, the jihadist group ISIS is a recent example of an idea-driven, crowd-funded organisation that quickly became sophisticated in terms of both cybercrime and campaigns of influence. In the space of cyber, the cost of entry is low, the risk of detection is negligible and the risk of accountability in any international judicial sense is virtually none, making this a cost-efficient way for agents to try to come by money, information (industrial espionage), to effectively disrupt services (sabotage), or to influence opinion of pressure groups or the electorate in a direction favourable to the antagonist. Because of the floating boundaries of whether an antagonistic state-sponsored act is considered an actual act of war, this is often referred to as grey zone problematique or hybrid warfare.

Moreover, approximately 90% of cyberspace resides in the private sector, which essentially means that the vast majority of cyberinfrastructure and operations have been designed, developed and put to operation without government involvement (Siers 2018). An attack against cyberinfrastructure in the private domain may thus, at least indirectly, be a threat against national security, but it also may not be. This adds to the complexity in terms of both governmental and organisational ability to map the risk and threat environment and take the necessary actions to withstand and deter attacks and to draw the line between what the responsibility of government and the responsibility of the private sector should be.

In order to manage this lack of governance, there has been a sharp rise in enterprise expenditure in cybersecurity, to a total cost of 124 billion USD (2019, see Table 1). This is interesting as it implicitly tells us something about corporations'

[3]One example of an ambitious and growing body of legislative exploration in this area is the Tallinn Manual, developed by, Estonia. The 2.0 version was published in 2017.

Table 1 Worldwide security spending by segment, 2017–2019 (Millions of US Dollars), Gartner (August 2018) (Gartner 2018)

Market segment	2017	2018	2019
Application security	2434	2742	3003
Cloud security	185	304	459
Data security	2563	3063	3524
Identity access management	8823	9768	10,578
Infrastructure protection	12,583	14,106	15,337
Integrated risk management	3949	4347	4712
Network security equipment	10,911	12,427	13,321
Other information security software	1832	2079	2285
Security services	52,315	58,920	64,237
Consumer security software	5948	6395	6661
Total	101,544	114,152	124,116

anticipation in terms of threat arena. Investment in this area shows that this is an area where antagonistic threats and attacks are anticipated. It seems organisations are more likely to anticipate threats in the security domain of their own organisations than in a wider strict geopolitical sense, meaning that their readiness to respond may be confined to threats of a certain magnitude, one which they can anticipate. But the level of anticipation is also dependent on what strategic outlook you have. At the same time, the focus on bolstering corporate security may also reflect spheres of responsibility and influence, where corporations are investing heavily in mitigating threats in domains they feel they can influence directly, whereas other areas of cyber defence are perceived to be outside of their spheres of influence (and hence regarded as subject to national cyber defence). Indeed, cybercrime alone costs nations more than $1 trillion globally, far more than the record $300 billion of damage due to natural disasters in 2017 (Mee and Schuermann 2018), an number which is destined to rise in the coming years.

5 Decline in Trust, the Regulation Tsunami and New Paradigms

5.1 The Decline in Trust in Technology and Institutions

As if the return of geopolitics and the ungoverned space of cyber were not enough, the recent decline in trust in technology and institutions should be a sobering moment for anyone conducting business in the digital age. Starting out like a promise to bring the world together, with free data access for all, recent developments have seen the trust in technology reversed. As the initial enthusiasm of the digital revolution begins to wane, people are beginning to understand the value of their personal data and the need for its protection. But the price for this insight has been a decline in trust in technology as such. For example, the exposure of the Cambridge Analytica events contributed to the electorate feeling estranged to the source of data—Facebook. This is both sobering and challenging, not least since companies are operating in digital markets where trust is essential in order to retain consumers and grow market shares.

5.2 Death by Regulation

The typical governmental response (both on national and supranational levels) to the declining trust in technology has been an ever-increasing flood of regulations in the digital domain, in order to regain public trust in the more and more digitised society. In one way, this regulatory effort is trying to address the nature of the ungoverned space of cyber discussed above. But at the same time, the need for regulation as such underscores the lack of trust, where the need for regulation itself points to the fact that unless regulation is in place, trust is by definition lost.

Apart from this, regulation has also become a means for governmental influence in the digital domain, where legal arrangements in order to operate in certain industries or territorial domains means that organisations need to give up on some of their demands (organisations their data or security) in order to be "compliant" and thus reap the fruits of the local market. Regulation has also become a way of limiting foreign access to strategic industries or markets to bolster influence in bi- or multilateral bargaining. This use of regulation is commonly referred to as "lawfare", a hybrid of the words "law" and "warfare".[4]

5.3 The New Paradigms of Information

In this new global environment, there is yet another aspect to be considered by those who aspire to a strategic outlook on the developments in the sphere of information and intangibles, namely the usage of technology and the shifting paradigms of information. Why is this important? Like with climate change, organisations need to understand how their usage of certain solutions serve to support or counteract against the competing paradigms of information, and in the end, what digital world we wish to leave behind for future generations.

There are currently two paradigms forming on the usage of technology and citizen data. The *Western paradigm*, led by the United States and the EU in the liberal tradition, is that of data and privacy protection. As the world becomes

---

[4]Lawfare is a form of war consisting of the use of the legal system against an enemy, such as by damaging or delegitimizing them, tying up their time or winning a public relations victory. The term is a portmanteau of the words law and warfare. https://en.wikipedia.org/wiki/Lawfare

digitised and digitally enabled, the data (most notably citizen data, but also open data) must be protected from misuse by antagonistic or predatory national, organisational or commercial interests. On the other hand, the *Eastern paradigm* is more authoritarian in nature, putting the stability of the state, and hence the control of its citizens, at the heart of technology usage, where citizen privacy becomes a trade-off to a system or regime stability. The most recent example is China, which is currently implementing a vast surveillance system to promote certain individual behaviour in its population, under the project name "leave no dark corner". This includes both high tech crime-fighting, generally thought of as something benign to the broader society, but also citizen ranking through a social credit system, meaning an encroachment on individual freedom under the state apparatus (Carney 2018). The line between these two paradigms underscores the fact that technology is never objective and that the application of the technology needs to be accompanied by a crucial understanding of its broader purpose.

6 Conclusions

As the main assets of organisational output and retention nowadays consist of intangibles (often digital), there is a need for a new and broader understanding of security and how these intangibles are to be protected. The intangibles are no longer just the IP, and the protective measures are not just IT.

In the digital era, the intangibles have become virtually all the strategic assets and information the company needs to run its operations internally and externally, including outsourced operations, supply chains and the access to strategic resources for production, such as energy, water, raw materials, etc. In order to safeguard these, organisations need to broaden their understanding of both intangibles and digital protection. The protection of intangibles is not a matter of IT, but a matter of information security, which as a term is both broader and includes all kinds of data/information, both digitally stored and physical, structured as well as unstructured. Legal measures that operated outside of the largely ungoverned domain of cyber will not suffice.

Further, to understand what needs protection, the organisation needs to map its strategic assets, categorise them and apply a structured level of protection to them through a strategically coherent (often risk-based) approach. The strategic outlook needs to be broader than the organisation, including the whole of the corporate universe, and (at best) the broader geopolitical domain, as well as the paradigmatic results of the applied strategy. This cannot be delegated to the IT department, but needs to happen at the C-level. Policies and guidelines on information security cannot simply address end-user behaviour and handling of internal IT tools, but must link to the broader security culture of the organisation and create an awareness in which all employees understand how their behaviour is protecting or risking the intangibles every day.

Strategic understanding and security awareness begin with the "tone at the top", meaning that unless the C-level understands that intangibles are more than digital assets and that the protection is more than IT, they may run the risk of failure. To include a CIO/CSO in the leadership team is a step in the right direction.

References

Carney M (2018) Leave no dark corner. ABC News. https://www.abc.net.au/news/2018-09-18/china-social-credit-a-model-citizen-in-a-digital-dictatorship/10200278. Accessed 17 Sep 2018

Cimpanu C (2019) China's cybersecurity law update lets state agencies 'pen-test' local companies. ZD Net. https://www.zdnet.com/article/chinas-cybersecurity-law-update-lets-state-agencies-pen-test-local-companies/. Accessed 9 Feb 2019

Gartner, Inc. (2018) Gartner forecasts worldwide information security spending to exceed $124 billion in 2019. https://www.gartner.com/en/newsroom/press-releases/2018-08-15-gartner-forecasts-worldwide-information-security-spending-to-exceed-124-billion-in-2019. Accessed 03 July 2019

Govt names the 10 agencies with powers to snoop on you (n.d.) India Today. https://www.indiatoday.in/india/story/government-snooping-order-1414231-2018-12-21

Hobbes T (2005) In: Klenner H (ed) Chapter 14: Leviathan. Meiner Verlag, Hamburg

Mee P, Schuermann T (2018) How a cyber attack could cause the next financial crisis. Harvard Business Review. https://hbr.org/2018/09/how-a-cyber-attack-could-cause-the-next-financial-crisis?utm_campaign=hbr&utm_source=linkedin&utm_medium=social. Accessed 14 Sept 2018

Probst L, Scharff C (2018) Upskill – 6 steps to unlock economic opportunity for all. reka print+, Luxembourg

Siers R (2018) Cybersecurity. In: Williams PD, McDonald M (eds) Security studies: an introduction, 3rd edn. Routledge, Glasgow

Stoltenberg J (2018) Why cyber space matters as much to Nato as land, sea and air defence. Financial Times. https://www.ft.com/content/9c3ae876-6d90-11e8-8863-a9bb262c5f53. Accessed 12 July 2018

Tallinn Manual 2.0 (2017) The most comprehensive guide for policy advisors and legal experts on how existing International Law applies to cyber operations. https://ccdcoe.org/research/tallinn-manual/

Wheeler T (2018) In cyberwar, there are no rules. Foreign Policy. https://foreignpolicy.com/2018/09/12/in-cyberwar-there-are-no-rules-cybersecurity-war-defense/. Accessed 12 Sept 2018

Wikipedia (2019) Lawfare. https://en.wikipedia.org/wiki/Lawfare. Accessed 03 July 2019

Wooldridge A (2015) The great disruption – how business is coping with turbulent times. The Economist. Profile Books, Great Britain, pp 19–21

World Economic Forum (2020) The global risks report 2020, http://www3.weforum.org/docs/WEF_Global_Risk_Report_2020.pdf

The Brazilian Development Bank Impact Thesis: A Methodology to Address the Development Goals of the Knowledge and Sustainable New Economy

Helena Tenório Veiga de Almeida and João Paulo Carneiro de H. Braga

In a world flooded with irrelevant information, clarity is power

Yuval Noah Harrari

Abstract The Development Finance Institutions (DFIs) must respond to the ongoing structural changes imposed by the new economy of the twenty-first century. These institutions should update procedures and foster the implementation of better practices by other economic agents. The Brazilian Development Bank (BNDES) case demonstrates that DFIs can develop tools that address these new challenges. We present the BNDES Impact Thesis for Investment on Projects (TIIP), a methodology to evaluate the expected impacts of development projects in nonfinancial variables such as knowledge and sustainability. It is inspired by the BNDES Methodology to Evaluate Companies (MAE), a tool to assess the client's intellectual capital in the concession of credit. Both methodologies translate a complex reality into an easy-to-read framework, which expands a manager's decision-making criteria to variables beyond the financial ones. Based on a case study, we detail the TIIP methodology to demonstrate it is a powerful instrument to adapt the BNDES to the challenges of the new economy. It translates nonfinancial benefits to a banking language and identifies opportunities to improve investment projects and enhance its benefits to development. The TIIP is a useful guideline for BNDES' action and a strategic tool to deal with the new economic challenges.

H. T. V. de Almeida (✉)
Banco Nacional de Desenvolvimento Econômico e Social (BNDES), Brasília, Brazil
e-mail: htv@bndes.gov.br

J. P. C. d. H. Braga
The New School for Social Research, New York, USA
e-mail: bragj553@newschool.edu

F. Matos et al. (eds.), *Knowledge, People, and Digital Transformation*, Contributions to Management Science, https://doi.org/10.1007/978-3-030-40390-4_16

1 Introduction

The twenty-first century economy imposes global challenges in many areas. Several debates have taken place on the impact of changes such as the new sources of knowledge, the labor market, the sustainable management of natural resources and ethics while using big data and artificial intelligence. The banks and credit markets are also challenged to adapt themselves to an economy in which the factors of production are inextricably linked to knowledge and to the so-called intellectual capital.

Nowadays, many are the names and concepts that define the features of the world economy. We are aware that we live in a very different economy from the one that formed the base of the industrial economy. The term globalization used for decades has become outdated and cannot define today's economy and net society. Terms such as post-capitalism, economy 4.0, postmodernity, digital economy, and green economy among others try to tackle the complex aspects of the twenty-first century economy. In this chapter, we focus on two ideas that we consider of paramount importance when talking about a development bank: the knowledge economy according to the conception of the New Club of Paris[1] and Sustainable economy based on the United Nations Sustainable Development Goals[2] (UN SDGs). We have chosen to break down the concepts into two in order to shed light toward them and the term new economy (Alexander 1983) encompasses everything that came afterwards the economy of industrial base.

In this chapter, we discuss the relevance of development finance institutions (DFIs) and its role in addressing the current challenges of the new economy. We set this discussion based on the BNDES (Brazilian National Development Bank) case. For this purpose, we present two methodologies, developed by the BNDES, aimed at adapting the institution to this new environment: the BNDES Methodology to Evaluate Companies (MAE) and the BNDES Impact Thesis for Investment on Projects (TIIP). Both methodologies enhance the bank's analytical skills. The former is used for a better evaluation of the client's intellectual capital in the concession of credit (assessment). The latter is aimed at invested projects as it provides a tool to evaluate its expected impacts for development (not only the financial returns). In Sect. 2, we discuss the role of DFIs and the potential contributions that such institutions, as the BNDES, have for a sustainable development path. In Sect. 3, we present the TIIP. Firstly, we briefly discuss the MAE, given that this methodology inspired the TIIP. Secondly, we give further details about the TIIP and its benefits to foster sustainable practices and knowledge creation and dissemination. The methodology intends to encompass into the development projects analysis the new economy challenges together with developing the countrys old challenges such as basic education and sanitation.

[1]See: http://new-club-of-paris.org/

[2]See: https://sustainabledevelopment.un.org

2 BNDES and the Role of Development Financial Institutions

The Brazilian Development Bank (BNDES) is the main financing agent for development in Brazil. Since its foundation, in 1952, the BNDES has played a fundamental role in stimulating the expansion of industry and infrastructure in the country. Over the course of the bank's history, its operations have evolved in accordance with the Brazilian socioeconomic challenges, starting from Brazil infant industrialization to today supporting for technological innovation, sustainable socio-environmental development, and the modernization of public administration.

The Bank offers several financial support mechanisms to Brazilian companies of all sizes and capital ownerships (private or public firms, as well as public administration entities), enabling investments in all economic sectors. In 2018, the BNDES's disbursements were R$69.5 billons (in Brazilian Reais, around US$18 billion), reaching 152 thousand clients. In any supported undertaking, from the analysis phase up to the monitoring, the BNDES emphasizes three factors it considers strategic: innovation, local development, and socio-environmental benefits and negative impacts.

BNDES is one of the most prominent public DFIs in the world. DFIs play a significant role in the sustainable development of the countries and regions where they operate. In middle-income countries, such as Brazil and China, DFIs have a wider scope, financing projects in almost all economic sectors. Furthermore, it should tackle developing countries' deficits such as education and sanitation. However, the current challenges for the new economy have been facing in both developing and advanced economies. Therefore, DFIs continue playing an essential role in economies such as Germany, France, South Korea, and Japan, where several sectors of production and the private long-term credit market have undergone significant consolidation.

Historically, DFIs finance the expansion of productive capacity, serving market segments whose needs are not adequately met by long-term financing instruments offered by the private sector. These segments largely correspond to those that generate positive externalities, not picked up or perceived by the market, and therefore often produce social returns in addition to private returns (Schmidt-Traub and Sachs 2015; Stiglitz 1994). As the private market is unwilling to finance investment with high social return, this kind of market gap must be filled by government action.

However, the importance of DFIs in boosting a country's progress goes beyond filling traditional market gaps (an argument used to justify more specific action to offset the deficiencies of the private financial system). In some cases, such as the initial stages of "disruptive" technologies, the level of uncertainty is such that they will hardly be financed by the private credit system (Mazzucato 2018). In this case, it is not a matter of filling a market gap, but of creating new markets. A further mission of these banks emerges in moments of economic crisis, when DFIs usually play a countercyclical role, contributing to maintaining systemic stability (Griffith-Jones and Ocampo 2018). The 2008 crisis was a good example of this mission. Therefore, DFIs are not only an unique institutions that support less developed economies, but they should also be recognized as key public instruments and potential partners of the private financing system for economies at various stages of development. This chapter discusses, based on the BNDES case, the DFI's role as relevant actors to foster a knowledge and sustainable dynamic economy in the face of the new challenges imposed on their own countries. We present, in the next section, two initiatives implemented by the BNDES to address the current challenges of the new economy.

3 New Analytical Instruments to Deal with the Knowledge and Sustainable New Economy: MAE and TIIP

3.1 The BNDES Methodology to Evaluate Companies (MAE): An Inspiration for a New Mind-Set

The traditional banking approach to evaluate a loan proposal basically considers the financial aspects of the borrower and the financial viability of the project and is based, essentially, on tangible assets—financial and physical assets. However, a development bank's operation demands a further analysis: it is vital to analyze in greater depth a firm's capabilities and its relations with the market. A company is made up of tangible and intangible assets. The latter should also be considered (Edvinsson 1997; Edvinsson and Malone 1997). Furthermore, these assets are key factors to guarantee one firm's competitiveness (Coutinho and Ferraz 1994). An analysis of strategy and competitiveness, based on a sectorial competitiveness pattern, should also be undertaken.

Contemplating these factors, the BNDES methodology to evaluate companies—MAE (Metodologia de Avaliação de Empresas in Portuguese) seeks to provide a single instrument to systematize this qualitative information for the beneficiaries of the BNDES (Almeida and Braga 2014; Almeida et al. 2018). The evaluation outcome is an easy-to-read figure and final score, in which a firm's intangible assets and competitiveness are summarized (Fig. 1). Such information is used consistently in all stages of financial support: from the review and approval of funding, up to the measurement of credit risk, reinforcing the use of nonfinancial indicators.

In the BNDES' point of view, the MAE represents a transformation in the traditional practice of project and company analysis. It adds a specific and systematic assessment of intangible assets and of the competitiveness of the companies in the bank's portfolio. Indeed, a single instrument is applied, and it generates information that can be used by different stakeholders in the process to grant financial support. Furthermore, adjustments of the procedures to assess these aspects substantially increase the bank's ability to finance companies with greater sustainable growth potential in the long run. Likewise, this innovative assessment increases its ability to

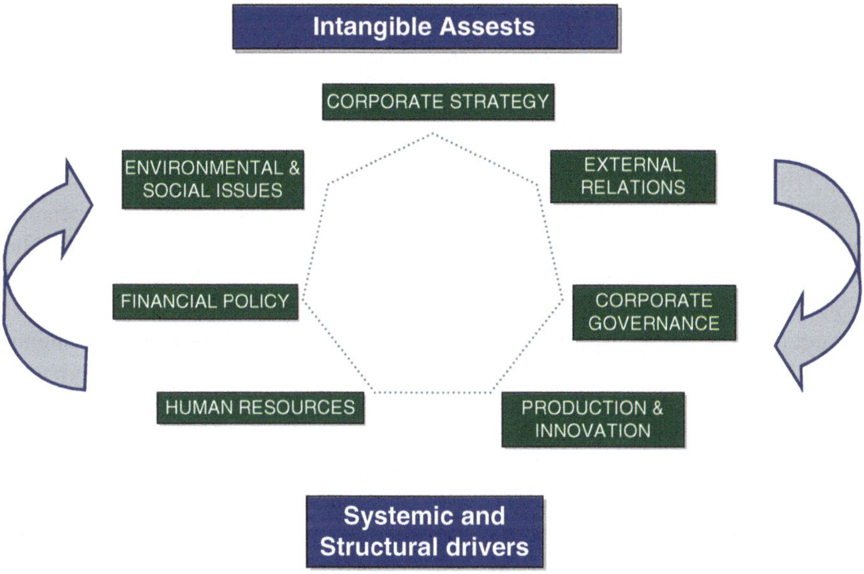

Fig. 1 MAE: BNDES firm evaluation methodology (Almeida and Braga 2014)

help strengthen the capacity building of companies in its portfolio. This approach legitimizes BNDES' role as a bank and as an agent of development policy, reinforcing each of its missions.

The experience of the BNDES in the development of the MAE methodology and its trailblazing aspect in the banking system were followed throughout the years by the think tank "The New Club of Paris" and reported by published articles[3] and by presentations during the annual seminar "Intellectual Capital for Communities".[4] Having said this, the current chapter will focus on presenting a second methodology, also developed by the BNDES and inspired by the MAE: the TIIP. The next section presents the TIIP and its benefits as a tool to address the challenges for the new economy.

---

[3]The MAE was already detailed in previous articles. See Almeida and Braga (2014) and Almeida et al. (2018).

[4]See http://new-club-of-paris.org/products/ic-conferences/

3.2 The "Impact Thesis for Investment on Projects" (TIIP): An Ex-ante Assessment Model

3.2.1 The Methodology

The TIIP was implemented in 2016 by the BNDES as part of the Impact Monitoring & Evolution Initiative (M&E). Its main objective is to assess the expected benefits and negative impacts to development in every intervention funded by the bank. The whole banking sector is facing the challenge to increase the disclosure regarding its ESG outcomes. There is a growing demand of private investors[5] for green and social impact assets while the national and international communities are also demanding larger transparency of government development targets and outcomes. Moreover, DFIs play a relevant role in implementing the UN 2030 Agenda for Sustainable Development, which increases the relevance of such a methodology. The TIIP was released to increase the BNDES commitment with these new demands and goals, adapting the bank's tools to the new economy challenges.

The in-house methodological development effort engaged the board and staff to answer one single question: "how are we able to turn explicit the BNDES' benefits to country's development challenges?". Also, the new method should provide a qualitative and easy-to-read framework to consider the desirable benefits of development projects in its eligibility process. In order to address this demand, the BNDES team searched for internal and external benchmarks in development agencies, banks, and social investment funds.[6] The reference cases should, at the same time, respond to the methodological demands, give theoretical benchmarks and fit with the bank's business model.

The TIIP is an ex ante impact assessment method based on the idea of "impact thesis," also used for social impact funds (Saltuk and Idrissi 2012). Every project should follow the expected impacts set by the investors, not only risk and return parameters (as shown in Fig. 2). An "Impact thesis" is a hypothesis, proposed by the project analyst and approved by the board, to be monitored and verified during and after every investment. In the methodology, "Impact" is understood as a positive or negative outcome, being primary or secondary and a result of direct or indirect

[5]Socially responsible investments grew by 34%, reaching $30.7 trillion globally over the past 2 years. Groups of investors (owning more than $33 tri in assets) have been engaged in fostering green responsibility in the capital market (e.g., Climate Action 100+, the IIGCC, and PRI). See: https://www.dw.com/en/myopic-stock-markets-deter-green-investments/a-49248966, https://climateaction100.wordpress.com/about-us/ and https://www.reuters.com/article/us-climatechange-investors/investors-managing-32-trillion-in-assets-call-for-action-on-climate-change-idUSKBN1O80TR

[6]Practices in organizations such as the OECD (2007), European Parliament (2015), European Commission (Helming 2009; Bach et al. 2008), International Finance Corporation (IFC) (World Bank 2007), the Brazilian Innovation Agency, Finep (Cavalcante and De Negri 2013), DAC—Development Assistance Committee (OECD 1991), Pricewaterhouse (PWC 2013), World Economic Forum (Drexler et al. 2014), and the KfW (2013).

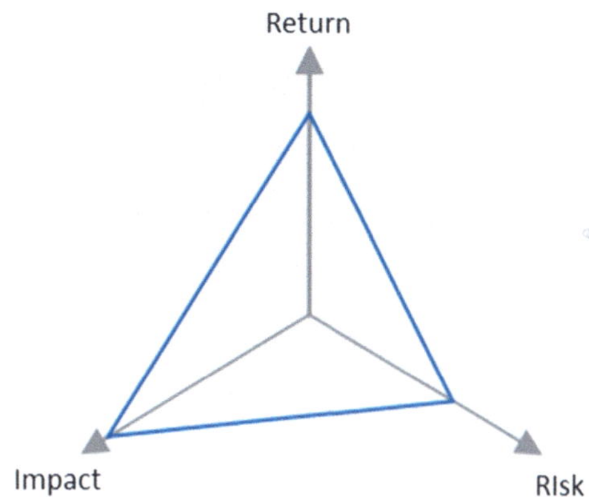

Fig. 2 Investment criteria adapted from the "impact thesis" framework (Saltuk and Idrissi 2012)

intervention, intentional, or non-intentional (OECD 2002). The concepts embedded in the methodology engaged the BNDES staff and board, together with the clients and the society, in the achievement of the development goals together with credit soundness targets.

The BNDES produces its own rating analysis for firms and projects. It means that the bank has already internal methodologies and procedures for credit analysis, which are accompanied in an ongoing basis by the Corporate Strategy and the Board. The TIIP provides the institution with an additional framework to the investment decisions. The methodology outcome was included in the investment reports, which are evaluated by the board before a project's eligibility and the definition of the effectiveness indicators that are accompanied by the M&E initiative. This comprehensive approach has been implemented in other institutions. The KfW, the German development bank, uses the Development Assistance Committee (DAC/OECD; OECD 1991) assessment. For every project, they provide a brief summary on their website that contains financial and nonfinancial information (Fig. 3). Indeed, a development bank analyst should be able to take account the risk parameters and guarantee a positive financial return for the bank and, at the same time, foster an increasing positive benefit to the society.

The BNDES developed its own methodology, based on the assumption that the new method should fit with the existent internal tools and with its internal procedures. The new method was also inspired by a market benchmark research. The Price Waterhouse Coopers' Total Impact Measurement and Management (TIMM) select variables to measure economic, social, and environmental impact of investments. It is used to increase corporate report disclosure and to support private investment decisions (based on the social return either). Also, the Bridge Ventures (a US$800 million fund, a case study presented by the World Economic Forum) uses a qualitative measurement to assess every investment's benefit. This assessment verifies whether the project is reaching the social targets set for fields such as education, health, welfare, and sustainability (Drexler et al. 2014). Alike these mentioned initiatives, 20 additional methodologies are compiled by Olsen and Galimidi (2008) for the Rockefeller Institute. They classify the distinct methods by

Overall rating: 3

The programme has made an important contribution to decentralising environmental policy and enhancing the capabilities of state-level environmental authorities. A particularly positive aspect of the programme is its sustained effect: virtually all the measures initiated under the scope of the programme are continued. Programme weaknesses were particularly evident in the area of efficiency.

Of note:

Almost all persons interviewed stressed the importance of the programme. The lessons learned in the programme – positive and negative – reportedly played a particularly prominent role.

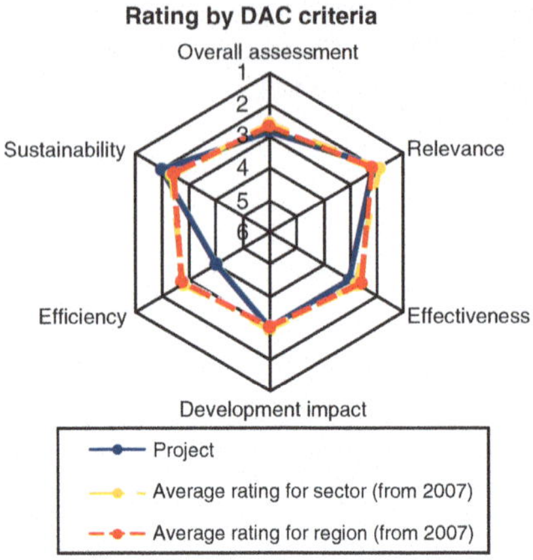

Fig. 3 Adapted from KFW project summary—DAC criteria (KFW 2013)

its objective (general or sector specific), by its scope (Rating, assessment, or management) and by the impact assessment stage (implied impact, proven impact, or optimized impact). The TIIP is a general rating assessment (based on a scorecard method) and evaluates the expected implied impacts in distinct dimensions.

The methodology is based on distinct criteria grouped in five dimensions: economic, social, environment, client management, and local development. In the economic dimension, we evaluate the benefits in terms of efficiency and value-added increase, taking account variables such as innovation, exports, productivity, knowledge, and supply chain. Regarding the environment, we verify the positive and negative impacts on resource use, emissions, and ecosystems at the national level. In the social field, we evaluate the positive and negative impacts on well-being and job creation. In terms of client management, we evaluate the client ESG management status and to what extent the skills built by their project enhance the firm's strategy in the long run. In the local development dimension, we check the investment potential in attracting workforce and additional economic activities for the region in order to reduce regional inequalities. The detailed criteria list is shown in Fig. 4.

As the main purpose of the TIIP is to obtain an easy-to-read evaluation, we also get a final score for every dimension and for every project. Every criterion is assessed via a unique scorecard, an increasing scale from the least desirable alternative (negative or neutral impact) till the most desirable alternative (the benchmark). The applied scale is modified for each variable to adapt it to its specificities (e.g., there is no negative impact on exports while there are several potential negative impacts in local development). However, the final dimension score is always given by a Likert Scale (from 1 to 5), a result of a weighted sum of each criterion. In the proposal scale, 5 is the highest positive impact while 1 refers to a negative impact and 2 to a neutral impact. We set the neutral level at two (closer to 1 than to 5) due to project analysis purposes. We are much more interested in differentiating projects with different positive benefits than projects with different negative impacts. A

	TIIP - Dimensions				
	Economy	Environment	Social	Local Development	Client
Criteria	Productivity and Economic Complexity	Negative Impacts in Resources Use, Emissions and Ecosystems	Employment	Direct Impacts by project	Management and ESG Practices
	Innovation	Positive Benefits in Resources Use, Emissions and Ecosystems	Positive Impacts in Well-being	Indirect economic benefits	Productive Capabilities
	Infrastructure		Negative Impacts in Well-being		
	Export				
	Supply Chain				
	Education and Culture				

Fig. 4 TIIP: criteria by dimension (Almeida and Braga 2017)

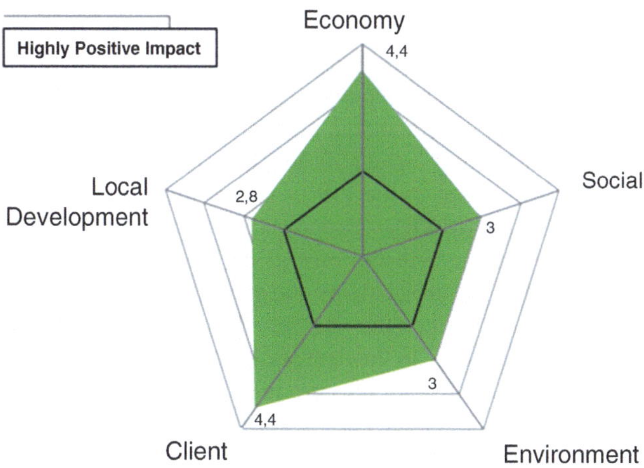

Fig. 5 TIIP: case study (Almeida and Braga 2017)

negative impact should be taken as a project drawback per se. Given the dimension scores, every project is classified as: Negative Impact, Neutral, Positive Impact, Highly Positive, or Benchmark. Figure 5 shows a project labeled as a "Highly Positive Impact" project (Box "TIIP Case Study: Capital Goods Industry", also explains this detailed case). We observe a high impact on the economy and client dimension (4.4 over 5) and that we have more social and environmental social benefits than negative impacts (as the grade is 3).

A project evaluation starts with the assignment of a score to every criterion, based on the given scale and ends with the final project classification. Every criterion generates a score which has a distinct scale of the one we obtain for the whole dimension. The reason is that we apply a monotonic transformation to reach a final score between 1 and 5 for each dimension: an item originally measured at a scale between A and B with n as a neutral is transformed for a scale between 1 and 5 with 2 as the neutral level. After we get the score for each criterion, we calculate a final weighted score for every dimension. The weights are exogenous given, developed by focal groups in BNDES followed by statistics consistency analysis. Having the final dimension score, we can classify the project based on the dimensions score.

The TIIP is a composite indicator and the statistical procedure of assigning weights is a key methodological feature. Composite indicators are often used to support multi-criteria analysis (e.g., Global Innovation Index—World Intellectual Property Organization, Cornell, Insead; Human Development Index—United Nations; Environmental Sustainability Index—World Economic Forum; and Betterlife Index—OECD. The European Commission has a permanent working group (Composite Indicator Research Group, Coin) in charge of setting methodological patterns for composite indicators. Saisana and Tarantola (2002) report the State-of-the-art methodological practices to build this type of indicators and give recommendations in this field. This report is a milestone reference for the TIIP development.

The TIIP management agenda has incorporated several recommendations from the Coin Report. One well-known disadvantage of composite indicators is that it requires a frequent tracking of its outcomes, based on statistical methods. The BNDES has already included semiannual methodological follow-ups in its working plan. The staff is often looking for criteria improvement opportunities and for new project benchmarks. Moreover, as the TIIP is part of the bank's strategy for impact Monitoring and Evaluation (M&E), we set a staff training program and an initiative to guarantee its coordination with the others M&E tools (such as efficiency and effectiveness indicators at the project level and external impact reports). The TIIP is a disruptive method that changes the staff mindset and workflow and requires a careful implementation strategy. In the next section, we detail how the methodology can guide the staff's mindset toward the current challenges of a new economy, such as innovation and sustainable initiatives.

3.2.2 The TIIP as a Guideline to Address the New Economy Challenges

Development institutions worldwide are engaged in implementing the UN SDG and in enhancing the country's capabilities to innovate and create knowledge. The BNDES, following the Brazilian federal government guidelines, has also a huge contribution to this effort at the national level. The past corporate planning documents set explicit targets for sustainability and innovation deliveries. Moreover, it encouraged the development of internal tools to improve staff's skills to identify and foster this type of benefit in every project. The TIIP is a key methodology to increase BNDES's contribution to new economy. In this section, we present the criteria in which this contribution is assessed based on examples and one case study (Box "TIIP Case Study: Capital Goods Industry"). First, we present how the methodology deals with the concept of knowledge and innovation. Later, we present the TIIP concepts and criteria for sustainability.

The TIIP takes knowledge as a relevant input to increase the value added and efficiency of the national productive system. For this purpose, we consider a broader approach based on three main concepts: (1) Innovation (based on the Oslo Manual—

OECD/Eurostat 2005); (2) Capabilities diversification toward complex industries and activities; and (3) Knowledge creation and dissemination. In the dimension "Economy," the TIIP evaluates the benefits of every project in six criteria that address those three concepts. The criteria are explained in the next paragraphs, based on the case study.

In order to assess the benefits for the criteria Innovation, the TIIP is based on the Oslo Manual guideline. Innovation is defined as the implementation of a new product or process to the firm or to the country, as the result of a previous technology development effort (e.g., R&D). The project assessment depends on the expected outcome and on the type of technological effort employed during the product development. We differentiate, for instance, projects that aim to create new products in the technology frontier versus initiatives to support the firm's R&D routines and update existent products.

For this purpose, the TIIP provides a group of indicators (such as the percentage of R&D in the firm's revenue or the number of employees hired for these activities) that should be obtained before the evaluation. Furthermore, it uses the bank's sectorial knowledge to identify how disruptive a technology is. The case study discusses the implementation of a new capital goods facility in the renewable energy sector. The facility will produce a capital good, new for the country and the firm, which demands new capabilities and a large R&D Effort. However, this product has been already implemented in a few projects in the world. This is one of the explanations to the fact that the project got a high score, although it is not a benchmark in the dimension "Economy."

In order to assess the diversification potential toward more complex sectors and activities, we use the idea of "economic complexity" (Hidalgo and Hausmann 2009). An economy is more complex depending on the ubiquity and on the diversity of the exported goods and services (i.e., more diversified economies with a higher share of goods and services with higher ubiquity, or higher scarcity, are more complex). Therefore, the project assessment depends on the type of good or service produced or exported as a result of the investment.

For this purpose, the TIIP evaluates the economic complexity in three criteria: Productive Capacity; exports; and supply chain. The main objective is to identify how much every project added to the economy in terms of added value. For every project, we evaluate how much it contributes in terms of productive capacity and exports taking account the type of good or service that will be produced or exported. Also, we evaluate the industry supply chain to identify to what extent the current domestic suppliers are able to respond to the needs of a more complex productive structure. In the case study, for instance, we have the relevant additional supply in a high-tech industry. However, the goodwill not be exported and the supply-chain still demands incremental improvements.

The TIIP assessment for Knowledge creation and dissemination is based on one unique criterion named "Knowledge, education and culture." Given the methodological challenges to measure knowledge, we evaluate the type of knowledge that is produced and its potential diffusion (by the type of sector and by the number of people able to obtain gains). We consider that initiatives like education expenses, information access, and the supply of cultural facilities can contribute to knowledge creation and dissemination. However, we understand that knowledge creation and dissemination are also assessed in other criteria such as innovation and productive capacity.

The TIIP also takes sustainability as a relevant project feature. It is explicit in three dimensions: environment, social, and local development. While the first two dimensions evaluate the project at the macro level, the latest discusses the expected benefits or negative impacts on social and environmental variables for the municipality and neighborhoods in which the project is implemented. During the 1980s, the Brundtland Commission qualified sustainable development as the one that fulfills the current generation needs without affecting negatively the future generation needs. This concept has been improved during the time to the idea of triple-bottom line: the sustainable development should be in harmony with economic growth, environmental responsibility, and social inclusion.

The TIIP assessment for sustainability evaluates, for each dimension, the expected positive and negative impacts in a group of variables. For the environment dimension, we consider natural resources use, carbon emission, and ecosystems. For the social dimension, we consider employment and quality of life (as defined in the OECD Better Life index[7]). In the case study, we observe positive benefits for the environment, social, and local development. However, these positive benefits are still low, indirect, and very restricted.

The case study reports the construction of a new site to produce solar energy equipment mainly to hospitals. In the environmental dimension, we understand that the environmental benefits exist, but their level will also depend on the equipment diffusion in the market (which is still uncertain). However, the project implementation per se has a very low environmental negative impact. In the social dimension, the investment creates low-skilled jobs and the equipment will improve health services. It means that we have a direct impact on job creation (although the jobs are in low-wage positions) and an indirect potential impact on social services improvement. This evaluation points out that there is room to increase the social and environmental benefits in this project, which should be considered by the BNDES project analyst.

One should notice that the case study is, purposely, a non-benchmark project. However, a list of benchmark initiatives is available for project analysts, so they can implement improvement in projects. For the sustainability dimensions, we especially find benchmark projects in the generation of renewable energy and on sanitation. During the implementation of wind energy sites in the Brazilian northeast, initiatives funded by the BNDES combined a high scale supply of low-carbon energy for the economy with social initiatives to increase social welfare in the low-income regions they were implemented. Several projects reached the highest ranking in environmental benefits and a score of around four in social and local developments. The score was not the highest for all the dimensions as many social gains were not

[7]See: http://www.oecdbetterlifeindex.org/

sustainable in the long run. On the other hand, sanitation projects are usually ranked as benchmarks in all the sustainability dimensions. This type of project generates highly long-term gains to the environment (as it sharply reduces waste and pollution), to the social welfare (as it increases, for instance, health benefits and water supply), and to the local development (the social gains are higher nearby the site and the project brings structural social and economic changes to several communities). Having a group of benchmark projects helps the analyst to maximize the externalities in projects since the beginning of the analysis.

Indeed, the TIIP is a powerful tool to accompany the BNDES contribution to the new economy. As the bank has a large database of development projects, the staff can diagnose the contributions of the Brazilian investments to knowledge creation and sustainability. These diagnoses must report the BNDES role in this effort. Moreover, as the methodology is applied before the loan eligibility decision, the staff has a guideline to negotiate project improvements with clients. These improvements should be especially encouraged when they chase larger gains in knowledge creation and sustainability.

TIIP Case Study: Capital Goods Industry

The Firm X produces capital goods and applied for BNDES financial support for the implementation of a new site to produce solar energy equipment. The machinery will be sold for the domestic market, having hospitals as the main clients. The TIIP evaluation was based on sectorial benchmarks, the data available for the project, and the firm and on a comparison between similar projects already financed by the BNDES. The TIIP evaluation for this case is shown in Fig. 2. We expect positive benefits in all the evaluated dimensions.

Economy (4.4): The investment will implement an equipment facility for domestic market supply. It adds a relevant productive capacity in a high-tech industry, which also contributes to the improvement of economic complement and productivity in Brazil. The good supplied is new for the country and the firm. Therefore, new capabilities in the renewable energy field will be developed in the firm and in the country. However, this shift with demand the development of a qualified supply-chain.

Environment (3): The investment will support the development of renewable energy supply-chain. After the equipment diffusion in the market, we expect an improvement in the country's energy matrix. The impact is indirect. Also, there the site construction has a low environmental impact.

Social (3): The investment will create a large number of job positions. However, the positions are mostly for low-skilled workers during the site construction and for the industry operation. We should also notice that the equipment will be supplied for health services, increasing this industry productivity, which also has a positive social impact.

Local Development (2.8): The site will be installed in the State of São Paulo, in a high development city but far from the state capital. There are

(continued)

several industries nearby the site, including key producers for the renewable energy supply chain. Therefore, the investment can enhance the productive networks in the regions and improve its productive structure.

Client (4.4): The investor is adding a new product to its portfolio in order to reach a market with higher profit rates and potential growth. The project will also implement a new project management system and improve firm's corporate governance practice. It increases the benefits of the project in the firm's competitiveness.

4 Conclusion

The DFIs should be aware of the global challenges the twenty-first century economy imposes and adapt its financial and nonfinancial procedures. In particular, the financial sector should adapt itself to the changes associated with the new economy, in which knowledge (as suggested by "The New Club of Paris") and sustainability (as defined by the UN SDGs) play a relevant role. Based on the BNDES case, we show that development banks can develop new tools and change its internal procedures to address these new challenges.

The MAE and the TIIP are methodologies implemented by the BNDES that sharply changes its staff's mindset and its rating and project eligibility procedures. Both methodologies here presented are concerned with translating a complex reality into something clearer to ease and improve the decision-making procedures by BNDES managers. Thus, achieving clarity through qualified information. The MAE presents, in a synthetic manner, the intangible capitals of credit borrowing companies, adding up to the traditional banking approach (based only on financial soundness). Beyond improving risk perception, the MAE allows the BNDES to act on its mission of development agent by promoting the improvement of the intangible capital of companies, notably the ones related to corporate governance. The TIIP, meanwhile, is an ex ante impact evaluation mechanism and therefore a tool in an investment project's decision-making process. Although it considers several complex economic, social and environmental factors in projects, the result is a straightforward and adequate analysis.

Moreover, based on a case study, we detail the TIIP' criteria to demonstrate it is a powerful instrument to adapt BNDES' procedures to the challenges of the new economy. The methodology has several criteria that assess a project's expected impact on knowledge, innovation, and sustainability. The case of a firm investment in a new site to produce renewable energy equipment shows that the methodology gives relevant information for a project eligibility decision and to enhance the project's benefits in knowledge and sustainability. Firstly, the gains in terms of economic complexity and innovation are explicit by the TIIP. Secondly, although the benefits for sustainability are also positive, the methodology addresses improvements that can be implemented in the project to enhance its contribution to the social and environmental dimensions. These improvements should have benchmark projects, such as investments in sanitation, as references. Therefore, the TIIP is a useful guideline for BNDES' action and a strategic tool to deal with the new economic challenges.

We can say that both the TIIP and the MAE are successful and powerful initiatives to reach their aims. Furthermore, as in any good method, they are flexible enough to adapt to the ongoing challenges of the knowledge economy and of the Brazilian development path. However, in an ever-changing world, we are deeply aware that, despite the successful innovative initiatives earlier described, the implementation of those tools should be complemented by other initiatives. The BNDES needs partners that will expose us to other technologies that are widely regarded as substitutes to the very own market we are part of: banking and credit. In the past few years, the BNDES began to align its operations with the reality of economies and institutions deeply connected with the technological transformation of banking activities.

An example of a partnership is the use of blockchain technology, together with the KFW and the Ethereum Foundation. This technology challenge is to use a stable coin to improve the traceability of the money lent (more transparency on the use of the loan) through the creation of a kind of cryptocurrency (called "BNDEStoken").[8] Another relevant initiative, an even bolder step, is the BNDES public call for fintech's services. Instead of considering fintech's as threats, the BNDES sets partnerships with them, offering financial education and credit loans to micro/small companies and entrepreneurs.[9] These initiatives, among others, aimed at adapting banking products and services, should complement the implementation of new assessment tools like the TIIP and the MAE. This is a required effort to establish the BNDES as a knowledge bank, capable of dealing with the kaleidoscopic nature of the new economic reality in the twenty-first century.

References

Alexander CP (1983, May 30) The new economy. Time Magazine. Retrieved from http://content.time.com/time/magazine/article/0,9171,926013,00.html

Almeida HTV, Braga JP (2014) Evaluating intangibles assets and competitiveness in Brazilian firms: the BNDES's approach. In: de Pablos PO, Edvinsson L (eds) Intellectual capital in organizations: non-financial reports and accounts. Routledge, New York, pp 253–262

Almeida HTV, Braga JP (2017) Explicitando as contribuições para o desenvolvimento no BNDES: a Tese de Impacto de Investimento em Projetos (Tiip) como método de avaliação ex ante. Text for discussion: 116. BNDES, Rio de Janeiro

Almeida HT, Viana M, Jannibelli G (2018) Afterword. In: Matos F, Vairinhos V, Selig PM, Edvisson L (eds) Intellectual capital management as a driver of sustainability: perspectives for organizations and society. Springer, Cham, pp 239–242

[8]For more details of those initiatives see Arantes et al. (2018).

[9]For more details of those initiatives see https://agenciadenoticias.bndes.gov.br/detalhe/noticia/BNDES-aposta-nas-fintechs-para-ampliar-acesso-ao-credito-de-micro-e-pequenas-empresas/

Arantes Jr GM, D'Almeida Jr JN, Onodera MT, Moreno SM, Almeida VR (2018) Improving the process of lending, monitoring and evaluating through Blockchain Technologies: an application of Blockchain in the Brazilian Development Bank (BNDES). Retrieved from https://ieeexplore.ieee.org/document/8726785

Bach H, Bakker M, Farrington J, Drillet Z, Duray B, Frederiksen P, Gyuró KÉ, Henrichs T, Jansson K, Jensen TS, Jombach S (2008) Indicators—methodology and descriptions. SENSOR Project Deliverable Report 2(2):3

Cavalcante L, De Negri F (2013) Índices compostos de inovação: uma proposta de cálculo de ratings para empresas e projetos. Working Paper 13. Ipea, Rio de Janeiro

Coutinho L, Ferraz JC (1994) Estudo da competitividade da indústria brasileira. Papirus/Unicamp, Campinas

Drexler C, Noble A, Leytes M (2014) From ideas to practice, pilots to strategy II: practical solutions and actionable insights on how to do impact investing. Report. World Economic Forum

Edvinsson L (1997) Developing intellectual capital at Skandia. Long Range Plan 30(3):366–373

Edvinsson L, Malone M (1997) Intellectual capital: realizing your company's true value by finding its hidden brainpower. Harper Business, New York

European Parliament (2015) Ex-ante impact assessment work in the European parliament: a compendium of initial appraisals of European Commission impact assessments. Retrieved from http://www.europarl.europa.eu/EPRS/IMPA_APIN_Compendium_July2014-December2015.pdf

Griffith-Jones S, Ocampo JA (2018) The future of national development banks. Oxford University Press, Oxford

Helming K (2009) Sensor sustainability impact assessment: tools for environment, social and economic effect of multifunctional land use in European regions. Report of Sixth Framework Programme. European Union

Hidalgo CA, Hausmann R (2009) The building blocks of economic complexity. Proc Natl Acad Sci 106(26):10570–10575

KFW (2013) Ex post-evaluation brief Brazil: Natural Resources Policy Project (NRPP), 2013. Retrieved from https://www.kfw-entwicklungsbank.de/PDF/Evaluierung/Ergebnisse-und-Publikationen/PDF-Dokumente-A-D_EN/Brasilien_NRPP_2013_E.pdf

Mazzucato M (2018) Mission-oriented innovation policies: challenges and opportunities. Ind Corp Chang 27(5):803–815

OECD (1991) Principles for evaluation of development assistance. Retrieved from http://www.oecd.org/dac/evaluation/

OECD (2002) Glossary of key terms in evaluation and results based management. Retrieved from https://www.oecd.org/dac/2754804.pdf

OECD (2007) Ex ante poverty impact assessment. Retrieved from www.oecd.org/dac/povertyreduction/38978856.pdf

OECD/Eurostat (2005) The measurement of scientific and technological activities. Oslo manual: guidelines for collecting and interpreting innovation data, 3rd edn. OECD Publishing, Paris

Olsen S, Galimidi B (2008) Catalogue of approaches to impact measurement: assessing social impact in private ventures. The Rockefeller Foundation, New York

PWC (2013) Measuring and managing total impact: a new language for business decisions. Retrieved from https://www.pwc.com/gx/en/sustainability/publications/total-impact-measurement-management/assets/pwc-timm-report.pdf

Saisana M, Tarantola S (2002) State-of-the-art report on current methodologies and practices for composite indicator development. European Commission, Ispra

Saltuk Y, Idrissi A (2012) A portfolio approach to impact investment. JP Morgan, London

Schmidt-Traub G, Sachs J (2015) Roles of public and private development finance. Sustainable Development Solutions Network. Retrieved from http://unsdsn.org/wp-content/uploads/2015/05/150529-The-Roles-of-Public-and-Private-Development-Finance.pdf

Stiglitz JE (1994) The role of the state in financial markets. The World Bank, Washington, DC

World Bank (2007) Development outcome tracking system (DOTS) indicator framework. World Bank Group, Washington, DC

Knowledge Decentralization in the Age of Blockchain: Developing a Knowledge-Transfer System Using Digital Assets

Marta Christina Suciu, Christian Năsulea, and Diana Năsulea

Abstract Disruptive technologies have reshaped the way governance, regulations and businesses plan their medium- to long-term development strategies, affecting our socio-economic and cultural environments in a number of ways. Blockchain in general, and its applications in corporations, medical services, archiving or investment, in particular, is a phenomenon whose significance is yet to be fully explored. Big corporations like Microsoft and Walmart are already integrating blockchain for cloud services, smart contracts or food chain databases. As the adoption of the blockchain is increasing, we will witness the discovery of more ways to make organizational processes run even more smoothly. The aim of our chapter is to challenge the traditional ways to perceive organizational knowledge by creating a model that allows the application of private Blockchains to knowledge evolution, ownership and transfer. Socio-economic and cultural aspects of integrating blockchain in the knowledge transfer systems would be discussed and our focus will be to explore the effectiveness of such a system and its impact on intellectual capital.

M. C. Suciu (✉)
Department of Economics and Economic Policies, The Bucharest University of Economic Studies, Bucharest, Romania
e-mail: christina.suciu@economie.ase.ro

C. Năsulea
Department of International Relations and Universal History, University of Bucharest, Bucharest, Romania

Institut de Recherches Economiques et Fiscales, Paris, France
e-mail: christian@nasulea.ro

D. Năsulea
Department of Economics and Economic Policies, The Bucharest University of Economic Studies, Bucharest, Romania

Institut de Recherches Economiques et Fiscales, Paris, France
e-mail: diana@nasulea.ro

F. Matos et al. (eds.), *Knowledge, People, and Digital Transformation*, Contributions to Management Science, https://doi.org/10.1007/978-3-030-40390-4_17

1 Introduction

Already well-established as a field of study, knowledge management leverages the most important intangible asset of an organization, human capital. Although knowledge management tools and systems are being constantly developed by companies, a lot of the practitioners seem to agree that the work culture and the people are the key drivers of a successful knowledge management initiative (Saint-Onge 1998).

Scholars such as Bratianu (2015), go even further to develop a theory based on a new metaphor of knowledge that consists on cognitive, emotional and spiritual knowledge. Knowledge is something more than information, because it carries behind the entire experience, culture and even feelings of the individual.

A fundamental part of the knowledge management is related to how can one make knowledge accessible, usable and transferable between individuals and then, organizations. Organizational knowledge in its dynamic form is one of the emergent research directions because transforming knowledge into a strategic resource became key to any successful company. Creating an environment that encourages and motivates employees to share knowledge is one of the drivers of competitive advantage.

Knowledge transfer and knowledge sharing are concepts backed by a lot of research but no universally accepted definition. However, a definition developed by Argote and Ingram describes knowledge transfer as (Argote and Ingram 2000, p. 151):

> The process through which one unit (e.g. group, department, or division) is affected by the experience of another.

In the digitalization era, the role of information technology is frequently mentioned as a solution to both inter- and intra-organizational knowledge sharing. However, without a proper organizational culture and an incentive for people to share their tacit knowledge, electronic systems remain only tools with no real value.

Blockchain is one of the hot discussion topics for governments and businesses alike, and this is continuously impacting the research within the field. As it promises to revolutionize many industries, a few researchers have started to discuss the impact of Blockchain in the area of knowledge management and more exactly, knowledge sharing or knowledge transfer. However, most of the academic research performed on this topic comes from an ITC and especially crypto-studies perspective, which ignores the social and cultural element that surrounds knowledge sharing between individuals. However, we strongly believe that the viability of the many proposed applications for Blockchain needs a socio-economic and even cultural assessment perspective as well. Knowledge transfer and knowledge sharing within organizations cannot be performed by machines if people do not trust them. Issues related to intellectual property or the need for maintaining one's position within the company are challenged when the intellectual capital is transferred in the cloud.

Our study develops on the technical side of the blockchain technology to create a social one that can be accepted and adopted by employees. Through our findings, the study contributes to the research on developing systems that help innovation and protect human and intellectual capital instead of replacing it.

2 Brief Literature Review

Bratianu and Orzea (2010) have analyzed knowledge sharing as a component of the organizational knowledge framework using the Romanian business environment as a case study. Their results show that, on an individual level, the barriers are trust between colleagues, lack of experience in knowledge sharing and motivation, while for the organization, rewarding systems, communication and the lack of corporate investment in employees seem to be the most noted challenges for knowledge sharing.

The research on knowledge transfer has recently started to include studies on the impact of digitalization on organizational performance from a KM perspective. For example, Rothberg and Erickson (2017) note the importance of big data for knowledge management and knowledge transfer. XLM systems facilitate the codification extraction, transfer and utilization of knowledge within organizations. However, scholars Lyu and Zhang (2016) agree that technology by itself cannot be sufficient for assuring the success of knowledge transfer in organizations. We argue that even if the technology is not per se the solution, its design can be more successful in offering the needed stimuli to employees. On the idea that incentives are a crucial factor for the success of knowledge transfer systems, we are noting the important works of Lee and Ahn (2007), Sundaresan and Zhang (2010) and Argote and Reagans (2003).

On the applications of blockchain within the organizational environment, we build on two major contributions. Gatteschi et al. (2018) have focused on the different applications for blockchain within government and enterprises and the reasoning behind it. Their results are rather descriptive, but helpful for the understanding of the already-acknowledged potential of the current technology. Li et al. (2018) went further and offered an overview of the blockchain technology from a managerial perspective, contributing to the theoretical research on the diffusion of the blockchain technology in socio-political and technical fields. Their practical results concern blockchain's market value, suggesting that although only 2% of the biggest 50 international corporations include blockchain in their annual reports, we are also witnessing an increase in the market value of this technology.

The model we developed builds on the concept of Knowledge Blockchains developed by Fill and Harer (2018) that aims to store knowledge in 'an immutable and temperresistant way', following the idea of creating a transparent system of knowledge proof that allows for transfer and delegation schemes within the organization. We are also noting the work of Lyu and Zhang (2016) that investigates the role of IT, incentives and organisational culture in knowledge management. They create both an analytical and a practical model that incorporates both the social and the organizational aspects. However, none of the aforementioned papers refer to both inter- and intra-organizational knowledge sharing and the relationship between them and intellectual property and incentives.

3 Methodology

Our research is mainly exploratory as it dives into a less studied interdisciplinary field, exploring different possibilities to integrate the Blockchain technology within the knowledge management systems within organizations. The structure of the study is composed of three main parts: the first section will explore the conceptual framework of knowledge management, transfer and sharing, with a focus on the problems current KM systems pose to intra-organizational and inter-organizational transparency and effectiveness. The theoretical part of our chapter deals with possible ways of integrating blockchain within the knowledge management research field, with a focus on knowledge sharing and knowledge transfer and it builds on the conceptual framework developed by Rubenstein-Montano et al. (2001), Bratianu (2015) and others.

The purpose of this first section is to explore the challenges a new system should overcome, not only from a practical perspective, but also from the perspective of the organizational culture of intellectual capital protection.

The second section will offer firstly, an explanation of the blockchain technology and secondly, an analysis of blockchain's potential applications within this framework, with a focus on the transition of the what, why, who and when knowledge processes from an in-person approach to an automatic digitally processable services that can be easily implemented and adopted by organizational structures. These two sections will create the framework for the third section dedicated to the development of our model that will build on Fill and Harer's (2018) knowledge blockchain prototype, taking it further from the perspective of (1) trust, (2) ease of use. We will also base our model on the work of Lyu and Zhang (2016).

Lastly, conclusions will be drawn on the advantages and challenges of implementing a blockchain-based knowledge sharing and transfer system.

4 Discussion

4.1 Knowledge Transfer

In a 1983 paper, Michael Polanyi (1983) has talked about the two types of knowledge individuals possess, namely (1) explicit knowledge—the type of knowledge that can be explained and easily transmitted and replicated; the know-what knowledge (Bratianu and Orzea 2010) and (2) tacit knowledge that is acquired through the individual's own experience and is affected by their own cultural attributes, feelings and beliefs. Managers should, therefore, harvest their employees, customers and

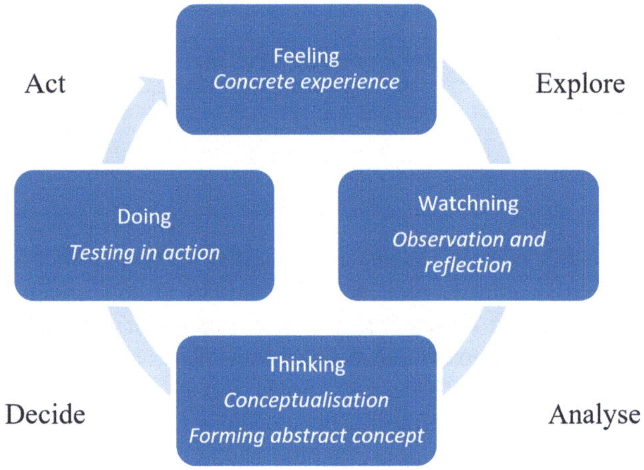

Fig. 1 Kolb's learning cycle (Kolb 1984)

stakeholder's tacit knowledge and try to transform it into added value for their companies (Riege 2005; Bratianu and Orzea 2010). Tacit knowledge is complex and thus, difficult to formulate and codify, although its impact on the organization's performance is significant (Nonaka and Takeuchi 1995).

Nonaka and Takeuchi (1995) SECI model of knowledge creation and transfer is based on the idea of a knowledge spiral. Socialization is based on the idea that human interaction and shared experience are vital for acquiring tacit knowledge.

Externalization refers to the process of articulating tacit knowledge into concepts by using language, metaphors and models through the scientific methods of induction and deduction. Combination is a social process (Bratianu 2015) that helps systemizing concepts into a knowledge system (Nonaka and Takeuchi 1995, p. 67). Internalization is the process of transforming explicit knowledge into tacit knowledge, at an individual level and the starting point of a new spiral of knowledge creation.

As the purpose of the chapter is to develop a model that allows both tacit and explicit knowledge to be shared or transform, we choose Kolb's learning cycle (Kolb 1984) model as a basis. According to the elicitation model, four phases need to be linked in order to undergo a process of experiential learning: feeling—a concrete experience watching—observation and reflection; thinking—conceptualization; doing—testing. As learning can start at any of these stages that are nevertheless adaptable and usually mixed for everyone, a knowledge transfer system needs to account for all this and not only offer a technical solution (Fig. 1).

Knowledge transfer is critical when employees retire, new ones are hired, when the organization is restructured or when mergers and acquisitions take place. Having an effective knowledge transfer system in place is one of the key aspects that make the transition flawless, with reduced costs. At the moment, for knowledge transfer organizations use different methods such as:

- Mentoring programmes
- Reference guides
- Online training programmes
- Internal forums
- Video training
- Guided practice
- Simulations

One of the main barriers is, however, the lack of resources for implementing a formalized knowledge transfer procedure. Regardless of how effective mentoring programmes are, the cost of relocating human capital for this task translates to increased costs for the company, since fewer individuals are actively contributing to the overall performance. Technology might just be the solution for all these barriers but implementing a software does not guarantee efficiency if employees (a) are not incentivized to use it or (b) do not trust it.

4.2 The Role of Blockchain for Knowledge Transfer

A blockchain is a distributed register or database that is organized as a list of immutable ordered blocks (Casino et al. 2018). Blockchain allows individuals to interact in a peer-to-peer network where non-trusting users can be automatically verified without the need of an authority. The blockchain technology, initially used as a solution for maintaining the order of transactions behind Bitcoin is now used for numerous applications such the banking sector (Peters and Panayi 2016; Ye and Liang 2016; Cocco et al. 2017), transportation and supply chain (Francisco and Swanson 2018), arts (De Filippi 2015) and governance (Beck et al. 2018; Atzori 2015; Shermin 2017). As its main characteristics are transparency, auditability and security, companies started to invest a lot in this technology that promises to create safer, more secure and transparent environments with lower costs.

Applications of Blockchain in the field of knowledge sharing have been developed, although not for or within organizational frameworks. Lunyr is a platform that offers a reward-based system for writing, editing and peer-reviewing information (Lunyr 2018). Similarly, Everipedia is a blockchain-based encyclopaedia that promises to decentralize Wikipedia by allowing editors to become stakeholders, thus incentivizing them to make sure their contributions are accurate (Everipedia 2019). Another example is Knowledge.io, a platform that wants to reward participants based on their knowledge (Knowledge.io 2019). Although not created for organizational knowledge transfer processes, what all these three platforms have in common is (a) the reward system that acts as incentive and (b) an intellectual property protection as the contribution or the distributed knowledge provenience is non-alterable. These two factors are extremely important for effective knowledge transfer.

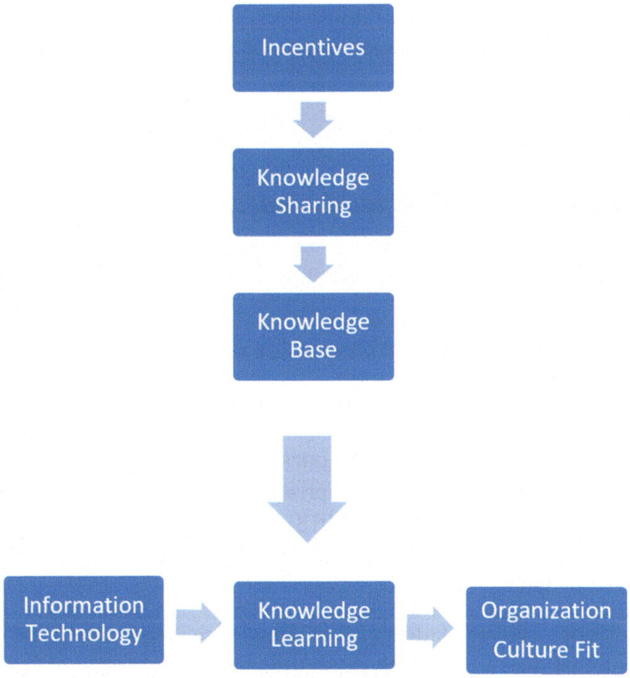

Fig. 2 Dynamic KM model developed by Lyu and Zhang (2016)

According to Szulanski (1996) incentives are key to developing an organisational culture that favoures knowledge transfer. Lee and Ahn (2007) have also studied the design of a reward-based system that encourages knowledge transfer at both an individual and group level.

Lyu and Zhang (2016) have built a dynamic model that captures the interactions between incentives, IT and organizational model (Fig. 2). Their model starts from the premises of an organisation that decides to offer incentives for voluntarily sharing their knowledge with their co-workers. Their results show that learning knowledge from the base allows culturally unfit workers to become culturally fit and that IT offers the right tools for workers to share their knowledge.

The relationship between knowledge transfer and intellectual property has been studied by researchers in the field of KM like Lee et al. (2010), but not a lot of studies refer to specific systems that are used for intra-organizational knowledge sharing. However, a study performed by Olaisen and Revang (2017) explores both knowledge transfer and intellectual property and their results, although referring to inter-organizational knowledge sharing, show that intellectual property rights are critical and imperative factors for creating trust in the team. Although one might argue that within the organization, the worker is not necessarily the owner of the knowledge they have, sharing that tacit knowledge is rarely performed if the organizational culture is not one that harnessed this practice and if the individual appointed to do this is not incentivized in any way. Furthermore, individuals are sensitive to knowledge they acquired through years of experience being shared with no personal attribution.

4.3 The Knowledge Blockchain Model

Fill and Harer (2018) have described the concept of knowledge blockchains. According to the two:

> The concept is based on the assumption that knowledge can—at least partially—be made explicit in the form of conceptual models.

For the moment, the existing knowledge-sharing platforms are merely used by big enterprises, as the small-to-medium ones do not have the resources for such a system. Although systems for cross-enterprise knowledge sharing have been created (Vatankhah Barenji and Hashemipour 2018), not a lot of them refer to the internal knowledge that is developed within a company. Three of the main challenges from this perspective include:

- Centralized non-scalable platforms. The knowledge is centralized and owned by a small group that does not incentivize sharing and poses challenges to controlling and saving the knowledge (Sedighi et al. 2016).
- Privacy and data leaks. As the number of users increases, there are ownership, access and control issues (Roman et al. 2013).
- Centralized platforms that do not motivate employees to share their knowledge as the information is centralized.

For storing and sharing knowledge, we propose a system based on a private Waves blockchain. We choose Waves because it is one of the most popular platforms and because users do not need to code complex smart contracts, but instead use plugins.

Intra-organizational Knowledge Sharing: Application 1
Figure 3 shows an overview of how the platform should function.

- We have a knowledge supplier—the employee—who wishes to share information about a specific procedure on the platform.
- A knowledge file is generated.
- The knowledge supplier needs to add a series of attributes for the file—job position; type of procedure and a series of keywords so the document is easily identifiable.
- The knowledge file gets encrypted and it transforms into a knowledge block that has a hash code and a timestamp.
- The generated hash code gets uploaded on the blockchain and stored in a decentralized manner, with no single point of failure. All the nodes (computers) within the blockchain validate the document.

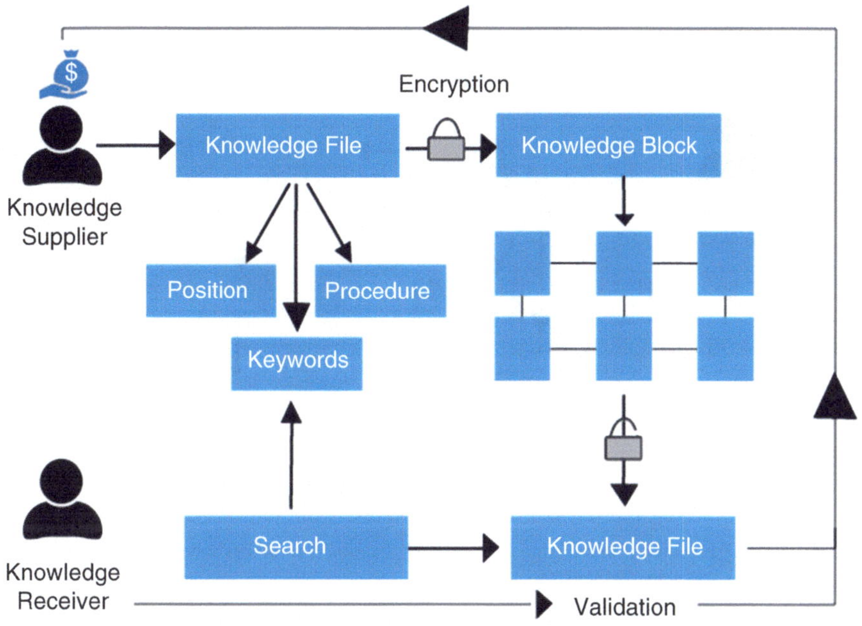

Fig. 3 Intra-organizational knowledge sharing—Application 1 (Authors' own work)

- The knowledge receiver—another employee—looks for information about a certain procedure by inserting keywords.
- The platform identifies the document—knowledge file.
- The knowledge file gets decrypted and downloaded on the knowledge supplier's computer.
- The knowledge supplier receives a certain amount of tokens in their own wallet, as decided in the smart contract.

Features

- *A token*—The company should launch an internal token that would be used to reward the employees who engage in knowledge sharing. The value of the token would be established internally.
- *File type*—Documents could be either text, or spreadsheet, presentations and even video recordings that show how a task is being performed in real time. This is key because it offers the possibility of observing and watching as described in Kolb's knowledge cycle.
- *Encryption*—This solves the privacy and intellectual property rights. However, some aspects need to be considered here. Firstly, if the information shared by one of the employees is no more than explicit knowledge gained through training and guided assistance, then the file uploaded on the blockchain can be freely used by anybody. However, if the knowledge that is being shared has a tacit nature, like a procedure that is developed by the employee and that makes them more efficient, then, the file gets encrypted. Encryption is the second stimulator the knowledge

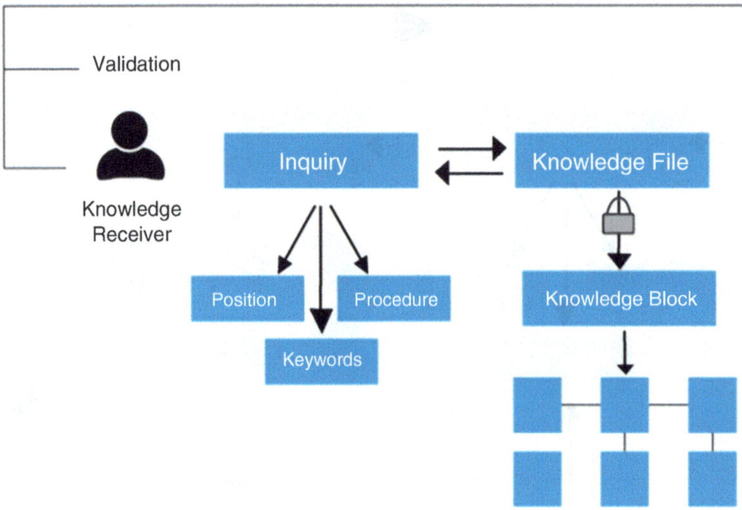

Fig. 4 Intra-organizational knowledge sharing—Application 2 (Authors' own work)

supplier has for engaging in knowledge sharing. Knowing that the information is decentralized and that nobody can access it without a key, makes it safe.

- *Smart contracts*—Contracts will be decided and uploaded on the blockchain from the very beginning. These contracts will stipulate the value of the tokens that are to be wired for each document that is being downloaded. Furthermore, a limit on the number of documents that an employee can download should be decided so that the system will not encourage employees to download each other's knowledge files just to make some more money.
- *Crypto wallet*—Each employee would own a crypto wallet that is theirs' to use. This means that even after the employee resigned or was dismissed from the job, they could still receive tokens if their knowledge file is being downloaded by somebody who took their position. Details are to be established by the smart contract.

Intra-organizational Knowledge Sharing: Application 2

The system can work both ways, meaning that users can ask questions that can be answered by one of the knowledge suppliers. Figure 4 shows how the platform should work.

- The Knowledge Receiver makes an inquiry referring to an issue they need assistance with. They select all the attributes, including the job position, the procedure they have issues with and keywords.
- A Knowledge Supplier claims the request and offers to answer.
- The Knowledge Receiver downloads the knowledge file.
- Once the receiver validates the file to make sure it is according to their needs, a certain amount of token gets mined and wired in the wallet of the Knowledge Supplier.

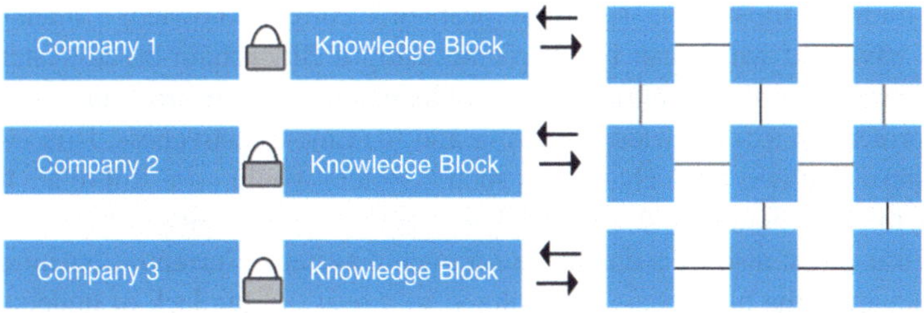

Fig. 5 Intra-organizational knowledge sharing—Application 3 (Authors' own work)

- The knowledge file gets encrypted and uploaded onto the blockchain so it can be used by others having the same issue.

Intra-organizational Knowledge Sharing: Application 3

When individuals working at two different companies exchange knowledge, there is an issue of intellectual property protection and security leak. However, in today's competitive market, companies are often exchanging knowledge through partnerships, agreements, consortia and joint ventures. Not following security procedures can turn out negatively for at least one of the involved parties.

Blockchain has the ability to solve this issue and to create an environment that encourages knowledge sharing and innovation without posing any risks.

The application of our model for Knowledge Blockchains starts from the idea that private blockchains can be linked with each other. Every company can upload their encrypted knowledge block into a common blockchain. This already means that data regarding ownership is now established with no possibility of disagreement, since the timestamp and the hash allow for information regarding ownership to be tracked. So intellectual property can de facto be established without the need of a third party.

Then, when another company wants to access a knowledge block, the owner company can choose to grant access or not, depending on how sensitive the information is. This already puts the basis for creating a sharing knowledge ecosystem that is safe, transparent and that allows for partnerships to take place (Fig. 5).

5 Conclusions

Effective knowledge transfer is one of the strategic resources of any organization. Developing trust between individuals and incentivizing knowledge sharing can only be performed if the organizational culture inspires people to do so. Developing trust between both co-workers and partner organizations used to be challenging. Moreover, intellectual property rights should be well established in all organizations in order to create an environment that is open to knowledge sharing. However, with the development of Blockchain technology, both the trust and the intellectual property issues can be easily overcome.

Our findings illustrate a series of problems current knowledge management systems have and which can be overcome using a Blockchain-based system, like (a) transparency in the monitoring of knowledge creation; (b) trust and intellectual capital protection; (c) knowledge sharing and (d) time-effectiveness. However, our results show that two main challenges such a system would pose still relate to costs for both implementation and training, but also to the possibility of rapid adoption. Ease of use might also be a challenge for such a system. Currently, businesses are still reluctant to the blockchain technology, as a result of the lack of understanding on how the system works, but this could and will probably change as technology evolves.

6 Practical and Research Implications

The implications of our research fall into three main categories. Firstly, the theoretical framework we develop can be further explored in a study of different digital KM systems and their implications on knowledge sharing and transfer within organizations. Secondly, our model can be built and tested by practitioners developing KM systems or integrated within the already existing ones. Results can then show the viability of the model and the perspective of the business environment towards it. Thirdly, as we have previously mentioned, we believe there is a lot to be discussed and study on the socio-economic and cultural side of implementing the Blockchain technology in different management processes within organizations, and especially in the ones connected to human and intellectual capital. Our study is merely exploratory as such a model was never implemented or tested. Furthermore, we have not studied the technicalities behind building such an infrastructure or the implementation costs. However, further research could dive more into employees' motivations for sharing knowledge. Quantitative and qualitative studies in this area could improve our understanding of the practical situation.

References

Argote L, Ingram P (2000) Knowledge transfer: a basis for competitive advantage in firms. Organ Behav Hum Decis Process 82(1):150–169

Argote L, Reagans R (2003) Managing knowledge in organizations: an integrative framework and review of emerging themes. Manag Sci 49(4):571–582

Atzori M (2015) Blockchain technology and decentralized governance: is the state still necessary? J Govern Regul 6(1). https://doi.org/10.2139/ssrn.2709713

Beck R, Muller-Bloch C, Leslie King J (2018) Governance in the Blockchain economy: a framework and research agenda. J Assoc Inf Syst 19(10). https://aisel.aisnet.org/jais/vol19/iss10/1. Retrieved 13 Mar 2019

Bratianu C (2015) Organizational knowledge dynamics: managing knowledge creation, acquisition, sharing and transformation. ICI Global, Hershey

Bratianu C, Orzea I (2010) Tacit knowledge sharing in organizational knowledge dynamics. In: Proceedings of the 2nd European conference on intellectual Capital, Lisbon, Portugal, 29–30 Mar 2010

Casino F, Dasaklis TK, Patsakis C (2018) A systematic literature of blockchain-based applications: current status, classification and open issues. Telematics Inform 36:55–81. https://doi.org/10.1016/j.tele.2018.11.006

Cocco L, Pinna A, Marchesi M (2017) Banking on Blockchain: costs savings thanks to the Blockchain technology. Future Internet 9(3):25. https://doi.org/10.3390/fi9030025

De Filippi P (2015) Blockchain-based crowdfunding: what impact on artistic production and art consumption? Observatório Itaú Cultural (19)

Everipedia (2019) Abgerufen am 18. 03. 2019 von https://everipedia.org/

Fill H-G, Harer F (2018) Knowledge Blockchains: applying Blockchain technology to Enterprise modeling. In: Hawaii international conference on system sciences. Waikola Village, Hawaii

Francisco K, Swanson D (2018) The supply chain has no clothes: technology adoption of Blockchain for supply chain transparency. Logistics 2(1):2. https://doi.org/10.3390/logistics2010002

Gatteschi V, Lamberti F, Demartini C, Prantenada C, Santamaria V (2018) Blockchain and smart contracts for insurance: is the technology mature enough? Future Internet 10(20). https://doi.org/10.3390/fi10020020

Knowledge.io. (18. 03. 2019). Von. https://knowledge.io/abgerufen

Kolb D (1984) Experiential learning. Prentice Hall, Englewood Cliffs, NJ

Lee D, Ahn H (2007) Reward systems for intra-organizational knowledge sharing. Eur J Oper Res 180(2):938–956

Lee P, Mann N, Wearing A (2010) Leadership and trust: their effect on knowledge sharing and team performance. Manag Learn 41:473–491

Li Y, Perron-Brault A, Marier-Bienvenue T, Wang X, Pare G (2018) Blockchain technology in business organizations: a scoping review. In: Presented at the 51st Hawaii international conference on social sciences

Lunyr (31. 01. 2018). Lunyr—Blockchain-based knowledge sharing platform launches open beta. Medium. Abgerufen am 18. 03. 2018 von https://medium.com/lunyr/lunyr-blockchain-based-knowledge-sharing-platform-launches-open-beta-11ba2e68d2d9

Lyu H, Zhang Z (2016) Incentives for knowledge sharing: impact of organisational culture and information technology. Enterp Inf Syst:1–20

Nonaka I, Takeuchi H (1995) The knowledge-creating company: how Japanese companies create the dynamics of innovation. Oxford University Press, Oxford

Olaisen J, Revang O (2017) The dynamics of intellectual property rights for trust, knowledge sharing and innovation in project teams. Int J Inf Manag 37(6):583–589

Peters G, Panayi E (2016) Understanding modern banking ledgers through Blockchain technologies: future of transaction processing and smart contracts on the internet of money. Springer, Heidelberg, pp 239–279

Polanyi M (1983) The tacid dimension. Peter Smith, Gloucester

Riege A (2005) Three-dozen knowledge sharing barriers managers must consider. J Knowl Manag 13(5):257–270

Roman R, Zhou J, Lopez J (2013) On the features and challenges of security and privacy in distributed internet of things. Comput Netw 57(10):2266–2279

Rothberg HN, Erickson S (2017) Big data systems: knowledge transfer or intelligence insight? J Knowl Manag 21(1):92–112

Rubenstein-Montano B, Liebowitz J, Buchwalter J, McCaw D, Newman B, Rebeck K (2001) A systems thinking framework for knowledge management. Decis Support Syst 31(1):6–16

Saint-Onge H (1998) Knowledge management. In: Proceedings of the 1998 New York business information technology conference, New York

Sedighi M, van Splunter S, Brazier F, van Beers C, Lukosch S (2016) Exploration of multi-layered knowledge sharing participation: the role of perceived benefits and costs. J Knowl Manag 20 (6):1247–1267

Shermin V (2017) Disrupting governance with blockchains and smart contracts. Strateg Chang 26 (5):499–509. https://doi.org/10.1002/jsc.2150

Sundaresan S, Zhang Z (2010) Knowledge sharing and learning in organizations: role of incentives and information systems. Working Paper. Rutgers-The State University of New Jersey

Szulanski G (1996) Exploring internal stickiness: impediments to the transfer of best practice within the firm. Strateg Manag J 17(S2):27–43

Vatankhah Barenji A, Hashemipour M (2018) Real-time building information modeling (BIM) synchronization using radio frequency identification technology and cloud computing system. J Ind Syst Eng 10:61–68

Ye G, Liang C (2016) Blockchain application and outlook in the banking industry. Financ Innov 2:24. https://doi.org/10.1186/s40854-016-0034-9

Digital Transformation and Additive Manufacturing

Florinda Matos and Radu Godina

Abstract The digital transformation in manufacturing, making processes fully automated and interconnected, using artificial intelligence, is transforming the industry, with impacts in the society in general.

The additive manufacturing technology is now a core component of modern smart manufacturing and is changing the products' life cycle with impacts in the way that products are designed, prototyped, manufactured, and used.

Additive manufacturing technologies are enabling new opportunities in business models, namely in production and in customization, and, also, in various aspects that affect people's lives.

In spite of additive manufacturing technology currently attracting a growing number of companies, organizations, and individuals, its challenges and impacts seem to remain unknown.

Exploring the literature that relates additive manufacturing and digital transformation, this chapter seeks to provide new insights into the impacts of additive manufacturing. It shows that additive manufacturing is playing an increasingly important role in the industrial–technological change, and that has effects on other activities and the people's life.

F. Matos (✉)
Instituto Universitário de Lisboa (ISCTE-IUL), DINÂMIA'CET-ISCTE, Lisbon, Portugal

ICLab – ICAA – Intellectual Capital Association, Santarém, Portugal

The New Club of Paris, Vienna, Austria
e-mail: florinda.matos@iscte-iul.pt

R. Godina
UNIDEMI, Department of Mechanical and Industrial Engineering, Faculty of Science and Technology (FCT), Universidade Nova de Lisboa, Caparica, Portugal
e-mail: r.godina@fct.unl.pt

F. Matos et al. (eds.), *Knowledge, People, and Digital Transformation*, Contributions to Management Science, https://doi.org/10.1007/978-3-030-40390-4_18

1 Introduction

In the digital transformation, additive manufacturing, associated with artificial intelligence, and big data, will transform manufacturing.

The automation and digitization, namely the developments in artificial intelligence, Internet of Things, robotics, automation, biotechnology, or additive manufacturing, are transforming the industry.

Initially known as rapid prototyping, additive manufacturing technology, known as 3D (also often referred in the literature as additive fabrication, rapid prototyping, layered manufacturing, and direct digital manufacturing) arose in the 1980s, as result of Charles Hull (1986, 2015) work's in stereolithography.

This is a professional production process that differs significantly from the conventional manufacturing methods. If until recently additive manufacturing technology was seen only as software-based tools for designing and prototyping objects or making special products or parts in small batches, nowadays additive manufacturing is seen as one of the technologies of factories of the future.

This new vision results from the new opportunities for freedom of design and the manufacturing flexibility of this technology, enabling mass production, and customization.

Additive manufacturing, also, serves as an intermediate step alongside conventional manufacturing methods, also known as hybrid production (e.g. in the jewellery industry).

The evolution of technology has allowed printers to emerge faster, more economical, and more capable of producing customized products and quality in large volumes. This process is changing the business models with undetermined impacts on society (Bogers et al. 2016; Ford and Despeisse 2016; Kohtala and Hyysalo 2015; Matos and Jacinto 2019).

The European Commission Report (2019) "A vision for the European Industry until 2030"[1] presents additive manufacturing as one of the emerging technologies with the most significant impact on the industry. According to this report, additive manufacturing technology "allows for shorter supply chains, more efficient use of production materials, and reduced time and cost in developing, designing and testing new products or improving existing ones".

Tuck et al. (2007), Holmström et al. (2015) and Bogers et al. (2016) stress that the transference from mass production to mass customization and the possibilities of personalized production also will transform the business models.

Additive manufacturing technology is increasingly used in many industries, such as aerospace, medicine, automotive, consumer products, etc. (Birtchnell and Urry 2012; Gao et al. 2015; Gibson et al. 2010).

Healthcare industries such as dentistry (e.g. dentures tailored directly from biocompatible materials. hearing aids, eye devices, or orthopaedic prostheses), audiology, orthopaedics, and ophthalmology are rapidly adopting additive

[1]See https://ec.europa.eu/docsroom/documents/36468

manufacturing technologies to produce end pieces that are tailored to specific patient profiles. This technology can increase the life expectancy and quality of life, with uncalculated impacts on society (Ford and Despeisse 2016; Jiang et al. 2017).

In other industries, like the shoe industry (e.g. Nike, New Balance, and Adidas), companies are combining additive manufacturing technology with other manufacturing methods to produce highly customized parts of products.

The impact of additive manufacturing technologies seems to be associated with the general impacts of digitalization. Some authors referred that these impacts will be relevant in areas such as labour (Chen et al. 2015; Matos and Jacinto 2019), namely with job losses and the development of new skills. Other authors argue that this technology could contribute to the gap between advanced economies and low-cost manufacturing economies.

The discussion about additive manufacturing impacts and challenges is still very incipient and if some impacts are indicated as positive (e.g. the increase of quality of life), others are indicated as negative, for example the facility of printing weapons for illegal purposes (Campbell et al. 2011; Rylands et al. 2016).

Since additive manufacturing involves several technologies at different stages of development, the prediction of its impacts becomes a complex challenge.

The aim of this chapter is to present a coherent vision for how additive manufacturing, combining with artificial intelligence, will transform the manufacturing and its impacts and challenges for society.

2 Literature Review

Linking digitization and additive manufacturing is the next milestone in the industrial sector that will completely revolutionize production. In this context, additive manufacturing, with its flexibility and freedom of form, is a clear example of how production technologies are developing in a customer-oriented, autonomous, and long-term aligned in order to attain greater efficiency and quality (Kritzinger et al. 2018).

Depending on the context, manufacturing parts in one piece, instead of subassemblies consisting of assemblies fabricated through conventional manufacturing, can generate a gain in mass and reduce the costs of materials and production significantly. The freedom of form that additive manufacturing allows and the lack of tools required for this purpose is a breakthrough technology for unique complex parts, such as parts with curves and odd cavities. It is also a breakthrough for parts produced in small series (Williams and Butler-Jones 2019). Additive manufacturing can save at least 50% of the time compared to conventional methods according to a recent study when compared to traditional fabrication (Dimensional Research 2019). Additive manufacturing signifies a profound revolution in design, which leads to the use of new software, new methods, and leads to the emergence of new professions. Since this is a relatively new technology, the fields of exploration and experimentation of 3D printing, or additive manufacturing, have yet to be deepened (Stavropoulos et al. 2018).

However, while additive manufacturing is one of the drivers of the digital transformation of businesses, 87% of French companies, for instance, report difficulties in driving this change according to a study (SmartLane 2018). Thus, while digital transformation is on the agenda of 90% of companies, structures with less than 500 employees are only 60% on average to have started this movement (SmartLane 2018). However, by being increasingly accessible financially and technically, additive manufacturing is becoming essential to every industry, in order to meet production needs of the near future; thus it will require both flexibility and customization (Öberg 2019). While additive manufacturing finds itself in a position to deliver solutions for the added-value processes and value chains, much has yet to be done (Eyers et al. 2018).

2.1 Industry 4.0

Industry 4.0 stands for intelligent machines that enable cyber–physical systems to communicate between all the units involved in the production. The goal of this relationship is to make the entire product development process more efficient by directly linking the individual steps in the value-added chain with computer science and modern communication technologies (Erro-Garcés 2019). Since the advantages of flexibility, personalization, and individual adaptation to production requirements can be found in additive manufacturing, the seamless workflows of Industry 4.0 are one of the valuable features of digital transformation (Dilberoglu et al. 2017).

Additive manufacturing could be a decisive Industry 4.0 element in industrial production by establishing 3D printers as the Internet of Things (IoT) compatible devices with full connectivity and data integration. Several enterprises are now incorporating CNC control systems in 3D printers. These types of changes will redefine additive manufacturing. A proper integration of 3D printers with full connectivity into existing production and automation systems can be achieved (Qin et al. 2017).

2.2 Health

Additive manufacturing has been drawing increased attention from researchers and technicians in the field of health (Javaid and Haleem 2019b), and this attention will only increase in the coming years. The world of health will be profoundly transformed by this technology as it will be by IoT and artificial intelligence. Additive manufacturing has become widespread in several medical and healthcare areas, such as dentistry (Javaid and Haleem 2019a), orthopaedics (Javaid and

Haleem 2019b), cardiology (Haleem et al. 2018), pharmaceutical products (Radcliffe et al. 2019), among others (Haleem and Javaid 2019).

Due to its characteristics, additive manufacturing offers the world of health several solutions that could allow fabricating prostheses at very low prices, and metal and ceramic teeth economically. Additive manufacturing could also be used in the preparation phase of surgical operations in order to make them more reliable and secure (Javaid and Haleem 2018).

In the near future, research shows that with the use of additive manufacturing, it will be possible to print better medicines and personalized for the patient (Pravin and Sudhir 2018). For instance, the Food and Drug Administration (FDA) of the United States has already approved the first printed drug, an antiepileptic (Di Prima et al. 2016). With additive manufacturing, it will also be possible to manufacture organs such as kidneys, liver, and heart by using the stem cells of the patient without risk of rejection (Moreno Madrid et al. 2019). Additive manufacturing will be essential to tissue engineering (TE) and has great potential in regenerative medicine; meanwhile, digital transformation will allow for precise and real-time monitoring.

2.3 Aerospace and Defence Industry

In civil aviation, companies are focusing on expanding production and other incremental product developments, including new, higher-performance engines. Defence and space companies are in a phase of strategic reorientation (Ceruti et al. 2019). With shrinking budgets and continual upheavals of new suppliers and new technologies, companies are forced to both adjust their cost structure and change their product offerings. Aerospace and defence companies develop platforms and systems that must meet the highest quality standards (Busachi et al. 2018). Individual states are investing large amounts in infrastructure, advanced security systems, and new defences. The driving force behind these state-of-the-art solutions is innovation that simplifies the collaboration, synchronization, and management of the life cycle, which is critical to the dynamically developing aerospace and defence industries (Kamal and Rizza 2019). Meanwhile, the space industry is still undergoing major changes that are likely to lead to further consolidation and vertical integration (Fateri et al. 2018).

Businesses operating in the aerospace and defence industry are increasingly realizing that digitization is not stopping at the forefront of the industry: nearly three-quarters (70%) of executives interviewed agree with the thesis that digitization is creating new business models, products, and services in Europe ("Luftfahrt- & Verteidigungsindustrie/Industrie erwartet steigende Verteidigungsbudgets in Europa" n.d.).

Responsible for these shifting dynamics are structural and strategic changes in the defence sector, the value chain in aircraft component manufacturing, revolutions in the space industry and, of course, additive manufacturing. Therefore, players in the sector have announced that they will work together to boost the use of additive parts

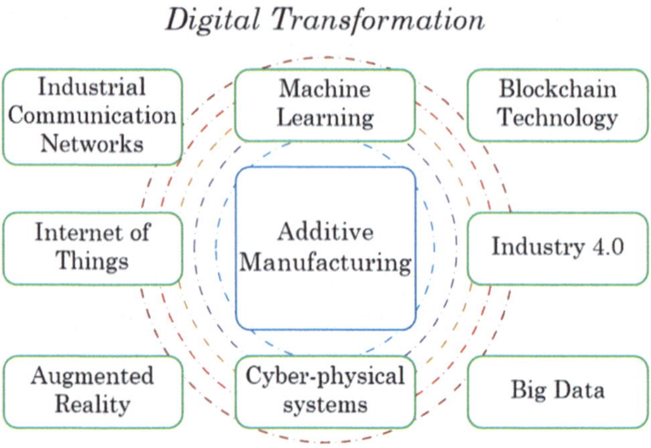

Fig. 1 Digital transformation's role in additive manufacturing

in the aerospace and defence industries (Kumar and Krishnadas Nair 2017). Both companies are important players in the industry and will use their combined expertise to address the most challenging aerospace challenges—greater efficiency and safety at a lower cost (Francis and Boyer 2019). The aim is to offer customers an end-to-end solution. The digital transformation, along with additive manufacturing, also provides opportunities to design, construct, manufacture, and make an accurate component inspection, all of which entail qualification opportunities (Froes et al. 2019).

3 Additive Manufacturing Shaped by Digital Transformation

The influence that digital transformation can have on additive manufacturing has the potential to bring many benefits. Figure 1 illustrates the digital transformation as the foundation of many modern technologies, including additive manufacturing, which will be influenced and shaped, at some level, by these technologies. Several advantages can be obtained by having a merger between digitalization and additive manufacturing technology.

Continuous data collection will provide the ability to reconcile real-time field information, such as contract values and inspection data from previous productions, with the customer's product or service requirements in order to provide personalized quotations. This integration of customer and empirical data into the production of Industry 4.0 distinguishes additive manufacturing, thus becoming an innovative advantage over conventional production technologies (Lemu 2019).

A clear advantage of merging digitalization and additive manufacturing technology is the production in real time and thus achieve significant cost savings in warehousing and logistics (Rosienkiewicz et al. 2018). Another advantage that results from the digitization of the production through additive manufacturing is the indication of leaking or wearing components in production. Consumption and wear data can be evaluated by means of the communication cycle prevailing between machines, and suitably adjusted order values can be forwarded to the additive manufacturing system (Comments 2017).

3.1 The Role of Industrial Communication Networks in Additive Manufacturing

The digitization of the industry is progressing. With it, the structures of industrial networks are changing. Even today, it is important to prepare existing productions for the upcoming tasks. In the future IoT, machines capable of communication will be by far the most common type of device. The IoT will enable a real-time optimization and monitoring of the additive manufacturing system, which will decrease the required time for maintenance. This will allow taking any required corrective measures, almost instantaneously ranging from human to machine/process. Therefore, also, the volume of data will grow significantly (Salama et al. 2019).

This development shows that digitization is only possible with powerful data communication. High-performance communication networks are an important prerequisite for digitization in the industry. Therefore, the industrial communication networks as the basis for digitalization. With them, all assets involved in value creation can be seamlessly integrated. They enable a seamless data exchange both horizontally and vertically. Moreover, they can grow with the increasing volumes of data. This makes them an indispensable prerequisite for all companies that want to go along the path to a digital future (Hammer 2019).

3.2 Additive Manufacturing and Augmented Reality

Augmented reality also plays a vital role in additive manufacturing. The simplistic way it functions is as follows: a sample is scanned three-dimensionally, then the scan is processed digitally and then transferred to a 3D printer that will produce the new spare part. Professional installation will be supported by an augmented reality headset that will project work instructions into the field of vision of an employee (Eiriksson et al. 2017).

The use of augmented reality offers many possibilities to accompany an additive manufacturing product throughout its entire life cycle. For instance, the production status could be verified through the augmented reality headset or visualized malfunctions. Likewise, the recognition of the device structure and required service information during maintenance is also a possibility (Ceruti et al. 2017). Augmented reality headset could also be used to observe the maintenance checklist for troubleshooting, or directly see the maintenance-needy part in front of the technician. He can first disassemble this virtually to implement these steps in reality. Considering the increased customer needs for better service quality, the technology significantly supports your service (Eckertz et al. 2020).

Augmented reality can completely redesign the workflow in additive manufacturing. With a solution developed at Cornell University (Peng et al. 2018), it is possible to construct in the physical room via the augmented reality headset and to print the design details on-site using a robotic arm. The future for a combination of augmented reality and additive manufacturing is auspicious, for example for the furniture industry or other fast-printed objects in a real environment. The advantage of the solution is that the robot can print the design in place and at the same time. Designers receive physical feedback in early design phases and can make adjustments (Peng et al. 2018). According to the authors, one can even construct and print directly on an existing object. This streamlines the process between design and manufacturing (Peng et al. 2018).

3.3 The Role of Machine Learning in Additive Manufacturing

Machine learning could play an important role in the additive manufacturing industry. New technologies could be developed, such as how machine learning can be used to optimize production processes and products and how new business models are created (Baturynska et al. 2019). The challenges for the successful use of artificial intelligence in additive manufacturing include the combination of complementary competencies that combine information technology and production engineering knowledge. One of the areas in which additive manufacturing still offers a great deal of innovation potential is quality assurance. The relationships between cause and effect of component defects must first be determined. This requires process-relevant data. Artificial neural networks can assign process deviations to possible component defects (Qi et al. 2019). As a result, they can independently make decisions without the direct influence of humans and, for example assign process deviations to possible component faults. Machine learning could also be used to solve tolerancing problems related to controlling geometric variations, which currently are a key bottleneck. Thus, in order to address shape deviation issues, machine learning techniques could be used to reach realistic simulations and predictive models (Zhu et al. 2018). Meanwhile, blockchain technology could offer valuable traceability applications for several types of industries. In a recent study, focused on the aircraft industry, a digital twin for additive manufacturing was built through the exploitation of blockchain (Mandolla et al. 2019).

3.4 New Business Models

A prerequisite for the successful implementation of additive manufacturing processes is the choice of an appropriate business model. In order to exploit the full potential of additive manufacturing, it is necessary to involve different business units and to coordinate their activities in the context of additive manufacturing (Lutter-Günther et al. 2016). Additive manufacturing has the potential to considerably interrupt the structure and operations of international business and impact their logic of capturing and creating value, such as, for instance, changing the traditional business models or mixing with digital models, as a direct result of digital transformation, which is almost indispensable for the future manufacturing processes.

Additive manufacturing is a particularly flexible technology that is able to deliver a vast array of personalized and customized products. This offers several opportunities and also challenges for creating new business models (Bogers et al. 2016). According to an article published in Harvard Business Review by Richard A. D'Aveni, six business models have emerged so far. Mass variety, mass customization, mass segmentation, mass modularization, mass complexity, and mass standardization (D'Aveni 2018).

Additive manufacturing also has the potential to reshape logistics—for example, by eliminating the stocking of spare parts, reducing storage area, and requirements and reduction of global to regional logistics, especially for products that are not sold on a daily basis (KPMG AG Wirtschaftsprüfungsgesellschaft 2015). Digital transformation could provide a permanent contact for analysis, design and implementation of a newer business model. In a multistage process, it could help companies to develop a significant solution for their specific business model involving additive manufacturing and show possible changes.

4 Upcoming Challenges

4.1 Interoperability

In the everyday professional processes used in the additive manufacturing, diverse heterogeneous systems are essential and thus require to be connected to each other, or a data exchange must be ensured, that is there is always a certain degree of interoperability (Forkel et al. 2018). Many requirements and limitations still exist in the additive manufacturing process chain, in particular, the limitations of classical exchange formats for additive manufacturing, starting with component design, through the manufacturing process to the reworking and the properties of the components made through additive manufacturing. Systems, devices, and processes for additive manufacturing processes must be securely integrated and coordinated. Consequently, accompanying processes such as quality management, design, and mapping the entire digital process chain are the focus of development.

Therefore, it must be guaranteed that materials and end products meet the required safety and industry standards (Monzón et al. 2019). As such, due to the complex interface existent in the process of additive manufacturing in terms of interoperability and security, meaningful standardization should be encouraged. The challenge will be to achieve an ecosystem in which numerous systems and subsystems, at distinct developmental stages, to capable of operating simultaneously in complex hybrid networks, thus ensuring sustainable corporate development (Forkel et al. 2018).

4.2 *Standardization in Additive Manufacturing in Face of the Upcoming Digital Transformation*

Professional users need clear criteria and verifiable quality features in order to be able to integrate additive processes into their production processes. They must be able to rely on the fact that similar components are produced during the manufacturing process with a uniform data basis and that the deviations are within the usual tolerances of conventional production. It is a logical step in the maturity of a technology that standards and standardization procedures must be followed to ensure widespread use (Lee et al. 2019). In the meantime, however, additive manufacturing has outgrown its infancy and is making an important step into the daily production in industrial plants. Standardization follows the know-how accumulated through practice and seeks to provide innovators with principles that guide current guidelines to avoid dead ends and promote business growth (Monzón et al. 2015). As the digital transformation process advances, the standardization system must be technologically placed on a new footing.

However, the definition of standards and guidelines, as well as certification, is a highly complex, international challenge that requires organizations, government agencies, and research to work together transnationally to arrive at generally accepted foundations. The materials used in additive manufacturing pose a challenge in terms of the quality of the products and are also a potential source of danger for the employees. Safety is extremely important, and new standards are being developed, which are addressing possible hazards related to additive manufacturing (Scime et al. 2018). Also, for many enterprises, certification is increasingly being used as a procurement criterion, making it an important tool in business strategy (Seifi et al. 2017).

At the same time, other standards describe procedures and methods that provide relevant parameters for powder characterization (Rudolph and Emmelmann 2017). This is intended to increase the reproducibility and process reliability of the entire additive manufacturing supply chain. It also deals with the quality assurance of additively manufactured components as well as with suppliers of measuring and testing technology for the characterization of powder materials (Jacob et al. 2018). For this purpose, the VDI 3405 guideline provides tangible parameters and application recommendations in order to qualify the materials for the application (Kumke et al. 2016; Kunkel et al. 2018; Yoo et al. 2016).

4.3 Data Security

Additive manufacturing is revolutionizing the entirety of the manufacturing industry. This disruptive technology will impact all the industrial players, from the global technology provider of high-end systems and solutions, an equipment manufacturer, developer, service provider, or (software) supplier to the 3D printing industry or a user of additive manufacturing and even a start-up with an innovative idea in the area of 3D printing. Therefore, the industry has to be forewarned regarding the protection of products against unlawful counterfeiting, including 3D scanning and 3D printing (Brown et al. 2016). As such, complex supply and service relationships within the additive manufacturing processes have to be rethought and the respective contractual performance obligations of the individual stakeholders, including the safeguarding of licence chains and liability issues, have to be taken into account, including the legally compliant application of technical standards and product safety issues.

As 3D printers are not only becoming more and more efficient, the price has also been steadily decreasing. Thus, a further increase in already increasing product piracy is to be expected. As a result, businesses need to protect their print templates and 3D models from becoming victims of piracy. Third parties that will obtain print templates will hold the blueprint for producing at least externally identical branded goods and industrial goods (Yampolskiy et al. 2018).

In addition, a 3D print template can also be created today by simply scanning the original product. No expensive devices are needed, just a standard mobile device and a simple optical character recognition (OCR) application (Appleyard 2015). The threats are not only from external hacker attacks, but could also be by dissatisfied employees who might leak the print templates. It is therefore strongly advised to treat the print templates as the flagship element of this technology and to protect them from unauthorized access by third parties. This includes not only the careful handling of data, but also adequate storage in a well-secured environment. Suppliers, service providers, and partners must also be contractually obliged to take the necessary technical and organizational measures to protect this type of data. If there is an unintentional outflow of data, the management can quickly get into a liability if it has not taken all the appropriate measures to secure the print templates ("13 Empfehlungen zur Additiven Fertigung" n.d.).

There is a need to be updated concerning the capabilities of piracy and the controllability of additive manufacturing. This technology can only be properly developed further when questions regarding data security are clarified, and when internationally recognized data formats exist. International norms and standards could be more up to date ("13 Empfehlungen zur Additiven Fertigung" n.d.).

4.4 Impact on the Workforce and Job Creation

The spread of additive manufacturing will have significant and disruptive effects on several industries, especially workforce disruption (Matos et al. 2019). It will, as it is a new process innovation, create job losses in a short-term period, particularly affecting unskilled labour (Kianian et al. 2015). Therefore, in order to cope with this challenge, classic occupational profiles of skilled workers ought to be extended by new qualifications for additive manufacturing technologies. Therefore, in the future, additive manufacturing could be used on an equal footing with other manufacturing processes in many industries. Digital transformation and additive manufacturing will have a longstanding impact on the qualification profile of skilled workers in industrial production, especially skilled workers. It will also create opportunities to work remotely, since it is already possible to operate additive manufacturing machines remotely while being able to create, also remotely, 3D printing design files (Eyers and Potter 2017). This development is determined by the two drivers—customer orientation and life cycle consideration. For customer orientation, new fields of design result from the digitization of industrial added value and the alluring networking of companies with customers (Nationale Akademie der Wissenschaften Leopoldina, Union der deutschen Akademien der Wissenschaften (Hrsg.) 2016). Also, the fast-changing landscape results in assessing whether the qualification of further education is to be limited in time in order to cope with the innovation dynamics of the digital transformation of additive manufacturing. A particular challenge is the rapid technological change: Digital platforms for teaching and learning as well as new approaches to knowledge transfer such as Massive Open Online Courses (MOOC) are to be realized in order to massively disseminate and strengthen these skills (Nationale Akademie der Wissenschaften Leopoldina, Union der deutschen Akademien der Wissenschaften (Hrsg.) 2016).

5 Conclusion

Industry 4.0 in the context of linking digital transformation and additive manufacturing is the next milestone in our industrial economy that will revolutionize production once again. In this context, Additive Manufacturing, with its flexibility and freedom of form, to name only two of the hundreds, is an exemplary piece of evidence of how our production technologies are developing in a customer-oriented, autonomous, and long-term direction to greater efficiency and quality. Consequently, digital transformation strategies for manufacturing enterprises could deliver several solutions in the face of challenges regarding additive manufacturing. The effect that digital transformation can have on additive manufacturing has the capacity to obtain many benefits. Several advantages can be obtained from the increasing link between digital transformation and additive manufacturing, such as production in real-time, real-time field information, wearing components identification, greater efficiency, and quality. The digitization of the industry will allow additive manufacturing to be improved by performance communication networks, augmented reality, machine learning tools, Internet of Things, and big data. However, also several challenges arise, such as the new guidelines and standards regarding additive manufacturing in face of the upcoming digital transformation as well as the increased complexity of the integration and interoperability due to the fast-paced digitized systems as well as the workforce qualification and job creation. Finally, the correct allocation of industrial property rights and liability issues are required as well as strong data protection systems should be put in place in order to prevent piracy and unlawful counterfeiting.

Acknowledgements The authors gratefully acknowledge (a) FCT grant (ref: grant UID/EMS/00667/2019) and (b) the funding of Project KM3D (PTDC/EME-SIS/32232/2017), supported by Fundação para a Ciência e Tecnologia, Portugal.

References

Appleyard M (2015) Corporate responses to online music piracy: strategic lessons for the challenge of additive manufacturing. Bus Horiz 58(1):69–76. https://doi.org/10.1016/j.bushor.2014.09.007

Baturynska I, Semeniuta O, Wang K (2019) Application of machine learning methods to improve dimensional accuracy in additive manufacturing. In: Wang K, Wang Y, Strandhagen JO, Yu T (eds) Advanced manufacturing and automation VIII. Springer, Singapore, pp 245–252

Birtchnell T, Urry J (2012) Fabricating futures and the movement of objects. Mobilities 8(3):388–405. https://doi.org/10.1080/17450101.2012.745697

Bogers M, Hadar R, Bilberg A (2016) Additive manufacturing for consumer-centric business models: implications for supply chains in consumer goods manufacturing. Technol Forecast Soc Chang 102:225–239. https://doi.org/10.1016/j.techfore.2015.07.024

Brown A, Yampolskiy M, Gatlin J, Andel T (2016) Legal aspects of protecting intellectual property in additive manufacturing. In: Rice M, Shenoi S (eds) Critical infrastructure protection X. Springer, Heidelberg, pp 63–79

Busachi A, Erkoyuncu J, Colegrove P, Drake R, Watts C, Martina F et al (2018) A system approach for modelling additive manufacturing in defence acquisition programs. Procedia CIRP 67:209–214. https://doi.org/10.1016/j.procir.2017.12.201

Campbell T, Williams C, Ivanova O, Garret B (2011) Could 3D printing change the world? In: Technologies, potential, and implications of additive manufacturing. Atlantic Council, Washington, DC

Ceruti A, Liverani A, Bombardi T (2017) Augmented vision and interactive monitoring in 3D printing process. Int J Interact Des Manuf 11(2):385–395. https://doi.org/10.1007/s12008-016-0347-y

Ceruti A, Marzocca P, Liverani A, Bil C (2019) Maintenance in aeronautics in an Industry 4.0 context: the role of augmented reality and additive manufacturing. J Comput Des Eng. https://doi.org/10.1016/j.jcde.2019.02.001

Chen D, Heyer S, Ibbotson S, Salonitis K, Steingrímsson JG, Thiede S (2015) Direct digital manufacturing: definition, evolution, and sustainability implications. J Clean Prod 107:615–625. https://doi.org/10.1016/j.jclepro.2015.05.009

Comments, 0 (2017) Digitalisierung – Industrie 4.0 – Additive Fertigung. 15 December. Steinbeis Transfermagazin website. https://transfermagazin.steinbeis.de/?p=2762. Accessed 6 Aug 2019

D'Aveni RA (2018) The 3-D printing playbook. Harvard Business Review (July–August 2018). 1 July. https://hbr.org/2018/07/the-3-d-printing-playbook
Di Prima M, Coburn J, Hwang D, Kelly J, Khairuzzaman A, Ricles L (2016) Additively manufactured medical products—the FDA perspective. 3D Print Med 2(1):1. https://doi.org/10.1186/s41205-016-0005-9
Dilberoglu UM, Gharehpapagh B, Yaman U, Dolen M (2017) The role of additive manufacturing in the era of Industry 4.0. Procedia Manuf 11:545–554. https://doi.org/10.1016/j.promfg.2017.07.148
Dimensional Research (2019) Current state of additive materials and 3D printing: a survey of 3D printing stakeholders in manufacturing [online]. Available https://cdn2.hubspot.net/hubfs/362383/additive-materials-and-3d-printing-jabil.pdf
Eckertz D, Berssenbrügge J, Anacker H, Dumitrescu R (2020) Work-in-progress: enhancing collaboration using augmented reality design reviews for product validation on the example of additive manufacturing. In: Auer ME, Kalyan Ram B (eds) Cyber-physical systems and digital twins. Springer, Cham, pp 244–254
Eiriksson ER, Pedersen DB, Frisvad JR, Skovmand L, Heun V, Maes P, Aanæs H (2017) Augmented reality interfaces for additive manufacturing. In: Sharma P, Bianchi FM (eds) Image analysis. Springer, Cham, pp 515–525
Empfehlungen zur Additiven Fertigung (n.d.) Produktion Online website. https://www.produktion.de/technik/id-13-empfehlungen-so-geht-erfolgreiche-additive-fertigung-357.html. Accessed 7 Aug 2019
Erro-Garcés A (2019) Industry 4.0: defining the research agenda. Benchmark Int J. https://doi.org/10.1108/BIJ-12-2018-0444
Eyers DR, Potter AT (2017) Industrial additive manufacturing: a manufacturing systems perspective. Comput Ind 92–93:208–218. https://doi.org/10.1016/j.compind.2017.08.002
Eyers DR, Potter AT, Gosling J, Naim MM (2018) The flexibility of industrial additive manufacturing systems. Int J Oper Prod Manag. https://doi.org/10.1108/IJOPM-04-2016-0200
Fateri M, Kaouk A, Cowley A, Siarov S, Palou MV, González FG et al (2018) Feasibility study on additive manufacturing of recyclable objects for space applications. Addit Manuf 24:400–404. https://doi.org/10.1016/j.addma.2018.09.020
Ford S, Despeisse M (2016) Additive manufacturing and sustainability: an exploratory study of the advantages and challenges. J Clean Prod 137:1573–1587. https://doi.org/10.1016/j.jclepro.2016.04.150
Forkel E, Baum J, Schumann C-A, Mueller E (2018) Smart interoperable logistics and additive manufacturing—modern technologies for digital transformation and Industry 4.0. 2018-01-1203. https://doi.org/10.4271/2018-01-1203
Francis HF, Boyer R (eds) (2019) Additive manufacturing for the aerospace industry, 1st edn. Elsevier, Amsterdam
Froes F, Boyer R, Dutta B (2019) 1—Introduction to aerospace materials requirements and the role of additive manufacturing. In: Froes F, Boyer R (eds) Additive manufacturing for the aerospace industry, pp 1–6. https://doi.org/10.1016/B978-0-12-814062-8.00001-7
Gao W, Zhang Y, Ramanujan D, Ramani K, Chen Y, Williams CB et al (2015) The status, challenges, and future of additive manufacturing in engineering. CAD Comput Aided Des 69:65–69. https://doi.org/10.1016/j.cad.2015.04.001
Gibson I, Rosen DW, Stucker B (2010) Additive manufacturing technologies: rapid prototyping to direct digital manufacturing. https://doi.org/10.1007/978-1-4419-1120-9
Haleem A, Javaid M (2019) 3D printed medical parts with different materials using additive manufacturing. Clin Epidemiol Glob Health. https://doi.org/10.1016/j.cegh.2019.08.002
Haleem A, Javaid M, Saxena A (2018) Additive manufacturing applications in cardiology: a review. Egypt Heart J 70(4):433–441. https://doi.org/10.1016/j.ehj.2018.09.008
Hammer M (2019) Digitization perspective: impact of digital technologies in manufacturing. In: Hammer M (ed) Management approach for resource-productive operations: design of a time-based and analytics-supported methodology grounded in six sigma, pp 27–68. https://doi.org/10.1007/978-3-658-22939-9_3

Holmström J, Liotta G, Chaudhuri A (2015) Sustainability outcomes through direct digital manufacturing-based operational practices: a design theory approach. J Clean Prod 167:951–961. https://doi.org/10.1016/j.jclepro.2017.03.092

Hull CW (1986) Patent No. US 4,575,330 A

Hull CW (2015) The birth of 3D printing. Res Technol Manag 58(6):25–30. https://doi.org/10.5437/08956308X5806067

Jacob A, Künneke T, Lieneke T, Baumann T, Stricker N, Zimmer D, Lanza G (2018) Iterative product development and production planning for additive manufacturing. ZWF Z Wirtsch Fabr 113(11):742–745. https://doi.org/10.3139/104.112005

Javaid M, Haleem A (2018) Additive manufacturing applications in medical cases: a literature based review. Alex J Med 54(4):411–422. https://doi.org/10.1016/j.ajme.2017.09.003

Javaid M, Haleem A (2019a) Current status and applications of additive manufacturing in dentistry: a literature-based review. J Oral Biol Craniofac Res 9(3):179–185. https://doi.org/10.1016/j.jobcr.2019.04.004

Javaid M, Haleem A (2019b) Current status and challenges of additive manufacturing in orthopaedics: an overview. J Clin Orthop Trauma 10(2):380–386. https://doi.org/10.1016/j.jcot.2018.05.008

Jiang R, Kleer R, Piller FT (2017) Predicting the future of additive manufacturing: a Delphi study on economic and societal implications of 3D printing for 2030. Technol Forecast Soc Chang 117:84–97. https://doi.org/10.1016/j.techfore.2017.01.006

Kamal M, Rizza G (2019) 4—Design for metal additive manufacturing for aerospace applications. In: Froes F, Boyer R (eds) Additive manufacturing for the aerospace industry, pp 67–86. https://doi.org/10.1016/B978-0-12-814062-8.00005-4

Kianian B, Tavassoli S, Larsson TC (2015) The role of additive manufacturing technology in job creation: an exploratory case study of suppliers of additive manufacturing in Sweden. Procedia CIRP 26:93–98. https://doi.org/10.1016/j.procir.2014.07.109

Kohtala C, Hyysalo S (2015) Anticipated environmental sustainability of personal fabrication. J Clean Prod 99:333–344. https://doi.org/10.1016/j.jclepro.2015.02.093

KPMG AG Wirtschaftsprüfungsgesellschaft (2015) Additive manufacturing—strategy & operations. Fokusanalyse—Revolutioniert der 3D-Druck die Supply Chain und das Geschäftsmodell der Unternehmen?

Kritzinger W, Steinwender A, Lumetzberger S, Sihn W (2018) Impacts of additive manufacturing in value creation system. Procedia CIRP 72:1518–1523. https://doi.org/10.1016/j.procir.2018.03.205

Kumar LJ, Krishnadas Nair CG (2017) Current trends of additive manufacturing in the aerospace industry. In: Wimpenny DI, Pandey PM, Kumar LJ (eds) Advances in 3D printing & additive manufacturing technologies, pp 39–54. https://doi.org/10.1007/978-981-10-0812-2_4

Kumke M, Watschke H, Vietor T (2016) A new methodological framework for design for additive manufacturing. Virtual Phys Prototyp 11(1):3–19. https://doi.org/10.1080/17452759.2016.1139377

Kunkel MH, Gebhardt A, Mpofu K, Kallweit S (2018) Statistical assessment of mechanical properties of selective laser melted specimens of stainless steel. Int J Adv Manuf Technol 98(5):1409–1431. https://doi.org/10.1007/s00170-018-2040-8

Lee BN, Pei E, Um J (2019) An overview of information technology standardization activities related to additive manufacturing. Progress Addit Manuf. https://doi.org/10.1007/s40964-019-00087-5

Lemu HG (2019) On opportunities and limitations of additive manufacturing technology for Industry 4.0 era. In: Wang K, Wang Y, Strandhagen JO, Yu T (eds) Advanced manufacturing and automation VIII. Springer, Singapore, pp 106–113

Luftfahrt- & Verteidigungsindustrie/Industrie erwartet steigende Verteidigungsbudgets in Europa (n.d.) Presseportal.de website. https://www.presseportal.de/pm/32053/3741071. Accessed 6 Aug 2019

Lutter-Günther M, Seidel C, Reinhart G, Baader A (2016) Geschäftsmodelle für den Einsatz der additiven Fertigung in der industriellen Praxis. Rapid.Tech 2015, Fachmesse Für Rapid-Technologie. Presented at the Erfurt

Mandolla C, Petruzzelli AM, Percoco G, Urbinati A (2019) Building a digital twin for additive manufacturing through the exploitation of blockchain: a case analysis of the aircraft industry. Comput Ind 109:134–152. https://doi.org/10.1016/j.compind.2019.04.011

Matos F, Jacinto C (2019) Additive manufacturing technology: mapping social impacts. J Manuf Technol Manag. https://doi.org/10.1108/JMTM-12-2017-0263

Matos F, Godina R, Jacinto C, Carvalho H, Ribeiro I, Peças P (2019) Additive manufacturing: exploring the social changes and impacts. Sustainability 11(14):3757. https://doi.org/10.3390/su11143757

Monzón MD, Ortega Z, Martínez A, Ortega F (2015) Standardization in additive manufacturing: activities carried out by international organizations and projects. Int J Adv Manuf Technol 76 (5):1111–1121. https://doi.org/10.1007/s00170-014-6334-1

Monzón M, Paz R, Ortega Z, Diaz N (2019) Knowledge transfer and standards needs in additive manufacturing. In: Pei E, Monzón M, Bernard A (eds) Additive manufacturing—developments in training and education, pp 1–13. https://doi.org/10.1007/978-3-319-76084-1_1

Moreno Madrid AP, Vrech SM, Sanchez MA, Rodriguez AP (2019) Advances in additive manufacturing for bone tissue engineering scaffolds. Mater Sci Eng C 100:631–644. https://doi.org/10.1016/j.msec.2019.03.037

Nationale Akademie der Wissenschaften Leopoldina, Union der deutschen Akademien der Wissenschaften (Hrsg.) (2016) Acatech – Deutsche Akademie der Technikwissenschaften. München, 64 Seiten

Öberg C (2019) Additive manufacturing—digitally changing the global business landscape. Eur J Manag Bus Econ. https://doi.org/10.1108/EJMBE-11-2018-0116

Peng H, Briggs J, Wang C-Y, Guo K, Kider J, Mueller S et al (2018) RoMA: interactive fabrication with augmented reality and a robotic 3D printer. In: Proceedings of the 2018 CHI conference on human factors in computing systems, vol 579, pp 579:1–579:12. https://doi.org/10.1145/3173574.3174153

Pravin S, Sudhir A (2018) Integration of 3D printing with dosage forms: a new perspective for modern healthcare. Biomed Pharmacother 107:146–154. https://doi.org/10.1016/j.biopha.2018.07.167

Qi X, Chen G, Li Y, Cheng X, Li C (2019) Applying neural-network-based machine learning to additive manufacturing: current applications, challenges, and future perspectives. Engineering. https://doi.org/10.1016/j.eng.2019.04.012

Qin J, Liu Y, Grosvenor R (2017) A framework of energy consumption modelling for additive manufacturing using internet of things. Procedia CIRP 63:307–312. https://doi.org/10.1016/j.procir.2017.02.036

Radcliffe AJ, Hilden JL, Nagy ZK, Reklaitis GV (2019) Dropwise additive manufacturing of pharmaceutical products using particle suspensions. J Pharm Sci 108(2):914–928. https://doi.org/10.1016/j.xphs.2018.09.030

Rosienkiewicz M, Gabka J, Helman J, Kowalski A, Susz S (2018) Additive manufacturing technologies cost calculation as a crucial factor in Industry 4.0. In: Hamrol A, Ciszak O, Legutko S, Jurczyk M (eds) Advances in manufacturing. Springer, Cham, pp 171–183

Rudolph J-P, Emmelmann C (2017) A cloud-based platform for automated order processing in additive manufacturing. Procedia CIRP 63:412–417. https://doi.org/10.1016/j.procir.2017.03.087

Rylands B, Böhme T, Gorkin R, Fan J, Birtchnell T (2016) The adoption process and impact of additive manufacturing on manufacturing systems. J Manuf Technol Manag 27(7):969–989. https://doi.org/10.1108/JMTM-12-2015-0117

Salama M, Elkaseer A, Saied M, Ali H, Scholz S (2019) Industrial internet of things solution for real-time monitoring of the additive manufacturing process. In: Borzemski L, Świątek J, Wilimowska Z (eds) Information systems architecture and technology: proceedings of 39th international conference on information systems architecture and technology—ISAT 2018. Springer, Cham, pp 355–365

Scime L, Wolf SD, Beuth J, Mrdjenovich S, Kelley M (2018) Safety and workflow considerations for modern metal additive manufacturing facilities. JOM 70(9):1830–1834. https://doi.org/10.1007/s11837-018-2971-4

Seifi M, Gorelik M, Waller J, Hrabe N, Shamsaei N, Daniewicz S, Lewandowski JJ (2017) Progress towards metal additive manufacturing standardization to support qualification and certification. JOM 69(3):439–455. https://doi.org/10.1007/s11837-017-2265-2

SmartLane (2018) Maturité digitale—Baromètre 2018

Stavropoulos P, Foteinopoulos P, Papacharalampopoulos A, Bikas H (2018) Addressing the challenges for the industrial application of additive manufacturing: towards a hybrid solution. Int J Lightweight Mater Manuf 1(3):157–168. https://doi.org/10.1016/j.ijlmm.2018.07.002

Tuck C, Hague R, Burns N (2007) Rapid manufacturing: impact on supply chain methodologies and practice. Int J Serv Operations Manage 3(1):1–22. https://doi.org/10.1504/IJSOM.2007.011459

Williams H, Butler-Jones E (2019) Additive manufacturing standards for space resource utilization. Addit Manuf 28:676–681. https://doi.org/10.1016/j.addma.2019.06.007

Yampolskiy M, King WE, Gatlin J, Belikovetsky S, Brown A, Skjellum A, Elovici Y (2018) Security of additive manufacturing: attack taxonomy and survey. Addit Manuf 21:431–457. https://doi.org/10.1016/j.addma.2018.03.015

Yoo IS, Braun T, Kaestle C, Spahr M, Franke J, Kestel P et al (2016) Model factory for additive manufacturing of mechatronic products: interconnecting world-class technology partnerships with leading AM players. Procedia CIRP 54:210–214. https://doi.org/10.1016/j.procir.2016.03.113

Zhu Z, Anwer N, Huang Q, Mathieu L (2018) Machine learning in tolerancing for additive manufacturing. CIRP Ann 67(1):157–160. https://doi.org/10.1016/j.cirp.2018.04.119

Afterword

One of the early distinctions of Intellectual Capital (IC) was "*Aha!*". This was an expression of the impact of the hidden assets and their implications. Later on, it was also simplified into the English phrase "*I see!*". The deeper meaning of IC might be *derived insights of head value*, nowadays also referenced to as the *in-between space.* This space is in a growing transition for which we need more understanding.

Intellectual Capital is multidimensional. In the age of digital transformation, IC taxonomy terms evolved, and one of the IC's dimensions is the Relational Capital. Today, this type of Capital is labelled as *Digital Networking*, on a global 24-h scale. For example, in the Chinese culture, it might be *Guanxi Networks*, with a lot of mutual tacit dimensions (i.e., Trust).

The core of this book is about these intersections and interrelated dimensions. All these chapters, on different aspects of IC, will hopefully add to your deeper "*Aha!*". For future generations, this means to *Navigate beyond Technology* and it is about addressing the unknown with intelligence and excellency procedures. NASA[1] did this "Navigation" with the *Apollo Project* 50 years ago. Looking into the very pedagogical film titled *"Mission Control: The Unsung Heroes of Apollo,"* presented in 2017, about the historical team in charge of reaching the Moon, we can see an illustration of the interplay of People, Knowledge, and Digital Development, on the different levels of a global society. Other illustrative cases of this, might be *Google, Baido, Spotify, Dr. Watson Artificial Diagnosis or Connected Health*, as well as, *Netflix.*

The Human Capital, another one of IC's dimensions, is surrounded by expanding global technology networks. A lot of implications are emerging for smarter sustainability knowledge navigation and impact questions. Will it be a Green Eco multiplier of Intelligence and Skills? Who is the owner of this relationship (human capital/global technology networks)? What are the Intellectual Property Rights (IPR) of an

[1]See: https://www.nasa.gov/

F. Matos et al. (eds.), *Knowledge, People, and Digital Transformation*, Contributions to Management Science, https://doi.org/10.1007/978-3-030-40390-4

idea? What protection is there for a Relation Capital Network? Who are the drivers of the Digital Transformation?

The emerging digital toolbox of IC is partially there to act upon the in-between space. Among others, there are the pioneering *IC Rating*[2] approach and the more elaborated *4-Leaf Model*[3] proposed by Aeropa, focused on the intersection spaces between the major dimensions of IC. In Japan, they refer to this approach as the *Pluralistic Economy.*[4] It is a "galaxy" of value-creating spaces, beyond the paradigm of a linear value chain. This idea was already explored in the 1990s and presented by Richard Normann in his book *Reframing Business: When the Map Changes the Landscape (2001).*

This foresighted approach is today more and more valid. The dynamic field of e-commerce is based on Relational Capital, or trade of ideas, more than trade of objects. This in itself is causing an exponential multiplier effect for the various value spaces to be explored. This is going beyond the *Recycling* and *Circular Economics*, with an *Economic Galaxy of Value Spaces* as the outcome of the IC Economics.

Intangible Assets (IA) might be a critical part of this process. But some questions arise: Do we have an IA policy for our enterprise or nation? Do we have a Ministry for these new expanding IA spaces? What legal framework do we have to cultivate further trade and knowledge on these important IC wealth dimensions? What is the International Patent Office (IPO) promoting? Is there any global meeting space of Macro Economics for IA and IC, beyond OECD and WICI[5]? What are the relationships between the Sustainability Development Goals (SDG), Ecology, and IC?

Facebook groups emerge to take initiatives globally for the Sustainability Development Goals. One impressive and awarded integrated SDG City approach has been emerging in Espoo, Finland.[6] Some of these new IC pioneers might be both the old well-acknowledged quality assurance enterprise DNV—Norske Veritas,[7] in Norway, as well as UNGSII[8]—a foundation that focuses on the acceleration of the SDG of Cities.

On the other hand, a deeper and softer dimension of the Relational Capital might be in the NeuroScience research developments. This is, what, in our perception, triggers our brains to express an "*Aha!*"? Professor Rizzolatti in Parma, Italy, developed a digitally detectable metrics system for *Mirroring Neurons.* Today, we know that there are some 30 muscles in your face reacting to the perceived signals. Using these perceived signals, seven different shapes of joy, grief, etc. are patterned. These patterns are included in the so-called *Body Language*. In microseconds,

---

[2]See: Edvinsson, L. (2000) *IC Rating*, Available at: www.intellectualcapital.se

[3]See: http://www.areopa.com/intellectual-capital-management/

[4]"Japan's Road to Pluralism: Transforming Local Communities in the Global Era" (ed. Shun'ichi Furkawa and Toshihiro Menju), Tokyo: Japan Center for International Exchange, 2003, pp. 21–45.

[5]See: WICI—World Intellectual Capital/Assets Initiative (see: https://www.wici-global.com/)

[6]See: https://urbanmillblog.files.wordpress.com/2015/04/eka_final_cover_hires.pdf

[7]See: https://www.dnvgl.com/about/index.html

[8]See: https://www.ungsii.org/

gestures might say more than words. Some research even indicates that gestures come before the brain has codified the gestures into words. Could it be that the Body Language Science discoveries will give IC an even more accurate taxonomy for the Relational Capital? How will this impact Coding, also said to be the language of the Digital Age?

This idea is a different and more evolutionary track for IC research than the *Accounting Metrics*, that often are based on the economic transaction paradigm. Nevertheless, these now softer dimensions of IC were already explored in Japan in the 1980s. A special *Softnomics Center*, in Tokyo, an alliance of the Ministry of Finance and some of the leading large enterprises, was established to address the *Softnomization of the Economy*. Continuing this work, today Japan has explored IC further based on learnings from the Germany experience (Wissenskapital[9]) and from the *WICI—World IC Initiative*,[10] among others. They have also taken it further in navigating the intersectoral *Pluralist economy* and in the quest for *Wisdom*[11] with *Wise Places*,[12] based on *Ba wisdom*[13] design. It might almost be a *Zen* quest for Future Generations.

The initial *Lab of IC and Organizational Explorations* was created by *Skandia Future Center*.[14] It started in 1996 and it was followed by a network of *Future Centers* in the *Future Center Alliance*.[15] Now it is time for a *Future Center 3.0*.[16] An example of this is the *EcoSyx Lab*,[17] a tentative next-generation *Lab of IC*, a platform for Society and Economy and a *Green Ba* and *Ecosystem for Future Prototyping*. Denmark is also pioneering with the *BLOXHUB*,[18] which was inaugurated in 2018 in Copenhagen.

There is a special need for such a prototyping space or *Platform Lab for Societal Innovation*. Today, we are said to be living in an era of Institutional Failure. How will, for example, the Federal Reserve Bank act, with its financial policy focused on interest rate fluctuations, in an era of new digital currencies like the Bitcoin? How can, for example, the Bitcoin shape the new Networks of Economies, such as *Business & Innovation Centers (BICs)*? What new working contracts will emerge for the digital generation? What new remuneration systems might emerge, related to

[9]See: http://wissenskapital.info/wp-content/uploads/2014/10/journal_of_intellectual_capital_08_03-2007_kivikas_edvinsson.pdf

[10]See: https://www.wici-global.com/

[11]Ability to think and act using knowledge and experience.

[12]See: http://www.futurecenteralliance-japan.org/en/innovation/wiseplace

[13]See: Nonaka, I., & Konno, N. (1998). The Concept of "Ba": Building a Foundation for Knowledge Creation. *California Management Review*, *40*(3), 40–54. https://doi.org/10.2307/41165942

[14]See: https://www.futurecenteralliance.com/single-post/2015/06/10/The-Pioneer-Skandia-Future-Center

[15]See: https://www.futurecenteralliance.com/

[16]See: https://drive.google.com/file/d/0B0ouzk5HIGWJQV9fYzY1cjF2Um8/view

[17]See: https://www.ecosyxlab.org/

[18]See: http://www.bloxhub.dk/

IC? What migration policies' prototypes might emerge? What new language will be the language of Future Generations? Will the above-mentioned NeuroScience research assist robots in detecting emerging weak signals long before the accounting framework?

In this book, some of these dimensions are addressed, but much more will need to be explored. What pattern might be seen in the in-between dimensions of the chapters? This might also be called the *Not Knowing Space* in further research. Can we sketch a 3D graphic? What are the missing points or perspectives related to Digital Transformation? The research on IC is still in its infancy. A lot of prototyping and research will be emerging. Hopefully, this is upskilling the Economics, like a "*T*", wider and deeper, to the benefit of Future Generations. The next generation of IC might be the *Green Multiplier*.

A "laboratorium" of IC is still to be established. In what city or country? It should be a network of research platforms like the *Weather Reporting Agencies*,[19] sharing coded data flow for local interpretation, from a central node.

Happy IC Future!

Leif Edvinsson

The World's First Professor Emeritus on Intellectual Capital

Co-Founder of the New Club of Paris[20]

[19]See: https://www.ecmwf.int/

[20]See: http://new-club-of-paris.org/

The manufacturer's authorised representative in the EU is Springer Nature Customer Service Centre GmbH, Europaplatz 3, 69115 Heidelberg, Germany. If you have any concerns regarding our products, please contact ProductSafety@springernature.com

Printed and bound by CPI Group (UK) Ltd, Croydon, CR0 4YY
05/10/2026
02228120-0009